© Noordhoff Uitgevers bv

Preface to the second edition

Organisational behaviour is an introduction to organisational psychology. It presents psychological and organisational theory in terms which can be used to describe and explain the behaviour of people in organisations. This knowledge can be applied by management to recruit, induct, train and motivate the right staff to perform satisfactorily and retain them.

This second edition pays attention to new developments in the digitization of our society. Recruitment and selection have become processes that can be conducted on-line; colleagues can take part in virtual discussions whenever and wherever, and stay up to date on all organisational matters.

This edition has been supplemented with new insight and recent studies. Various case studies, examples, illustrations and exercises have also been updated.
In our introduction, we show that organisations are complex systems that can be described from four different perspectives, being the open system, the technical system, the financial-economic system, and the socio-political system. This division serves as a broader framework for the perspectives covered in this book.

This book is accompanied by the website www.organisationalbehaviour. noordhoff.nl, which offers test questions to test the reader's knowledge of the study material and concepts covered in each chapter. The answers to the assignments that are part of the various chapters can also be found on the website. Additionally, the website offers links to interesting tests and experiments, as well as background information about individuals, topical subjects, and (doctoral) studies.

Groningen, Autumn of 2018

Gert Alblas
Ella Wijsman

Contents

© Noordhoff Uitgevers bv

Organisational Behaviour

Gert Alblas
Ella Wijsman

Second edition

Noordhoff Publishers Groningen/Utrecht

© Noordhoff Uitgevers bv

Cover design and illustration: 212 Fahrenheit, Groningen

Any comments concerning this or other publications should be addressed to Noordhoff Uitgevers bv, Afdeling Hoger Onderwijs, Antwoordnummer 13, 9700 VB Groningen, The Netherlands, or via the contact form at www.mijnnoordhoff.nl.

The information contained in this publication is for general information purposes only. No rights or liability of the author(s), editor or publisher can be derived from this information.

0 / 19

© 2021 Noordhoff Uitgevers bv Groningen/Utrecht, The Netherlands

This publication is protected by copyright. If you wish to (re)use the information in this publication, you must obtain prior written permission from Noordhoff Uitgevers bv. More information about collective arrangements for education can be found at www.onderwijsenauteursrecht.nl.

ISBN 978-1-032-04807-9 (hbk)
ISBN 978-90-01-89895-3 (pbk)
ISBN 978-1-003-19473-6 (ebk)

NUR 801

© Noordhoff Uitgevers bv

Introduction

It is hard to keep a bird's eye view of everything going on in an organisation at all times. The reality of organisational life is simply too complex. There are too many processes influencing the business activities that are needed to achieve the organisation's goals and to ensure its continuity. Looking at the complexities of that reality from an independent perspective allows us to make organisational reality somewhat more accessible; allows us to map it, to study it. Four of those perspectives are briefly described below, followed by an indication of the ones that are the central themes of this book.

The organisation as an open system
Organisations and companies are regularly faced with difficulties. Consider a clothing company collapsing as a result of customers turning to the world wide web for their shopping needs, or healthcare institutions finding themselves in financial troubles due to changes in healthcare acts. The circumstances under which organisations have to function can change to such an extent that these changes begin to threaten an organisation's continued existence if they are not addressed in time. This goes to show that organisations interact with the environments in which they operate. Organisations may be considered open systems, since they have to deal with customers, suppliers, capital providers, unions, regulations and legislation, competitors, and technical and economic developments, to name a few. As such, managers find themselves confronted with a variety of questions and issues, including:
- Which developments in our environment are the biggest sources of influence?
- Which changes in development are we faced with, and what are the resulting opportunities and risks to our organisation?
- How should we respond to those opportunities and risks if we are to ensure the continuity of our organisation?
The greater the number of changes and the faster those changes occur, the more alert management needs to be.

The organisation as a technical system
Place an order at a restaurant, and you set off a chain of work processes. The waiter who provides you with a menu initiates a data flow that starts with the customer's order. That order is relayed to the bar and the kitchen. Once those departments have finished their activities, the waiter is informed that the order is ready for pickup and delivery to the table. Organisations rely on countless data flows to steer and calibrate the activities of their employees. Preparing the order is only possible if prior requirements have been met, such as drinks for the bar and resources and ingredients for the kitchen having been puchased. The supply of those products initiates a goods flow that starts with the supplier of the raw materials and ends with the customer.

© Noordhoff Uitgevers bv

The order placed with the waiter also initiates a transformation process consisting of pouring drinks and preparing dishes. Whether it is producing goods or providing services, an organisation can be considered a technical system which houses data flows, goods flows, and transformation processes. Properly structuring these flows is essential for optimum customer service.

The organisation as a financial-economical system

Money is an important requirement for initiating and continuing goods flows and transformation processes. Organisations rely on a monetary flow that starts with obtaining materials, labour, and capital. There are resources to be bought from suppliers, staff to be recruited, business space to be rented, production resources to be procured, and energy consumption to be paid. Costs precede benefits, and organisations are often required to invest before they can produce. This results in an outgoing monetary flow. Monetary resources required for this flow may first need to be borrowed through debt capital markets.

The transformation process results in products or services being made available for the sales market. Once these products or services are purchased and paid for, they result in an incoming monetary flow. Eventually, the incoming monetary flow should be large enough to accommodate the outgoing one. The existence of the organisation depends on its ability to obtain enough money to be able to afford its business processes. To that end, the organisation needs to produce products or services that are sufficiently appreciated and valued. On the one hand, value generates sufficient revenue; on the other hand, it ensures the credit rating required to borrow money through the debt capital market remains viable. A restaurant needs to achieve a certain level of turnover to offset its costs - and to possibly turn a profit. That is the only way to safeguard its continuity.

The organisation as a socio-political system

The production of goods and services involves people. These people perform operational activities, exchange information, consult and discuss, align their activities, perform managerial tasks, and solve problems - together. The division of labour is generally a fixed affair, covering who does what when with whom and as part of which department, division, or team. There are identifiable standardised activity patterns and prescribed contributions that make it possible to control and predict collaboration and interplay within the organisation. These are characteristics that establish the organisation as a kind of social system.

Many members of an organisation feel closer to the group or the department within which they operate than to staff members throughout the remainder of the organisation. Group members derive their status from their own group, which can be a source of information, aid, and social support. These positive gains are not established automatically. They require group members to work together properly and offer pleasant work circumstances: not an easy task.

The relationship between the individual and the organisation is considered a reciprocal relationship. The individual contributes to the organisation's functioning, and the organisation in turn contributes to the individual in the forms of money, status, security, social contact, and appreciation or valuation. These contributions are not inexhaustible, and the individual strive to maximising gains can come to stand at cross purposes to the organisation's objective of maximising profits. Members of an organisation emphasize the interests of their own group over those of other groups or over that of the organisation as a whole. Differences in vision or interest between groups with respect to the distribution of scarce gains can soon lead to groups considering each other to be in competition. An organisation can therefore be considered a collection of parties whose interests are partly aligned and partly at conflict. Faced with situations like these, it falls to management to establish a balance between the different visions and interests. This makes an organisation a political system.

Organisational behaviour
Organisational Behaviour focusses on the organisation as a socio-political system from the perspective of organisational psychology. It deals with the behaviours of people in organisations. How do people interact? How do they influence each other? How do they align their interests to each other's and the organisation's goals?
These questions are approached from four different perspectives, being the individual perspective, the group perspective, the organisational perspective, and the environmental perspective.

Interrelated factors of influence on the behaviour of people in organisations

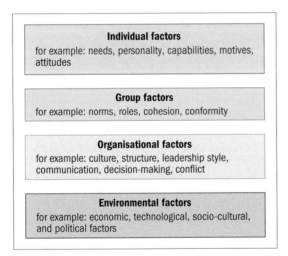

Source: Mullings, 2008 (edited)

1

Individual and organisation

- What motives do people have for working?
- How does motivation differ from one person to the next?
- What other personal characteristics play a role at work?
- What is the nature of the relationship between individual and organisation?
- What attitudes do people have towards work?

© Noordhoff Uitgevers bv

Maya applies for a job

Maya has applied for a job as assistant receptionist with a large transport company. She was very enthusiastic about the interview. She found the interviewers friendly and open. Unfortunately, during the guided tour of the building, she saw many older people. She also found the building to be gloomy and poorly maintained. However, her positive contact with the staff made her decide to accept the job. In an interview with the company magazine she says: "I like working with people and I can work 36 hours in four days. I then have a day off for my training at college."

Tom is looking for security

After ten years of working in industry, Tom is looking for a job in the non-profit sector. Now that Alma is pregnant with their second child, he wants to be at home more. He is looking for a less hectic job with shorter working hours. It seems sensible to him to choose a job with more job security, especially now that Alma has taken the risk of starting her own business. His eye is caught by an advertisement; perhaps he could work in IT for the municipality?

◀1.1▶ Behaviour and motivation

In the first example, Maya accepts a job offer because her future colleagues seem to be friendly and open. In the second example, Tom opts for a new job because it provides more security. Maya and Tom have different motives for choosing a certain job. These motives have to do with their motivation for working.

In this chapter, we provide an in-depth discussion on the subject of Motivation. But first, we turn our attention to behaviour.
The concept of behaviour deals with the perceivable interactions between human beings. Colleagues joining each other for coffee, checking their smart phones or sharing a joke; a door slamming in the distances; a friend running past without saying hi: there are many types of behaviour. The kind that managers like, is productive behaviour.
Human behaviour is a subject of interest to psychology and other sciences, such as sociology, anthropology, and political science. Psychology is interested in the scientific study of human behaviour as well as the mental processes at the basis of that behaviour. Mental processes are processes within the brain, thoughts and memories, perception, sensation, and so on. Studying behaviour involves more than explaining behaviour. It also deals with predicting and influencing behaviour. Relevant questions in the context of a work organisation would be: Why is this employee calling in sick so often? What can management do to prevent absenteeism and lower staff turnover rates? How can productive behaviour be encouraged? How do we stimulate staff collaboration? How do we motivate people? What type of behaviour should our executives display?

Motivation means the sum total of motives applicable to an individual at a certain time. These motives can lead to the willingness to make certain efforts. Motivation is derived from the Latin word "movere", which means: to put into motion.

Motivation

There are different theories as to the origin of motivation. These can be divided into three categories, which dictate that motivation is determined either by:
- Internal forces (needs).
- External forces (situation).
- A desire to balance internal and external forces.

The following paragraph first addresses these three schools of thought, after which we discuss two types of motivation: intrinsic and extrinsic.

1.1.1   Motivation through internal forces

Since ancient times, people have been seeking answers to the questions: Why do we behave in a certain way? What inspires us? Is it gods or spirits? Or is it primitive forces within ourselves?
Freud, the founder of psychoanalysis, calls these internal forces "tendencies". These tendencies are innate, have a physical origin. They are the wellsprings of behaviour. Modern psychologists usually call internal forces "needs".

Needs

There are different theories about needs. Here, we outline the theories of Maslow, Alderfer and McLelland.

© Noordhoff Uitgevers bv

1

Maslow's theory

Maslow (1943, 1954) argues that there are five needs which form the basis for any person's behaviour (see Figure 1.1):

FIGURE 1.1 Maslow's needs pyramid

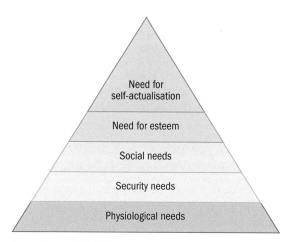

Source: Maslow, 1943, 1954

1 **Physiological needs.** These are things that are necessary to sustain life (food and water, sleep, and a certain body temperature).
2 **Safety needs.** These are safety, security and protection.
3 **Social needs.** These include human contact, friendship, love and a sense of belonging.
4 **Need for esteem.** Esteem encompasses appreciation and respect by others.
5 **Self-actualisation needs.** These are knowledge, the pursuit of truth and wisdom, self-development and personal growth.

EXAMPLE 1.1

Needs

For Maya, her social needs are the most important at work. She also seeks self-development but she does so primarily in her free time. Tom used to need recognition, appreciation and respect, but now these things have become less important. He has built up sufficient self-confidence. Now, he is primarily looking for financial security, pleasant working conditions and time with his family.

Maslow's theory is based on two premises:
1 **Deprivation** of needs leads to activation. If there is perceived deprivation, an unsatisfied need, people will take action (activation). They take measures to satisfy this need. The strength of the activation depends on the degree of deprivation. Once the need is satisfied, the activity level subsides.
2 Needs are **hierarchically structured.** Maslow is of the opinion that there is a hierarchy of needs that is the same for all people. Lowest in the hierarchy

are the most fundamental needs (physiological needs). When these are satisfied, safety or security needs become dominant; next, the social needs, and so on. People can experience a need for recognition, for example, only once their underlying needs have been satisfied.

The first premise applies to the first four needs, which is why they are also called "deficiency needs". This is not the case with the last need, the need for self-actualisation, which is of a fundamentally different nature. People reaching this level are no longer driven by a deficit but by the wish to develop themselves into their "best" version possible. Maslow is of the opinion that by no means all people achieve their full development potential. According to him, only a small group of people achieve the highest level of self-actualisation.   *Deficiency needs*

Maslow's theory has received a great deal of criticism. For example, there is disagreement as to the hierarchy of needs. Some critics believe that different types of needs can be present at the same time. Maslow's grouping or classification of needs has also been questioned. Research has undermined the classification used by Maslow (Wahba & Bridwell, 1976). Moreover, the concept of self-actualisation has been criticised as being vague and therefore difficult to measure (Herman & Hulin, 1973). Finally, Maslow's hierarchy of needs is not applicable to non-Western cultures. For Chinese people, the need to be part of a group is greater than any other need. The need for self-actualisation is interpreted differently by the Chinese: it refers to the individual's contribution to society, rather than striving for individual goals. In general, research indicates that people's needs as they themselves perceive them can be better classified by a simpler system. An example of a simple system is Alderfer's ERG theory (1969, 1972).

Alderfer's theory
According to Alderfer, there are three types of needs. These are:
1 **Existential needs.** These relate to material security. The needs for good working conditions and a regular salary are existential needs. Existential needs are comparable to Maslow's physiological and safety needs.
2 **Relational needs.** These are the needs for good relations with other people and for love and friendship. People like to belong and they strive for appreciation and recognition. Relational needs can be compared with Maslow's social needs and need for recognition.
3 **Growth needs.** These are linked to opportunities for self-development. Growth needs correspond largely to Maslow's self-actualisation needs. The need for self-respect is counted among the growth needs by Alderfer, but for Maslow this need is part of the need for recognition.

Unlike Maslow, Alderfer argues that different types of need can be present simultaneously. There is no fixed order. Moreover, he posits the frustration-regression hypothesis: the more the satisfaction of higher needs is frustrated, the more important the lower-level needs become. Like Maslow, Alderfer is of the opinion that deprivation of needs leads to activation. People are primarily motivated to action if they perceive a deficit.   *Frustration-regression hypothesis*

American research based on the ERG theory yields interesting data (Hellriegel et al., 1989). People whose parents enjoyed higher levels of education turn out to have stronger growth needs than people whose parents had lower levels of education. Men turn out to have more existential needs and fewer relational needs than women. Women have more relational needs than existential needs.   *ERG theory*

© Noordhoff Uitgevers bv

Social needs: a party with colleagues.

McIelland's theory

In every organisation, differences can be seen in the effort put in by different employees. There are people who slack off and others who always work hard. One person is ambitious and wants to get ahead while another is satisfied with what they have. According to McLelland (1971, 1976), every individual develops their own profile of needs in the first years of life. In such a profile, there is a dominant need, and this dominant need determines a person's orientation, independently of the situation in which persons find themselves. It becomes a stable characteristic. McLelland identifies three needs profiles:

Profile of needs

1 **Need for achievement.** If this need is dominant, people to which it applies are primarily focused on performing well. They will look for challenging situations that allow them to demonstrate their capabilities.
2 **Need for power.** People in whom this need is dominant strive for influence and control over others. They try to attain positions in which these can be achieved.
3 **Need for affiliation.** If this need is dominant, people are focused on the creation of good relationships with others.

The dominance of a certain need has been established through research. Andrews (1967) found that among middle and senior management, the need for power is primarily dominant. Kotter (1982) carried out research among 15 higher managers and found strong achievement and power needs. Among lower-level management, the need for affiliation is dominant (Kolb, Rubin & McIntyre, 1984). The question is whether the results of these studies prove that people have a stable dominant need. At first sight, it seems as though people ascend to a management position in an organisation due to a strong need for power. However, the situation can also be looked at from from the other way round. Through a higher position, people obtain power and consider it important for exercising their authority. This situation makes their orientation dominant towards power. Lower-level management generally has little power. To achieve anything, they must enter into good relationships with their subordinates. They can then use these good relationships as a source of influence.

This reasoning fits in with McLelland's view that a dominant need is learned or acquired. In the learning process, the rewarding of behaviour reinforcement plays a major role. A manager who achieves something by exercising power has the tendency to repeat this approach. If 'being friendly' produces the desired effect, this style of approach can become dominant.

Reinforcement

Unlike the preceding theories, McLelland's assumes that needs are not innate but learned. He does, however, assume that learning takes place at a young age and that the dominant pattern, once developed, thereafter remains stable. This is open to debate. What has been learned can be changed or unlearned – for example, by training managers in a different approach. Research is necessary to provide a decisive answer to this question.

1.1.2 Motivation through external forces (the situation)

Behaviour is driven not only by need but also by the a person's situation. A growing child still has much to discover and learn before it can function purposefully. This learning partly takes place by trial and error, through a process of trial and error. In order to achieve something, a child will try out different behaviours. These do not always produce the desired results but occasionally, certain behaviours have the intended effect. Behaviour followed by a desired effect is more likely to be adopted in another similar situation compared to behaviour that elicits no effect or a negative effect. In this way, even a baby can learn that it can get attention simply by crying loudly. Thorndike calls this the law of effect: the consequences of an action determine whether someone has the inclination to repeat the action or not. If the consequences are attractive, there is positive reinforcement. If the consequences are unattractive, there is negative reinforcement.

Trial and error

Law of effect

Positive reinforcement

Negative reinforcement

Crying often has an effect.

EXAMPLE 1.2

Positive and negative reactions

Maya cracks jokes during her first progress meeting with her new colleagues. Her colleagues look offended and do not respond to her witticisms. They do respond, however, when she delivers a substantive contribution to the discussion. Maya stops making jokes after a while and acts in a more businesslike manner.

Conditioned

A certain action that is always followed by positive reinforcement will, after a time, automatically be taken in a similar situation. This action has become conditioned and is included in the behavioural repertoire. However, this action does produce the same effect in every situation.

EXAMPLE 1.3

Modifying behaviour

Maya discovers that she should not make jokes during the progress meeting. However, during coffee and lunch breaks, this same type of behaviour is very much appreciated.

Stimuli

Conditioning

The consequences of a certain action dependend on the characteristics of the situation. These characteristics are called stimuli. A new employee learns to distinguish between an official situation and a coffee break. In the first case, serious behaviour is expected and in the second case a less professional attitude is appreciated. In the process of conditioning, a link is first created between a stimulus (situation) and a response (action). Once this link has been established the situation automatically elicits the conditioned action. A large part of human behaviour is automatically elicited by a situation.

EXAMPLE 1.4

Automatic behaviour

William has worked on a milling machine for years. When he arrives in the morning, he has a long list of set actions, which must take place in a fixed order. First, he goes to the changing room. There, he takes overalls from his locker and changes into them. Subsequently, he greets his colleagues, chats with them, gets a cup of coffee from the machine and goes to the milling machine. There are all the order tickets for the orders he has to complete. He goes through the motions and subsequently programs his machine.

The type of behaviour elicited or not elicited by a given situation is connected to the process of reinforcement. The consequences of the behaviour of employees in an organisation have a notable effect on colleagues and line managers. The latter can elicit the desired behaviour or eliminate undesired behaviour by using positive or negative reactions. Positive reactions include offering attention, compliments, a smile help, information, more assignments, more freedom to organise work and promotion. Negative reactions are ignoring, giving disapproving glances, offering criticism or giving low assessments, and showing anger, or nagging.

By means of systematic reinforcement, the behaviour of an employee can be conditioned. In organisations this learning process can be used to make sure that (new) employees behave in the correct manner and so make a worthwhile contribution to the team.

1.1.3 Motivation through a desire to balance internal and external forces

The first two motivations for behaviour are, in a sense, opposites. On the one hand, people display behaviour because it is elicited by the situation. This is a pulling force. On the other hand, people are encouraged into behaviour by their needs. This is a pushing force. Both approaches suggest that people have no choice: either they follow their needs or they are conditioned into certain behaviour by the situation. In a number of cases, however, the behaviour that people display is the outcome of a process of consideration and choice. Here, both the needs of the person and the possibilities that the situation offers play an important role.

Pulling force
Pushing force

EXAMPLE 1.5

Ambition

Sonia is very ambitious and wants to advance a step in her career. The question is how she should proceed. Are there in fact higher positions to be attained within the bank where she now works? If so, how might she attain them? By working even harder and by establishing better relationships with the senior managers? By networking informally? Or would it be better to apply for a higher position somewhere else?

Before people make a choice, they consider the situation they are in, and also consider the opportunities they have of achieving certain goals or results. They also estimate the likely consequences of certain behaviour. The motivation to display or not to display certain behaviour is the result of a process of deliberation. Two theories describe the considerations that form the basis of behavioural choice: the expectancy theory and the attribution theory.

Expectancy theory

The process of deliberation that determines a certain behaviour is described by Vroom (1964) in his expectancy theory. According to this theory, whether people are inclined to make an effort in their work depends on various considerations:

Expectancy theory

1 The **connection between effort and performance.** This is the estimated likelihood that a certain effort will lead to good performance.

2   The **connection between performance and returns.** This is the extent to which someone believes that good performance will actually lead to attractive returns. Sometimes that connection is clear, because there is a clear reward system, but in many cases it is a matter of waiting to see if certain efforts lead to more appreciation, job security or promotion, for example.

3   The **value of the returns** that certain efforts produce. Work can provide various positive returns, such as good pay, high status, good social contacts and possibilities for growth. There can also be negative returns, such as frustration, physical discomfort, conflict and stress. The value of the returns is the sum of the advantages and disadvantages these extra efforts produce. Extra hard work can lead to a positive evaluation from the boss but a poorer relationship with colleagues, because they see it as showing off. Promotion can produce more salary and status but also more work pressure, worries and responsibility.

The value of the results of work is not the same for everyone. As we discuss in section 1.2, for some employees salary is the most important return, while for other employees challenging work, responsibility and appreciation have greater value. Research has shown that simply having work contributes to people's happiness (see the following example).

BUSINESSWEEK, MARSHALL EN KELLY GOLDSMITH

How Adults Achieve Happiness

How does an adult achieve a high level of contentment while living a frenetic and distraction-packed life? The two of us have just reviewed results from our new survey designed to elicit insights into short-term satisfaction (happiness) and long-term benefit (meaning) – both at work and away from it. Our respondents weren't randomly chosen. They're well-educated managers, entrepreneurs, and professionals, numbering over 3,000.

Our findings were in many cases unexpected but clear-cut. There is an incredibly high correlation between people's happiness and meaning at work and at home. In other words, those who experience happiness and meaning at work tend also to experience them outside of work.(...) Overall satisfaction at work increased only if both the amount of happiness and meaning experienced by employees simultaneously increased. (...) What can companies do differently? They might stop asking, "What can the company do to increase employees' experience of happiness and meaning at work?" which encourages dependency. Instead, managers can encourage employees to ask themselves, "What can I do to increase my experience of happiness and meaning at work?" This strategy may produce a higher return in employee commitment – and do so at a lower cost.

According to expectancy theory, the more likely people estimate there to be a likelihood of achieving positive returns and the more valuable they consider those returns, the greater their effort will be. A student works hard for the upcoming exams, for example, thinking that by so doing they will pass (effort–outcome expectancy) and, by doing so, expecting to have more chance of obtaining work (outcome–return expectancy). Obtaining work has a high value (valence) for the student. If passing the exams is not a means to obtaining more attractive work and earning more money, the student will begin to wonder whether it makes sense to make any effort for the exams. Success is then not connected to attractive returns.

The relationship between effort, returns and values is shown in Figure 1.2.

FIGURE 1.2 The expectation model

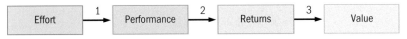

The motivation for someone to make an effort is a function of:
1 Effort-performance expectation
2 Performance-returns expectation
3 Value of the returns

Employees within an organisation like to know whether their efforts lead to positive outcomes and thereby to other returns they consider valuable. How an organisation can take advantage of this fact and thus increase employees' motivation to perform is discussed in chapter 2.

It would seem as though Vroom's expectancy theory is about the more or less objective consideration of the chances of success and the value of returns. This is, however, not the case. It is primarily about subjective considerations and estimates – in particular:
1 the extent to which the relationship between effort and returns (equitability) is thought to be reasonable
2 the extent to which people regard themselves as capable of producing a good performance (self-image).

Attribution theory

The attribution theory (Vroom, 1964; Kelley, 1972) explains why people are willing to make an effort. If people think that they can achieve success with their efforts, they will make those efforts. They are less willing to make efforts if they think that they no positive results can be achieved, whatever they do. How do people arrive at a positive estimation of their potential? This occurs through attribution. Attribution is a process by which people try to find out the causes of their own behaviour and the behaviour of others. Say that a manager of a large export company, for example, is annoyed to find that his excellently prepared proposal receives no support at all at a meeting. He has spent more than six months putting his plans on paper, and now everything seems to have failed. How can this be possible? The manager will want to find cause for the painful situation he finds himself in. The first thing he will ask himself is: "Am I the cause of this issue, or is it due to factors other than myself?" People will try to find out the causes of their failure or success. They do so by comparing themselves to others in the same situation and considering whether there is possibly a set pattern to their failure or success. In determining the causes of success or failure, people take the following into consideration:
- Whether they frequently fail or succeed in similar situations. This enables them to establish whether there is a fixed pattern (when I go out of the door, I always forget to turn off the lights) or whether it happens only occasionally.

Attribution theory

Attribution

© Noordhoff Uitgevers bv

- Whether others fail or succeed in the same situations. If others make the same mistakes, it must be because of the circumstances – for example, because it is very difficult to do well. If only they make mistakes, it will be because they are not as good as others.
- Whether they frequently fail or succeed in other situations.

Internal attribution

The results of the considerations above determine whether a person should seek the cause of their success or failure in themselves or in the circumstances. If someone comes to the conclusion that he is the only one who does something wrong or does it well, and that this is frequently the case, then he will seek the cause in himself. We call this internal attribution.

External attribution

If others also regularly fail in comparable circumstances, then the causes should rather be sought outside oneself. The task was too difficult, for example, or there was too little time. There is external attribution if people ascribe their success or failure to circumstances.

Self-image

When people ascribe their success or failure to themselves, this influences their self-image. Self-image consists in the characteristics that people assign to themselves. For example, people can consider themselves sporty, jovial, modest or intelligent. If someone is regularly better than others in a certain area, e.g. sprinting, that person will ascribe this to their own ability. This

Self-confidence

produces a positive self-image in this area and thus gives self-confidence. The person will not avoid new situations involving sprinting and trusts that

they will again perform well. Someone with self-confidence does not avoid challenges. Someone who always performs poorly in certain situations in comparison to others will feel incompetent in that area and will have a tendency to shy away from those situations.

As people prefer to have a positive self-image, their internal attribution does not always be entirely objective. They have a tendency to be selective and attribute positive characteristics to themselves and negative characteristics to environmental factors. We call this a self-serving bias. In addition to this self-serving bias, there is fundamental attribution error. This error arises from the tendency to attribute someone else's behaviour to their characteristics rather than to external circumstances. If a manager finds that an employee is delivering an assignment late again, they will tend to attribute this to certain characteristics of the employee (laziness, inefficiency) rather than to circumstances (pressure, lack of data and suchlike).

Self-serving bias

Fundamental attribution error

People strive after a positive self-image, since it helps them meet their need to feel capable. Giving them the opportunity to demonstrate their competence increases their motivation to commit. Therefore, it is important for management to ensure that there are situations in which employees can implement their work abilities in a positive manner.

Self-image influences one's performance expectancy. Someone who feels competent will expect their efforts to generate better results than someone who does not feel competent.

1.1.4   Intrinsic and extrinsic motivation

To motivate people to perform well, it is important to have insight into their motives. What motives play a role in the work situation? We can identify two types of motive: intrinsic and extrinsic.

Work-intrinsic motives to perform well relate to the challenge posed by the work itself and to satisfaction in the work. People do not do their best because they expect to be rewarded with greater recognition, a bonus or promotion, for example. They do their best because they like the work and derive satisfaction from performing well. To them, it is more about taking part than about winning. Intrinsic motivation is connected to the previously mentioned need for self-development, the need to be good at something and the need for independence and responsibility.

Work-intrinsic motives

Work-extrinsic motives to perform well relate to the returns that can be achieved, such as money, rewards, good working conditions, high status and promotion. It is more about winning, and less about taking part.

Work-extrinsic motives

Guzzo et al. (1985) analysed more than a hundred studies and came to the conclusion that work-intrinsic motives have a greater motivational effect in organisations than work-extrinsic motives. Organisations can take advantage of this fact (see also chapter 2).

EXAMPLE 1.6

Needs during different life phases

Tom has a need for financial security, favourable employment terms, and good working conditions in this phase of his life. This is because Alma has become self-employed and has no protection against dismissal, no right to unemployment benefit, no pension fund, no collective labour agreement, no sickness benefit and no limitation of liability in the event of losses. She doesn't mind because she likes being independent, wants to take responsibility for her own work and finds the work challenging. The challenge of Tom's work is also important for him.

As seen in example 1.8, both types of motive can be present at the same time.

Employees who are primarily work-extrinsically motivated have an instrumental attitude towards their work. People used to say: "Having work means being able to put bread on the table." We describe this attitude in section 1.6.

People have different needs and interests (motives). All kinds of factors affect these, such as their health, the psychological and relational problems with which they are confronted, their social environment and culture. Motives can also change during one's lifetime. At 60 years old, a person usually has different needs from when they were 20. At 35 years old, one cannot indefinitely keep postponing a decision about whether or not to have children. Having a family changes one's needs and interests.

How people function in organisations is dependent not only on their needs but also on their abilities and competences, personality, attitudes and values.

1.2 Abilities and competences

Employees can be motivated to get a job or acquire a better position, but if they are not sufficiently competent, their efforts will fail. Intelligent people and people who are skilled socially and communicatively often have an advantage.

Abilities
Intelligence

People can have specific abilities, but there is a more general ability: intelligence. People differ in intelligence. Some learn more easily than others. Intelligent people are often quicker at resolving difficult problems and understanding situations. Intelligence is established with an IQ test. A high score in an IQ test suggests that a person will be able to learn a new job quickly, for example, and be successful at work (see also chapter 2). Nevertheless, an IQ score does not tell you everything: it establishes only the person's ability for reasoning, absorbing and processing information, thinking logically and analytically and having spatial awareness. For success at work, other abilities are often also important. An employee should have specific knowledge and skills, for example.

EXAMPLE 1.7

Communicative skill

As a journalist, Alma has frequently reported on events in Eastern Europe. She speaks several Slavic languages, engages with people easily and is able to put her thoughts into words accurately. Now that she has started her own communications consultancy firm, these skills come in very handy.

Competence is not only about specific knowledge and skills necessary to perform well at work. Other abilities, personality traits and motives also play an important part (Kessels, 2011).
As a journalist, Alma's competence in Slavic languages comes in very handy. Her oral and writing skills are also up to standard. Her extroverted nature and ability to empathise with others allows her to easily connect with other people, and intrinsically motivates her to take care in managing and maintaining her relationships.
The skills that are required for a certain position are often listed in job advertisements in newspapers.

Competence

EXAMPLE 1.8

Job application?

Tom reads an advertisement in the newspaper which clearly specifies the abilities he must possess. He is expected to be able to work in a team, to be persuasive, to be independent and to be good at problem-solving. He thinks he has three of these four abilities. Teamwork is not his strongest point: he would rather work solo. He detests 'chatty' people who prevent him from getting rapid results.

1

1.3 Personality

People can differ greatly from one another. Some are impulsive, cheerful and exuberant, while others are serious and cannot express themselves easily.

EXAMPLE 1.9

Clashing personalities

Tom is easily irritated by his colleagues, whom he calls 'chatty'. These cheerful and exuberant colleagues are in turn irritated by Tom's serious behaviour. They also think that he shouldn't work so hard.

Personality

The pattern of characteristic thoughts, feelings and behaviours by which one person distinguishes themselves from another, and which remains fairly constant over time and in different situations, is called their personality.

Attempts have been made to describe the individuality of a person in terms of a number of personal characteristics, also called 'traits'. In terms of what personal characteristics can people be adequately described? Cattell (1973, 1982) identified 16 traits. Nowadays, the Big Five, an internationally known personality test (Goldberg, 1992), is widely used to establish a person's character. As its name suggests, this personality test has five dimensions:

1 Extraversion
At one extreme of this dimension is extraversion and at the other introversion. Extravert people are talkative, spontaneous and exuberant. They like to laugh and touch others. Introverted people are closed and taciturn. They keep their distance. Extravert people can cope with many stimuli. They like dealing with others. Introverted people screen themselves off from too many stimuli. They want to work in peace and quiet.

2 Agreeableness
At one extreme of this dimension is agreeableness and at the other self-absorption and disagreeableness. Agreeable people are gentle, kind-hearted, obliging and peaceful. Disagreeable people are unbending, unyielding and stubborn. Agreeable people are focused on the needs and interests of other people. Disagreeable people push for their own way and cut discussions short.

3 Conscientiousness
At one extreme of this dimension is conscientiousness and at the other laziness. Conscientious people are scrupulous, orderly, precise and careful. They work systematically and purposefully. They like to turn up on time. Lazy people are disordered, careless and frivolous. They lose things and do their work at the last minute.

EXAMPLE 1.10

Creative and immune to stress

Carlo has achieved a low score on conscientiousness in the Big Five test. It's true that he is a bit nonchalant, he says. He likes change and is not very focused on details. He begins all sorts of projects but is not so good at finishing them. Carlo can take on a lot of tasks at once without suffering any stress. He likes to improvise.

---

4 Emotional stability
At one end of this dimension is emotional stability and at the other end emotional instability (neuroticism). Emotionally stable people are imperturbable and cool-headed. They can detach themselves from problems and are immune to stress. Emotionally unstable people are panicky, anxious and emotional. They can quickly be overcome by emotion and have vivid imaginations.

5 Openness to experience
At one end of this dimension are people who are open to experience and at the other people who shut themselves off from new experiences. People who are open to experience are imaginative, creative and reflective. People who shut themselves off are over-polite and do not undertake anything on their own initiative. They agree with everything.

EXAMPLE 1.11

Social and careful

Natasha has not scored highly on openness to experience. It is not surprising. On the one hand, she doesn't like surprises and prefers a predictable environment. On the other hand, however, she does like variety. This can cause difficulty because the two desires are often incompatible.

What is the purpose of this personality test? For the individual employee, self-knowledge is important for making the right choices when selecting a profession or career and for personal development. People who are highly introverted and score low on agreeableness would be unwise to choose a profession in which they have to be around people. Examples are care professions, sales and management positions.

Big Five scores can also be used by employers in the selection process, in order to establish who is the right person for a certain position. A candidate should score highly on the characteristics that are required for the position in order to be considered (see chapter 2).

1.4 Attitudes

EXAMPLE 1.12

Car pooling?

Stimulated by some remarks made by his manager, Duncan is considering car pooling. He makes a list of positive factors: it saves costs; it is good for the environment (and the organisation wants to improve its performance in this respect); his manager is in favour of it.

But he also feels car pooling doesn't suit him because he does not want to sit in a car with the same colleague every day; he would rather be on his own; he wants to be able to decide when to travel himself; the organisation should not force him to car pool. Therefore, I will not do it.

Attitude

The position that Duncan adopts with regard to car pooling in example 1.12 can be called an attitude. An attitude is a reasonably stable position with regard to other (groups of) people, types of behaviour, things or ideas.

Cognitive considerations

Affective or emotional considerations

How do people arrive at a certain attitude? Two factors play a part. In listing the advantages and disadvantages of car pooling, Duncan is using cognitive considerations. In allowing his feelings to come into play – for example, his reluctance to be forced – he is using affective or emotional considerations. Emotional considerations are often decisive in the attitudes that people adopt.

Attitudes elicit behaviour. If Duncan adopts a positive attitude to car pooling, there is a good chance that he will join in. However, the relationship between attitude and behaviour is not a direct one. Other factors intervene on the way from desire to action.

EXAMPLE 1.13

Impediments

In principle, Duncan intends to start car pooling, but in practice nothing comes of it because he has flexible working hours, so it is difficult to make regular arrangements

with others. It is also difficult to find colleagues who can pick him up without having to make a big detour. The issue therefore remains problematic.

Behavioural intention

As the example shows, an attitude produces only a tendency to adopt certain behaviour. We call this a behavioural intention. Whether someone actually transforms this behavioural intention into behaviour is dependent on several factors. Three factors are set out in Kok's ASE model (De Vries, Mudde and Strecher, 1991): one's own attitude, the influence of the environment (society) and one's own effectiveness, i.e. the perceived likelihood of impediments to the adoption of the intended behaviour (see Figure 1.3).

FIGURE 1.3 The ASE model

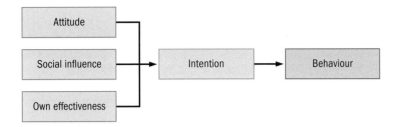

According to the ASE model, the likelihood of adopting certain behaviour, such as car pooling, increases if:

- a person has a positive attitude towards car pooling;
- the person's social environment also has a positive attitude and pressure is put upon the individual to join in (e.g. if the majority of colleagues do it and they emphasise how financially beneficial it is and how it helps the environment by, for example, reducing traffic jams);
- a person finds that they can make the necessary arrangements with they colleagues. If this turns out to be difficult, they quickly give up.

People can experience uneasiness if their attitudes and behaviour are contradictory. This creates cognitive dissonance. For example, Duncan wants to help the environment and should therefore start car pooling, but at the same time he would like to decide for himself how he goes to work. Cognitive dissonance causes uneasiness and tension. This creates a need for 'dissonance reduction' and the brain attempts to reduce this dissonance.

Cognitive dissonance

EXAMPLE 1.14

How to eliminate cognitive dissonance

Duncan knows that he should start car pooling, but he doesn't do it. He combats his uneasiness by telling himself that sharing a car with a colleague doesn't make much difference to the environment, or that he is actually not particularly in favour of car pooling.

1.5 The relationship between individual and organisation

People generally like to be part of an organisation. This often produces a great deal of value, such as income, status and social contacts. These rewards do not just happen: people have to invest time and energy into the work that they do and they must adapt to the demands the organisation imposes on them.

EXAMPLE 1.15

In the organisation's interests

Carla, the head of the Marketing and Sales Department, is happy with her new employee, Johan, because he has a lively personality and the right skills. But she also wants Johan to exhibit appropriate behaviour and, for example, give the right impression to clients and external contacts.

Exchange relationship

The relationship between individual and organisation has the character of an exchange relationship. The employee helps to achieve organisational goals through their contribution. They make an effort, contribute time and energy to their work and place their physical and mental abilities at the organisation's disposal. The organisation can profit from those abilities, skills, personality and motivation. It offers rewards (benefits) in return. The organisation ensures that the employee benefits from such rewards as a good salary, interesting work, agreeable colleagues and attractive prospects.

Table 1.1 shows what can be exchanged between employees and organisations. For employees, the benefits are essentially of two types: economic and affective.

TABLE 1.1 Contribution and benefits of people in organisations

Contribution	Benefits
• Time	• Salary and perks
• Effort	• Interesting work
• Knowledge	• Social contacts
• Skills	• Appreciation and status
• Social support	• Training, education and career prospects

People turn a situation to their own advantage as much as possible, in order to make the exchange as favourable as possible for themselves. March and Simon (1958) therefore posit that an individual decides to work for an organisation on the basis of a negotiated contract (see chapter 2).

Mutual dependence

A result of the exchange relationship is mutual dependence. Individual and organisation need each other to achieve their goals. The organisation can function well only if it has employees who are prepared to achieve the desired results. The employee needs the organisation to achieve their individual goals, such as a good salary, meaningful work and self-development.

The mutual dependence is not complete. People can leave an organisation if the exchange no longer suits them. Organisations can replace people with other people. An employee spends only a certain amount of their time in the organisation; they have time to do other things, which may also bring them rewards.

Working with interruptions.

EXAMPLE 1.16

Leisure activities

Tom goes jogging with a neighbour twice a week and every Thursday evening he plays music in a band. He also tries to find the time to go swimming and play with his daughter every week. And perhaps he go on that dance course with Alma?

Not all of a person's abilities are always relevant to a position. The organisation has an interest in the employee making as much effort as possible, but too much personal investment in his work can lead to problems. The organisation uses people for part of their time and part of their potential. The relationship is therefore characterised by partial commitment on both sides.

This explanation of the exchange relationship suggests that people's commitment to organisations is based solely on economic considerations. This is not always the case. According to Etzioni (1961), three types of commitment are possible:

Commitment

1 **Obligation**. The employee's contribution is made under obligation. This can be the case in prison or in the armed forces.
2 **Use**. The employee's contribution leads to the results that the organisation wishes to achieve.
3 **Norms and values**. The employee's contribution is made for ideological or religious reasons. This is the case in a political organisation, for example.

The commitment of people to organisations can, of course, be based on several considerations. These considerations determine people's attitudes towards their work and the organisation.

1.6 Commitment

The emphasis on the exchange-based relationship between employees and their organisation suggests that employees consider whether to continue working for and put an effort into an organisation base their decision solely on rational considerations. This is not the case. Emotional considerations also play a role. How do employees become involved in the organisation they work for? The concept of commitment refers to the bond between a person and an organisation. The greater the level of commitment, the more the employee identifies with the organisation and they more they wish to remain part of it. Meyer and Allen (1997) distinguish between three types of commitment:

- Affective commitment. The feeling that one is part of an organisation (sense of community).
- Normative commitment. The feeling that leaving the organisation would not be the decent thing to do.
- Continuity commitment. The consideration that it would be too difficult to re-accumulate all that has been invested in the job so far (training, pension plan, promotion) at another company.

The first two types of commitment involve emotional considerations. The latter is to do with a rational one. Employees only experiencing continuity commitment remain in an organisation based on a cost-benefit analysis. Should they find out that they could do better elsewhere, they will leave the organisation. They are not prepared to offer additional effort or to help their colleagues. They put in just enough work to make sure they do not lose their job.

All three types of commitment influence the extent to which an employee is inclined to stay with an organisation. Affective commitment also relates to other factors. Employees with high levels of affective commitment show less absenteeism and a greater tendency to put in an effort for the organisation. What are the factors that determine the extent to which an employee shows commitment? The first is personal characteristics. Some individuals are more sensitive to their social environment, whereas others have a greater interest in their income or job security. The second is relational factors. Affective commitment increases as employees experience greater appreciation from their colleagues. The third factor is the nature of the work. Employees fulfilling functions that require a greater skill set, that offer them a sense of responsibility, and that they are able to perform to some level of personal discretion experience greater commitment than employees performing short-cycle routine jobs that require little training and whose activities have been strictly prescribed.

1.7 Job satisfaction

If commitment describes the extent to which someone feels bound to an organisation, work satisfaction means the extent to which someone perceives their work and working conditions as pleasant or enjoyable (Locke, 1976). How positively people view their work and working conditions is connected with the following factors:

1 **Work characteristics.** How someone perceives their work is often dependent on the extent to which the work is dull or varied, the extent to which it

appeals to their own character, the extent to which it is possible for them to influence the way in which the work is done, and the social status of the work.

2 Nature of the **social environment**. The social environment comprises colleagues and management. They can be pleasant or unpleasant to work with. They can also provide or fail to provide **social support** in situations where there is a need for it (see also subsection 10.4.2). Quite a few professions are hazardous or require emotional commitment. Consider police officers, firemen, prison wardens, nurses, social workers and teachers. In these professions, employees can be exposed to harassment, aggression, violence, accidents, illness and death. In these situations, social support helps the employee to achieve acceptance. But social support can also be beneficial in less serious situations, such as periods of work overload.

3 Nature of the **reward**. If an employee considers that the reward they derive from their work is commensurate with the effort that has to be made to carry out the work, there is said to be equitability (see also section 1.9).

Social support: a safety officer monitors the welfare of his colleagues as they extinguish a fire.

Research shows that it is primarily the characteristics of the work itself that influence work satisfaction (Judge and Hulin, 1993; Taber and Alliger, 1995). People with a high degree of work satisfaction have a high affective commitment to the organisation in which they work, have less inclination to leave the organisation, and perform better than people with low satisfaction (Arnold et al., 1998; Meyer et al., 1993).

1.8 Equitability

The attitude of people towards their work and the commitment that results from it are partly determined by the relationship between their efforts on behalf of the organisation (costs) and the results obtained (rewards). People make a cost-benefit analysis and strive for equitability.

Cost-benefit analysis

Equitability   Equitability means that the efforts people put in must be in proportion to the rewards they obtain. When people make a great deal of effort, they expect greater rewards than when they invest much less effort.
But what is a fair relationship between costs and rewards? In general, it is difficult to establish this objectively.

EXAMPLE 1.17

Comparing oneself to others

William earns a modal average income. He finds that he has to work hard in comparison with people in public service. They have it a lot easier, in his view. Still, he is reasonably satisfied with his salary, certainly if he compares his job to others that are physically more demanding, which sometimes pay even less.

What an employee considers a fair relationship between his efforts and his rewards is often arrived at by comparison. The process involves two types of comparison (Thibaut & Kelley, 1959):
- **General comparison level**. This arises from comparison with other people. It produces a norm that indicates the lower limit of a fair relationship between costs and benefits.
- **Comparison level for alternatives**. The cost-benefit relationship of the employee's current position is then compared with that of available alternatives.

Everyone has their own norms for determining whether their efforts are reasonable for the rewards they receive. These norms are primarily created by comparison with other people. From that process of comparison a lower limit for the cost-benefit ratio is established. If the costs are too high or the benefits too low, people will perceive the relationship as unfair. If the relationship between costs and benefits is more favourable or reasonable, then people see it as fair. People not only apply general norms, but also look at what alternatives are on offer.

EXAMPLE 1.18

Alternatives

William has heard that in another factory employees doing the same work have better conditions and more opportunities to progress to a higher position. This alternative is thus more attractive in terms of the cost–benefit ratio.

Balance theory   The equitability theory can be regarded as a balance theory. If a lack of equitability is perceived, a feeling of tension arises. People will try to reduce this tension until a new balance is achieved (see Figure 1.4).

FIGURE 1.4 Reduction of equitability

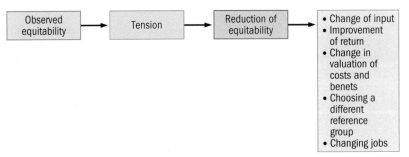

Source: Thibaut & Kelley, 1981

When people perceive a lack of equitability, they can act in various ways:
- **Adaptation of effort.** If the rewards obtained are too low, people can decide to make less effort, thereby making the relationship between costs and rewards more equitable. If people find that they are getting too many rewards, they can increase their efforts.
- **Improving the rewards.** People can try to obtain better rewards, for example by asking for the working environment to be improved by reducing noise nuisance or providing better ventilation. Demands for pay increases are another example of this type of action.
- **Change of appreciation.** A lack of equitability can also be countered by a different appreciation of costs and rewards. People can, for example, perceive a lack of equitability because more rewards are obtained than is reasonable. In this case, they are overpaid. This can lead to a re-evaluation of the situation. The employee can convince himself and others of the special value of his contribution to the organisation. The employee may also consider the contributions of his colleagues. He can raise or lower his evaluation of their contributions until he finds it reasonable that they receive more or fewer rewards than he does.
- **Choosing a different reference group.** An employee can choose different people to compare himself with. He may realise that it is not realistic to keep comparing himself with colleagues who used to work with him in the department, for example. These colleagues now have very different tasks and are categorised at different functional levels.
- **Leaving or changing jobs.** If an employee continues to perceive a strong sense of a lack of equitability, he can opt to look for another job and resign.

In general, people are inclined to act sooner when they perceive themselves to be disadvantaged by a lack of equitability than when they perceive their rewards to be too great.

1.9 Changing relationships

Various organisations are working on reorganising their employees working conditions. Whereas employee work activities were formerly tied to particular fixed hours and locations, the introduction of New World of Work (NWW) has changed all that. This change involves the implementation of four principles (Baane et al., 2010):
1 Employees are able to perform their activities independently of place and time. They are largely able to determine when and where they work

themselves. This means: no fixed working location and fixed groups of colleagues working together at the same times. Flexible work means employees being able to determine where, with whom, and how they work. The core concept is that of flexibility in terms of time, space, and working method.

2 Direct supervision and control of employee activities are no longer possible. This means employers need to make agreements with their staff in terms of targets (results-based management).

3 Whenever and wherever they are at work, employees should be able to freely access the information and tools they require to do their job. Proper ICT-support is essential. Whether employees are working from home on during their commute, they should be able to sign in from anywhere to receive direct access to required information, or to contact colleagues, supervisor, or other parties (customers, project members, suppliers, etcetera).

4 Employees have flexible working relationships and contract types. Employees enter into arrangements dictating the degree of freedom with regards to their places and times and work.
   In practice, this freedom comes in different forms. Some employees enjoy full freedom, others are required to spend at least 50% of their time at a predetermined location; some companies set a maximum to the number of virtual meetings, with face-to-face contact being required at specified times.

EXAMPLE 1.19

The case of Microsoft

Microsoft introduced flexible working without using blueprints or multi-annual planning. Director of Human Resources Management Ineke Hoekman-van Hasse: 'The idea was for the human being to become the central axis in the age of working, independently of time or place. Another pillar was that there should be sufficient attention for cooperation and mutual communication. Top level management was the first to learn how to manage for results, learning to let go and trust their employees. This was followed by training modules that were open to all interested employees.' At the same time, Microsoft was able to move to new offices. There were no fixed work stations or landline telephones, and all office spaces also doubles as meeting spaces. Employees are not subject to fixed office days, and teams themselves determine the number of physical meetings required to optimise their virtual collaboration. Some teams meet three times per week, others meet once every three months - which is made possible by everyone having learned to make use of the available technologies as efficiently as possible.

The New Way of Working: no fixed work stations or landline telephones.

The office no longer houses fixed locations that are the 'property' of a single employee. Those wanting to work at the office can make use of any work site not yet occupied. The office is less of a work location and more of facility promoting social interaction and cohesion and preventing detachment.

The introduction of NWW has changed something fundamental about the relationship between the individual and the organisation. Organisations that have implemented NWW are no longer the same types of social environments which can used to derive support, appreciation, and social contacts. The question is whether this will influence the exchange-based relationship between individuals and organisations and attitudes with regard to work. Proponents of NWW are promoting its implementation by emphasising the expected resulting benefits:
• improved employee satisfaction and commitment;
• improved employee performance;
• improved collaboration between employees and between organisational units;
• improved utilisation of available knowledge;
• improved customer satisfaction;
• reduced housing, travel, and ICT expenses;
• reduced absenteeism and unwanted staff turnover.

Sub-paragraph 2.5.3 discusses whether these positive effects will occur, what the negative (side-)effects are, and what conditions need to be met in order to make NWW a success.

Changes in relationships are also shown by the increasing numbers of company and organisational employees with a flexible employment contract instead of a permanent position. In the Netherlands, for example, the percentage of flex(ible) workers was only at 15% in 2004, but had gone up to 22% by 2014. The reasons for making use of flex workers differ per company. Firstly, flex workers can be used to compensate for fluctuations in production or service scope. Flex workers can easily be hired or let go as situations require (i.e. whenever they are or are not needed). Secondly, flex workers can be employed to meet a temporary demand for certain highly specialised work which the organisation does not have on its permanent payroll. This usually involves hiring self-employed workers.

Flex(ible) workers

NRC HANDELSBLAD, CAROLA HOUTEKAMER

Shifting flexibility

DAF lowers production due to collapsed export to Russia; flex workers the first to be sent home.

Each of the 140 lorries manufactured every day by DAF Trucks in Eindhoven is different. Different cab, different gear box, different coupling high, different colour.

You will not find robotic clamps holding the tools in the factory - just human hands. With the inevitable result being that, if fewer lorries are produced, fewer hands are required.

Per this month, DAF has lowered production from 164 to 140 trucks per day: a 15 percent drop compared to last year. A

© Noordhoff Uitgevers bv

weak rouble; a poor Russian market; a Western Europe that is only slowly picking up. And this is not the first drop in production - there was a drop from 212 to 164 lorries in 2014 already.

DAF's collective agreement, 'established by union agreement', demands that no employee shall have performed more than 45 hours over or under their contract the end of the year. Any excess is to be paid out or waived. But over the course of the year, the 'balance' can grow to as many as 80 hours. And waiving the hours sometimes leads to inequality in the workplace, says Schippers.

DAF also employs flew workers; nearly one thousand. That number will be the first to be lowered now that production has gone down. Schippers: "We do not think Russia is anywhere near their normal levels. A more temporary dip would have been solved by looking at working hours. This is more of a structural issue." During brief dips and peaks, DAF prefers to retain the permanent crew. "Training somebody to work on the floor takes at least 120 hours. It is an expensive process."

Organisations using flex workers need to determine the ratio between the core of permanent employees and the scope of the flexible workforce. The continuity of production requires a sufficient number of staff members in the permanent core to perform those tasks that require substantial experience and/or specialised knowledge - since those can only be fulfilled by flex workers following a long training period, which costs time and money. The extent to which organisational culture and desired 'look' towards customers in terms of quality and (the provisions of) service are maintained are also factors that are influenced by the relative sizes of the permanent core and the flexible workforce. Employees with a flexible contract will feel less committed to the organisation by which they are employed, unless there is the possibility of a permanent contract. And those

employees may also feel less motivated to conform to the company's
standards of performance (see paragraph 2.5.3).

One aspect of flex working is job insecurity; this insecurity may lead to
certain levels of stress. The occurrence and severity of that stress depends on
people's motives for choosing to perform flex work. We can distinguish
between voluntary and involuntary motives. People who choose flex work
because they do not want to commit to a permanent position, and who
enjoy switching jobs regularly, do so from a voluntary motive. People who
would prefer a permanent contract but are unable to obtain one, even
though they still need an income, will be forced to agree to a flexible
contract; their motive is involuntary. Only 20% of flex workers prefers a
flexible contract. The remaining 80% is aiming for a permanent position.
Research shows that, compared to permanent employees, flex workers who
work from a voluntary motive are better motivated to deliver a solid
performance than flex workers whose motive is involuntary (Koeman, 2006).

Job insecurity

Voluntary and
involuntary
motives

1

© Noordhoff Uitgevers bv

Tips for managers

As a manager, you have an interest in motivating employees. By holding regular performance appraisals, you will obtain an insight into the sources of motivation and needs of your employees.

Obtaining insight into sources of motivation
Ask your employees how they like their work and what their needs are. Ask the following questions:
- Are you instrumentally or emotionally involved committed to your work?
- Are you extrinsically or intrinsically motivated?
- How can I best satisfy your needs?

If you do not know exactly how your employees regard their work or what needs they have, you can ask the following questions:
- Why do you work for this organisation and what would you like to achieve?
- What do you like best about your work and working conditions?
- What do find most annoying in your work and working conditions?

Subsequently, adjust your means of motivation to your employees' preferences and needs.

Giving appreciation
Appreciation seems to be an important reward for just about everyone, and it also stimulates emotional involvement. Regularly offer compliments and social support as a token of appreciation. If you do not know whether that is sufficient, ask, for example, at every performance appraisal:
- What are good tokens of appreciation for you?

Discontented employees – i.e. those who perceive a lack of equitability between their efforts and their rewards – can be asked the following questions in a performance appraisal:
- To what extent are you satisfied with your salary and the appreciation you receive?
- Do you consider that you are sufficiently rewarded for the work you do here? If this is not the case, ask why.

Motivating discontented employees
If you have a discontented employee, the following applies:
- Take criticism or complaints seriously. Do not brand someone as a 'complainer'. Listen, ask lots of questions and see if anything can be done about the problem. Managers who never listen have complaining employees.
- See whether adjustments to the work are necessary. Does the work need to be more interesting or easier? Is there a lack of tools or facilities?
- Consider whether you yourself should handle the employee differently. Should you provide more appreciation and support? Should you show more interest in his problems? Should you direct your employee less and leave him alone more, or should you make it much clearer what you expect from him?
- Your employees wish to be rewarded equitably. This does not mean giving everyone exactly the same rewards. People are different and thus should be rewarded differently. Rewards can be given in the form of money or promotion, but there are other types of reward that your employees might appreciate, such as compliments, a dinner, flexible working hours or a week's holiday.

Summary

▶ People have different motives for making efforts for an organisation. These motives can result from internal forces, also called needs.

▶ Needs can be:
- inborn
- situation-dependent
- a combination of inborn and situatio-nal factors.

▶ A person's functioning in an organisation is also dependent on:
- personal characteristics
- abilities
- employee values and attitudes

▶ Types of commitment:
- affective commitment
- normative commitment
- continuity commitment

▶ Job satisfaction is determined by:
- the nature of the work
- the relationships with colleagues and the manager
- the rewards

▶ Types of rewards are:
- economic (salary, bonus, company car)
- affective (appreciation, status, good working relations, meaningful work)

▶ The relationship between the employee and the organisation is an exchange.

▶ The employee's contribution consists of:
- time
- energy
- abilities

▶ The organisation's contribution comprises:
- provision of work
- rewards

▶ People strive for an equitable relationship between their efforts and their rewards. A lack of equitability leads to tension.

© Noordhoff Uitgevers bv

Assignments

1.1 Motivation, ambition, and commitment

John Paul is intrinsically motivated to work hard for his company, because he feels proud at helping to manufacture such wonderful products. He feels connected to the organisation, and believes that his work allows him to make good use of his skills. He is also ambitious, however, and has set his sights on a higher step on the corporate ladder. Will he be successful? He feels he is capable enough, but he is not looking for a management position by way of favouritism or sucking up. But those, it would seem, are exactly the types of behaviour that lead to success in his organisation.

a Do you think John Paul will put in effort to achieve a higher position? Use Vroom's expectancy theory in your answer.

b If John Paul chooses not go for a higher position, will that impact his commitment to and satisfaction with his work?

1.2 Personality and the Big 5

The staff of a medium-size ICT-company is spending a weekend of survival activities in France. The first assignment for the teams is to go rafting on a large float. John is an outgoing, social character, quick to take charge. Jerry is quiet, reserved, helpful and friendly, and keeps his eye firmly on the ball. Abby is talkative, restless, and masks her fear by cracking jokes. Chris is adventurous and creative. As far as she is concerned, the faster and the more thrilling the ride, the better. Eventually, the team manages a very good performance.

a Does that have to do with the combination of their personalities and abilities?

b Characterise the four individuals using the five dimensions of the Big Five.

1.3 How to reduce unfairness

Two young individuals (Ann and Bernie) started with a medium-sized organisation on the same day. Their education has been similar, and they are both highly motivated to explore the organisation and to develop their own skills. Ann receives extra attention from her managers, while Bernie receives her on the job training courtesy of two senior-employees. Ann is given many extra opportunities and is asked to take part in different projects. Bernie is not given the same opportunities, and he feels he is being treated unfairly. He becomes more and more withdrawn, and his commitment is waning. He starts to doubt his own capabilities, and becomes convinced that Ann is much better than he is.

a In which two ways can Bernie reduce the unfairness he experiences in the situation described?

b Imagine you were in Bernie's shoes. What would you do? Would you become upset and fight for your position? Or would you look for employment elsewhere? Study the book and find out how you might deal with this situation.

1

1.4 The New World of Working

NWW does not suit all employees equally. Research by Van Yperen (2012) shows that this philosophy is best suited for male supervisors who are able to work independently, exhibit strong autonomous qualities, and require less social interaction in the workplace.

a What types of needs do these supervisors have according to Alderfer?
b What types of personal characteristics do they probably exhibit on the dimensions of the Big Five personality test?

2

Integration and motivation

- How can the right people be recruited and selected?
- How are new employees helped with integrating and what resources are available for integration?
- How can employees be motivated to make an effort?
- What effects do the different forms of motivation have?
- How can employees be retained?

© Noordhoff Uitgevers bv

Recruitment and selection

2

Erdal is an experienced personnel officer with many years of service. He is proud of having gained a degree in HR management in his spare time. Now he has a great job as a senior personnel officer and puts his heart and soul into his work. He recently hired a number of new people, including Maya. During job interviews, he primarily looks at personality factors, motivation and the appropriate skills for the job. "If you have to work with clients, you need a pleasant and calm manner. You must be able to listen and show that you understand. And you must also be sure of yourself, in order to cope with difficult clients."

Recently, there has been a high outflow of personnel. A number of people have taken sick leave after experiencing aggressive clients, and many people still in their 30s have found other jobs or started their own businesses.

2.1 Recruitment and selection

In the above example, personnel officer Erdal is hard at work attracting employees. In his company there is a high outflow of personnel and the vacancies must be filled.

Attracting employees involves a process of recruitment and selection. Various recruitment activities must be undertaken to make potential candidates aware of the vacancy. If several people wish to be considered for the job, Erdal needs to find out which of the applicants is the most suitable via a meticulous selection process.

2.1.1   Job requirements and job descriptions
Before commencing recruitment, it is necessary to gain a full understanding of the nature of the job for which you wish to hire someone. The following details should be clear at the very least:
- the title and the purpose of the job;
- the place of the job in the organisation;
- the tasks that go with the job;
- the authority and responsibilities that go with the job;
- the internal and external contacts that must be maintained;
- the specific circumstances in which the work has to be carried out, such as the working hours and the workplace.

Filling in these details results in a job description at the task level.   *Job description*

A job description at task level is by no means always complete. It describes not only the work employees have to do, but also how the work should be performed and in what employees are required to conduct themselves when working with others, such as colleagues, management or clients. In an organisation in which people must collaborate and consult a great deal, it is unwise to attract a person who possesses the right skill set but prefers to work alone and takes little notice of others. In addition to a description of   *Job-specific requirements*
job-specific requirements there must also be a description of person-related requirements, such as the ability to work well in a group, resistance to stress,   *Person-related requirements*
flexibility, customer-orientation and dynamism. These person-related requirements are also called skills.   *Skills*

These days, recruiting no longer revolves around the use of job profiles. Such profiles are mainly useful for filtering out unsuitable candidates, but less suitable when trying to predict the capabilities of the applicants that do meet the criteria. Attracting good candidates involves taking a good look at rewards, personal and career development possibilities, and organisational culture.

EXAMPLE 2.1

Competences

Care workers in a self-guiding team need to be competent in terms of oral communication, customer orientation, and flexibility. Being result-oriented is a competence that applies to many professions, from sales agents to lawyers to teachers to 3D artists. But an artist also needs creativity, and a lawyer is well served by the ability to cope with stress and the ability to convince others. Managers who include the competence of organisational sensitivity in their competence profile need to be able to display the knowledge, skills, and personal characteristics associated with that competence. But how do you measure these competences? How exactly is such a manager expected to behave?

2.1.2 Methods of recruitment

Recruitment

Organisations can recruit internally or externally. Internal recruitment means looking for suitable employees within the existing pool. Advantages of internal recruitment are reduced costs and management's existing knowledge of the nature, knowledge, and skills of the employee applying to the new position. It may serve as a motivational tool for involved employees. One disadvantage is the risk of selection bias and favouritism.

External recruitment occurs through various channels. Traditional recruitment through job adverts happens less and less, whereas recruitment through on-line resources happens more and more. There are several examples of recruitment methods:
- the organisation's own website, which can be used to present the organisation's working climate and offer an overview of outstanding vacancies. Dedicated job recruitment pages on the website may also be used to encourage applicants to send in unsollicited application, attracting a motivated, high-initiative audience;
- recruiting new staff with help from the old (referral recruitment). Referral recruitment is an appealing option because it saves on recruitment costs. The chance of a successful match is also very good, since employees are often very capable of assessing someone's suitability;
- social media platforms like LinkedIn, Facebook or Twitter;

View vacancies online.

- recruitment websites, job vacancy search engines, or job boards. Searching those sites is not always the most user-friendly process - but a meta-crawler such as Monster.com can be helpful;
- on-line recruitment. Recruitment using classifieds is on the decline, whereas recruitment using on-line resources is on the rise. Finding suitable applicants through social media is less successful than using company, recruitment, or job vacancy websites. The average rate of success for these sites is 73%, whereas the success rate via social media is 40%. When looking for high-potentials to fulfill specialist functions, social media can be a helpful source of information for recruiters, since those platforms offer the unemployed a way of presenting themselves, their competences, and their job experience. And they allow recruiters to approach suitable applicants directly.
- guerilla marketing. an unconventional way of attracting the attention of a relevant target audience, for example through playful or unusual advertising campaigns.

EXAMPLE 2.2

Guerilla marketing

Guerilla is the diminutive form of the Spanish word guerra: war. Heineken was the first to make use of this type of marketing in the 1970s, when they had 100 pretty women and 100 handsome men visit all bars in New York to order a Heineken. Bartenders who could not help them were met with an outrageous display of discontent. Within the next month, Heineken had become a supplier for 72% of all of New York's hospitality providers. A recent example is the painted image of a boa constrictor that appeared to strangle the life out of several of Copenhagen's public transport buses, in an effort to promote the local zoo.

Promotional image for Copenhagen Zoo on a public bus.

This list is by no means exhaustive. Other recruitment methods include approaching possible candidates through meetings, presentations and events at schools, universities, conferences, or conventions. Radio and TV adverts are also possible.

© Noordhoff Uitgevers bv

2.1.3   Selection

Selection

Selection usually begins with the assessment of written texts: a CV and a letter of application. Sometimes a candidate has to fill in an additional questionnaire on the internet.

Interview

Unstructured
interview

The most important means of selection is usually the interview. This interview is usually unstructured in form. The interviewers have established the questions they wish to ask the applicant in broad outline, but this is only a framework for the interview. Depending on the candidate's responses and questions, the interview will run its own course. The interview has two goals:
1 to provide information about the nature of the organisation and the requirements of the particular job
2 to obtain information from the applicant in order to make a prediction about his/her suitability.

The interview in part exists to enable an applicant to decide whether the organisation fits in with their own ideals, while giving the organisation the opportunity to establish whether the candidate fulfils the organisation's requirements. Whether job-specific requirements can be met is usually already clear from the letter of application. In the interview, therefore, it is primarily the 'soft' criteria, such as personal characteristics and interpersonal skills, that are evaluated. Will the person be able to well in a team, be flexible enough, fit in with the way we interact with one another, display sufficient application? If the person has to work in a team, it is sensible to have one or more team members present at the interview. They may well be able to sense whether the applicant would fit into the team.

Will this applicant be hired?

Because the interview is not about 'hard' criteria and usually does not take long, it is not easy to obtain a true picture of the candidate – on the one hand because it is a tense situation for that person, so that they perhaps behave differently than they would in a familiar situation, and on the other hand because the applicant is able to emphasise their best points and hide weaker ones. What people say about themselves is not always entirely true. As a result, the predictive value of an interview is variable. First impressions may or may not accurately indicate how a person will behave in reality.

People can easily make errors of judgement. A candidate could make a wonderful first impression in an interview, for example, but later turn out to be entirely unsuitable for the job. In other words, there could be a 'halo effect' (see example 2.2).

EXAMPLE 2.3

Halo effect

A new candidate impresses Erdal as enthusiastic and knowledgeable. His first impression has inclined Erdal to think that the candidate also has other attractive personal characteristics ('image'). He thinks, for example, that this candidate is also sociable and knowledgeable and that they has initiative and courage. In reality, the new candidate is a person who can present themselves well but has little more to offer, is not very knowledgeable and, furthermore, is rather lazy.

Selective perception always plays a part: you miss things or see things that are not there. You can interpret a person's behaviour incorrectly. Everyone is selective in their observations, and for different reasons. A person from another culture, for example, often behaves differently in an interview. If a woman lowers her eyes, that does not necessarily mean she is shy and unsuited to working with clients or unable to deliver good performance.

An unstructured interview thus has certain limitations. People therefore often opt for other means of selection, such as a structured interview, psychological test or assessment centre.

2.1.4   The structured interview

A job interview is usually unstructured. Certain points that must be discussed are fixed but the further course of the interview depends on the applicant's responses and the incidental questions he raises. This gives the applicant the opportunity to emphasise their strong points and lead the interview in a desired direction. With a structured interview, the discussion is more strongly directed by the organisation and the questions are more precisely focused on the characteristics and behaviour that are essential for the job. The structured interview, which is also called the criterion-oriented interview, requires a great deal of preparation.

Criterion-oriented interview

First, the essential skills required for the job for which the company is recruiting must be established. For this, a task analysis is necessary, in which the skills are divided into two areas (Borman and Motowidlo, 1993):

1 **Task skills**. These are the skills necessary to properly carry out the tasks that are part of the person's job.
2 **Contextual skills**. These are the skills necessary in order to become a good and committed member of the organisation.

© Noordhoff Uitgevers bv

PW, LOEK VAN DEN BROEK

Further questioning

Applicants generally talk easily about their experience. Often, however, they talk at the 'we' level. 'We did this' or 'We did that together'. This says little or nothing about the behaviour of the applicant themselves. In a selection interview, it is important to get the candidate off this we level and make them talk about their own contribution.

Questions like 'Who took the initiative?', 'What was your role exactly?' or 'Which responsibilities were yours?' provide more insight into the potential of the applicant. The chances that they will repeat such behaviour in his new job are good. The more recent the behaviour, the greater the chances of repetition. Circumstances also play a part. The more the new job resembles the old job, the greater the chances of identical behaviour, but it is never a guarantee. Behaviour depends on several variables: the new job and the situation, but also knowledge, motivation, personality and experience. Furthermore, behaviour in itself is not everything; even more important are the results that the person has achieved. After the formulation of questions at the 'I' level, it is important that you ask for the results of the applicant's actions. Questions like 'What was the effect?', 'How did that turn out?', 'What did you achieve?', 'What happened then?', 'What did that produce?' or 'What was the reward?' give more insight into a person's qualities. Questions involving examples also generally produce answers at the results level.

Experience-oriented questions produce even more if further questioning takes place. This is in essence nothing more than continuing where the candidate left off. Most interviewers have the tendency, once the candidate is talking, to think about the next subject they wish to broach. If the candidate so much as takes a breath, they have already started talking about a new subject.

A good listener follows the speaker and asks questions through which they show that they wish to go into the subject in greater depth. Such questions are, for example: 'What do you mean, exactly?', 'Could you explain that a little more?' or simply 'Mmm, mmm' or 'Yes, yes'. This prevents the interview from jumping from one topic to another and the candidate is given sufficient room to elaborate.

This further questioning technique is exactly the opposite of the 'shooting arrows' technique, where questions – often closed – are asked in rapid tempo. Only if you are looking for factual answers (how often, how many, etc.) does this technique work well. Suppose a person says: 'I implemented a system that brought about a 20% cost-price reduction.'

In that case, you could respond

- Tell me something about the old system.
- What did you change?
- What problems did you encounter?
- How did you resolve them?
- How do you arrive at 20%?

Drs L.C. van den Broek was a director at van den Broek & Partners in Breda.

Once these skills have been established, questions must then be devised to measure them. The questions must be as precise as possible and provide an opportunity for further questioning. This prevents the applicant from giving too general and too positive an image of himself.

2.1.5 The psychological test

A psychological test comprises various assessments. The applicant must, for example, complete an intelligence test, an interests test and various ability tests. Personality tests or personality questionnaires are also used to obtain a picture of the applicant's personality structure.

Figure 2.1 illustrates some (possible) questions from a personality test.

Psychological test

FIGURE 2.1 The Big Five questionnaire

Introversion/extraversion	
timid	self-assured
quiet	talkative
subservient	assertive
inhibited	spontaneous
introvert	extravert
Atruism and friendliness	
cool	cordial
unfriendly	friendly
selsh	unselsh
uncooperative	cooperative
rigid	exible
Conscientiousness	
inaccurate	accurate
inattentive	meticulous
negligent	thorough
careless	careful
idle	diligent
Neuroticism/emotional stability	
restless	restful
nervous	relaxed
wound up	wound down
irresolute	resolute
hotheaded	calm
Openness to experiences	
unintelligent	intelligent
unwise	wise
unimaginative	imaginative
uncreative	creative
disinterested	studious

Source: Brysbaert, M. (2006, p. 556)

People differ greatly in their personal characteristics. Some are timid, closed and apprehensive; others are self-assured, open and relaxed. Many combinations of personal characteristics are possible.

An organisation can opt to select people primarily on personal characteristics. These characteristics can be different for every job or profession. It is possible to make a profile for every job and therefore establish whether a person fits the desired profile for a particular job.

In chapter 1, we described a much-used questionnaire by which someone's personal characteristics can be established, namely the Big Five. This questionnaire measures five dimensions (characteristics) of someone's personality: extraversion, agreeableness, conscientiousness, emotional stability and openness to experience (see figure 2.1).
The scores from the Big Five can be used to analyse whether the applicant has the personal characteristics that the organisation believes are necessary to carry out the work in a proper manner.

EXAMPLE 2.4

The introverted entrepreneur

Mark Zuckerberg is a computer programmer and an Internet entrepreneur. In 2004, he founded Facebook: a new way of connecting and sharing information with others on-line. In 2010, he was named Time magazine's person of the year. The New Yorker describes him as distant, somehow a strange mixture of self-conscious and arrogant. People have joked and complained about his robotic or even alien personality, with one of his best friends calling him 'overprogrammed'.

Because the Big Five questionnaire is filled in by the person involved, it is questionable how reliable this form of measurement is. Firstly, it requires that the person thoroughly understands himself. This is by no means always the case. Secondly, the person must be honest and not try to paint themselves as favourable as possible. It is to be expected that people in a selection situation wish to represent themselves as favourably as possible.

2.1.6 Assessment centre methods

Assessment centre

In an assessment centre, a candidate is tested in a situation that resembles the future work situation. As part of the interview and psychological testing, characteristics and behaviours must be derived from what the person asserts about themselves. This does not always produce a truthful picture. An assessment centre is intended to establish how an individual actually functions, preferably in a situation where skills and behaviours considered relevant to the work can be measured.

● www.vkbanen.nl (edited)

Group applications: party time?

A group application enables employers to select candidates more efficiently. 'Ideal if you are looking for people with similar profiles,' says project coordinator Gwenda David for Randstad Holding, a Dutch multinational human resource consulting firm. She is currently looking for over 400 employees to man the hospitality areas, cash registers, and wardrobes at the Ziggo Dome, a new concert venue in Amsterdam which will soon be opening its doors to the public.

Group application is more fun, faster, and offers more comparison material.

Randstad first makes a selection based on 'killer requirements', such as long-term availability and maximum wages. The selected candidates are given a short introduction to the company in groups of twenty. Then, they take part in a 'selection game', with each candidate being offered an assignment which is to remain a secret for the other candidates. David: 'These types of games quickly show you how people address certain issues, and what kind of role would be best suited to them.' Functions with tougher training demands are also eligible for group applications. Henk Reijnen, the head of HR for Food Retail at the Dutch Sligro Food Group, was looking for suitable managers for the Emté chain of supermarkets. He organised applications with five to six candidates at a time. Reijnen had the candidates perform IQ and personality tests at home, attend a company presentation together, and individually present their own plan of improvement for an Emté supermarket of their own choosing.

'Group applications are more fun, more dynamic, and offer employers more possibilities for comparison between candidates,' says Reijnen. 'The process of individual talks often still quite dependent on personal mood.' Are group applications not too intimidating for applicants? Reijnen does not think so. 'It really is party time. At the end of the day, everybody heads home with a spring in their step. The applicants agree. One applicant says: 'Of course we all wanted a position, but it did not feel like we were at each other's throats.'

This takes the form of a dramatised or role-playing situation. For example, a candidate may be confronted with tasks like:
- A **coaching task**. The candidate has a half-hour interview with a subordinate who has recently performed less well than was formerly the case. This subordinate is a professional actor, who produces all kinds of excuses and reasons for his under-performance. It is up to the candidate to arrive at a proper resolution of this problem with the subordinate (see the following example).

- A **team task**. All the candidates are asked to prepare a presentation in 10 minutes on proposals for economising they have just received. After 10 minutes, they are told that the management has decided that not all the proposals can be presented, but only one. The candidates must decide together which proposal will be presented. They are given half an hour to come to a decision. Thereafter, each candidate is asked to produce minutes on this decision.

Depending on the skills you wish to measure, the assessment can be extended by adding other tasks. The candidate may be asked, for example, to collect all kinds of information in order to resolve a problem. This test resourcefulness and creativity. Instead of the coaching task, the candidate sometimes has to conduct a different type of interview. In addition, the candidate can be asked to participate in a group discussion or give a presentation.

EXAMPLE 2.5

Assessment exercise

Dutch railway company NS presents six to eight potential candidates with a problem that needs to be solved within a certain amount of time. Following that, the group needs to assign two individual members the responsibility of presenting the solution to two members of the NS board of directors. Assessment specialists observe the group process and note the roles that the candidates assign to others and themselves.

The premise behind the assessment method is that behaviour during the assessment is a better predictor of a person's overal behaviour than a self-completed questionnaire.

Designing an assessment requires a good understanding of:
- the characteristics the person needs to have;
- the situations in which these characteristics can be established;
- the means by which these characteristics can be established.

Measuring people's characteristics through an assessment centre usually takes one or two days. The person is exposed to different situations and his behaviour is observed by trained assessors. The assessors make an evaluation of the candidate's characteristics and skills on the basis of the ways in which he behaves.

An abbreviated form of assessment requiring less investment is the task-based assessment. This differs from the assessment centre method in the following points:

Task-based assessment

- Only the core activities of a job are tested.
- After the test, only an overall assessment is given and not an assessment of the individual components.
- No trained assessors are necessary. An assessment manual is used.
- The scores of the assessors are averaged. No agreement between assessors is necessary.

As of yet, little is known about the reliability and the predictive value of these assessment methods, though the available data give a positive impression.

2.1.7 Validity of selection methods

The selection process is intended to single out employees who will function and perform well. It is therefore important to find the selection method that is most suitable for this. A method has validity in this regard if it can predict whether a selected candidate will actually function well within the organisation. Validity has been the subject of many studies in recent decades. Because these studies often involve small numbers of research units, an attempt has been made to combine them and perform a meta analysis of the results. One of the best meta analyses was performed by Schmidt and Hunter (1998) and Robertson and Smith (2001). As a criterion for predictive value, the general performance scores that managers gave to their employees were used. Their data on predictive value is reproduced in Figure 2.2. Individually, the specific work test (capacities test), the intelligence test and the structured interview score the highest. Next come the personality test (conscientiousness) and the assessment centre. The unstructured interview has no predictive value.

Validity

Conscientious-ness

FIGURE 2.2 The predictive value of various tasks to establish the suitability of applicants for a particular function

The higher the correlation, the greater the predictive value. The highest correlation is .100 and the lowest correlation is .000

1	IQ test in combination with a structured interview	.63
2	IQ test in combination with specific trial assignments	.61
3	Specific trial assignments	.54
4	IQ test	.51
5	Structured interview	.51
6	Personality test	.31 / .40*
7	Assessment centres	.37

* The predictive validity of the personality test scored .31 in a study by Schmidt and Hunter, and .40 in a study by Robertson and Smith

A few marginal comments may be made on these data. First, they present average scores from a combination of several studies. Some studies show lower and others higher scores, depending on the situation in which the research was carried out. Second, it has been established that certain groups of candidates score less well on intelligence tests; that is to say, they are proportionately less often selected than one would expect. This is the case with certain ethnic minority groups, for example. Finally, with regard to intelligence tests, the measurement of general intelligence (G-factor) is a better predictor than the separate measurement of different intelligence factors.

© Noordhoff Uitgevers bv

In 2011, a study conducted among 156 organisations showed that, for purposes or recruitment and selection, organisations most frequently used their own website (nearly 58%), other websites (47%), and offered internships. Organisations also advertise in newspapers and magazines, and recruit new employees through job conventions and open house events. Information from the Dutch National Job Market Research Foundation (NOA) shows that students generally look for jobs on-line (nearly 70%). 50% uses a career or job vacancy website. Notably, only 8% of students applied for jobs through a social media platform.

A study among 50 companies in the Dutch city of Utrecht (Joust, 2015) showed that placing a job description on a company owned website (58%) was the most frequently used and successful recruitment method. There had been a solid increase in the use of social media (42%), and the retention of quality interns came in third (34%). Recruitment and selection agencies proved successful in filling trickier vacancies (30%).

Drenth (1988) established the following trends in recruitment and selection that still apply today:

- A shift in choice is observable. The choice is shifting from selection of the 'best' candidate to selection of the candidate that best suits the work situation.
- It is not just the organisation that makes a choice. The candidate must also decide whether the work suits him.
- Selection focuses not only on the entry job, but also on the wider career.
- Selection is increasingly seen as the beginning of a series of assessment processes related to career planning and guidance.

2.1.8   Employability

Until recently, it was quite usual for people to work for one employer for an extended period of time. In exchange for job security, people put in an effort out of loyalty to the organisation. We call this lifetime employment.

Employability

Nowadays, people change jobs more frequently and organisations demand not only loyalty, but also increased flexibility and mobility. Employability refers to a person's capability of gaining initial employment, maintaining employment, and obtaining new employment. Training is important in this context. Employees who have many skills and much knowledge are deployable in several places and therefore flexible. If an employee wants to have high employability, they must also be prepared to be mobile. It can be important for the organisation to have a constant supply of 'new blood'. This can lead to innovation and change. Being mobile can also offer benefits for the employee: getting to know different places of work, meeting new challenges and developing different skills. The organisation and the employee therefore both have an interest in employability.

An employee with high employability can, however, leave to work somewhere else at any time. The organisation is thus faced with a paradox: they would like their employees to develop themselves and be mobile but employees also thereby increase their opportunities on the (external) labour market, and so they leave again all too quickly.

In the context of the New Way of Working, the organisation offers a working environment that makes flexible working possible.

EXAMPLE 2.6

Disappointment

Erdal, in charge of recruitment, has just had a disappointing experience. One of his highly qualified employees has left after only a year. Yet he and his director did everything to retain the man including offering him a chance of specialist training.

Organisations would therefore be wise to require employees, in exchange for the offer of training and education, to remain with the organisation for a certain length of time.

2.2 Integration

Once a person has been hired, they must be integrated into the organisation. Activities must be developed within the organisation to ensure that the person does what the organisation expects of them. Integration therefore means ensuring not only that the work for which a person is hired is done in the correct manner, but also that the person's behaviour fits in with what people in the organisation are accustomed to. The prevailing values within the organisation are guidelines for such behaviour. In this section, we explore the values within an organisation and the socialisation of new employees.

Values

© Noordhoff Uitgevers bv

2.2.1 Values within an organisation

On an individual level, values can be regarded as personal wellsprings that give direction to choices and behaviour. These values are related to different areas in life, such as family, work, leisure interests and groups of friends. Values are acquired through what one hears from parents, teachers, friends, colleagues, the mass media and other influential sources. Once values have been learned, they are relatively stable and determinative for just about all types of social behaviour, ideas, judgements and goals. During the integration process, staff strive to ensure that the new employee adopts as many as possible of the values existing within the organisation.

Congruence It is presumed that congruence or agreement between the values of the employee and the organisation makes the employee feel committed to the organisation. Meyer et al. (2010) found that strong similarities between the values of individuals and of organisations are closely linked to strong affective commitment.

In a family business, strong affective involvement often prevails.

Managers set great store by the values existing within an organisation. Consequently, in recruitment procedures, they often select people whose personal values fit in with the prevailing values. This promotes homogeneity within the organisation. Judge and Ferris, in their research into recruitment procedures (1992), found evidence that management seeks homogeneity above all. Values within the organisation are related to different areas, such as what performance is expected, what reward is equitable, how interaction should take place among employees and between employees and management, what goals are important and what commitment or loyalty is expected. However, it is not always possible to achieve agreement beforehand in all these areas via such selection. After an employee has been hired, the process of socialisation commences, in which the employee and the organisation both play a part.

2.2.2 Socialisation

New employees find themselves in a situation with many uncertainties. They do not yet know exactly what is expected of them or what types of behaviour are appropriate. Uncertainty makes them dependent on the information supplied by their colleagues and managers and on the reactions their behaviour evokes in others. If they are prepared to largely accept the prevailing values in the organisation and allow themselves to be influenced, then a process of socialisation begins.

If a new employee wants to belong to the organisation, they will begin directing their behaviour towards the requirements and expectations of the organisation in advance. This process is called anticipating socialisation. Before people can become part of a social system (organisation), they must accept certain norms and types of behaviour.

Anticipating socialisation

Anticipatory socialisation is sometimes also seen in people who have worked for an organisation for years. An example is an employee who achieves a more senior management job. His appearance changes: he begins buying more expensive suits and acquiring new habits. His behaviour also changes. He used to come into the department for a chat but now sits alone in his office, letting people come to him. This may be characteristic behaviour of senior managers in the company. He is thus preparing for the (different) role expectations that are linked to the job of a senior manager.

Advance adjustment does not always take place, but the process of socialisation can begin only after the employee has been hired.
The following are necessary for proper socialisation:
- The employee must pick up the knowledge and skills to do the work properly.
- The employee must get to know the organisation well. They must come to know and understand communication lines, rules, customs and procedures, and decision-making processes.
- The employee also has an interest in good social contacts and finding his place in the group or department.

In this initial period, one's boss and colleagues are important sources of information: on the one hand through the behaviour they display and how they model themselves and on the other through the manner in which they react to the behaviour of a new employee. They can direct this behaviour by indicating what is right and what is not. When they succeed in getting the new employee to function as desired, socialisation is complete.

Initially, it may seem as if a new employee must adjust to the wishes of the organisation. This does not necessarily mean, however, that they endorse the values the organisation is based on. It is nonetheless difficult for a person to adopt the organisation's values over a long period without also becoming convinced by them. Usually, a person will accept the applicable values and internalise them after a time. Internalisation has then occurred.

Internalisation

They will, in turn, play an informative and guiding role with new employees, in order to integrate them into the organisation as well. After internalisation, an employee is truly integrated and the manner in which they must behave has become obvious.

2

EXAMPLE 2.7

Adjustment problems

Sonia walks into her new company's offices wearing violet trousers and a lilac jacket. She notices that most people are dressed in grey, brown or black. The women usually wear skirts. Her boss shakes her hand and introduces her to her new colleagues. They make some jokes that she doesn't understand. He takes her round the building and points out the office in which she will work. He then leaves for an urgent meeting.

Sonia very quickly realises that she will have to rethink her wardrobe where work is concerned. In this company, there are clear norms governing the way employees dress. Other norms and rules are not yet clear to her, however. Why are her future colleagues laughing or making jokes? Does it have something to do with her behaviour? Do they expect her to show initiative or do they want her to adopt a more cautious attitude?

An organisation has an interest in successful socialisation and internalisation. The employee must therefore behave in accordance with the applicable rules and also communicate them to others.

2.3 Methods of integration

An organisation's most important goal with respect to integration is to ensure that employees function properly. We have already indicated that the organisation expects the employee to acquire all kinds of knowledge and skills that are relevant to the job. They need to know what agreements there are, what procedures must be followed and what customs and types of behaviour are appreciated. The employee will have to display social (role) behaviour that is appropriate to the situation. They will need to adjust their behaviour to that of their colleagues and boss. What methods can be used within the organisation to achieve this? There are four types of method: information and guidance; reward and penalty; demonstration; and training. We shall explore these methods in this section.

2.3.1   Information and guidance

An organisation passes on information to a new employee in a variety of ways. For example, the employee receives a job description, an organisation chart, an annual report and a list of commonly used abbreviations. The formal contract sets out a number of responsibilities and obligations. Colleagues will also make these clear. Often, one person is specially entrusted with the guidance of the new employee. They act as a mentor. The person appointed mentor is responsible for training the new employee. They supply the information necessary for the proper performance of the work and for insight into the applicable values. Furthermore, they offer feedback on the functioning of the new employee and can also be approached by the employee if they should need more information.

Guidance

Mentor

American companies have used mentoring for years. Often, the employee themselves selects a more experienced (older) employee as an advisor and guide. The choice is made on the basis of impression, conversation and feeling of affinity. Organisations in other countries are also increasingly opting for the mentoring system.

Mentoring system

EXAMPLE 2.8

Inspirational guidance

'Pamela Bouwmeester shows that she is enthusiastic and driven when it comes to helping 'her people' develop. She takes time for them, and listens attentively and sincerely. She has taught me a different way of looking at things', says Wout van der Heijden (NPC consultant). She inspired him to solve certain troublesome issues help him to regain his motivation for one of his project. 'But the greatest source of inspiration was her way of asking questions, which she used to help people gain new insights into themselves... . It is a wonderful thing to experience the effect of a good question when it comes to clarifying matters. I have tried to emulate her way of talking to others in an attempt to ask others those questions that will help them reach a clearer perspective.' Pamela Boumeester was the CEO for Dutch NS rail, and is now an independent supervisor for several companies, chairperson of the jury for the Dutch Chairwoman of the Year foundation, and and Executive Coach.

Sources: Lückerath-Rovers, 2008, LinkedIn 2016, a.o.

2

The mentoring system offers all kinds of benefits, such as providing emotional support, preventing errors, and learning the proper strategies for tackling work. There are also disadvantages: the mentor and the new employee may not be compatible with each other, for example. Sometimes, excessive dependency arises. The mentoring system has also recently been used for the guidance of employees in higher jobs. In this case, it becomes an instrument in the framework of 'management development'. In addition to a mentor within the organisation, qualified external people are also used. An organisation may have other means of communicating with new employees, such as an induction programme or a company or staff magazine.

2.3.2   Reward and penalty

The behaviour of new employees can also be directed through a system of rewards and penalties.

EXAMPLE 2.9

Sending the new colleague to Coventry

A new employee has enthusiastically set to work in the stockroom. After an hour, he has already completed the assignment he was given. He diligently starts on the next task. His colleagues watch him for a while and then begin to comment. They make remarks like 'if you carry on like that you'll hurt your back', or 'trying to suck up to the boss already, are you?' When these hints don't work, they send him to the canteen to buy something for them and obstruct him so that he can't get on with his work. During the coffee break, they make jokes about how keen and hardworking he is. Eventually, if the new employee takes no notice of them and continues to go his own way, they will simply ignore him. As a result, he becomes more and more estranged from the group and is no longer included in social activities.

A boss can also respond positively or negatively to the behaviour of a new employee. It is possible for them to praise or condemn this behaviour. They have the power to give an employee more latitude or recommend them for promotion and a bonus. The reactions of other people in the organisation to a new employee's behaviour often have the character of a reward or penalty.

Reward
Penalty

When desired behaviour is displayed, the organisation can ensure that it is suitably rewarded. Reward and penalty, as we explained in chapter 1, can both reinforce and eliminate behaviour (see section 2.5.1).

2.3.3   Demonstration

People can serve as examples to a new employee. How should you behave here if you want to be accepted? How can you obtain good results? In other words: what social behaviour leads to favourable results? The people with whom a new employee associates can be important examples (role models)

Role models
Identification

for him. Role models (or references) are people to whom they compare and identifies themselves. Their example is worth following because the colleague finds them attractive or because they have important knowledge, expertise or relationships. The colleague is inclined to allow themselves to be influenced by others and imitate their behaviour.

The organisation can also use employees as examples by putting them under the spotlight or publishing positive articles about them in the company magazine.

EXAMPLE 2.10

Do examples motivate?

Josh Jones thinks we should institute an 'Employee of the Month' award. This, he feels, will attract more attention to all the people who work so hard to give our clients a pleasant experience. Josh used to work for McDonald's, where he was often voted Employee of the Month. He proudly shows us photos of how pleased he looked. When Josh became Employee of the Month for the second time, he was given a limited edition mobile phone.

German Federal Chancellor Angela Merkel is an important role model for women.

2.3.4   Training

Introduction programmes are used by organisations to familiarise employees with an organisation and stimulate them to adjust and assume the desired characteristics. To ensure that new employees have the skills that are relevant to a certain job, organisations can also opt for specific education or training programmes. New employees, as well as those who have been working in the organisation for some time, have the opportunity to take occasional courses individually or in groups. Many organisations send their employees on internal courses. Through these, they try to direct the behaviour of their employees and teach them the desired behaviour. For example, they train their personnel in customer orientation, teamwork or handling confidential data. This training involves not only the technical knowledge and skills that are necessary to accomplish a task, but also the concepts, attitudes and behaviour that are desired within the organisation.

Some organisations take training to great lengths – such as a well-known American fast-food chain that has founded a 'university' for its employees.

An organisation therefore has various resources available to ensure that employees are properly integrated. When socialisation proceeds successfully, the new employee accepts the values, norms and behaviour applicable within the organisation. The foundation has then been laid for the employee to function properly. Integration is important, but thereafter the employee will need to be motivated to produce good performance. It is also important to retain good employees. These topics are discussed below.

EXAMPLE 2.11

Hamburger University

At McDonald's, training and education are considered to be very important. McDonald's requires its employees to be versed in the local language, to be quality-conscious, and to be able to work in a team. Employees and managers together follow an internal training program at McDonald's academy in addition to their regular duties. Graduates leave with a vocational training or bachelor's certificate. In 2000, McDonald's opened its Training Centre in Amsterdam, the Netherlands, where future managers advance their understanding of values such as quality and crystal clarity. The emphasis that McDonald's places on being crystal clear was demonstrated by the dismissal of an employ who, counter to protocol, grew a beard - and this was an assistant manager who had been working for McDonald's for six years.

McDonald's Hamburger Universities are found in many countries the world over, including Great Britain, Brazil, Russia, and Japan. In 2001, McDonald's opened a university in Shanghai (China). Every year, over 5,000 students are registered at the main branch of Hamburger U in Chicago. They are trained in marketing, communication, operations, and human resources.

Source: www.mcdonalds.nl, 2015

2.4 Motivation

For the organisation, it is important to have employees who will make adequate efforts to complete the tasks they have to perform. If they do not do this by themselves, it is necessary to motivate them – particularly if additional effort is necessary from time to time, for example because more orders are received, or because a number of employees have called in sick. In chapter 1, it was established that people are motivated to perform activities by work-intrinsic and work-extrinsic factors.
In this section we discuss motivation through reward, attractive work and challenging goals.

● www.randstad.nl

Money and flexible hours increasingly popular

Dutch workers still feel a pleasant work atmosphere is the most highly valued factor when it comes to (choosing) an employer. Financial security and flexible working hours are gaining in popularity. This information comes from the annual employer reputation-study conducted by the Dutch Randstad employment agency. According to a group of 15,300 respondents (men and women between 18 and 65 years old), career prospects have become less important, whereas more employees feel the 'quality of the product' has become an important factor in looking for a new employer. Training opportunities remain important for 16% of the interviewees. This year, TNO (the Netherlands Organisation for Applied Scientific Research) and Amsterdam Airport Schiphol were the winners of the award for most attractive employer in the Netherlands.

The top 10 of the most important employer aspects according to employees:

1	Pleasant working atmosphere	65%
2	Salary/(secondary) benefits	62%
3	Job security	52%
4	Balance between work/private life	43%
5	Financial viability	42%
6	Flexible working hours	40%
7	Interesting work	40%
8	Accessible location	36%
9	Career prospects	29%
10	Training opportunities	16%

Age group preferences
The younger job seekers (18-24 years) are relatively less focussed than older employees on atmosphere, salary, job security, and the balance between work and private life. Younger people are looking for an interesting and substantive job, with good training opportunities and (international) career prospects. In addition, the lower age brackets feel more strongly about the importance of management and reputation than the older employees. The 25-to-44-year olds often find themselves at a period of their life in which more emphasis is placed on parenthood. This makes the possibility of flexible working hours more attractive. Older Dutch employees experience difficulties with finding new jobs, and prioritise job security and stability. Location is also important; the distance between work and home should not be too great.

2.4.1   Motivation through reward

The principal work-extrinsic motivation is money. Motivation by financial reward links the performance of employees and their salary or bonuses: the so-called **pay-for-performance** system. This is a **variable payment** or **variable reward system**, which is different from the traditional reward system, where the reward is established in advance. There are different forms of pay-for-performance. In the purest form of this reward system, **piecework**, employees receive a fixed amount for every unit of product; for example, the number of articles sold by a salesman or representative. There is a total link (**complete coupling**) between performance and reward. Usually, however, there is a partial link (**incomplete coupling**). A basic wage is agreed and an extra reward is given if production (performance) is above a certain level. The extra reward can be linked to **individual performance** or related to the performance of a group, such as a department or work team. In that case, it depends on **group performance** (see the following example).

Bonuses
Profit-sharing

Other financial stimuli are bonuses and profit-sharing. There is then a basic wage and a supplementary, one-off payment (bonus) per year, based on the performance of the employee or on the collective performance of all the employees thanks to which profits have been made. Part of these profits can then be paid out to every employee (profit-sharing). In Lizzy Firm's article there is a partial link between performance and reward, where a bonus is paid out once a year based on the group performance of the business unit.

The advantage of a partial link is that dips in performance that have very little connection with an individual person's efforts (such as seasonal slumps, stoppages caused by machinery failure and declining markets) are not charged entirely to the employee. A certain basic salary is still guaranteed. Insecurity about income is thereby reduced. In the commercial sector, a partial link is very common, especially in the case of sales personnel, for example (50% in 1991). They receive a bonus that is dependent on the size of the orders brought in. This type of pay-for-performance scheme has a favourable effect on performance only if the results of a person's efforts can be properly measured and if the bonus is sufficiently large. A degree of equitability must be perceived between the extra effort produced and the extra reward (Guzzo et al., 1985).

Pay-for-performance schemes can work only if performance can be adequately measured. This condition means that pay-for-performance is more difficult to apply to jobs in which objective measurement of performance is difficult.

In 2012, mismanagement by the Vestia housing cooperative was the cause of great commotion. The cooperative had gotten into major financial difficulties through speculation with derivatives. The affair resulted in the bonus of a former top executive being reclaimed.

In many cases, an objective determination of performance is impossible. This is true of jobs which are not concerned with measuring production but of assessing qualitative matters such as flexibility, effort, customer orientation, innovation and capacity for teamwork. Subjective matters, such as the relationship with the person doing the assessment, can, in these cases, dominate the assessment. This means that a mediocre or poor assessment will not readily be given if the relationship has to remain good or, conversely, that a mediocre or poor assessment may be given because a boss cannot get along with a subordinate.

Pay-for-performance does not always have the desired effect. This is clear from the following example.

DAILY NAUK, SIMON DUKE

Bank governor Mervyn King blames credit crunch on 'unattractive' City bonus culture

The culture of greed engulfing the City has been criticised by the Governor of the Bank of England. In an unprecedented assault, Mervyn King pinned the blame for the growing crisis in credit markets on fat-cat pay in the banking sector. The prospect of multi-million pound bonuses had fostered a decade of 'excessive risk-taking' by banks, sowing the seeds for the current turmoil, said Mr King. (...) "Banks are paying the price for designing incentives packages that are not, in the long run, in the interests of the banks themselves." Bulging pay packets in the Square Mile have caused a damaging brain drain from other parts of the economy, Mr King warned. "It's unattractive that so many young people, when contemplating careers, look at the compensation packages in the City, and think these dominate almost all other careers," he said.

The excesses of the banking industry have been most apparent on Wall Street but the effects have been felt sharply all over the world. Huge rewards encouraged U.S. bankers to lend to low-income customers, who had little realistic chance of repaying their mortgages. (...)

Pay-for-performance applies exclusively to monetary rewards. There are, however, several other forms of reward. One example is the 'cafeteria system'. In this system, employees can opt for the rewards that are most attractive to them, according to their needs. The options are:

Cafeteria system

- **Money for time.** Unused or saved vacation time is paid out.
- **Time for money.** Employees can retire early or purchase extra days' off.
- **Work arrangements.** Employees arrange their own working hours.
- **Insurance options.** Employees can opt for certain pension schemes.
- **Monetary arrangements.** Employees receive part of their pay in savings schemes or shares.
- **Additional arrangements.** Employees receive a company car or a grant towards their children's education.

The growing popularity of the cafeteria system is illustrated in the following example.

ELSEVIER (TRANSLATED)

Rewarding flexibly

He's still visibly basking in the afterglow. 'During the second week of March I was enjoying time off work, just as the weather had turned so wonderful. I am the proud owner of a two-acre stretch of woodland, so I spent all of my time out of doors, cutting wood for the fireplace.' Now that his kids have left the nest, Wim Gosselink wanted to spread out his vacation time across the year: one week in spring, one week in autumn, and three weeks in summer. 'But when I did the math, I found that I was coming up short on days off.' His employer Centraal Beheer Achmea's flexible reward system offered a solution. 'I took a pay cut, which means that I can regularly take Friday afternoons off as well.'

2.4.2 Motivation through attractive work

Extrinsic motives

If pay-for-performance is primarily a work-extrinsic motivation, the provision of attractive work is work-intrinsic.

Work-extrinsic motivation

The attractiveness of work, according to Hackman and Oldham (1976, 1980), can be increased by giving work more quality. Their Job Characteristics Model (JCM Model) – see figure 2.10 – indicates that the intrinsic motivation to work can be increased if the activities that go with a person's job have the following characteristics:

Job Characteristics Model (JCM Model)

- **Skill variety.** The skills required of the employee should be varied.
- **Skill significance.** The tasks should call for significant skills.

Intrinsic motives

- **Identity.** The tasks should form a complete and cohesive whole and not be just a link in a long chain.
- **Functionality.** The tasks should be interrelated and influence each other.
- **Autonomy.** The employee should have sufficient scope to organise the performance of the tasks himself.
- **Feedback.** The employee should receive sufficient information about the results of his work.

These qualities should ensure that employees regard their activities as meaningful, attractive and sufficiently challenging. They will also feel more responsible for the proper performance of their work.

Initial testing of the model produced contradictory results, so control variables were later added to validate the model. It was found that the desired consequences of ensuring that a job has the characteristics outlined in the model will occur only if employees have the qualities shown in Figure 2.3.

FIGURE 2.3 The Job Characteristics model

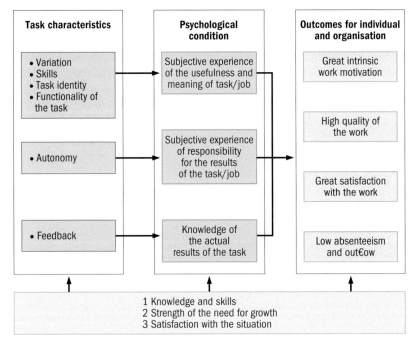

Source: Hackman & Oldham, 1975

a   The appropriate **knowledge and skills** for the work. If this is not the case, the
    task may be too onerous and the opposite effect generated.
b   Sufficient **growth needs** to perceive the tasks as challenging.
c   **Satisfaction** with the working environment. Dissatisfaction about pay,
    leadership or relationships with colleagues, for example, will have a
    braking effect on the expected results.

To increase intrinsic motivation, it is thus not sufficient to change the job
characteristics in the direction of greater variety and autonomy, etc.
Attention also has to be paid to employees' training, growth needs and
working environment.

2.4.3   Motivation through challenging goals

Another way to increase intrinsic motivation is to set challenging goals.   Challenging
A person is not challenged by a simple task, but may be challenged by a   goals
difficult one. If the person manages to perform the difficult task well, this
increases his feeling of competence. A number of conditions must be
fulfilled, however, to make people feel challenged:
- The goals must be concrete, specific and measurable.
- The person must be sufficiently competent to achieve these goals.
- The person must accept the set goals.
- Proper feedback on the results is needed.

2

People do not attempt a difficult task if they think they will not succeed. They will also not let themselves be challenged by a difficult assignment if they do not approve of it themselves but regard it only as a form of exploitation. Two factors previously described in chapter 1 thus play a part: self-image and, in particular, the ability that a person ascribes to himself determine whether he believes that a difficult task can be properly completed. People with a low self-image will not attempt a difficult task. The reward that is linked to the extra effort must also be perceived as equitable.

In Japanese industries, these ideas are widely applied by presenting work groups with high and concrete goals and giving plenty of feedback on the progress and results of the work. A combination of increasing the attractiveness of work and increasing the challenge by setting high goals is, of course, also possible.

2.5 Effects of motivation

A great deal of research has been done into the effects of the different forms of motivation on the performance of employees. It turns out that they may or may not be in line with expectations and, in many cases, the results are ambiguous.
In this section, we discuss the effects of pay-for-performance, attractive work and challenging goals.

2.5.1 Effects of pay-for-performance

A number of factors can ensure that pay-for-performance encourages better performance. These factors are derived from the conditioning theory described in chapter 1, the equitability theory, the expectancy theory and the attribution theory:

- According to the conditioning theory, behaviour is reinforced only if the reward quickly follows the demonstrated behaviour. This is the reason that an annual supplementary payment, in the form of profit-sharing or a bonus, for example, cannot be a daily stimulus to work harder.
- The reward must have sufficient value to be attractive (expectancy theory).
- There must be an equitable relationship between the extra effort and the extra rewards that come from it (equitability theory). If a person receives only 5% more salary for 40% extra effort, this can be perceived as inequitable by the person involved. Pay-for-performance is then ineffective.
- The person must consider himself able (self-image) to produce the desired performance (attribution theory).

To ensure equitability, performance must be well defined and it must be possible to measure it adequately. The performance of salesmen or production staff can be assessed relatively objectively, through the number of articles sold or produced by that person, for example. With other employees there are no such objectively measurable qualities; instead there are characteristics like communication skills, flexibility, customer-orientation, carefulness and problem-solving ability. These qualities cannot be measured in any strictly objective manner. Rather, quantification involves the assessment of others, which is a subjective issue.

Before instituting pay-for-performance, management needs to know what employees regard as equitable, feasible and valuable. Young et al. (2012) found that the effects of pay-for-performance are optimised if employees feel that its implementation does not result in any negative influence on individual autonomy or other positive work aspects. These conditions require management to involve their employees in the implementation of a pay-for-performance system.

Pay-for-performance can also have negative consequences. This is the case, for example, if the reward is individual but good performance is dependent on effective collaboration. Under these circumstances, employees no longer seek the best solution for the group (team, unit), but the solution that produces the most for them personally. Saturation can also occur. After a time, employees become accustomed to the bonus or profit-share and begin to see it as a right. Through the emphasis on rewarding effort, employees learn that the organisation cares primarily about making money (instrumental attitude) and not about other things, such as providing challenging work or involvement in the organisation (see the following example). Due to this, their intrinsic motivation and affective commitment declines. It is affective commitment that leads to an increase in the effort put into work.

HP/DE TIJD

A good team really is more important

Bonuses often have adverse effects, psychologists Ellemers and De Gilder (2012) have concluded based on their own studies. In their experience, managers in the Netherlands still massive flock towards to the idea of the individual reward, such as money or promotions, to encourage their employees to work harder. But when asked what really motivates them, most employees answer that they enjoy being part of a team that works well together. Emphasising personal opportunities for gains contributes to individualist, short-term oriented behaviours. Such behaviours often involve working at the expense of others – which can be a killing blow for the collegial atmosphere people

feel is so important. People who feel emotionally involved with their team are willing to go the extra mile for good results. And they put in effort for others as well. Especially during times when things are tough, a company needs committed employees more than some cock of the walk whose motivation is merely extrinsic – since those will be the first to start hunting around for something better elsewhere. In fact, the current approach is often still to reward individualism, conclude Ellemers and De Gilder. People who are intrinsically motivated are taught that their approach is flawed, unless it helps you achieve your targets. And that is unfortunate.

Research into the effects of pay-for-performance on the productivity of employees or on the organisation as a whole has produced variable results. Pay-for-performance sometimes has a positive effect, but not always (Guzzo et al., 1985). Furthermore, the researchers concluded from almost 100 studies in the field of motivation and work performance that the following three types of approach are the best methods of increasing motivation:

- the training/education of personnel;
- making the work more varied and meaningful;
- setting specific and challenging goals.

The last two, unlike pay-for-performance, are concerned with work-intrinsic motivation.

2.5.2 Effects of attractive work and challenging goals
The effect of providing attractive work can be explored by establishing to what extent employees' work matches the characteristics of the JCM Model and how it connects with the motivation, work satisfaction and performance of these employees.

Hackman and Oldham (1975) developed a tool for measuring and determining the attractiveness of work. From an overview of 31 studies into the relationship between the task characteristics of the JCM and their supposed effects, it emerged that higher work satisfaction and motivation were measured in all these studies, but there was higher performance only in a limited number. Morgeson and Campion (2002) found that redesigning jobs around autonomy, identity, task-based skills, and significance improved the task motivation of employees. Providing more autonomy (self-management) for employees and teams does not always lead to better performance. Manz (1992) concluded that the effect of increased autonomy is dependent on the circumstances (contingency factors). First, the

Characteristics of the employees

characteristics of the employees themselves: they must have a need for autonomy and feel sufficiently competent. Second, the nature of the task:

Nature of the task

more autonomy is primarily meaningful with non-routine tasks and tasks that are not yet fully established. Third, the environment: if the environment

Environment

is dynamic and requires continuous adaptation of the work, autonomy is

Nature of the organisation

important for a rapid response. Finally, the nature of the organisation: its information and communication systems must be geared towards autonomy in the workplace and the style of leadership must provide room for self-management.

In a great many studies it was shown that setting challenging goals leads to higher performance (e.g. Locke et al., 1988). This can be explained by the fact that employees commit themselves to challenging goals and will make efforts to achieve them. However, they will commit themselves to these higher goals only if they consider themselves able (self-image) to achieve them (attribution theory). This can be achieved on the one hand by convincing employees that they can succeed and on the other by involving employees in establishing the goals. Research has shown that these conditions amplify the effect of setting challenging goals (Sue-Chan & Ong, 2002).

2.5.3 New World of Work, flexible working, and motivations
Proponents of New World of Work (NWW) indicate that one of the arguments in favour of this philosophy is that it would lead to greater employee performance. NWW has motivational characteristics that would seem to support this argument. Where extrinsic motivation is concerned, it is possible to conclude that NWW conforms to the so-called 'cafeteria-plan'. Employees are given more freedom to perform their activities where and when they see fit. With regards to intrinsic motivation, it is possible to conclude that the autonomy in performing these activities makes them more appeal.

The question, however, is whether these motivational characteristics lead to improved performance. Various studies into the introduction of NWW have failed to show an improvement in performance (Bailey & Kurland, 2002; De Croon et al., 2005; Batenburg & Van Der Voordt, 2008). Yet these studies do show that employees appreciate the increase in freedom and flexibility. How can this be explained? Research by Van Yperen (2012) and Slijkhuis (2012) shows that NWW is not a work philosophy that suits all employees equally. Their conclusion is that NWW is especially suitable for employees with the following characteristics:

- A need for autonomy and responsibility;
- An ability to properly plan and schedule their activities;
- Discipline and the ability to self-manage;
- A below average need for social workplace interaction.

These characteristic do not apply to all employees. Some employees do not thrive on autonomy and responsibility; they prefer a more structured working life and prefer to be managed by a superior. They may also have a greater need for social workplace interaction. Employees like these are not intrinsically motivated through the implementation of NWW. But what does motivate them? According to Slijkhuis (2012): 'The presence of a supervisor. Clear guidelines, concrete road-maps - diametrically opposed to NWW.' They need clarity and predictability, and find it hard to cope with ambiguous situations.

According to 2014 research by TNO, the Netherlands Organisation for Applied Scientific Research, people's productivity can be somewhat improved by allowing them to spend part of their working day working outside office grounds, and by permitting them to work flexible hours. This approach also leads workers to have somewhat greater than average appreciation for their employer. But too many hours spent working outside the office, as well as having to work in too many different locations leads to a slightly negative effect on employer appreciation by employees.

NRC HANDELSBLAD

Rather be at the office

'I began looking for a new job when my previous employer implemented NWW. The offices in the north and south of the Netherlands were closed, and only the central office remained open. I was based in the north, which meant I would have had to start working from home full-time. I did not enjoy the prospect. Not because I lack the discipline, but because I do feel the need for a certain degree of structure. Moreover, I feel it is important to talk to one's colleagues regularly. I like to bounce some ideas off of others, or watch more experienced colleagues in action. Besides that, my partner's work means his shifts are irregular. He is at home during the day a lot as well. In that type of situation, having to work from home full-time has a major impact on your relation. I do work from home part of the time right now; occasionally I leave for home at four, enjoy a relaxed meal with my family, and that do a little work in the evening when my son is in bed. And that works very well. But having to work from home exclusively? No, that does not suit me at all.'

2

The way in which telecommuting and home-based working are introduced and supervised by management have a determining influence on their effect. Allowing managers their own office while simultaneously requiring staff to work in large open plan offices, is not beneficial to overall motivation.

In paragraph 1.9, we described how employees who are part of an organisation's flexible workforce are often only under a temporary contract. If those employees voluntarily choose a temporary position, this does not have any adverse effects on their motivation and performance, as has become evident from previously discussed research. A large segment of the flew workers has not found themselves in this position voluntarily, however - their motivation and performance fall behind when compared to employees under a permanent contract. Thus, we are faced with the question of how to motivate the second group of flex workers. There are two possible ways for an organisation to address this issue. The first is by improving the motivation of involuntary flex workers by offering them the prospect of a permanent position. These flex workers consider permanent employment to be an appealing reward, leading to increased extrinsic motivation. In many cases, however, the flexible workforce is actually intended as a temporary one, which means this form of motivation is irrelevant. The second possibility is to increase extrinsic motivation by offering workers more of a challenge, and allowing flex workers greater autonomy and responsibility.

2.6 Intrinsic and extrinsic motivation: conclusions

Some people perform well because they find their work pleasant and challenging. They work not for the gain but for the game, as it were, and are work-intrinsically motivated. If they do not care about the work itself but only about the rewards connected to it, such as appreciation and salary, they are extrinsically motivated. These different types of motivation are shown in Table 2.1.

TABLE 2.1 Forms of intrinsic and extrinsic motivation

Extrinsic motivation	Intrinsic motivation
• Pay-for-performance	• Quality of the work
• Cafeteria system	• Challenging goals

As we learned earlier from research by Guzzi et al. (1985), intrinsic motivation has a stronger effect on work performance than extrinsic motivation.

2.7 Retaining people in an organisation

Retention

Retaining people in an organisation can be important in two circumstances:
1 If it involves the retention of people with qualities that are valuable to the organisation.
2 If there is a labour shortage and it is difficult to recruit people.The outflow of personnel will then exceed the inflow.

A high outflow is dysfunctional if employees who are valuable to the organisation leave. Outflow also sometimes leads to the necessity of reallocating tasks or recruiting and training new people. It can therefore be important to slow the outflow. If the outflow is high and the organisation wishes to do something about it, it will first need to establish the causes. Exit interviews are a good method of discovering these causes. These are interviews with employees who have indicated that they wish to leave, with the purpose of finding out what factors have led to their decision. Depending on the factors mentioned, various measures can be taken to combat outflow. These can include higher rewards, the offer of training, the option of part-time employment, prospects of a different (more senior) job or different job content.

Exit interviews

2

EXAMPLE 2.12

Low staff turnover

Dutch employers who are best appreciated by their employees suffer lower staff turnover than employers whose staff members are less positive (Effectory, 2010). Commitment is seen as an important predictor of staff turnover. The increasing number of 'job shoppers' has meant that commitment has become less of a given. Pride in one's organisation has been found to be to an essential condition for commitment. Another is that employees have to be able to identify with the organisation's goals. Other important factors are: appreciation, a stimulating work environment, and confidence in management, as well as job enjoyment. These are all factors that contribute to commitment levels.

Source: Suzanne Mancini, http://www.effectory.nl, August 2010

The organisation can retain employees through a good staffing policy. The following factors are instrumental in doing so:
• career guidance
• range of education and training opportunities
• age-aware personnel management
• attention to diversity ('minority groups')

Ensuring employee commitment to the organisation is not relevant when it comes to employees on a temporary contract. The idea, after all, is that those employees leave the organisation once their contract expires. This raises the question of what sort of psychological contract employers offer their temporary workers, what the organisation can offer them, what they can offer the organisation, and how the organisation can sustain cultural consistency in the face of many flex workers. Gallagher (2005) concludes that more research into this area is required if we are to form a proper insight into the answers to these questions.

© Noordhoff Uitgevers bv

Tips for managers

To assess employees and establish rewards suited to the performance produced, managers must have insight into how employees function.

Assessing people

Making assessments of people is more difficult if the qualities you wish to assess cannot be objectively measured and relationships and mutual dependencies play a part.

In this situation, the following errors can occur in the assessment process:

- Being too wary of offending a person or harming the mutual (working) relationship.
- Taking your pound of flesh because you don't like a person.
- Giving a person a label and no longer looking properly at the quantity and quality of their performance.

When making important assessments of how well a person is functioning, ensure that you utilise several sources. Not only your assessment is important, but also the opinions of others, such as the colleagues of the person being assessed. Questions addressed to relevant colleagues in the organisation often produce a fuller picture. Clients, customers and other contacts can also be asked for feedback.

Performance and reward

Rewarding people can be difficult for an employer to do well. Employees usually think that their performance is improving. They also often think that they function better than their colleagues. However, reality can be very different.

- Use information (feedback) from several sources to establish the quality of a person's performance.
- Ask what important results they have achieved.
- In many cases, a kind word, a compliment or just showing interest is reward enough for many employees.
- Intrinsic motivation works better than extrinsic motivation. Pay-for-performance reduces intrinsic motivation and this can lead to people only being prepared to to do their best for extra rewards, such as bonuses.

Bringing in the personnel department

Regularly ask the advice of HR staff and, if possible, involve them in important discussions. They often have the knowledge and skills to advise you, mediate and conduct difficult interviews.

Always conduct an interview in the presence of a third party. This will provide a great deal of information, which can be obtained in two ways:

1 Ask for feedback at the end of the interview: What did the third party think of the interview? Did you miss any opportunities?
2 If you involve a third party in the interview, you can also prepare for it together. In the subsequent discussion you can evaluate your roles and ask questions like 'What went well and what went less well?' 'Why was this?'

Regularly record interviews and listen back to them. See if you achieved what you set out to do.

Investing in growth and development
Stimulate people to develop themselves. Develop a careers policy and take into account the ages and interests of different groups of employees. For example, you could hire a mentally disabled employee. This is not only good for that employee, but has also an effect on the whole organisation: 'we care about people' and 'this could be you'.

© Noordhoff Uitgevers bv

Summary

▶ The need for good personnel imposes requirements on the recruitment and selection of new employees. These requirements are established in a job description.

▶ The job description contains:
  • job-specific requirements
  • person-related requirements

▶ Selection methods used:
  • unstructured interview
  • structured interview
  • psychological tes
  • assessment centre

▶ Requirements imposed on new employees:
  • to carry out the tasks required by the job description
  • to adapt to the culture of the organisation

▶ Adaptation to the culture of the organisation is achieved through:
  • informing
  • guiding
  • exemplary behaviour (mentor and role models)
  • rewards
  • punishment
  • training

▶ Motivation of the employee:
  • extrinsic (pay-for-performance, attractive work arrangements such as the cafeteria system)
  • intrinsic (attractive and challenging work)

▶ Attractive work:
  • is varied
  • calls for skills
  • has identity
  • provides responsibility
  • provides autonomy
  • is subject to feedback

▶ Challenging work:
  • has high but achievable goals
  • requires employee's acceptance of challenge
  • requires feedback on results

▶ Retaining valuable employees in the organisation can be achieved through:
  • good career guidance
  • staffing policy sensitive to employees' needs

Assignments

2.1 Young people: recruiting and commitment

In March of 2012, there were 465,000 people unemployed in the Netherlands. The lower age brackets were hit hardest by that unemployment.
Organisations have an interest in recruiting young people into their workforce – but in times of economic recession they are often only able to offer flexible (temporary) contracts.

a What could an organisation do to improve the numbers of young people they recruit and commit to their organisation? What tools are available for online recruiting? Would you recommend a job aggregator website? How can the organisation use personal contact for recruitment purposes? What are good measures when selecting appropriate candidates?

b What is the best way for an organisation to coach young people with a flexible contract? What options can you come up with?

c What was are there for making sure young people with flexible contracts become invested in (or committed to) the organisation? What sort of arrangements is the organisation likely to stimulate? Also use the information from chapter 1 in your answer.

2.2 STAR method job interview

Finn has applied for the position of law enforcement officer for an average-sized municipality. Part of the job description entails interpreting indicators of fraud, drafting risk profile assessments, and independently performing checks and house calls. Other requirements a strong though flexible personality, an inquisitive nature, and excellent communication skills. The municipality is accustomed to conducting their application interviews using the STAR method, which is a method for conducting behavioural-based interviews.

a Study the STAR method; use, for example, online resources. Also read Loek van den Broek's 'Further questioning' in paragraph 2.1.4. What does a STAR method interview look like?

b Name two important competences Finn should be able to show. What sort of behaviour matches those competences? What should Finn do, what should he demonstrate?

c Draft a setup for the interview. Create a list of questions, and practice the interview with a colleague or fellow student.

2.3 Pay-for-performance and motivation

Jimmy and Maria have worked for their company for several years now, to the satisfaction of all parties involved. Lately, however, it has been suggested that they be stimulated to up their performance.

– Jimmy is a senior administrative worker at a major transportation company. He frequently feels bored and takes long breaks. He is often at loggerheads with his

© Noordhoff Uitgevers bv

2

colleagues, specifically with regards to his commitment and behaviour. In the past, Jimmy was proven to be susceptible to extra money as an incentive to work harder.
- Maria is a good sales representative, who is values highly by her team members. Her recent sales figures, however, have been disappointing. This is limiting her team's ability to achieve their desired targets. There do not appear to be any unusual circumstances in Maria's situation. Does she need a bit of a pick-me-up?

a   Would pay-for-performance be a viable tool in both situations? What are the conditions for using pay-for-performance?
b   There are other ways of motivating Jimmy. What are they? Pick a strategy that falls under the heading of 'motivating through appealing work'.
c   The sales department uses targets and bonuses. Would you recommend Maria be valued individually for her performance, or would you opt for a team reward?
d   Maria could also be motivated by employing the 'setting challenging goals' strategy. Wat are the requirements for this strategy. Does it match Maria's self-image?

3

Groups in organisations

- How can one distinguish a group from a collection of people?
- What groups can be identified in organisations?
- What functions does a group fulfil for its members?
- How do group members influence each other?
- How do groups develop and what structural characteristics can be identified?
- How do groups relate to each other?

© Noordhoff Uitgevers bv

Team meeting

The employees in Section A of the Family Care Department get together every Monday morning for a progress meeting. They discuss the allocation of work for the coming week with their team leader. Because one team member is sick, her work must be taken over by the others. They discuss who will take on which tasks and how the additional work can be fitted into their own work schedules. They also discuss specific problems that have arisen with clients and ask whether these problems require extra care. One team member would like to go on holiday in three weeks' time, and they decide to discuss the consequences of this in the next progress meeting.

New policy

At a company board meeting, the board and the heads of the departments are discussing policy proposals for the next few years. The board wants the departmental heads to explore the consequences of the proposed policies for each individual department at operational level with their staff. They must then bring concrete plans for policy implementation to the next board meeting.

3.1 The group concept

An employee is seldom involved with all of the other employees in an organisation. The first example suggests that the employees in Family Care consult and collaborate primarily with colleagues in their own team. They seldom meet employees in other teams or departments. The departmental heads in the second example are primarily in contact with the employees in their own department and with the heads of other departments.

People who work in organisations spend most of their time in a group context. Their group may consist of colleagues in their own department or shift, members of their team or members of the various consultative groups and committees in which they participate.

What do we understand by a group? Do five people waiting for a bus constitute a group? What about people watching a play in a theatre or patients in a doctor's waiting-room?

EXAMPLE 3.1

A group?

The news shows images of an impromptu student strike. Students are protesting the increase in the number of compulsory class hours.
Using text messages, they have urged others to gather in the inner city, where they are drawing quite a crowd. Some of them seem to be enjoying their little rebellious streak: they are throwing eggs, setting waste paper bins on fire, and provoking police officers. The newsreader is referring to it as a 'protest' by a group of students.

In day-to-day conversation, we generally use the word group to refer to people who remain in each other's vicinity. In psychology, however, a group is more than a random collection of people who are located close to each other. The people waiting for a bus look like a group from a distance, but these people have little to do with each other. Most of them probably do not know each other. There is only a group if the following conditions are met:

Collection

Group

- If two or more people regularly intercommunicate in a direct manner.
- If the people have common goals.
- If the people are to a certain extent dependent upon each other to achieve these goals.
- If the people feel that they are part of a group (Paulus, 1989) (see Figure 3.1).

No strict dividing line can be drawn between a group and a collection of separate individuals. People who meet only four times a year in the Works Council will regard themselves less as a group than those colleagues they interact with on an almost daily basis.

© Noordhoff Uitgevers bv

FIGURE 3.1 Characteristics of a group

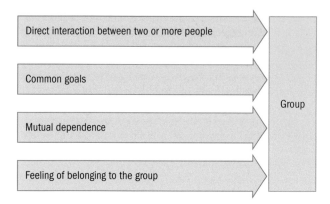

3.2 The organisation as a collection of groups

As organisations grow, it becomes necessary to divide the work into sales tasks, production tasks, storage and shipping tasks, administrative tasks and so on. These tasks are then allocated to units called departments, teams, or shifts. Usually, such a group consists of a small number of people. If a department is large, sub-departments are usually formed. The distribution and grouping of the activities by Stichting Thuiszorg, a Dutch foundation for home care, is shown in Figure 3.2.

FIGURE 3.2 Organisational structure of Stichting Thuiszorg

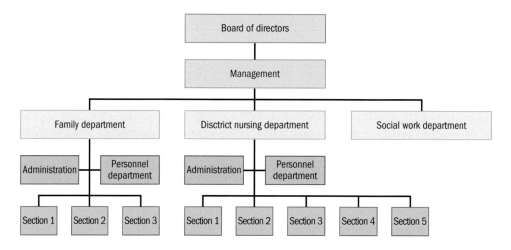

Stichting Thuiszorg comprises three departments: District Nursing, Family Care and Social Work. The Family Care Department comprises three regional sections and the District Nursing Department has five regional sections. Each section has around 10 employees and a team leader.

The Social Work Department has a team leader and 12 employees. There is also a board of directors and a management team. Because the Social Work Department is not very large, it comprises only one team. The District Nursing and Family Care departments are much larger and are divided into several smaller teams.

In view of the manner in which tasks are distributed and grouped in the Stichting Thuiszorg, this organisation can be regarded as a collection of groups. This is, however, also true of most other sizeable organisations.

Collection of groups

3.3 Types of groups in organisations

3

Organisations can house different types of groups, with the main distinction being between formal an informal groups.

3.3.1   Formal groups

Formal groups are groups that are part of the organisational structure. There are administrative groups, executive groups, self-managing teams, and virtual teams.

Administrative groups

If the group's function is to determine the goals of the organisation, how the organisation should be structured, how activities should be planned, managed and coordinated and how problems in the organisation should be resolved, we call this a management group or administrative group. Such groups include management consultation groups, the departmental heads, the board of directors, the works council, committees, teams and project groups. Committees and project groups can be temporary, brought together to resolve a single problem.

Management group

Administrative group

EXAMPLE 3.2

Project group for a new building

A hospital is being expanded by creating a new department. To that end, the construction of a new building has been scheduled. Management has put together a project group comprising members from various disciplines, each with their particular expertise, who are to make recommendations for the construction and equipping of the new building. The project group is of a temporary nature: once the new building has been completed, the group will be disbanded.

Executive groups

If executive activities are carried out in teams, we call these work groups. They have a common goal and a need to allocate and coordinate activities.

Work groups

EXAMPLE 3.3

Divide and calibrate

A group of four roofers has to construct a new thatched farm room. One roofer is engaged in fetching and carrying materials (reeds, laths). Two roofers are on top of the building, removing the old thatch. The fourth roofer brings down the material that has been removed and, while the new roof is being constructed, makes sure that the new reeds are in the right position to enable the other two to work uninterrupted.

Many work groups have a degree of self-management. They can therefore be regarded as a hybrid between administrative and work groups.

Self-managing teams

Self-managing team

The idea of forming semi-autonomous or self-managing teams in organisations arose in the 1970s. The idea was to make production work less monotonous by allowing the employees to work in teams and giving them executive, planning and supervisory tasks. It was assumed that work satisfaction would increase, performance would improve and absenteeism would decrease. The addition of a planning role meant that the team would not only have to carry out the work, but also have meetings to discuss how it should be carried out.

To carry out

To discuss

The introduction of self-managing teams has slowly gained ground and is no longer limited to production contexts. The premises for making use of self-managing teams have been extended. Self-managing teams may be set up for various reasons. The first aim is to increase the quality of the work, by giving employees more varied tasks and greater responsibility.

Quality of the work

EXAMPLE 3.4

Life insurance company

Customers of a certain life insurance company who wished to take out or change an insurance policy used to have to deal with different departments. It was often unclear who was responsible for handling particular requests or enquiries. The company therefore decided to start using self-managing teams, which were responsible for everything concerning a particular group of clients. This led to better client contact and quicker decisions. For the clients, it was also clearer to whom they should direct their questions or complaints and they were no longer sent from pillar to post.

Customer-oriented

Secondly, the formation of self-managing teams can derive from a desire to work in a more customer-oriented manner and be able to respond better to the demands of the market.

Flexibility

Thirdly, self-managing teams may also be formed in order to increase the flexibility of the production process or of service provision. Such flexibility must make it possible to respond more quickly to production breakdowns or changing customer requirements (see the following example).

NRC HANDELSBLAD (TRANSLATED)

Small-scale care

Mr and Mrs De Blok of the Netherlands, both district nurses, lost their faith in the system and in a management that dictates the way they should be doing their jobs. The couple resigned.

District nurses are quite capable of determining who does what and when. The De Bloks are convinced that they should be the ones to organise and plan their own activities instead of some gaggle of managers and declaration systems. Thus was established the fundamental idea behind the 'self-managing' teams: groups of district nurses who sort out what needs doing. Visits to patients, number of required hours, etcetera. And any team that grows beyond twelve members automatically splits up into two or more new groups. This ensures the continued existence of the human dimension; both for patients and for employees.

Since 2006, many home-care contractors have signed up of their own accord with 'Buurtzorg', the neighbourhood home-care initiative – they share the indignation the De Bloks feel at the 'intensive human farming' perpetrated by long-term care companies. The 'Buurtzorg' setup has proven to be more than something bodged together by a group of well-meaning amateurs. At the heart of 'Buurtzorg' is a sophisticated automation system.

Despite the different reasons for their formation, self-managing teams should have a number of common characteristics:

1 The team's tasks must include both executive and planning or controlling activities. The group members must all be able to do multiple tasks (multi-utility), so that they are able to take over each other's work. This gives the work more variety and quality.
2 As few decisions as possible should come from above, so that the team's own planning capacity is maximised. What can reasonably be determined by the team must be left to the team. This improves the speed of reaction to changes in performance requirements and changes in what customers want. The organisation becomes more customer-oriented and flexible.
3 The team must constitute a 'family', where social contacts are possible and where people can learn from each other. Its size should be limited accordingly.

Virtual groups

New World of Work has led to colleagues being less dependent on each others proximity, and has meant that they have experienced an increase in electronic methods of communication. Coordinating activities, taking part in discussions, managing, and solving problems are no longer processes involving frequent or even any face-to-face contact. Discussions and decision-making processes between department colleagues or project group members, or in meeting sessions that are conducted entirely through electronic means are known as virtual groups. But virtual groups do no nearly always restrict themselves to fully virtual contact; some groups use a hybrid of virtual communication interspersed with face-to-face meetings.

© Noordhoff Uitgevers bv

EXAMPLE 3.5

Product innovation project team

A new project team has been assigned the task of proposing new products to be developed and marketed. The project team consists of members from the Purchasing, Production, Development, and Sales departments. Since their working hours and locations are so different, their discussions mainly take place through electronic means.

The project leader feels that he is losing his grip on mutual communication between the team members. Proposals and responses are only given if and when group members feel like it. This is slowing down the overall process. Therefore, the leader suggests the group takes part in weekly face-to-face meetings. This makes the project group both a virtual and a non-virtual group.

3.3.2   Informal groups

Informal group

There are also informal groups in organisations. These groups can develop spontaneously, such as groups based on friendships or certain common activities like sport, cooking or self-development. Informal groups can also arise as a consequence of issues that elicit common emotions, such as the threat of dismissal or functional changes due to reorganisation.

The different groups that can be identified in an organisation are shown in Table 3.1.

TABLE 3.1 Formal and informal groups in organisations

Formal groups	Informal groups
• Administrative groups • Work groups • Self-managing teams	• Groups formed spontaneously around common activities/interests

3.4 Functions of groups

Evolutionary explanation

Psychological explanation

Cognitive explanation

Useful function

Why do people spend a large part of their lives in a group context? Different explanations are given for this. First, there is an evolutionary explanation, which states that groups offer the individual protection in dangerous situations and the opportunity to breed. Second, there is a psychological explanation, which states that people need to have contact with other people so that they feel they belong and are valued and accepted as a member of a group or society. Third, there is a cognitive explanation, which states that people perform better in combination with others than individually. All these explanations illustrate that the group has a useful function and can fulfil certain needs of the individual. See Figure 3.3.

FIGURE 3.3 Three functions of groups

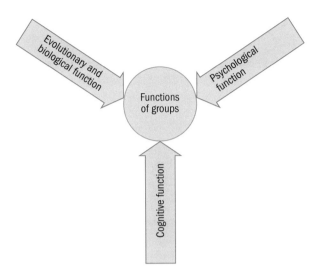

3

3.4.1   Evolutionary and biological function
Our early ancestors lived in a dangerous environment. Wild animals, diseases, hostile tribes, bad weather, scant resources and natural disasters constituted threats to their existence. By living in groups, people could better withstand these threats and thereby also better ensure the survival of their own species.

Living in a larger group, such as an extended family, tribe, or village community, means increased available manpower - which comes with various benefits:
- communal hunting and gathering;
- communal agriculture and food preparation;
- communal effort in constructing housing, land clearing, and constructing defensive perimeters;
- improved vigilance in unsafe circumstances;
- improved protection against outside threats;
- greater care for the young, sick, and elderly;
- greater opportunities for reproduction.

According to Darwin's theory of evolution, living organisms are subject to natural selection. Living organisms whose properties help improve their chances of survival can pass those properties on to later generations. People who tend to live in groups with others have a better chance of surviving threatening circumstances than people who do not have this tendency. This property will eventually be passed on to their offspring and, eventually, will become a property that is *biologically* ingrained into the species.

In organisations, groups can also offer protection to their members. This has been shown by research described by Mayo (1945). See example 3.6.

© Noordhoff Uitgevers bv

EXAMPLE 3.6

Seeking protection

In a study carried out in the last century, a company's employees who had to solder the links in a chain were observed. They were paid according to performance and they had to record how many links they had soldered every day. It was observed that they recorded about the same number every day but their actual production varied. At the beginning of the week they did more than they recorded and at the end of the week they did less. The total production reported over a week was thus correct. When they were asked why they did this, they said they wanted to protect themselves against unforeseen problems, such as delays in the supply of components. They also liked being able to take it a bit easy later in the week. Furthermore, their method enabled them to protect and support team members who were unwell or made mistakes. They protected the team as far as possible against interference from the boss. Despite being paid according to their performance, they did not work as hard as they could, because they were afraid that if they did, the minimum production level for which they were paid would be increased. They would then have had to work harder for the same reward.

3.4.2   Psychological function

People live in groups because this helps them fulfill a number of psychological needs. These needs include the need for social support, identity and status, and information.

Ad 1 Social support
Group members can be an important source of social support to each other. This support can take various forms:
- Emotional support. This consists of showing empathy and caring for another's wellbeing.
- Advice and assistance. This consists of offering guidance and support.
- Positive feedback. This consists of showing one's appreciation for the behaviour and qualities of others. People need to feel positive about their self-image, and giving and receiving contributes to this feeling.

EXAMPLE 3.7

Time of crisis

Police officers are frequently confronted with high-threat, stressful situations – anywhere from being attacked by a hostile individual, or defending themselves with their sidearm. Following these types of events, officers receive help and support: from colleagues to official support agencies. This allows them to blow off steam and express their emotions.

The importance of social support from others is shown in the fact that this type of support offers a resilient buffer for the negative consequences of stressful situations. People who receive adequate social support from their colleagues and their managers do not suffer from mental or physical problems as frequently as people who go without this type of support.

Ad 2 Bestowing identity and status
People who are asked to describe themselves will often refer to the groups
they belong to, in addition to their personal characteristics. From a role in
the managing board to playing in a football team to a family to mountain
biking with friends. According to the theory of social identity by Tajfel and
Turner (1986), a person's self-image contains both a personal and a social
identity. The groups to which an individual belongs are a major influence in
determining their social identity.

*Theory of social
identity*

Social identity

Ad 3 Information
The events that take place in an organisation are open to interpretation.
Think of rumours of reorganisation. What are the consequences for any given
person's position? How do others experience the performance of a new
manager? What will the performance interviews be like, and what factors will
be addressed? Employees often need to depend on other colleagues in their
team for answers to these questions. In that respect, a team or group is an
important information resource. The longer one is part of a group, the more
one's views of the organisation will shift to the average perspectives held by
that group - with regards both to work and to the world outside of work. The
group that solders chain links (example 3.6) was quick to inform new
colleagues about the prevailing thoughts concerning managers, proper forms
of collegial conduct, and production capacity and expectations. Those
expectations were rather precise, and consisted of 'a substantial performance
for a substantial reward.' With regards to mutual collaboration, group
members were expected to have each other's backs, and swap tasks if things
got a little dull. Those who did not conform to group etiquette were called to
order in any of a number of ways. Several preconceptions also have direct
consequences for the behaviour that should or should not be displayed. In
many groups, the junior member (either in age or experience) tends to be the
one who is assigned the less enjoyable tasks. Employees who are new to a
company or group will take notice of the behaviour of others in establishing
their behaviour in a group or department. What is the road a new employee
should take to get something done in the organisation? What is the right way
of approaching a manager is they have a suggestion about their work? What is
the right way to respond when a machine blows a fuse? By looking at how
other group members act in these situations, or by asking them directly, an
individual lets other group members dictate their own behaviour. Those
other group member become behavioural models', as it were. This way,
employees learn how best to adapt to their new work environment, and what
the ruling philosophies and modes of conduct are.

EXAMPLE 3.8

Crisis situations

Members of the police force sometimes
face threatening, aggressive and stressful
situations. This is the case, for example,
when a policeman has shot someone in
self-defence. The police officer is supported
after the incident so that he can let off
steam, express his feelings and receive
help.

© Noordhoff Uitgevers bv

3.4.3   Cognitive function

People need others in order to achieve the goals they have difficulty achieving on their own. If more than one person shares the need to achieve a single goal, this is known as a collective need. Collective needs can only be developed by individuals uniting in a group. Various collective needs can serve as the basis for group formation, such as organising work strikes, calibrating activities producing goods or services, practicing team sports, performing a show, or expressing one's religion.

EXAMPLE 3.9

Collaborating to achieve goals

The team in Family Care Section B is responsible for care in the southern region. The care requirements of this region are so great that there are 12 employees in this team. Even this is on the tight side and they would like to have an additional employee.

They need each other not only to carry out the executive work, but also for their expertise in tackling difficult cases. In progress meetings, people can benefit from the others' insights to help them handle difficult situations better.

Working towards the same goal together.

People try to engage with groups whose goals appeal to them. Whether they remain as group members depends on the appeal of the group's activities, its mood or atmosphere, or its success. If the goals are appealing by the mood is not, then an individual may decide to leave the group. If the group is not very successful but still offers pleasant activities, then an individual may decide to stay on. In short, people can have various cognitive considerations when it comes to deciding whether or not to remain a group member.

EXAMPLE 3.10

Making music together

At her music school, two students approach Aimée with the idea of joining them in a music group. The girls are looking to play chamber music. Even though she is not that fond of chamber music, the idea of harmonising together does appeal to Aimée. And so, she decides to join in.

Playing music together is great fun, and the interpersonal contact is very worthwhile. Even though chamber music still is not Aimée's favourite genre, the joy of making music together is enough reason for her to stay in the group

Participating in the labour process nearly always means working as part of a group. This participation is primarily intended to acquire an income. In addition, a group (team, department) may provide social support, identity, and status or information. Working as part of a group can be appealing for several reasons, but if the work is dull and monotonous and the mood of the group leaves something to be desired, group members may decide to switch jobs.

3.5 The group as a social environment

People are seldom if ever alone. At work, with the family, during their studies and in their free time, people belong to groups. These groups form their social environment. As we have shown in the previous section, belonging to groups provides people with all kinds of benefits. They receive information, help, appreciation, support and protection from the group. Membership is not automatic but must be earned.

Social environment

3.5.1   Active and passive influence

EXAMPLE 3.11

The jury is out

A jury of twelve is meeting up for the first time. Their task is to pass their verdict on the guilt of an accused party. The first meeting proceeds fairly chaotically. Various arguments are offered, both acknowledging and rejecting a guilty verdict. On top of that, the jury members occasionally switch sides, repeat earlier arguments, and barely listen to what the others are saying. Thirty minutes in, and chaos reigns supreme. One member sighs: 'This is not getting us anywhere'.

By the final day of the jury sessions, the discussion has become discipled. A chairperson lists the various arguments both pro and con, and then asks whether there are any new arguments. Each member of the jury is given their turn to speak, one at a time, after which there is time for final statements. The matter is put to a vote, and the group reaches a conclusion.

Group members influence each other's notions and behaviour. The jury in example 3.11 influenced each other not only in terms of notions (guilty or not guilty) but also in terms of behaviour. The jury members together decide on the best method of discussion. There is *social influence*; which, in time, results in a certain extent of agreement on, for example, the group's goals, shared notions, and desirable behaviour.

Social influence can occur both actively and passibely. Active influence is a form of conscious influence. One group member is trying convince another member of a certain opinion or notion. Passive influence is another possibility. Passive influence occurs if group members do not set out to influence each other, but still end up doing so anyway. Passive influence is unintended and happens without being notives. This form of social influence was already demonstrated in an experiment by Sherif in the previous century (1951).

EXAMPLE 3.12

Sherif's experiment

People looking at a fixed point of light on the wall of a dark room will start to see this fixed point move about. This movement is caused by involuntary twitches of the human eye, which moves about unprompted if asked to look at a fixed point. The resulting perceived movement of the fixed point of light is called the auto-kinetic effect. People differ in their estimate of the extent to which

this movement occurs. Sherif made use of this effect and put together people in groups of three in a dark room. He asked the group members to estimate aloud the extent of the movement of light, switching around the order in which participants gave their answers every time. The answers given by the group members showed that the differences in estimates were greater at the start of the experiment than towards the end. The responses given by the group members moved closer and closer together, until there was very little difference between them.

The majority of the participants indicated that the responses given by the other participants had not influences their estimates. These participants had been influenced passively.

FIGURE 3.4 Scores of participants in Sherif's experiment (1936)

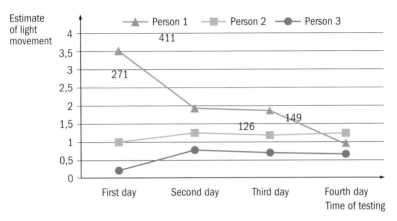

Source: Stangor, 2004

3.5.2   Conforming

The 'price' for belonging to a group is that a person must conform with the accepted ideas and models of behaviour within the group. A person is accepted into the group only if they adapt those ideas and ways of behaving. It is not always necessary for the group to actively and openly enforce conformity. In many cases, group members adapt to each other unconsciously.

Conformity

The extent to which one's needs to belong and be accepted play a part in adaptation to others is revealed by a famous experiment carried out by Asch (1950).

EXAMPLE 3.13

Asch's experiment

Students were asked to take part in research into visual skills. They were placed in a group and were asked to indicate which of the three lines on the right-hand side of 18 cards matched the line on the left-hand side of the card (see figure 3.5).

The task is very simple. If students are tested individually, they always give the right answers. In this experiment, however, the other group members were accomplices of the researcher. They were instructed to give the right answer the first six times and thereafter unanimously to give a wrong

© Noordhoff Uitgevers bv

answer every time. The procedure was that the group members always answered in turn, from left to right. The genuine student (the only one who was not an accomplice) was always placed next to last.

FIGURE 3.5 The lines in Asch's experiment

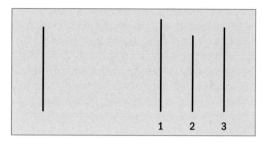

Determine which line on the right (1, 2 or 3) is the same as the line on the left.

The Asch experiment. The second student from the right hears all the other members of the group unanimously giving the wrong answer. Will he conform with the group?

The goal of the experiment was to find out to what extent a person is influenced by the answers of others. Although the visual task was very easy and, under normal circumstances, most participants produced correct answers, in this case 76% of the 'genuine' students gave a wrong answer one or more times. They joined in with the wrong answer given by the other group members. Only 24% did not adapt to the group.

Why does a person give a wrong answer because others do? From interviews afterwards, it turned out that many participants knew they were giving the wrong answer but they did so in order to belong to the group. They felt uneasy about adopting a different standpoint and could assuage their feelings of unease only by agreeing with the rest. Their psychological need to belong and be accepted won over their against honesty.

Deviance

In groups, pressure is often exerted on group members who are different or display different behaviour (also known as deviance). The way in which group members deal with deviant behaviour, was shown by Schachter (1951) in a revealing experiment. See example 3.14.

EXAMPLE 3.14

Group pressure

Discussion groups each consisting of 10 people were asked to determine a penalty for a young delinquent who had committed a minor offence. The penalty had to be determined after considering a list of seven proposals. These proposals varied from very light to quite severe penalties. Each group contained three accomplices of the researcher. The first accomplice had to advocate the most severe penalty, the second accomplice had to advocate a moderate penalty and the third accomplice had to advocate a fairly severe penalty but then modify his opinion towards the direction of the group.

3

Observation of the groups' discussions showed the following pattern:
- At first, repeated attempts were made to convince the member of the group who had advocated the most severe penalty that he was wrong.
- If the deviating group member adapted, communication with him became the same as communication with the others in the group.
- If the deviating group member did not adapt and stuck to his standpoint, the attempts by the other members of the group to influence him decreased and his contribution was ultimately ignored.

Group members who maintained a deviating standpoint slowly but surely found themselves outside the group. They assumed a peripheral position.

If the group's members were asked who they would like to sit on a committee with, the deviating group members were never chosen.

3.5.3   Conformity-influencing factors
Which factors influence the extent to which group members conform to one another? The following paragraphs describe three factors that reinforce or weaken conformity:
1 the scope of majority and unanimity;
2 task or subject characteristics;
3 personality characteristics.

Ad 1 The scope of majority and unanimity
Does majority's influence increase the larger the majority is? Asch varied the number of accomplices in his experiment; groups had between 1 and 16 members who intentionally gave the wrong answers. The results showed that an increase in the scope of the majority led to a higher degree of conformity. This increase was most apparent in the region from 1 to 6 accomplices. Any more than 6, and the increase flattened out. In the experiment with estimate the length of a certain line on paper (see example 3.12), the accomplises unanimously gave a wrong answer. If, however, Asch instructed one of the accomplices to devite from the standpoint of the others, then the test subjects would only conform to the incorrect answer in 5% of cases. The precense of a deviating ally caused a significant drop in conformity. How can this be explained? Why does unanimity have such a major influence on degree of conformity?

© Noordhoff Uitgevers bv

Stangor (2004) offers three possible explanations:

a *Discomfort*. In cases where all group members are in agreement, a deviating group member is on their own. This is when the feeling of deviation is greatest. This leads to a maximum feeling of discomfort.

b *Uncertainty*. The more people are alone in their notions or behaviours, the more their uncertainty about the accurace of these concepts decreases.

c *Allies*. The more allies there are who deviate from the rest of the group, the lower the feelings of discomfort or uncertainty, and the greater the chances a deviating group member will retain their position.

Ad 2 Task or subject characteristics
If a task that is part of an experiment is difficult, and the correct answer is not immediately apparent, conformity with other group members will increase. A *difficult taks* causes more uncertainty about the accuracy of a solution, increasing the tendency to take notice of the opinions of others. Opinions and notions which are very important and belong to the *ingrained* convictions of a group member are less easily incfluences by other group members. In these cases, conformity will not increase as quickly.

Ad 3 Personality characteristics
Not nearly all of participants in Asch's experiment conformed to a unanimous majority. A quarter of the participants stubbornly stuck to their own perceptions. What makes one person more susceptible to social influence than others? According to Bornstein (1992), there are three personality characteristics which influence the extent to which people allow themselves to be influenced:

a *Self-esteem*. People with low self-esteem will conform more to others than people with high self-esteem. People with low self-esteem tend to be more insecure about the accuracy of their own notions and perceptions, causing them to conform to others more easily.

b *Needs*. People with a strong need to be accepted will be quicker to feel uncomfortable and conform to others more easily than people who feel less need to be accepted.

c *Commitment*. People who feel strongly committed to a group and to whom the group matters dearly will be quicker to conform to other group members than people who are less committed.

Figure 3.6 indicates the factors which conform group conformity.

FIGURE 3.6 Factors that cause conformity to increase

Personal characteristics • low self-esteem • high requirement for acceptance • strong group commitment	Increase in conformity
Task characteristics • high task difficulty	
Group characteristics • unanimity • size of unanimous group	

3.6 Phases in group development

When people do something together, they are initially more of a collection of people than a group. It takes some time before they display the characteristics of a genuine group.

EXAMPLE 3.15

Exploration and probing

An educational organisation decides to adopt project-based learning. A committee of five teachers is appointed to produce a plan for implementing this decision. They have four months to do so. In the first meeting, they probe each other's opinions and ideas. They do not yet know quite what they can expect of each other and how they can best collaborate.

Research into group formation has been going on for more than 50 years. It has shown that new groups undergo a development in which certain phases can be recognised. The nature of these phases is described in various models. Although these models differ in detail, they also have many similarities. In general, five phases of group development can be identified (Forsyth, 1990; Wheelan, 2004): orientation (forming), conflict (storming), stabilisation (norming), performance (performing) and dissolution (adjourning). See Figure 3.7.

Phases

FIGURE 3.7 Phases of group development

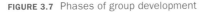

| Orientation phase | Conflict phase | Stabilisation phase | Presentation phase | Termination phase |

3.6.1   Orientation phase (forming)

When people first become involved with each other, uncertainty dominates. What does everyone want from the group? What are the attitudes of the group's members? How should I behave? How will others respond to me? This uncertainty provokes tension, which in turn ensures that group members behave cautiously. They will be more inclined to take a cautious attitude than to push themselves forward. By acting cautiously and not revealing all their cards, they can better discover what ideas, desires and intentions other group members have. This cautiousness prevents unpleasant surprises.

Uncertainty

Tension

If there is a leader in the group, people will focus primarily on this leader to determine their own behaviour and the goals of the group. People expect moral support from the leader. If there is no leader, people will focus on themselves.

Focus

© Noordhoff Uitgevers bv

EXAMPLE 3.16

Uneasiness

The teachers on a project-based learning committee all have the same status and their first meeting proceeds rather chaotically because no one proposes an agenda. The discussions do not lead to conclusions or decisions. People jump from one subject to another. Some rather vague ideas are put forward about project-based learning and the role of teachers therein, but they are not elaborated upon.

By not immediately expressing clear points of view, people avoid conflicts over what the group should be trying to achieve. Not displaying any distinctive behaviour prevents others from perceiving you as dominant, bossy or a chatterbox. By acting cautiously, people give each other the opportunity to explore whether they can and will work together and whether the group is viable. Viability in two areas must be investigated: task-oriented and social–emotional.

The two areas will be intermingled in this first phase. After a hesitant beginning, the group members will exchange rather more information about who they are and what they think about all kinds of things on a personal level. It also slowly but surely becomes clear what ideas and desires people have in the task-oriented area. Group members will become more open towards each other and reveal more about themselves.

3.6.2   Conflict phase (storming)

Opposition

As it becomes clearer how the group's members will behave and exactly what they want to do within the group, the likelihood of opposition increases. This leads to conflict.

EXAMPLE 3.17

Differences of opinion

In the second meeting, one teacher proposes appointing a chairman and a minutes secretary. Another teacher thinks that a chairman is unnecessary for this small group. Everyone is adult enough to work together in a properly structured manner. When other group members give their opinion, it sparks an argument about the need for a chairman.

Conflicts

Difference of opinion

Easy to resolve

Conflicts can arise in many areas – sometimes just because people misunderstand each other. In this case, a better explanation of each person's intentions can quickly lead to a solution. In this type of situation there is not so much a conflict, more a difference of opinion. Sometimes, conflict arises over something that is fairly easy to resolve, e.g. by agreeing who will take the minutes, who will lead the discussion, at what time everyone must arrive and what activities each group member must have carried out before the following meeting. Clear agreements often prevent people from becoming irritated with one another because certain things have been left unresolved for too long. Differences of opinion within the group can also arise over important things, such as how people should treat each other and what the group's goals should be. When the differences in important areas are great and people stick to their positions stubbornly, there is an escalating conflict.

Escalating conflict

The occurrence of conflicts is a natural phenomenon. Conflicts are unavoidable and necessary to reaching ultimate clarity about the goals people wish to achieve, the methods they wish to use and the manner in which they should interact with each other. If group members are able to openly discuss and resolve these contradictions, this contributes to the better functioning of the group and to greater unanimity over goals and methods.

Group members will sometimes avoid conflict because they are afraid of hindering collaboration. Apathy, lack of effort, unexpressed irritation and a lack of effective collaboration then arise. The group remains stuck in the conflict phase and goes no further in its development. Despite the fact that conflicts have negative connotations, they are necessary for further development, unless they escalate to such an extent that the group's members are unable to resolve them satisfactorily. The resolution of conflicts contributes to shaping a group into a workable unit. However, the resolution of conflicts costs time and energy, which are not invested in accomplishing the task. An effective approach to tasks is possible only when most of the conflicts have been satisfactorily resolved.

3.6.3 Stabilisation phase (norming)

The solution of conflicts brings greater clarity within the group about goals and methods. This enables the group to devote itself wholly to the tasks it needs to accomplish.

EXAMPLE 3.18

Flexible consultation

In their second and third meetings, the teachers thoroughly discussed the form they wanted their collaboration to take as well as their ideas about project-based learning. In the fourth meeting they adopted an agenda and a chairman. They are now focusing on the things that need to be developed further in order to produce a sound proposal on project-based learning. The matters that need further investigation are divided among the group's members and a long-term schedule is drawn up.

The resolution of conflicts within the group takes place largely through trial and error. Group members try out all kinds of behaviour (participation, contributions) in the initial phase and find out how the other group members respond. This testing of behaviour is not completely random. They make use of their experience in other groups. The teacher's proposal to appoint a chairman came from her positive experience in a chaired group. Through the manner in which different members of the group react to the various contributions and proposals, slowly but surely more insight is gained into what is possible and desirable within the group.

Trial and error

In a new group, there is greater variety of behaviour among group members than there is in the stabilisation phase. Behaviour and ideas that do not elicit positive reactions will slowly disappear from the group's repertoire, while behaviour and ideas that receive positive reactions will begin to dominate (law of effect, see paragraph 1.1.2).

This process of regulation leads to clarity in many areas of group behaviour, answering questions such as:
- How openly should we be in expressing our wishes, feelings and ideas?
- How should we take decisions? Must they be unanimous or can we also take majority decisions?
- How should we handle members who do not behave properly?
- Who is in charge of the group?
- How often and for how long should we meet?
- How should we divide among ourselves the activities that need to be carried out?

As more matters are satisfactorily resolved, fewer differences of opinion or conflicts occur. Mutual confidence increases and a feeling of unity arises. Group members present information and put forward their wishes and views more readily. Open communication is created.

3.6.4   Performance phase (performing)
Groups enter the performance phase when their members have reached sufficient agreement about goals, methods and how they will interact with one another. The group's members no longer need to invest so much time and energy in resolving conflicts and differences of opinion, with the result that more time remains for working on group tasks.

Nevertheless, during the performance phase, not all the contributions will be focused on group tasks. From time to time, members of the group will have differences of opinion about their approach to tasks and the goals they wish to achieve with the group. Sometimes, irritations arise. Energy then has to be invested in removing these irritations. Research (Bales, 1970) has shown that groups that have reached the performance phase spend about 60% of their time on tasks and 40% on maintaining a good atmosphere and resolving differences of opinion.

By no means every group reaches the performance phase. Various studies into different types of group show that this phase is reached by only 10-25% of groups.

3.6.5   Dissolution phase (adjourning)
Groups can cease to exist for various reasons. Some groups are formed for a clearly defined task. Once this task has been completed, the group's members go their different ways. This is the case with the committee of teachers that has to produce a proposal for the introduction of project-based learning (see example 3.16).
Groups can also dissolve because they become mired in conflict or because they have had so little success that, after a time, members simply give up. The costs invested in the group are becoming or have become too high and the rewards received too low. Deciding no longer to participate or to dissolve the group is not an easy matter. In these cases, a great deal of stress is experienced and negative feelings and a sense of failure can predominate.

3.7 Structural characteristics of groups

The development of a stable manner of collaborating and interacting occurs in the previously mentioned stabilisation phase. In this phase, a natural selection process takes place, in which unsuccessful forms of collaboration disappear and successful forms remain. Weick (1979) regards the development of a group not so much in terms of the individual contributions that are or are not successful, but rather in terms of an interactive model. Effective collaboration is based on a series of diadic interactions between group members. A diadic interaction is the smallest unit of interaction that can take place in a collaboration between two people.

Diadic interactions

3

EXAMPLE 3.19

Whether or not to respond?

Suppose you are sitting at a bar; you do not know anybody else there but you would still like to have a conversation with someone. You can start a conversation by saying something to the person sitting next to you. This person can either respond and say something in return or pretend they did not hear and not respond. If the person responds, you can continue by saying something else, or you may think 'what nonsense' and keep quiet. Whether a conversation starts up therefore depends on mutual responses and whether those responses contribute to what one considers to be a good or friendly conversation.

The display of behaviour, someone else's response and responding to that response is called a diadic interaction (see Figure 3.8).

FIGURE 3.8 Double interaction between A and B

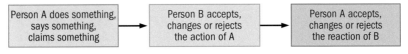

Source: Alblas & Van de Vliert, 1990

Whether a diadic interaction is successful and leads to a good conversation or to effective collaboration depends on the desires and viewpoints of the participants. People try to exercise influence by the manner in which they respond to each other. Often, a series of diadic interactions is necessary before one can decide whether the collaboration will lead to the desired result for the parties involved or whether it is better to terminate the collaboration. According to Weick, a shared objective is not the most important thing. A successful diadic interaction arises if party A contributes to the desires of party B, and if party B in turn contributes to the desires of party A. According to the previously mentioned law of effect, successful diadic interactions will be repeated in group behaviour and a pattern will become distinguishable in the group's collaboration and mutual relationships. A stable pattern of relationships and behaviour between group members is called a group structure.

Group structure

Structural characteristics

Differences in the way groups function are determined by their structural characteristics, such as:
- the pattern of contributions made by group members;
- the influence exerted by group members;
- the roles adopted by group members;
- the relationships between group members and the team spirit or cohesion they produce;
- the norms and values that regulate the behaviour of the members.

These characteristics are discussed in the following subsections.

3.7.1 Participation

Anyone who has ever observed collaboration in a group over an extended period is able to confirm that some group members participate and contribute more than others and also exercise more influence on what happens. This inequality in the input and influence of the group's members is one of the most striking characteristics of group behaviour. Bass (1954) and Bales (1953) demonstrated this by experiment. Bass put together groups of people of about the same age, educational level and status. The groups were asked to discuss problems and find solutions to them. Differences in input quickly developed. Some group members contributed a great deal and others very little. Bales came to the same conclusion. The differences in input arose in the very first discussion session and the pattern remained stable in the subsequent sessions. Whoever contributed a lot in the first session continued to do so in the following meetings. Bales's observations suggest that in groups of three to seven members the group member who contributes most produces around 40 to 50% of all the input (see Figure 3.9).

FIGURE 3.9 Difference in input of group members in different group sizes

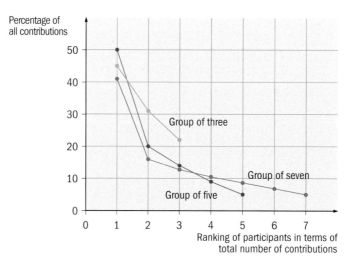

Source: Alblas, 1983

In larger groups, two to three members together usually account for more than 60% of the input. If we look not just at the amount contributed but also at the communication flow, a pattern can likewise be identified (Bales, 1953). This pattern is as follows:
- Group members who contribute little primarily ask for information,disagree or agree with something. Group members who contribute a lot primarily produce information, opinions and suggestions. These group members influence the content, direction and results of the discussion to a large extent.
- Group members who contribute a lot focus primarily on the group as a whole, while group members who contribute little focus primarily on the group members who contribute most. Due to this upward communication, the group members who contribute a lot also have the opportunity to respond to remarks directed at them, which reinforces their dominant position.
- In large groups, the group members who contribute a lot focus primarily on each other. They pass each other the ball, as it were, and thereby ensure that other group members hardly participate at all.

The observations of Bass and Bales on patterns of communication in groups show that these patterns arise fairly quickly. Characteristic of these patterns is the inequality of input and the fact that the members who contribute most pass the ball to each other.

3.7.2   Influence and status
If, at the end of a meeting, group members are asked who has had the most influence on the direction and outcome of the discussion, those who have contributed the most are always named.

Influence

EXAMPLE 3.20

Leading in knowledge and experience

The committee of teachers tasked with producing a project-based learning plan has now been in existence for two months. They have chosen as their chairman a member of the group who is also chairman of the expertise team and fulfils this role well. Two teachers on the committee turn out to be primarily content experts in the field of project-based learning, not only because of

their field of study, psychology, but also because they have already included project-based learning in their teaching methods from time to time. They can therefore contribute their experiences. For these reasons, they contribute a great deal of information and dominate the discussions on this point.

How does the pattern of unequal contribution and influence arise? We can explain it using the expectancy theory of Berger, Conner and Fisek (1974). When group members collaborate, they have certain expectations about their own behaviour in the group and also about the behaviour of the other group members. These expectations are based on:
- **Past behaviours**. Every group member has a picture of their own behaviour in groups and sometimes of that of other group members as well. The teachers' committee knew that one of the group's members would be a

Expectancy theory

© Noordhoff Uitgevers bv

good chairman and that two other members had experience with project-based learning and could therefore contribute more on this subject.
- **Status.** Every group member has a general or specific image of their own status and that of others in the group. In a formal group, it is often clear who is the team leader or coordinator and who is an expert in a particular field. Experience of one's own and other people's behaviour and the status of the group's members determine the **expectations** that people have of each other's contributions and influence.

How these expectations can lead to the emergence of a pattern of unequal input, influence and status has been described by Berger, Conner and Fisek (see figure 3.10). According to them, communication within groups can be understood as a series of behavioural opportunities and contributions.
- **Behavioural opportunity.** Every silence or pause in the discussion and every question that is asked offers group members the opportunity to make a remark, observation or reaction.
- **Contribution.** Every time a person makes use of a behavioural opportunity, they make a contribution to communication within the group.

The contributions of group members elicit reactions in and from others. These reactions can be positive or negative. Positive reactions consist in further questioning, agreement, elaboration or approval. Negative reactions consist in ignoring, disparaging, attacking or changing the subject.

FIGURE 3.10 The relationship between expectation and behaviour in groups

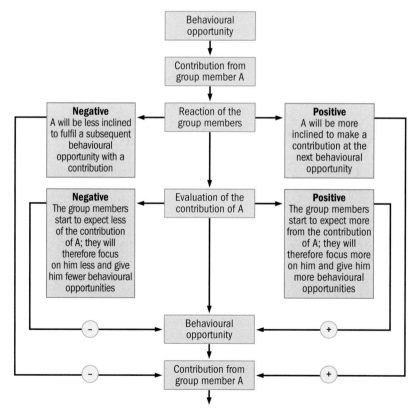

Source: Alblas & Van de Vliert, 1990

According to the previously mentioned law of effect, a person will be more disposed to seize a behavioural opportunity to make a contribution if his contributions in the past have been positively received. Not only do group members respond to each other's contributions, they also determine whether those contributions have any value in terms of collaboration within the group.

If people expect a positive contribution from a certain person, they will focus their questions and remarks on that person, react more positively to their contributions and reinforce them. Naturally, expectations about the value of a person's contribution can also be formed in advance, based on knowledge of their status.

3.7.3   Roles

After a while, group members acquire a certain role in the group, due to their specific input and function. Expectations arise about this role and these provide the opportunity to repeat the behaviour appropriate to the role, as explained in the previous subsection.   *Role*

A role can be created in two ways. It can be linked to the function a person has in the group. A person can be appointed as the coordinator of the group, for example. When the organise a progress meeting, they are expected to lead the discussion, request information, give instructions and, if necessary, take difficult decisions. Ideas exist about the behaviour that corresponds to this role, so the role of the coordinator in the group is predetermined.

Roles can also arise from the interaction between group members in the course of group development. In a new group, some members take a cautious attitude. Other members soon start making all kinds of proposals and thinking actively when a decision needs to be made. There is also generally a group member who tries to direct the discussion and take a leading role. In a group where the members fulfil the same position in the organisation, different roles arise from a process of mutual interaction. Which roles emerge from this depends on how group members wish to present themselves and on the reactions of the other members of the group.   *Interaction*

Problems with role fulfilment

Problems can arise with respect to role behaviour. One reason for such issues is the existence of role ambiguity. This is the case if a person is unsure about how they should fulfil the role because there are insufficient clues, e.g. no clear role definition.   *Role ambiguity*

EXAMPLE 3.21

Vague roles

The introduction of teamwork in a distribution centre involved a period of adjustment. The team members had previously been allocated their duties by a boss. Now they had to divide the work among themselves and take turns to inspect and process orders and to drive the forklift truck. At first, it was not clear exactly how they should do this: who, for example, should take the initiative in consultations about the division of work, how should they make a decision about this and what should they do if there were differences of opinion? The roles that people were required to fulfil during the collaborative process were vague.

Role conflicts There can also be role conflicts within a group. These are conflicting requirements or expectations regarding the role a person should fulfil.

EXAMPLE 3.22

Role expectations

A group expects its leader to pass on all the information obtained in meetings with the head of the department, but the departmental heads sometimes requires the group leaders to keep certain

information to themselves. The group also expects the leader to represent their interests, while the heads of the departments expect them to represent the interests of the department.

Role conflicts often arise if someone has several jobs in an organisation. With every job goes a specific role and this can lead to conflicting demands being made on a person.

Functional and dysfunctional contributions
Groups can function well only if certain contributions are made. These are:
- **Task-oriented contributions.** These are contributions which ensure that the group can work on its tasks effectively. In the committee for project learning, the group would benefit from people who could fulfil the roles of planner, minutes secretary, panel chairman and expert. Through their contributions, the collaboration can proceed in a goal-oriented manner.
- **Group-oriented contributions.** These are contributions that make pleasant collaboration possible. When conflicts and opposition in the group threaten effective collaboration, there is a need for a person to fulfil the role of mediator, who can break through the tension and make differences of opinion productive.

Functional contributions Task- and group-oriented contributions are called functional contributions. There may also be contributions that hinder the progress of the group. This is the case, for example, if group members focus exclusively on their own interests. They are then making:
- **Self-oriented contributions.** These are 'contributions' such as slacking, being obstructive or domineering, seeking recognition or going one's own way without taking account of others.
Self-oriented contributions are **dysfunctional contributions**. Proper collaboration is possible in groups only if task- and group-oriented contributions are forthcoming and self-oriented contributions are absent.

3.7.4   Group cohesion
Another characteristic of group structure is expressed in the pattern of mutual attraction and repulsion, in the **affective relationships** between group members. Moreno (1943) was one of the first researchers to map out the affective relationships between group members. He developed the **sociometric method** to this end. This method consists of a written questionnaire, through which group members indicate who they wish or do not wish to work on a future task and who they like or do not like. On the basis of these answers, he was able to discover the pattern of affective relationships and represent them in a **sociogram** (see Figure 3.11).

FIGURE 3.11 Sociogram

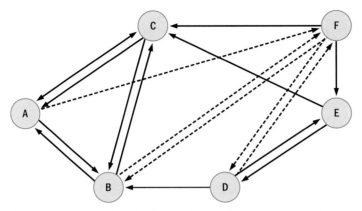

The solid arrows ──▶ indicate the direction of someone's preference with regard to other group members.
The dashed arrows ---▶ indicate the negative attitude with regard to other group members.
If there is no arrow, people feel neutral towards each other.

Source: Meertens & Von Grumbkow, 1988

The sociogram shows that the group comprises two more or less separate subgroups. It can thus be concluded that the group does not form a unit. The extent to which group members form a whole, feel attracted to each other, want to work together and find the group important determines the cohesion of the group. Several factors can strengthen cohesion within a group:
- **Success with the group task**. If a football team plays well and often wins its games, the group becomes attractive to its members and cohesion increases. If they subsequently lose a lot of games, mutual irritations and differences will lead to conflicts, and cohesion will decline.
- **Good interpersonal relationships**. If group members like each other and get along with each other well, cohesion increases.
- **Size of the group**. In general, the likelihood of subgroups forming increases as the group increases in size. Group members feel connected to a subgroup more easily than to the group as a whole. Therefore strong cohesion is more likely in small groups than in large groups.
- **Common enemy**. If the group is threatened by others or has to compete with other groups, its members are forced to help and support each other. Cohesion then increases.

The factors that contribute to cohesion are shown in Figure 3.12.

EXAMPLE 3.23

Common enemy

Sherif and his colleagues (1961) installed two groups of boys in a holiday camp. The groups lived in separate houses. They each received a number of group tasks, such as preparing food on a wood fire. After some time, activities were organised in the form of competitions between the groups. These competitions gave rise to rivalry. The members of each group regarded the other group as a common enemy and Sherif found that cohesion within the groups was strengthened. At the end of the week, the groups were given a number of tasks that this time required collaboration between the groups. The result was that cohesion within the groups declined to the level at which it had been before the competitions.

FIGURE 3.12 Factors that promote cohesion in a group

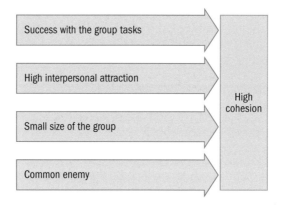

3.7.5 Group norms

Norm

After a time, when group behaviour has stabilised, the manner of collaboration that has been established becomes the norm.
Norms can be regarded as informal rules that determine group behaviour. Unlike role expectations, which apply to specific people or jobs, norms are applicable to all group members. Norms must be distinguished from the formal rules that exist in organisations. These formal rules are usually laid down and imposed from above. Group norms, on the other hand, develop within the group itself and consist of a system of commands and prohibitions. The commands prescribe the kind of behaviour to be demonstrated by all group members, while the prohibitions indicate behaviour that must be avoided. In many cases, group members are hardly aware, or even completely unaware, of the norms they follow. That there are norms is often apparent only when they are violated and the other group members take steps to eliminate the offence.

EXAMPLE 3.24

Norms in the group

A new employee has joined a production group. He notices that a machine is not working properly, so he gets some tools and begins to repair it himself. Two colleagues rush over and ask: 'What are you doing?' The new employee is surprised at this reaction and asks: 'Am I doing something wrong?' His colleagues then tell him that it is not usual for people to repair machines themselves; it should be done by the maintenance service.

What norms develop in a group is dependent on a number of factors. Feldman (1984) describes these factors as follows:

a **Start situation**. What happens during the first group meeting(s) often sets the tone for how people interact with each other – for example, how businesslike or informal their interaction is.

b **Past**. The group's members bring with them certain preferences and desires based on their experiences in other groups.

c **Explicit statements**. A boss or a colleague can make a clear statement about 'the way we do things around here'. They may do so with new group members who need to find their place in the group, for example.

d **Critical events**. If a group member reveals confidential information to a boss or another group, the other group members may perceive this as an offence. From this situation, the norm can arise that certain information may not go outside the group. Through such a critical event, what people want and do not want becomes clear, and a group norm is created.

3

The outsider in a group is often easy to spot. Which kind of group norm can you see here?

Group norms can apply to anything. For example:
- the manner in which group members interact;
- the things that can and cannot be said to a boss;
- how punctual group members are in the performance of their work;
- how group members interact with clients or other departments;
- how hard they must work.

Group norms need not agree with the formal rules and regulations that exist within the organisation. In many cases, group norms can deviate from these, either because the formal rules and regulations are not appropriate for the situation or cannot be implemented properly, or because the group's members do not agree with these regulations and develop their own norms instead.

EXAMPLE 3.25

Autonomous norms

At a university building, it was noticed that coffee machines in several staffrooms were sometimes left on all weekend. This not only resulted in extra electricity costs but also increased the risk of fire. The decision was made that machines would no longer be provided and employees must get their coffee from the canteen. In many departments, this decision was seen as a restriction of staff autonomy and a violation of the tradition of making one's own coffee. The norm that staff should be allowed to drink good-quality coffee prevailed and people sought their own solutions to the problem – for example, putting large coffee machines in one or two rooms, which everyone within the department could use.

3.8 Relationships between groups

We have described organisations as a collection of groups, usually in the form of departments, services and committees.

EXAMPLE 3.26

Departmental interests

In a meeting of departmental heads, the head of the sales department advocates giving priority to a large order from a new client. According to her, this new client can only be retained by complying with the desired delivery time. The production planning manager sighs deeply and looks worried. The schedule for the coming week has already been agreed and must now be changed. The head of the production department is not very happy either. The new order will require overtime working if the delivery times promised to other clients are to be met. It is questionable whether his staff will want to work even more overtime than they have been doing recently. Perhaps this is the moment to stand firm and not give in to the sales boss.

Groups in organisations form functional units, which can function properly only if they supply each other with adequate information, knowledge, and materials. The production department can operate only if the sales department brings in orders, the planning department specifies when and in what order production must take place and the supplies department delivers the components or raw materials necessary for timely production. There is therefore mutual dependence among groups in organisations.

Mutual dependence

Mutual support is not always automatic. Various factors can hinder it. These are: differences in identity and vision between groups, differences in interests between groups, and the extent to which there is differentiation between in-groups and out-groups.

3.8.1   Differences in identity and vision

Groups are formed to contribute towards the objectives of the organisation and every group has responsibility for a specific part of the organisation's activities. To this end, people are recruited who have certain knowledge or skills. The people in production planning have had different training than the salesmen. They collaborate primarily with the production department. The salesmen on the other hand, who are always on the road, have contact primarily with clients; they work independently of their colleagues and come into the factory only every now and again. Salesmen therefore regard themselves as independent operators, who have little to do with the rules and regulations imposed from above. They think that they are the pivot on which the organisation turns; after all, they are charged with providing the orders that give the organisation its reason for existing. The production planning staff, on the other hand, think that work in the organisation must be firmly bound by rules because otherwise there cannot be efficient production, and that requires strong and central leadership. All the other groups must therefore be subordinate to them.

Groups in organisations can also differ from each other in their area of expertise, their place of work, the problems with which they are confronted and the people and groups with which they have to interact. They consequently develop their own place and identity in the organisation, but also their own vision of how the organisation should function. The resulting differences between groups arise in a number of areas (Lawrence & Lorsch, 1967):

a Differences in **goal orientation**. The people in sales focus on different goals than the people in product development.

b Differences in **time orientation**. In some departments people are more focused on resolving day-to-day problems, while the product development department, for example, is occupied with long-term issues.

c Differences in **interpersonal orientation**. The style of interaction can be highly businesslike and formal in one group, while in another it is more personal and informal.

d Differences in **structure**. In one group, such as the production department, activities may be much more prescribed and standardised than in the sales department, for example, where the salesmen plan their own activities.

Due to these differences, groups develop their own vision of organisational reality. Organisational problems are usually analysed and resolved from each specific viewpoint. If there is a decline in the sales of a certain series of products, the sales department will usually see the problem and solution from a market-oriented perspective. The decline in sales may be related to

Own vision

the actions of their competitors, to the changing tastes of the public or to a lack of effective advertising. In the product development department, they are more of the opinion that this series of products is at the end of its life-cycle, that it has gradually become technologically obsolete and therefore has to be updated. These differences in vision can easily lead to conflicting ideas as to the right way to resolve common problems and so can constitute a source of conflict between groups.

3.8.2   Differences in interests

Interests

Groups are not only focused on the interests of the organisation as a whole, but also – or even primarily – have their own interests at heart. The production planning department has an interest in avoiding unexpected changes. They therefore ask the salesmen to take this into account in their negotiations with clients over delivery times. The salesmen, on the other hand, want to be free to act as they see fit and would rather not be bound by rules. After all, they are highly customer oriented and they can only accomplish their role if they fulfil the wishes of their clients. Production wants to know well in advance what orders have to be met, in order to arrange for the correct materials to be delivered, set up the machines in time and, if necessary, recruit temporary staff. It is obvious that these interests do not always run parallel with each other and are sometimes contradictory. Conflicts can be expected where interests clash.

Competitors

In many cases, groups in organisations are each other's competitors. This is the case if people, materials or resources must be shared.

EXAMPLE 3.27

Rivalry between groups

Section B of Family Care has been struggling with personnel problems for some time. This is a consequence of the long-term sickness of an employee and of an increase in the number of clients requiring care. The employees in Section B are envious of Section C, because this section has more staff and fewer clients. In terms of work

pressure, they are clearly better off. In fact, the employees in Section B think that Section C should surrender an employee to them, to reduce their work pressure. Section C is fiercely opposed to this, since its employees have an interest in seeing that their work pressure does not increase.

Shortages

In many cases, organisations have to cope with shortages of cash or resources. Not every 'justified' request can be fulfilled. The allocation of more people to one group inevitably means that other groups will not receive any more for the time being. The organisation can therefore also be regarded as a conglomeration of parties (Lammers, 1983). These parties have interests that are partly shared and partly in conflict. The conflicting interests can be a major source of conflict between groups.

Conglomeration of parties

3.8.3   Differentiation between in-groups and out-groups

A supplementary problem for collaboration between groups is the in- and out-group phenomenon. Under certain conditions, this can create stereotypical images of each group and hinder collaboration.

The regular collaboration between people in a group results in identification with their own group. The more closely the members feel allied to their own group, the more they regard it as the 'in-group' and other people in the organisation as the 'out-group.' Differentiation between an in-group and an out-group has certain psychological and behavioural consequences (Koomen, 1988):

a   There is a difference in **involvement**. People in the in-group keep a better eye on affairs and information than the out-group.

b   There is a difference in **observation**. People in the in-group more clearly observe mutual differences than the out-group. This can easily result in general statements about members of the out-group, such as: 'Those people in the product development department are arrogant.' By overlooking differences, everyone in the out-group is treated as the same.

c   **Stereotyping** arises. The homogeneous conception of the characteristics of people in the out-group easily leads to stereotyping and prejudice.

d   There is a difference in **assessment**. Behaviour in the in-group is generally assessed more positively than behaviour in the out-group. A certain characteristic – for example, the finance department not readily spending money – is perceived within that group as good management but by other groups as being stringy or tight with money.

In-group
Out-group
Behavioural consequences

How is it that one's own group is more positively assessed than groups in which one takes no part? The more positive assessment of one's own group is explained by the social identity theory (as described in paragraph 3.4.2).

Social identity theory

In- and out-groups: rivalry between groups.

It appears that people need to construct and maintain a positive self-image. To obtain or retain a positive self-image, people define the groups of which they are part, the in-groups, as positively as possible. This can be done by interpreting and designating the characteristics of these groups primarily as positive. This bias in favour of one's own groups need not *per se* lead to negative stereotyping of the out-group. There are, however, circumstances that quickly result in this and lead to a deterioration in relationships between the in-group and the out-group. This is the case if groups regard each other as competitors or enemies.

As shown by the above, groups within organisations can easily end up in conflict due to differences in interests. These conflicts result in more acute differentiation between the in-group and the out-group (Sherif et al., 1961), increasing cohesion and solidarity within the in-group and negative stereotyping of the out-group.

When there is conflict between groups, the members of these groups become increasingly involved in their own group. People start to observe and assess the other group more negatively and contact between the groups deteriorates. There is a negative spiral, which seriously hinders collaboration. This negative spiral proceeds as follows (Schein, 1988):

Negative spiral

a Each group in a conflict situation is inclined to observe only the best aspects of itself and overlook its own weaknesses. At the same time, primarily the weaker aspects of the out-group are observed. This selective observation leads to negative stereotyping of the out-group.

b Communication and interaction with the out-group declines; as a result, it is easier to maintain the negative stereotyping and more difficult to correct the distorted perceptions of the out-group.

EXAMPLE 3.28

Competence contest

The executive office in a company makes use of advanced equipment. Technical departments handle maintenance and advise on the purchase of new equipment. Purchasing decisions are taken by the managing director in consultation with the heads of the two services. In recent years, the technical departments have become more influential because the equipment coming onto the market has become increasingly complex and requires more specialist knowledge. In the past, it was the executive office that specified what equipment it needed, but now it is the technical departments. The technical departments collect information and data about the function and use of new equipment, then assesses what equipment

is suitable and subsequently advises the managing director. This has led to more and more resistance from the executive office, which has been accustomed to deciding for itself. The result is that the services end up in a competence contest. Accusations are thrown back and forth, negative images (stereotypes) arise, mutual irritation increases, contact between the services reduces and there is stagnation in the decision-making process. The people in the executive office accuse the technical departments of 'extraordinary arrogance', while the executive office is characterised as 'passive and unreasonable'.

Source: Mastenbroek, 1986

---

c People primarily defend the interests of their own group, to the exclusion of those in the out-group, due to which the contradictions become more pronounced and hostility increases.

These effects make it extremely difficult for groups to extricate themselves from a negative spiral. Communication and collaboration between groups can be hindered for a long period and it is not easy to remove the obstacles. People are inclined to prejudge each other's behaviour in the light of their prejudices and negative stereotyping, due to which it is not easy to create a better and more effective image. If contradictions between groups in organisations lead to such negative images, collaboration can be seriously hindered and thus threaten the continued existence of the organisation. Several factors can hinder collaboration between groups. These are shown in Figure 3.13.

FIGURE 3.13 Factors that can impede cohesion between groups

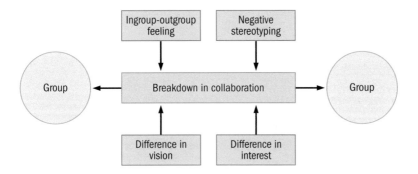

3.9 Improving relationships between groups

When collaboration between groups is impeded due to the in-group/out-group problem, it is necessary to break through the negative images each group has of the other. This can be done by increasing contact between the groups. Allport (1954) has formulated a contact hypothesis for this in which he assumes that under certain conditions the negative images will disappear if there is more mutual contact. Conditions that can play a positive role in this are:

Contact hypothesis conditions

- **Equality**. Groups that are brought into contact with each other must not have too many differences in social and economic status. This ensures that contact can more easily be established and that people will perceive each other more or less as equals.
- **Collaboration and mutual dependence**. The groups should work on a task that can be accomplished only through joint effort. The joint effort weakens the group boundaries and mutual communication increases.
- **Informal contact**. The group members must be placed in a situation in which informal contact is possible, so that people from the two groups get to know each other better.
- **Necessity**. The importance of collaboration between groups must be emphasised as a common interest in the organisation. This can ensure that people focus less on the interests of their own group and more on the common interest, through which the strict boundary between the in- and out-groups disappears.

A manager can try to create one or more of the above conditions, so that the relationships between groups improve. Use can also be made of team coaching by hiring someone from outside the organisation.

© Noordhoff Uitgevers bv

Tips for managers

New groups are regularly created within organisations. Examples are project groups or committees. It is important to keep an eye on whether group development is proceeding well.

Impediments to group development
There are several possible impediments to group development. They can be identified by asking the following questions:
- Has the group achieved a clear formulation of its objectives, which has been accepted by all group members?
- Is there sufficient agreement about the tasks and functions everyone must fulfil?
- Is communication between group members lively and open?
- Can group members cope with differences in goals, insights, desires and methods?
- Is there a relaxed atmosphere?
- What is the relationship between the energy devoted to the task and the energy spent on mutual relationships within the group?

If the first five questions are negatively answered and people put more time into group upkeep than into the task itself, then the group is still in the conflict phase. If the group stays there too long, outside help is needed to move the group to the next stage (see 'Tips for managers' in chapter 4).

Breakdowns in relationships
The functional relationships between groups in the organisation must be good. Breakdowns in these relationships and too much in-/out-group differentiation must be identified as promptly as possible. Watch out for the following behaviour:
- There is little communication (information, consultation) between groups that are mutually dependent.
- There is a great deal of grumbling about other groups and only the weak and annoying characteristics of people in the other groups are mentioned.
- People think everyone in the other group is the same.
- People think their own group is perfect and never does anything wrong.

If these phenomena occur, it is important to intervene quickly to improve mutual communication and functional support (see practical tips in chapter 4).

Improving communications
Improvement in the relationships between groups can be accomplished by promoting communication between them. For example:
- by organising informal activities (sports, days out) that intensify contact between the members of different groups;
- by devising an assignment (project) that requires intensive collaboration between two or more groups.

Summary

- A collection of people constitutes a group if they:
  - regularly interact directly with each other
  - strive for a common goal
  - need each other to achieve that goal
  - feel that they are a group

- There are three types of functional group:
  - administrative groups
  - work groups
  - self-managing teams

- Spontaneous, informal groups can also arise.

- Functions of groups for the group members are:
  - offering protection
  - providing information
  - achieving goals
  - providing social support, identity and status

- A valued member of a group conforms with the ideas and behaviour that are seen by the group as correct and desirable. After some time, a certain uniformity of ideas and behaviour emerges.

- Group members who do not conform are sidelined or take a peripheral position.

- The phases of group development are:
  - orientation (forming)
  - conflict (storming)
  - stabilisation (norming)
  - performance (performing)
  - dissolution (adjourning)

- There are five ways in which a group structure becomes visible:
  - in the differentiation between the contributions of group members
  - in the differentiation between the status and influence of group members
  - in the differentiation between the roles that group members fulfil
  - in the degree of cohesion within the group
  - in the norms of the group

- Formal groups in organisations can function well only if they receive sufficient functional support from other groups (mutual dependence).

- Collaboration between groups can be disrupted by:
  - differences in identity and vision
  - differences in interests
  - differentiation between in-group and out-group

- Differentiation between an in-group and an out-group has certain psychological consequences:
  - differences in commitment to one's own and other groups
  - differences in observation of one's own and other groups
  - stereotyping
  - differences in assessment

- The in-/out-group differentiation can be overcome and relationships between groups improved by:
  - equality of treatment
  - collaboration and dependence
  - informal contact
  - emphasis on the importance of collaboration

3

© Noordhoff Uitgevers bv

Assignments

3.1 Observe a meeting or discussion group. Find out the pattern of contributions and the direction of communication in the group. Do this as follows:

a Make a diagram of the places in which the group's members sit at the table.
b Use a watch with a second hand (or keep counting up to five) and every five seconds see who is saying something to whom. Indicate with an arrow who is speaking to whom. If a person says something more general to the group as a whole, mark this with a dash.
c Afterwards, use the dashes and arrows to work out what pattern the communication has followed. Find out whether this corresponds with the pattern identified by Bales, as defined in subsection 3.7.1. Do the dominant group members pass the ball to each other?

3.2 Read the following example.
A computer company has approximately 200 employees. The production department is divided into parallel teams of 14 to 18 people. These production teams have responsibility for the whole of production, from the input of raw materials to the transport of finished products. There is a team meeting every day to discuss production, distribution of work, work structuring, raw materials and the intake of team members. They determine their own working hours, do their own scheduling and check the quality of the products. Each team has a coordinator, with a supporting and coaching role.

What characteristics of self-managing teams do you recognise in this example?

3.3 Everybody is part of various groups. So are you.

a List three groups of which you are a member.
b For each group, list the group characteristics.
c Are these characteristics in your groups present to a strong extent or to a weak extent?
d How did you come to be a member of these groups? Can you explain your membership?
e What are each group's most important functions to you?

4

Collaboration and decision-making in groups

- What is effective group performance?
- What conditions encourage collaboration?
- What conditions hinder collaboration and what can be done about them?
- What is effective decision-making?
- What conditions hinder decision-making?
- How can decision-making be improved?

© Noordhoff Uitgevers bv

Difficult decision-making

The Social Work team meets weekly. Their meetings are about such matters as the allocation of new clients to team members, progress, and problems that have arisen. Personnel matters, such as reductions or increases in staff numbers, are also discussed. Once a month there is a case discussion, with the aim of increasing professionalism within the team.

Some team members are unhappy with the level of collaboration and the decision-making process within the team. They think the decision-making process is too slow and delivers too little. The decisions that are taken are often vague and are frequently not implemented or implemented too late. Some employees do not do their work properly, as a result of which other members of the team are becoming overloaded. The team could do more to reduce the client waiting list by working a little harder and more efficiently, for example. The team leader intervenes too little and does not have the courage to cut through logjams or tackle people about their responsibilities. The monthly case discussion produces insufficient insight because the meeting is too non-committal. People are not critical enough of each other's working methods.

4.1 Effective collaboration in groups

The example above shows that collaboration in a group context is not always problem-free. The criticism made by some team members is that a number of their colleagues should work harder and more efficiently because otherwise the collaboration cannot be effective.

When do we speak of efficient cooperation or effective collaboration, and what criteria for judging efficiency of effectiveness can be identified? We shall illustrate the answers to these questions by looking at two teams of social workers. One team covers the North region and the other the South region. The North team functions satisfactorily. They provide good care for their clients, are satisfied with the team atmosphere and the level of collaboration and are able to keep the waiting list short. In the South team there are always problems: the decision-making process is ineffective and the waiting list continues to grow. Group performance in the North team is markedly better than that in the South team. Some member of the South team are so discontented that they are already looking for jobs with other organisations.

Effective collaboration

Criteria

The differences between the teams show that effective collaboration is based on two criteria. These are:
- **Productivity**. This concerns the quantity and quality of the work that is done by the team.
- **Satisfaction**. This concerns the team members' satisfaction with each other and with their collaboration.

These two criteria are independent. High levels of production need not always go together with high levels of satisfaction. Conversely, high satisfaction levels do not automatically lead to high production levels.

Good teamwork demands that members learn to listen to each other very carefully.

4.2 Process losses in executive groups

Indivual
performance

Process losses

The efficiency of collaboration in work groups sometimes leaves much to be desired. In experimental research it has been established that groups by no means always obtain optimum productivity from their members. This optimum can be established by adding together the peak performance of each individual group member. In practice, however, there are usually 'process losses.' The performance of the group as a collaborative unit is generally lower than the sum of the maximum performances of the group members individually.

EXAMPLE 4.1

Poor performance

Latané, Williams and Harkins (1979) set up an experiment to establish the maximum a group was able to achieve, based on the individual potential of the group's members, and to compare it with the actual **group performance**. Participants in the experiment were first individually asked to shout as loudly as possible following a cue. They were then assigned to a group and told, once more, to shout as loudly as possible

following a cue. The groups ranged in size from two to six participants. The results showed that, during their individual phases, participants produced greater levels of noise than during the group phase, and that, the larger the group, the smaller the individual contributions to the overal noise level. The groups were therefore dealing with process losses.

That people in groups produce less than they could on their own can be ascribed to three factors: coordination problems motivation problems and low performance standards (see Figure 4.1).

FIGURE 4.1 Factors leading to low team performance

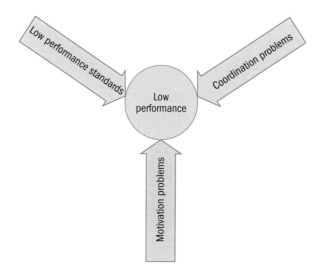

4.2.1   Coordination problems

Sometimes, the proper performance of a task is dependent on coordinating the contributions of several team members. In a tug-of-war competition, for example, synchronising everyone's efforts is an important condition for optimum performance. All must pull on the rope at the same time. For other tasks, the correct sequence of contributions from team members is important. This is the case if a group of three people have to put up scaffolding together, for example. One group member has to supply the right materials to the other group members on the scaffolding at the right time. For the two group members on the scaffolding, it is important to achieve the right combination of actions. One of them needs to hold a scaffolding component in the right place, for example, so that the other can bolt it together. If coordination falters, process losses occur.

Synchronising

Sequence

Combination

4

EXAMPLE 4.2

Carelessness

In the social workers' meeting, an hour was set aside for a case discussion. It had previously been agreed that Anya would lead the discussion and bring along a difficult case. When it came to the discussion, however, it turned out that Anya had forgotten. Because it was not the first time that Anya had forgotten something, she was outright attacked by some group members. This led to the meeting ending in an unpleasant atmosphere. As a result, the team forgot to appoint anyone to lead the next case discussion.

4.2.2   Motivation problems

Team efforts can fall below what the team is truly capably of, if the members of the team are not fully committed – this means their motivation is suboptimal. The existence of suboptimal effort was proved using experiments conducted by Williams, Harkins and Latané (1979) (see also Example 4.1).

EXAMPLE 4.3

Scream at the top of your lungs

Participants in this experiment were told to scream as loudly as possible while on their own. This was used as the benchmark for their optimum performance. Next, they were told that they had to scream again, but this time as part of a team of two or more individuals. Their efforts, the experimenters told them, would contribute to the team's overall performance. The participants were blindfolded and told to wear headphones which would prevent them from seeing or hearing the other participants. In reality, there were no other participants; all that was measured, was their individual performance under the new circumstances.

The outcome of this experiment was that participants who believed they were shouting as part of a team would shout less loudly than participants shouting on their own. 'Team members' would shout at only 74% to 82% of their maximum capacity.

The researchers came to the conclusion that working in groups can lead people to feel less motivated to put in their maximum effort. Their term for this phenomenon was social loafing. There are various factors which can influence the extent of social loafing in groups:

Social loafing

- **Group size**. The larger the group, the harder it is to determine the contribution of individual effort to the whole. As a result, group members feel less responsible (diffusion of responsibility) for the outcome, thereby increasing the extent of social loafing.
- **Visibility**. If it is less clear what each member is meant to contribute, or if it becomes difficult to determine what these contributions should entail, the extent of social loafing increases.
- **Appeal and importance**. As the tasks to be performed by the group become less appealing or important to individual group members, the extent of free riding increases.

Free riding

The concept of free riding is a special form of social loafing. Free riding occurs when an individual contributes little to the group's results, but still incurs benefits from those results.

- -

EXAMPLE 4.4

Free-riding

For their graduation assignment, a group of students is assigned the task of investigation the viability of real estate agents in the future, and what new services realtor might start offering in this era of online communication. Over the course of

Not every student provides the same contribution.

two meetings, the students discuss the nature and contents of the assignment, and draw up a schedule for various activities, such as studying relevant literature, designing interviews, researching current realtor tasks, assessing the usage of the internet in the industry, establishing trend in the housing market and the like. The tasks are subdivided between group members.

During task assignment, Peter keeps a low profile. He eventually voluteers for a very short and simple task. And during the remainder of the collaboration, Peter also picks the easiest jobs exclusively. He offers little input or quality ideas, nor does he perform any organisational or coordinating task during group meetings.
Not all students contribute equally.

Too much free-riding can result in others feeling exploited and also doing less.

- **Attractiveness** of the task. The less attractive the tasks that must be carried out in the group, the greater the chance of poor input. Perhaps Anja did not forget that she had to lead the case discussion; she simply did not want to do it because she thinks that the case discussions are a waste of time.
- **Conscientiousness.** Lack of input can also be caused by free-riding. This is the case if a group member is lazy, in which case his motivation for achieving the group result will inevitably be low.

4.2.3   Low performance standards
The coach of a losing football team will, when faced with sports journalist, occasionally bemoan their performance, along the lines of: 'They just stood there. No passion or fight in them at all.' Good team results can only be achieved if every member is fully committed.

The scope of team member contributions is determined to a large extent by the performance standards developed by the group.

EXAMPLE 4.5

A new job

Barbara has started work at her new company with vim and vigour. Her assignments are finished rapidly, because she is used to working hard. She is motivated to show that she is an achiever. Initially, her colleagues watch her have at it. But in a little while, they begin making snide

remarks. They start sending Barbara to the warehouse, to pick up random errands. It takes Barbara a week to figure out that, according to her colleagues, she is working too hard – which is not workfloor etiquette. Once she begins slowing down her pace, her colleagues start to let up.

The extent to which existing performance standards influence group member contribution was shown in an experiment by Mitchell, Rothman and Liden (1985).

EXAMPLE 4.6

Experiment by Mitchell, Rothman and Liden

Employees were hired to perform a certain task. Part of this group of employees was given written notice of the productivity of other employees beforehand. Another part of the group only found out about employee productivity in practice. The results from the experiment showed that employees lend more weight to how they perceive their colleagues to perform than to written information on that subject.

People who start in a new position soon find out what the working pace in their team is, and what the ruling norms about that pace are. These norms perform a regulatory function with respect to the performance by team members. If group members are used to taking things easy, then an overachieving newcomer will be influenced in an attempt to taming their productive spirit. The norms concerned rarely specify exact levels of performance but relate more to the outer limits of what is felt to be acceptable (see Figure 4.2). Pass those thresholds, and group members will be encouraged to modify their behaviour. New employees who throw these encouragements in the wind, become outcasts.

Low performance standards in a group can be caused by various factors, being:
- *Lack of challenge.* This can occur if the work is dull and requires little in the way of skill from the members of the group.
- *Lack of authority.* This can occur if group members are told exactly how to perform their tasks top-down (by a supervising authority).

FIGURE 4.2 Normative reactions to performances

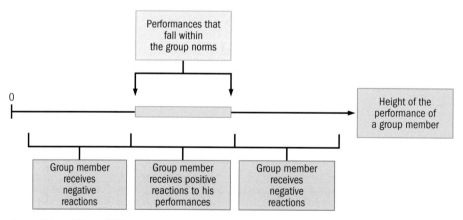

Source: Alblas en Wijsman, 2009

- *Lack of commitment.* This can occur if group members are hardly if at all involved in work planning or work implementation methods.

(4.3) Optimising group performance

Chapter 3 covered the factors that can prevent group performance from achieving its optimum output. This paragraph details the interventions required to improve good group performance. What can be done to maximise the satisfaction and productivity of executive teams? Various researchers have developed a model which indicates the circumstances that contribute to an optimum collaboration (Hackman & Morris, 1975; Fuller & Aldag, 2001; Stangor, 2004). This model shows the different ways in which collaborative performance can be improved (see Figure 4.3), being through:
- optimising team composition
- optimising planning and organisation
- optimising performance standards
- optimising cohesion

FIGURE 4.3 Procedures which improve the effectiveness of group collaboration

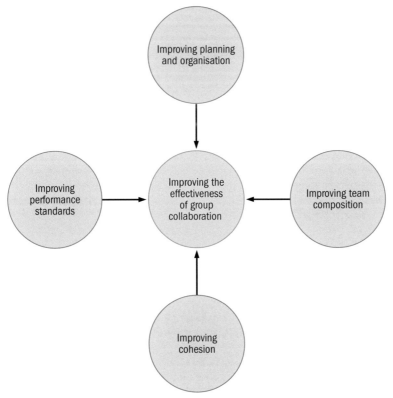

Source: Alblas (2010)

4.3.1   Improving team composition
Depending on the tasks it must accomplish, a group will need to have sufficient members with the required knowledge and skills to carry out the tasks properly.

Knowledge and skills

Some tasks can be succesfully performed with individually specialised group members, allowing each member to excell at one of the sub-tasks. Some tasks benefit from group members with multiple skills, allowing group members to assume each-others tasks or lend a helping hand where needed. Good group collaboration can only be realised if group members get along reasonably well. If there are group members with personality differences which are irreconcilable, chances are that too much time will be spent on individual conflicts, with those group members offering (each other) insufficient support. In that case, it would be preferable to transfer one or more members to a different group.

Good task performance can be affected by taking the following into account when putting together a group:

- Group together people whose knowledge and skills are sufficient to complete group tasks.
- Ensure sufficient overlap in knowledge and skills so that team members can replace and support each other.
- Group together people who get along reasonably well.

4.3.2   Improving planning and organisation

Coordination problems can be avoided through improved planning, organising, steering and adjusting of work in a team. Sometimes, a good approach to activities becomes impossible because team members have not been properly informed of how to perform. To remedy this issue, better planning and organising are required. To that end, the following matters need to be sorted out properly:

- *Establishing targets.* A team should be made aware of which concrete performance targets they are expected to achieve.
- *Planning.* A team should be made aware of the allowable time-frame of particular tasks.
- *Dividing and assigning.* Team members should be made aware of which persons are responsible for which (partial) tasks.
- *Aligning.* Team members should be made aware of how they can best tie-in their activities.

EXAMPLE 4.7

A welding job

A team of welders is in the process of applying a new steel cover to a submerged portion of a ship. Jerry has established the size and dimensions of the steel plate that is to be welded on and passes the information on to Harold. Harold cuts the steel plate as indicated, and molds it into the correct shape. Roland positions the plate next to the ship with his crane, and then helps Cisco weld it in place. Meanwhile, Jerry has begun measuring for a new steel plate.

- *Monitoring and adjusting.* Every one in a while, team performance should be evaluated to ensure it is processeding according to planning and that targets are achieved. Deviations from the desired situation can be a cause for making adjustments, for example by updating the goals or the planning, by reorganising the assigned tasks, or by improving calibration.

The extent to which these activities should be managed by a team leader or by the team itself depends on the organisation's style of manament and on group members' need to be able to influence their own cooperative effort. The various activities required for a smooth process of planning and organising has been depicted in a schematic overview in Figure 4.4.

FIGURE 4.4 Planning and organisation characteristics

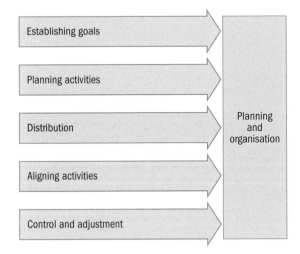

4.3.3   Improving performance standards

Quality team efforts can only be achieved on the performance standards within that team are high. How can these standards be improved? Chapter 3 covered the improvement methods of increasing job appeal and by setting challenging goals (see paragraph 3.5). The productivity of executive teams partly depends on the extent to which group members are willing to put in effort in the group task. The quality of team member efforts can be affected by:
- improving the appeal of the group task (see paragraph 2.5.2);
- setting challenging goals (see paragraph 2.5.2);
- combatting and preventing free-riding.

Work appeal can be improved by increasing work quality. Quality is established through an adequately varied task package, requiring the team members to use their different skills and this letting them influence the way in which they can perform their activities.

Challenging goals are established by setting high targets for the team. These high targets can challenge teams to perform better, provided the goals are specific and measurable, achievable and accepted, and the subject of proper feedback in terms of achieved results

Commitment to intended targets is of particular importance. Research by Sue-Chan & Ong (2002) shows a strong positive relationship between commitment and performance.

Both work appeal and challenging goals contribute to an increase in the work intrinsic motivation of team members and, as a result, to an improvement in performance standards (see paragraph 2.5.2).

Free-riding is defined as having one team member contribute less to the group's result than the other team members, while still profiting from that result. The lack of commitment of this team member can cause other team members to lower their contribution. As a result, performance standards are lowered.

Free-riding can be prevented by:
- clearly indicating what each team member is expected to do;
- visualising individual efforts by team members and evaluating those efforts;
- increasing the commitment to the group taks. This is done by increasing the involvement of group members in the intended targets and in establishing the best work methods for the group.

4.3.4 Improving group cohesion

Many studies have looked into the relationships between group cohesion and group performance (Beal et al. 2003; Craigh & Bischoff, 2007). These studies show that groups characterised by high levels of cohesion often perform better than those with low levels of cohesion. The relationship between high cohesion and group performance is strongest in groups in which group performance is highly dependent on a proper calibration of contributions. This is the case in, for example, certain team sports, such as basketball, volleyball, and football. High cohesion also goes hand in hand with good mutual communication and greater mutual influence. A stronger level of mutual influence causes group members to contribute an improved performance if group performance standards are high. If performance standards are low, then high cohesion results in decreased performance. Low cohesion causes group members to be less concerned with ruling performance standards.

The relationship between performance standards and cohesion is shown in Figure 4.5.

FIGURE 4.5 The relationships between performance standards, cohesion, and performance

	Cohesion	
	High	Low
High	High performance	Moderate performance
Low	Very poor performance	Poor performance

Improving cohesion in teams is not a simple task. However, there are some methods by which cohesion can be improved. These methods are:

- *Team composition.* Do not group together people with irreconcilable character traits. Allow people to choose their own partners in a team.
- *Success.* Promote a team who that successfully manages to complete its tasks and compliment them on their achievements.
- *Competition.* Let teams compete against one another, thus creating a competitive situation.

Hackman and Wageman (2005) studied the factors which proved decisive in the effectiveness of collaboration in executive teams. The concluded that the following factors contribute to effectiveness:
1   The extent to which group members put in an effort to perform their tasks (motivation, performance standards).
2   The extent to which group members are able to arrive at a good task approach and internal calibration (planning, calibration, control).
3   The extent to which group members possess the correct knownledge and skills.

The factors here identified largely correspond to the factors indicated in Figure 4.5.
The theory discussed above indicates that there are various possibilities for arriving at an effective execution of tasks in groups. These possibilities are also indicated in Figure 4.6.

FIGURE 4.6 Prerequisites for effective operations in groups

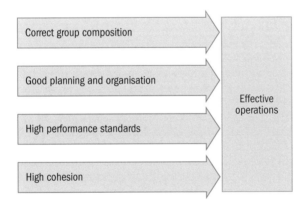

4.4 Effective decision-making in groups

All kinds of events that make decision-making necessary take place in organisations. Not only must the work be done, but people also need to hold regular meetings to resolve problems and make decisions. People can be confronted with an unexpected machinery breakdown, due to which production is delayed and the schedule has to be adjusted. Someone can fall ill, making it necessary to redistribute work. Sometimes these problems are resolved on the spot through consultation between colleagues or by a boss who makes a decision.

Consultation

EXAMPLE 4.8

Differences of opinion

In a factory making electric motors, the managing director meets with the heads of all the departments on one morning a week. On the agenda for this week are a number of specific problems. The order book for the coming six months is not full, resulting in a risk of overproduction. What is to be done? Furthermore, a number of large machines have reached the end of their normal life. Should they be overhauled or replaced? Is it possible to switch to a more computerised method of production? At the end of the morning, no decision has yet been taken and the managing director suggests further investigation of the advantages and disadvantages of a number of solutions, putting these points on the agenda for the following meeting.

Many problems may prompt various solutions. People by no means always agree on the best solution. This sometimes causes long discussions and friction.

Decision-making in a group context is not a simple matter. It takes time and effort and can cause disagreements and irritation between the members of the group. Should problems actually be resolved in the group context? Can certain problems be tackled in a simpler manner or by delegation to a sufficiently knowledgeable person?

4.5 Advantages and disadvantages of a group approach

A great deal of research has been done into the question of whether problems can better be resolved by a group than by one person. The results of these studies show that this question is not easy to answer.

Type of problem

Estimation

In the first place, it depends on the type of problem. If the problem is one for which a solution can easily be established (calculated), it can be delegated to one person with the appropriate expertise. If it involves an estimation, such as predicting the development of the housing market or guessing the benefits of a marketing campaign, then it is better left to a group.

EXAMPLE 4.9

Do groups do better?

The pupils in a classroom are asked to estimate the temperature in the room. First, they are asked to write down their individual estimates; then, they should discuss their ideas; and lastly, they should present their answers as a group.

Research into this type of estimation task indicates that the group solution is better than the vast majority of the solutions proposed individually by group members. In the discussion process, people tend to shift to a middle position, by means of which estimations on the high and the low side are cancelled out.

A group approach is also the best choice if the problem is one where several insights must be combined to reach a solution and where it cannot easily be established what the best solution is.

EXAMPLE 4.10

NASA experiment

Groups are asked to resolve a problem relating to space travel. This problem is as follows:
You are one of a group of five astronauts assigned to join the mother ship on the sunlit side of the moon. Due to technical difficulties, your capsule has to land 300 kilometres away from the mother ship. In the landing, a lot of equipment is destroyed. Your survival therefore depends on reaching the mother ship on foot. You can take with you only what is absolutely necessary. There are 15 undamaged items. Your task is to assess how important each item is for your journey. Number the most important item 1, the second most important item 2, and so on. The scores that the participants individually and the group as a whole give to the items are compared with the scores that NASA experts have awarded. From this comparison, a quality assessment of the solutions is made.

The results of NASA's experiment in example 4.10 are that the quality of the group solution – that is to say, the extent to which the group solution agrees with that of the experts – is always higher than the average quality of the individual solutions of the group members and, in most cases, even better than the best individual solution.
From these findings, two conclusions can be drawn:
1 If it is clear what specific knowledge or expertise is required for the resolution of a problem and it is clear which group member has the most expertise, the solution can better be left to that group member than to the group as a whole.
2 If it is not absolutely clear what specific knowledge or expertise is required or if it is not clear which group member has the necessary skills, the problem can better be resolved in a group context.

Why does the group do better than any individual in the majority of cases?
- In a group there is usually more knowledge, insight and skills than any one person possesses.
- In a group, new ideas and new solutions are easier to arrive at because of the discussion process. One idea elicits another. This produces more ideas.
- People can more easily notice errors in the solutions of others than in their own solutions. The critical capacity of the group is thus greater than that of any one individual.
- With tasks for which the correct solution cannot be calculated but must be estimated, group members are inclined to meet in the middle. Because it can be expected that some group members will err on the high and the low side, such errors will cancel each other out.

Research has shown that in estimation and combination tasks a group often arrives at a better solution than an individual. For this type of problem, people in an organisation would thus do better to opt for a group approach. This takes time, however, and time is often an expensive and scarce commodity in organisations. It is therefore important for the group to tackle these problems as efficiently as possible.

4.6 Criteria for effective decision-making in a group context

Organisation can only function successfully if the decisions taken (in the context of groups) are good decisions. What criteria does a decision need to meet to be classified 'good'? Paul et al. (2000) classify the quality of a decision using three criteria. These criteria, listed below, are essential for good decision-making.

- **Effectiveness.** A decision should lead to the solution of a problem. Whether this has been the case can only be established in hind-sight. This criterion therefore does not offer any direct instruction for the way in which the decision-making process should be conducted.
- **Efficiency.** Decision-making takes time and manpower, and can therefore be a precious process. The efficiency of a decision-making process is increased the less time and manpower it takes. The same applies to the implementation of the decision. A decision is more efficient if its implementation takes less time, manpower, and finances.
- **Legitimacy.** A decision needs to be legitimised in order to obtain support from the employees tasked with implementing it. If the decision that is made is impopular in terms of acceptance and support among employees, there is every chance that its implementation will be delayed, adjusted, or outright prevented.

The three criteria established by Paul e.a. should be complemented with a fourth one:

- **Practicability.** There should be adequate resources in order to implement the decision. Do the employees involved have time, energy, knowledge, and skills in order to implement the decision? Will this implementation be possible within the time indicated? A plan can look excellent on paper, but their practicability may be the subject of debate.

EXAMPLE 4.11

Good solution?

Policy officials for the Ministry of Education felt they had come up with a good solution to the problems of high rates of dropout and low rates of success among applied university students. They chose to implement a new method of financing applied universities, which linked financing to the number of students that was registered and the number of students that made it to the finish line.

Was the decision by the policy officials in example 4.11 effective? In certain respects it was, but in others, it was not. The new method of financing did lead to greater numbers of registered and graduated students. The unintended side-effect was that (some) applied universities began cheating with their number registered students to their own advantage, and ensuring that even the weakest students left the university with an undeserved degree. These side effects mean that the decision-making had been less effective than possible.

EXAMPLE 4.12

Should we check?

In a company board meeting, the problem of high levels of sick leave is discussed and a procedure decided upon, although some departmental heads are not happy with it. It is decided that the departmental heads must visit the sick employees at home as soon as possible. The departmental heads believe that this will appear to be controlling and will contribute little towards a good atmosphere in the department. Those heads of department who are unable to accept the solution will not readily cooperate in implementing it.

It is impossible to establish beforehand which of the criteria described will be the most decisive for the quality of a decision. It differs from one problem and one situation to the next. However, it is always important to consider whether the positive effects of a decision are not outweighed by their possible side-effects in implementation (see example 4.12).

In many cases, the favourable effect that is expected from a chosen solution depends on the enthusiastic performance of those involved. This can occur only if they genuinely believe in the solution. If the solution has been chosen against their will, they have countless opportunities to delay, compromise or even sabotage its implementation.

The four criteria for good decision-making are shown once more in Figure 4.7.

FIGURE 4.7 Criteria for good decision-making

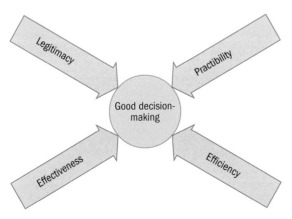

Source: Alblas e.a. (2012)

© Noordhoff Uitgevers bv

🔴4.7 Process losses in decision-making

It has already been established that, in a number of cases, a problem can better be resolved by a group than by an individual.

In the discussion of problems and decision-making in a group context, optimal use is by no means always made of the knowledge and awareness of the group's members. This is known as process losses. The group performs below its optimum capabilities. The question is why. We shall describe a number of cases in this section and thereafter propose methods of improving decision-making processes in groups.

Process losses

4.7.1 Process losses through unequal contributions and influence

Unequal input and influence

In the previous chapter, we indicated that unequal input and influence from group members are a characteristic of the collaborative process. Some group members dominate discussions and often determine their outcome. The shortcomings that can result can now be explained, as follows:

- The non-dominant group members contribute little. If they have important information and knowledge and do not contribute it, it is lost to the group.
- The dominant group members contribute a great deal. Their information and knowledge will to a great extent determine which solution is selected. If these dominant group members are not very competent, this will lead to a poor solution.
- The dominant group members enforce their preferred solution, and there is a risk that the non-dominant group members may not support the solution.

Inequality of input and influence can mean that insufficient use has been made of all the insights of group members and that the chosen solution has insufficient support.

It certainly does not seem as though he appreciates my creative input.

Often, people of unequal status participate in discussion groups. A progress meeting, for example, takes place between the boss and his subordinates.

The managing director and heads of department take part in a management meeting and the managing director often gets the solution he prefers accepted, though this is due more to his status than to his specific expertise.

Process losses resulting from uneven contributions and influence are shown schematically in Figure 4.8.

FIGURE 4.8   Process losses resulting from uneven contributions and influence

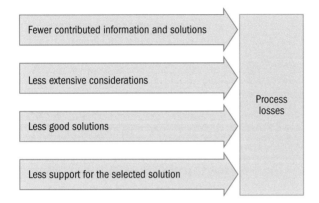

4.7.2   Process losses through self-censorship

Sometimes, group members have certain insights that they do not put forward. This is the case if they estimate that their contribution will have negative consequences for them or for the progress of the discussion. They then practise self-censorship. Self-censorship can be expected under two conditions: a very bad atmosphere and a very good atmosphere.

Self-censorship

If there is a bad atmosphere in the group – for example, caused by disagreement, mistrust and conflict – group members with 'abnormal' insights or preferences run the risk of being attacked. The atmosphere can consequently worsen and the discussion can sink deeper into the mire. A group member may then decide simply to keep his mouth shut.

Bad atmosphere

EXAMPLE 4.13

High staff turnover

Management is discussing the high rate of staff turnover in the Home Care sector. Eva feels this is a problem caused by the unrelenting authoritarian leadership of the Head of Home Care. She does not put her ideas forward, however, since she knows they will land her in hot water with the Head of Home Care – an easily offended individual, known for his exceptionally blunt responses.

Group members who are not assertive and who are inclined to concede easily are more likely to self-censor than the more dominant and assertive group members. Poor atmosphere usually comes with a lack of openness, causing potentially valuable insights to remain unshared with the rest of the group.

© Noordhoff Uitgevers bv

Good atmosphere

Self-censorship can also occur when there is a good atmosphere. In groups with good mutual relationships and strong cohesion, the group members exert a great deal of influence on each other and this leads to a large degree of conformity. Under certain conditions, strong cohesion can be detrimental to the discussion process. We will illustrate this through the results of a study by Janis (1972).

The motive for the research was the failed invasion of Cuba by the USA in 1961 ('Bay of Pigs'). Janis wondered how it was possible that the then president of the United States and his advisory group decided to deploy 1,400 Cuban exiles against a trained army of 200,000 men. To find out how they came to this decision, he interviewed the members of the advisory group. On the basis of his findings from the interviews, he came to the conclusion that there had been 'groupthink'. The factors that lead to groupthink are the following:

Groupthink

- **Feeling of invulnerability.** The members of the group were so convinced of their power and ability to succeed that dangers were ignored.
- **Selective handling of information.** They ignored information that did not fit in with their preferred solution.
- **Moral rightness.** They believed that their own goals were ethically correct and the opposition was acting wrongly.
- **Negative stereotyping.** The opposition was too stupid to be taken seriously.
- **Pressure to conform.** Group members with different opinions were called to order by intimating that they risked finding themselves outside the group or that their attitude showed disloyalty. Research by Postmes et al. (2001) indicated that group members who are placed under severe pressure to come to an agreement are often incapable of discussing effectively during the decision-making process.
- **Self-censorship.** Group members who had criticisms or doubts minimised their own importance and did not voice them in order not to shake belief in the rightness and authority of the group.

It is strong cohesion in a group, together with the belief that it is right and has power, that leads to excessive conformity and self-censorship. The groupthink that results means that insufficient use is made of the knowledge and insights of group members, on the one hand because some of these insights are too quickly reasoned away, on the other hand because they are not put forward due to self-censorship. Maintenance of the unity of the group is thought to be more important than careful and critical consideration of the solutions proposed.

Turner and Pratkanis (1998) created an overview of 25 years of research into group thinking. They concluded that there is a strong relationship between high cohesion and group thinking. The strongest relationship they identified was that between directive leadership and group thinking. If a directive leader begins by submitting their ideas and voicing their preference for a particular solution, then group members will contribute fewer deviating conclusions and fewer alternative solutions.

4.7.3 Process losses through poor structuring

When a problem is complicated and the group is large, discussions soon become disorderly or even chaotic. All kinds of suggestions are put forward in quick succession and people jump from one idea to another. While one group member is still analysing the causes of the problem to be resolved, another member is already making proposals for its solution. Points of view are rapidly exchanged, but not a single one is sufficiently discussed or agreed upon. Certain viewpoints come up again and again and the discussion is repeated without any progress being made. Repeated discussions cost time and in many cases produce no new information or new points of view.

Which viewpoints are ultimately sufficiently discussed in such an unstructured process is more likely to be a matter of who introduces them and when, than to be related to their relevance to solving the problem. In a disorderly process, which of the proposed points (information, viewpoints, solutions) is adopted often seems arbitrary. The impression is given of a game in which the objective is to put forward a certain viewpoint several times with vigour and to exercise sufficient influence at the right time. The right times can be:

Unstructured process

- when the group loses track and is briefly reorienting;
- when group members get tired and need something to focus on;
- when the group needs to take a decision.

Whoever comes up with a clear and well substantiated proposal at such a moment and is able to communicate it convincingly can determine the decision to a significant extent. The exact reasons for choosing a given solution are often unclear. The possible shortcomings of an unstructured discussion can are shown in Figure 4.9.

FIGURE 4.9 Process losses resulting from poor structuring

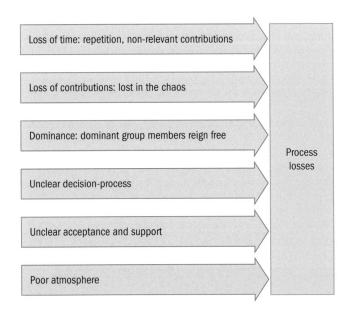

4.7.4   Process losses through conflicts

During the Social Work team meeting, it turns out that the members of the team differ in their insights, ideas and wishes on many points.

EXAMPLE 4.14

Differences in vision

When it comes to the allocation of new clients, people think first of the team member with the fewest clients. She objects. She has fewer clients but many difficult cases that require a great deal of attention. Other team members don't consider this a good argument. Everyone has difficult cases, so that is no reason to refuse new clients. The work load must be distributed fairly. On the subject of case discussions, a team member remarks that previous discussions have been unproductive. If they are unable to be more critical of each other, the case discussions should be removed from the agenda. This remark elicits many reactions. Some members of the group find case discussions beneficial and think that they are not about criticising one another but about providing constructive feedback. Others feel that 'being kind to each other' only reinforces existing methods of working with clients, which they do not always find effective. In their view, most of the clients are treated much too gently or patronisingly. This does not encourage initiative or lead to greater self-sufficiency among clients.

Conflicts

Differences in insights, ideas and preferences can have positive and negative consequences. Expressing these differences can result in better solutions to problems and innovation in one's approach to work. These differences can also lead to conflicts (see also chapter 10). There is a conflict if a group member feels thwarted by one or more of the other members.

EXAMPLE 4.15

A quarrel!

When the social worker who remains convinced that she has many difficult cases is opposed by the group, she refuses to accept two new clients. A conflict is created. The other group members criticise her for not organising and carrying out her work better. If she did, she could easily take on two more clients. In turn, she criticises them for not doing their work carefully enough or supporting their clients adequately.

The following process losses can arise due to conflicts between group members:
- **Polarisation.** Belief in their own ideas becomes increasingly strong and there is a tendency to denigrate those of others. Owing to this, ideas and preferences differ from each other more strongly. Polarisation then occurs.
- **Widening.** The conflict widens to involve other conflicts.

Differences in conception can lead to conflicts.

The conflict over the allocation of clients widens to a conflict about methods of working with clients, resulting in:

- **Loss of time**. During the conflict, the different viewpoints and ideas are merely repeated, as a result of which there is no further progress in the discussion.
- **Blame and threats**. The hardening of viewpoints makes the atmosphere even worse. Group members fire accusations at each other and threaten to take certain measures if the other party does not concede.
- **Defective decision-making**. Due to polarisation, it seems as though there are only two possibilities to choose from and both of them elicit resistance. Sometimes, because of this resistance, the group simply does not take a decision, or postpones it. In other cases, the logjam is broken and one of the parties in the conflict gets what it wants at the cost of the other party. The parties no longer look for a compromise (see chapter 10).

Process losses by conflict are illustrated in Figure 4.10.

FIGURE 4.10 Process losses due to conflict

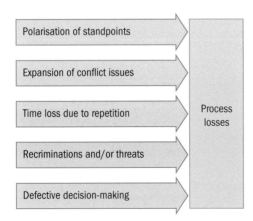

© Noordhoff Uitgevers bv

4.7.5   Virtual group discussions

How do discussions run their course in virtual groups? Does it matter for the outcome of the proceedings whether a discussion takes place face-to-face or via some electronic means? Research shows varying results, some indicating positive effects and some indicating negative ones. A study by Mesmer-Magnus et al. (2011) indicates that, in virtual groups, participants experience a greater sense of anonymity, and feel less pressured into showing compliancy. This allows for a greater level of freedom, as we will discuss in the next paragraph on the delphi-technique, and for improved group member participation and for a greater input of diversified ideas. The down-side is that the anonymity is less conducive to the interpersonal connections and team identity-building processes, and less conducive to mutual trust. This is detrimental to the development of cohesion, and makes is more difficult to reach a consensus in decision-making when dealing with differences in preference or insight (Hertel et al., 2005). However, if the teams taking part in a virtual discussion already benefit from good existing mutual relationships, then the negative effects are not of any consequence.

Dube and Robey (2008) conclude that team-building activities and regular interim face-to-face meetings can improve discussions in virtual teams. Peters and Manz (2007) indicate that discussions in virtual teams are improved if those teams, prior to the virtual sessions:
- Ensure the creation of mutual trust (building trust).
- Work on the improvement of mutual relationships.
- Clarify the team's goals and working methods.

EXAMPLE 4.16

Virtual teams at IBM

Based on personal experience, a number of IBM managers indicate that virtual team discussions are not suitable for all situations. The first of those is discussions about complex subjects; in this instance, a 'richer' form of communication, i.e. a face-to-face discussion, is better. The second type of situation is when the project to which the discussion relates is subject to severe time pressure. Communications at a distance and time lag between the different responses by group members can result in delays in the decision-making process. Thirdly, virtual discussions are less suitable if there are social conflicts within the team. Those types of conflicts are more easily solved through face-to-face communication; IBM's managers recommend that, in situations like these, team members should occasionally meet up in person.

4.8   Improving decision-making in groups

In recent decades, various methods have been developed to make discussions within and between groups more effective. We shall describe a number of these methods and indicate how process losses can be countered. We begin by offering methods that are primarily focused on improving decision-making within groups. Thereafter, we show how leadership of the discussion can contribute to efficiency, and finally we describe a method for improving discussions between groups.

4.8.1   Brainstorming

The brainstorming method was developed in 1953 by Alex Osborn. This approach focuses on increasing the input of information, ideas and possible solutions. To this end, a number of guidelines were developed to give shape to the process within groups. These guidelines are as follows:

- Participants are encouraged to devise as many possible solutions to a problem as they can (quantity).
- Unusual or crazy solutions are encouraged (anything is possible).
- Participants are allowed to collaborate in modifying proposed solutions or proposing related solutions (cross-pollination).
- Participants must not to comment on or criticise (judge) each other's contributions.
- All the possible solutions devised must be written down and presented to the group. Only after that can there be a discussion about the usefulness of the solutions.

Brainstorming method

Brainstorming: inventing and writing down as many ideas as possible and not immediately judging or dismissing anything as crazy.

With this approach people try to avoid process losses arising from hasty assessment, over-simplification and reluctance to propose anything too radical. This increases the quantity of possible solutions that are offered. Initially, quantity is the prime concern. Conformity and self-censorship are discouraged by explicitly stating that unusual solutions are desired. This is the result of ruling that anything is possible and that cross-pollination is desirable. Because a distinction is made between thinking up solutions and assessing them, there is less risk that solutions that initially have little support will disappear from the process. The no-judgement rule applies here. The premise for the brainstorming method is that quantity leads to quality. The more solutions that are devised and proposed, the greater the chance that a good solution will be found. Research shows that through brainstorming more ideas and possible solutions are proposed by group members than in comparable groups that do not use this method. At first, the ideas and solutions that are proposed are fairly obvious and

Quantity

Anything is possible

Cross-pollination

No-judgement rule

© Noordhoff Uitgevers bv

conservative. Only after conventional solutions have been exhausted and people realise that they can introduce anything without criticism do innovative and unusual ideas emerge. The psychological freedom and safety to propose something unusual must first be created and perceived if the method is to work. Two conditions are important for the application of the brainstorming method:

1 The problem must be well defined. If there are different ideas about the nature of the problem, the method does not work.
2 There must first be a number of practice sessions to allow group members to experience the freedom of thought and input and to break down conformity and self-censorship.

NRC HANDELSBLAD

Bad ideas eventually fade away

It seems contradictory, but nothing needs a firmer guiding hand than a group of people attempting a brainstorm.

1 Seize control
Pretend as though you know less than you do at the start of the 'creative process'. Tell others you can rarely ever come up with any nice ideas at all, but that you would be more than happy to take on the role of chairperson to make this brainstorming business does not run out of hand.

2 Divide and conquer
Never brainstorm with large groups. A group of ten or more will soon give rise to the wrong sort of dynamic, with overly dominant people on the one hand and overly submissive people on the other. During the first phase of the session, form groups of three people. Studies show that three is the ideal number, the best way of encouraging an atmosphere of 'one good idea begets another'.

3 There are no bad ideas
Negative criticism of volunteered ideas is strictly prohibited. Keep silent if you find an idea to be poor, and it will eventually fade away. Ask questions i fan idea does not immediately leap out at you. But make sure never to say: yes, but...

4 More from coarse to fine
Once you have let everyone have their say in their three-person-group, have them all sit together in a circle. Each group is then given a chance to present their best ideas in five minutes. First force the groups to sift their own wheat from their chaff before getting everyone else involved.

5 Make a list of greatest hits
Make a list of the nine best ideas and let the group discuss those ideas. There may be some ideas that are rubbing shoulders – try to rephrase those into a single idea.

There can also be disadvantages to brainstorming. Association occurs verbally and this gives the faster thinkers and responders in the group the opportunity to dominate. For people who think rather more slowly or respond somewhat hesitantly, it is then difficult to get a word in edgeways. It is therefore questionable whether the maximum thinking potential of the group members is extracted with this method. Do they have the opportunity to bring in everything they can think of? Bouchard, Barsaloux and Drauden (1974) set up an experiment to answer this question. They composed two groups, one of four and one of seven members, and had them think of as many solutions as possible to a creative problem using the brainstorming method. At the same time, they had 11 other people work on the problem individually. Afterwards, they compared the quantity of solutions produced in the group context with the number of solutions from the 11 individuals. The results (see Figure 4.11) show that individual brainstorming produces more solutions than brainstorming in groups.

The results of the research show that groups do less well than an equivalent number of people working individually. The presence of others probably has a limiting effect on group members thinking up or proposing solutions. Variations in this method have therefore been devised. The brainwriting **Brainwriting pool** pool is one such variation. With this method, each group member must first (individually) come up with as many ideas and solutions as possible and write them down on a form. Once their inspiration has dried up, people exchange forms with another person in the group. They can then react associatively to the other person's solutions. This exchange process continues until everyone has seen everyone else's form.

FIGURE 4.11   Comparison in performances between individuals and brainstorming groups

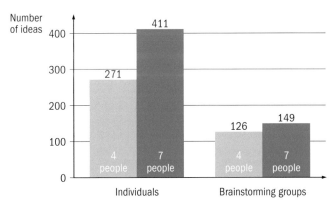

Source: Bouchard, Barsaloux & Drauden, 1974

4.8.2   The Delphi method
The brainstorming method is designed to maximise the number of ideas and solutions that are considered in a discussion. Ultimately, only one solution can usually be chosen. The more that are proposed, the more difficult the selection process becomes for the group's members. It is also to be expected that there will be unequal input and influence, and conflict in the phase of consideration and selection. The Delphi method (Delbecq, Van de Ven & **Delphi method** Gustafson, 1975) attempts to combine the advantages of an exhaustive contribution of ideas and solutions with a form of consideration and choice that counters or minimises the shortcomings of this phase. The Delphi method is carried out in writing and has the following steps:
1   The chairperson or guide asks the group's members to put as many solutions as possible on paper. These are then collected by the chairperson and the entire list submitted to the members in writing.

© Noordhoff Uitgevers bv

2 The group's members have the opportunity to supplement this list with possible new solutions. These are then added and the whole list is again offered to every group member.
3 Each group member must indicate their preferences from the list of solutions. They do so by ranking their preferred solution in order of preference: first choice ranked 1, for example, second choice ranked 2, and so on.
4 Each group member receives the rankings of the other group members in writing and may modify their own ranking.
5 The chairperson collects the data and chooses the solution with the highest average ranking.

This method prevents the choice process from being influenced by dominance, self-censorship, conflict and conformity. The push-and-pull that usually plays a part in the decision-making process is eliminated with this method.
Research has shown that the Delphi method leads to an improvement in the problem-solving process for certain types of problem (Willis, 1979). However, group members miss the discussion and the process is perceived as sterile.

The members of a virtual group can take part in brainwriting and in the Delphi-technique via electronic means. There are specialised computer programs available to this end, which allow team members to contribute individually to submitting as many possible solutions as possible, to establishing criteria required for solutions, and ordering preferences for submitted solutions. The Delphi-technique addresses and overcomes the earlier mentioned issue of problems in decision-making in virtual groups (see paragraph 4.7.5).

4.8.3 Structuring decision-making

Proper problem-solving and decision-making are promoted by an approach which addresses the discussion process in a gradual, established order. The application of *structure* to the process is described in the *phase model*. This approach model is shown in Figure 4.12.

FIGURE 4.12 Phase model of problem-solving and decision-making

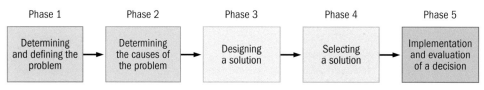

Source: Alblas (2010)

There are five phases:
1 establishing and defining the problem;
2 establishing the causes of the problem;
3 devising solutions;
4 selecting a solution;
5 implementing and evaluating the decision (solution).

Ad 1 Establishing and defining the problem
A problem is classified as a current situation that differs from the desirable situation. Team members tasked with addressing a problem are often too

quick to look for solutions, even though the nature, severity, or scope of the problem have hardly been established. This may result in team members having different opinion as to what the problem actually is. These differences can lead to confusion when discussing which solutions to the problem are suitable. Johnson and Johnson (2008) indicate that the process of defining a problem should take three steps:

1 Establishing what group members consider the desired situation.
2 Establishing the current situation.
3 Establishing the differences between the desired and current situations, as well as the significance of these differences. Are these differences large or severe enough to warrant intervention?

EXAMPLE 4.17

Combating staff turnover

The management team meeting concludes that staff turnover needs to be brought down to a maximum of 3%. Current turnover for this year was 15%; something management considers to be much too high. This calls for action, as soon as possible.

Ad 2 Establishing the causes of the problem
Before any solutions can be considered, team members must first chart the factors causing and/or maintaining the problem. This is not always easy. Complex problems may be the result of various factors; the most important of these cannot always be distinguished from the others. The proper approach to this phase comprises finding the answers to the following questions:
• Which causes can be established?
• What is the influence of these causes on the problem?

Since devising a solution is largely a continuation of establishing the supposed causes of a problem, these causes should first be tracked down and defined in detail.

Ad 3 Devising solutions
Even if the causes of a problem are known, the best solution is not always evident. Multiple solutions may present themselves; all may have their own distinct advantages. Certain circumstances may limit to possibility of submitting solutions, for example self-censorship and conformity, or a team lead who dictates which solutions would be good ones. When devising solutions, all group members should be made to feel free to submit their suggestions.

Ad 4 Selecting a solution
Before a solution is selected, the submitted solutions should be carefully weighed based on the criteria involved in taking a good decision. This means that considerations should involve expected effects, costs, practicability, and legitimacy. Only if these aspects are more or less clear for all suggested solutions should the focus move to the actual decision-making. In that case, the question becomes: how should the decision be made? By unanimous vote? By majority rule? By order of the team lead?

© Noordhoff Uitgevers bv

A unanimous vote is impossible in many cases, and striving for unanimity can lead to a lengthy process of to-ing and fro-ing, thus limiting the efficiency of the process. Whatever the method, it is vital that team members who would have preferred a different solution still throw their weight behind the solution that is selected. This is something that must be discussed.

Ad 5 Implementing and evaluating a decision (solution)
A group can only define the quality of a selected solution following it implementation. A good decision causes the problem to disappear and/or the desired situation to be reached. This requires an evaluation of the effects of the implementation. Evaluation can relate to two aspects:
1 *Process evaluation.* This considers whether the implementation of a decision is proceeding/has proceeded according to plan. If this is not the case, it may be necessary to review and improve the implementation process.
2 *Product evaluation.* This considers whether the desired effects are being/ have been reached. If this is not the case, it may be necessary to select a different solution.

EXAMPLE 4.18

It is not working

In order to decrease absenteeism figures among the production teams, team leads had been given a two-day term to contact employees calling in sick. During this contact, they were to ask they employee after the nature of the issue, and establish a projected timeline with regards to the duration of the absenteeism. The team leads did not enjoy this task and were afraid it would come across as an excessive form of scrutiny. As a result, they started phoning it in. The solution that was selected to address the problem of absenteeism was being implemented by the team leads barely if at all (process evaluation). In hind-sight, the desired decrease in absenteeism was not achieved (product evaluation).

The phase model describes the best possible way to address problem-solving and decision-making. It is, however, subject to a few critical side notes. As an approach, it is costly in terms of time and manpower. If both are limited, following the steps described in the phase model will not be possible. The same applies for situations where group members have different individual interests and goals: having too many differences leads to endless debate and conflict. Every subjected solution has its appeal to one group member while simultaneously being detrimental to the interests of others.

A phased and accessible group discussion is not something that simply happens. It is a process that requires proper steering, with a chairperson supervising the members to make sure they follow the required protocol, and that each phase is completed as prescribed. This is only possibly if the discussion is headed by a chairperson with adequate leadership skills.

4.9 Leadership in decision-making

Effective decision-making in groups can be promoted by two main types of input: task-oriented and group-oriented input.

Task-oriented input is necessary in order to structure the process in accordance with the sequential phase model. The chairman, team leader or coordinator must do the following:

Task-oriented input

- Ensure that the problem to be tackled is defined as clearly as possible by giving and/or asking for information about the nature of the problem and the factors that cause or perpetuate it and working towards a common conception of the problem.
- Stimulate the proposal of different possible solutions.
- Ask for criteria that are important in assessing the usefulness of the solutions offered, encouraging as many criteria as possible to emerge.
- Encourage careful consideration of the usefulness of the proposed solutions.
- Work towards a decision that receives the widest possible acceptance and support and is feasible, ensuring the clear formulation of the chosen solution.
- Keep the solution process clear, orderly and goal-oriented. This can be encouraged by regularly indicating how far the group has advanced in the decision-making process, for example by summarising the different proposals, indicating which phase of the process the group is in and explaining what is still to be done. The leader also needs to monitor the time and, if necessary, cut short discussion not directly related to the problem in question. Group members who are too verbose or repeat too many of their own ideas must also be curbed.

Group-oriented input is necessary to ensure that process losses due to unequal input and status, self-censorship, groupthink and conflict are minimised. The chairman, team leader or coordinator must do the following:

Group-oriented input

- Encourage group members to contribute as much as possible by curbing dominant group members and stimulating diffident group members to voice their insights, ideas and wishes.
- Encourage open communication by indicating that every contribution, even if it is rather unorthodox, is valuable.
- Encourage group members to take each other's contributions seriously.
- Indicate that differences in ideas and wishes must not be perceived as threats but as motivation to investigate them further.
- Ensure that polarisation in conflicts is reduced so that the parties can be conciliated.

Good leadership of the decision-making process is possible only if the leader has no strong interests or views with respect to the problem to be resolved or with respect to the parties in a conflict. The leader should be neutral and not use their position to push through through own ideas and interests or favour one of the parties in a conflict. Regardless of the decisions taken, they should primarily be a process leader. If the leader has strong ideas and interests, impartial process leadership is almost impossible. Someone else will then have to be asked to lead the discussion.

Neutral

Process leader

If everyone in the group has taken sides in a conflict, someone will need to be recruited from outside to mediate in the conflict (see chapter 6).

4.10 Collaboration and consultation in self-managing and virtual teams

In self-managing and virtual teams, team members must both perform the work and make decisions. When a new team has been put together that does not yet have any experience of the new manner of collaboration, various problems can arise that can destroy the supposed positive effects of self-management (see the following example).

EDUCATION AND DEVELOPMENT

Behavioural change

Working in self-managing teams means a new type of task performance, a new role, and new competences for employees and supervisors. The focus is a top-down behavioural change. Van Dijk: 'There are two important aspects: people need to be more employable, and it should be possible to overview, to monitor, multiple aspects of the work. Self-management adds quite a number of elements to existing tasks: others start to involve themselves with your work, you are a co-responsible team member – nobody tells you exactly what it is you need to do any longer. There are no more clearly delineated tasks, which can lead to tensions. Not everyone is immediately sold on the idea of working in teams; there are doubts, particularly amount part-timers: is this really what I am looking for? Coping with group processes is seen as troublesome, and sometimes also as threatening.

Executive skills

Teamworking

This two-fold task of performance and decision-making means that members of self-managing and virtual teams are faced with a number of demands. They must have sufficient executive skills to perform all the activities assigned to them. They must be able to develop themselves and their skills via a programme of education and training. They must make all kinds of arrangements themselves, and so must have sufficient teamworking skills. They must be able to conduct meetings, cope with differences of opinion and make decisions that have the support of the team. It is not likely that these skills will be fully available in new teams. Team members will therefore need to be trained and supervised in this area. The responsibilities of the team should not initially be too great and the latitude for adjustment must be well demarcated (see the article 'Self-management').

Performance norms

Responsible

Finally, self-management can only lead to the intended positive effects (high performance) if all team members feel responsible for collaboration and have high performance norms.

PW

Self-management

Print and document solutions company Xerox has seen changes to the concept of self-management in the Customer Service Organisation (technical maintenance). Although the teams had been operating successfully, their freedom also came with an excess of responsibility. Fully planning and implementing maintenance, combined with administration, data analysis, complaints handling, and the requirement to keep up with developments in the field proved too taxing for the individual technicians. In the end, they relinquished the planning and complaints handling aspects back to the central organisation themselves.

These conditions will not always be present. In view of the influence team members can exert on each other, particularly in the area of effort and performance, careful consideration must be given to the composition of teams. Norms will need to be developed to regulate the behaviour of team members. These norms need not coincide with the requirements of the organisation. The improved possibilities for self-management allow teams to create a solid front, and lets them close off very well from the outside world.

Collaboration in virtual teams does not always proceed swimmingly. Various studies (Hughes et al., 2000 Carletta et al., 2000 Baltes et al., 2002 Axtell et al., 2004) demonstrate the vulnerability of these teams:
- Interaction at a distance means fewer social exchanges. As a result, there is less mutual trust, less solidarity, less openness in terms of communication, and fewer exchanges of informal organisational information.
- Interaction at a distance causes more misunderstandings in communication, resulting from a lack of non-verbal cues and a lack of immediate feedback.
- Interaction at a distance negatively affects the effectiveness of problem-solving and decision-making, task completion, and satisfaction with mutual collaboration when compared to face-to-face teams.

Axtell et al. (2004) offer the same reccomendations as the previously indicated researchers (see paragraph 4.7.5), being that virtual teams should schedule and attend regular face-to-face meetings as well as make sure that the informal exchange of information is improved. Informal contact can be stimulated by, for example, organising fun get-togethers outside of work. They also recommend the use of group sessions aimed at improving mutual trust and dealing with mutual conflicts before actually compiling a virtual group.

© Noordhoff Uitgevers bv

Tips for managers

4

As a manager, you want the groups for which you are responsible to collaborate effectively and perform well. This does not always happen automatically, since group members are different.

Diagnosis of effective collaboration
The effectiveness of a group can be established by asking the following questions:

Productivity:
- How high is the group's productivity?
- Is their productivity too high or too low compared with that of other groups doing the same work?
- Are clients satisfied with the products or services supplied?
- Are the group's objectives being achieved on time?

Satisfaction:
- Are the group's members satisfied? Keep an eye on the amount of sick leave, job interviews and conflicts within the group.

Improvements in executive activities
With groups that do *executive work*, you should pay attention to the following and possibly improve them:

Knowledge and skills:
- Do group members have the necessary knowledge and skills for the proper performance of the task?
- What knowledge and skills are insufficiently represented and what training or education is necessary?

Norms and cohesion:
- What performance norms are present in the group?
- Does the group know what norms they must comply with and is the group able to do this?
- Is there sufficient cohesion within the group? Changing the composition of the group or engaging in communal activities outside work can promote this.

Role definition:
- Is there sufficient clarity and agreement about the roles within the group?
- Is role analysis required?
- Are the functional roles within the team adequately filled?
- Are dysfunctional roles present? If necessary, reduce the dysfunctional roles and increase the functional ones.

Task structure and goals:
- Is it clear how tasks must be tackled?
- Are the goals clear and sufficiently challenging?

Motivation:
- Are all group members making the same amount of effort? Or are some group members freeloading on the efforts and contributions of others? If so, this must be discussed and a better division of work devised.

Resources:
- Does the group have sufficient resources to perform its tasks properly?

Improvements in decision-making groups

With groups that are responsible for *making decisions*, you must pay attention to the following:

Type of problem:
- Which problems can best be tackled by the group and which can be delegated to one person?

It is important to avoid unnecessary group discussion, which costs time and energy. For complex problems it is worthwhile to involve several people in the decision-making process.

Group composition (for project groups, self-managing teams and committees):
- Are there people with sufficient expertise and adequate collaborative skills in the group?
- Have the functional roles in the group been fulfilled?
- Are there any dysfunctional roles present?
- Is the group too large?

Quality of decisions:
- Has attention been paid to the feasibility of the decision in terms of cost, resources and knowledge?
- Can adequate support for its execution be expected?
- Have the risks been sufficiently discussed and what are the chances of success?

Observation forms

Shortcomings in the decision-making process can be established using observation forms (see website):
- Shortcomings due to unequal input and influence (observation form 1)
- Shortcomings due to self-censorship and groupthink (observation form 2)
- Shortcomings due to poor structuring (observation form 3)
- Shortcomings due to conflicts (observation form 4).

Mediation

Process losses can be prevented or stemmed by appointing a person with sufficient skills to counter them and increase the efficiency of the decision-making process. Have one or more people undergo training in this field. In the case of persistent conflicts, employ a mediator (see paragraph 10.10.2).

© Noordhoff Uitgevers bv

Summary

4

▶ The criteria for effective collaboration in executive groups are:
- productivity
- satisfaction

▶ There are four conditions for the effective performance of work in groups:
- adequate knowledge and skills among group members
- high performance norms and strong cohesion within the group
- role clarity and agreement about roles among group members
- a clear task structure and challenging goals

▶ The Role Analysis Technique (RAT) can be used to clarify and reach agreement on roles.

▶ Process losses in the executive work of groups is the result of coordination and motivation problems.

▶ The likelihood of motivation problems increases as
- the group becomes larger
- the group's tasks become less attractive

▶ Criteria for effective decision-making are:
- adequate time frame
- adequate consideration of opportunities and risks
- feasibility of selected solution
- acceptance of and support for selected solution

▶ For estimation and combination problems, a group solution is generally better than individual solutions.

▶ There are for reasons for preferring a group approach:
- A group has more knowledge and awareness than one person.
- In a group, one idea elicits another.
- The critical capacity of a group is greater than that of one individual.
- Estimation errors are cancelled out in a group.

▶ Causes for process losses are:
- unequal input and influence of group members
- self-censorship and groupthink
- poor structuring of discussion
- conflicts within the group

▶ Decision-making in groups can be improved by:
- brainstorming
- brainwriting
- the Delphi method
- clear structuring

▶ Conditions for effective collaboration in self-managing teams are:
- adequate skills
- good mutual understanding
- high performance norms, accepted by the group
- sufficient resources

Assignments

4.1   Coca-Cola's market share was being increasingly eroded by its rival Pepsi. Coca-Cola's President and COO Roberto Goizueta decided to do something about it. The company developed three new flavours and tested them on 200,000 people. The research took over four years and cost $4 million. (Fewer than 40,000 people could taste the difference between the old and new flavours.) How consumers would react to the introduction of a 'new Coke' was also investigated. Various specialists and external advisors were consulted. On the basis of the research results and the estimated financial return, it was decided to bring new Coke onto the market in 1985. This event was given excessive coverage.

Soon after the launch, it became clear that the public was not satisfied. People telephoned to complain and wrote angry letters. Consumers formed protest groups and demanded the return of the old and familiar Coca-Cola. Distributors and bottlers complained to the head office. Sales went into drastic decline. The response of consumers surprised Coca-Cola's management. Apparently, the old brand belonged to a certain lifestyle or was a symbol of earlier times. All the market research had apparently failed to reveal these aspects of the product. Too much attention had been focused on the new product.

Within three months of the launch, the new product was withdrawn and supply of old Coca-Cola resumed. This decision took little time and no further research.

   a   Which phases of the sequential phase model were properly observed and which were not?
   b   In which phase(s) were significant errors made?
   c   What shortcomings in the decision-making process most probably caused the wrong decision to be taken?

4.2   Barack Obama surrounded himself with teams of astute, skilled and highly critical people. He encouraged them to disagree with him.

   a   What process losses are thereby avoided? Explain your answer.
   b   Obama set high performance goals for himself and his staff. What can you say about the quality of the resulting performance if his team had been dealing with weak cohesion?
   c   What can you say about the quality of the performance if he had a highly cohesive team?
   d   Under what conditions will challenging goals result in high performance?

4.3   The management team meeting at a certain company discusses the agenda topic of 'high rate of sick leave'. The chairman of the meeting opens the discussion stating that this kind of absenteeism in the production teams is caused by the lack of a proper approach by the supervisors of these teams. He calls it a problem of leadership. Considering his diagnosis, he feels that the obvious plan of action is to draft a better plan for approaching employees who all in sick. Team leaders should

© Noordhoff Uitgevers bv

contact any ill members of staff and ask them about the nature and cause of their illness. They should also ask the staff member when they expect to be fully recovered and ready for work. Weak protests against this diagnosis are ignored by the chairman, who is also unwilling to address the reservations the team leaders have with regards to the usability of the suggested solution.

a Which identifiable process losses have occurred during this meeting?
b Which phases of problem-solving and decision-making are address inadequately?
c Which criteria for proper problem-solving and decision-making have or have not been met?

4

5

Communication in organisations

- What is communication?
- What forms of communication are there?
- What does the communication process consist of?
- What are the functions of communication?
- How is communication in organisations organised?
- What impediments to communication can occur?
- How can impediments be removed?

© Noordhoff Uitgevers bv

Keeping in touch

Lisa begins her working day by opening her email inbox. A lot of new messages have come in. One student asks if she can still join the forthcoming practical exam and, if so, what she must prepare. Four other students have handed in a term paper that she will need to assess and comment on. A colleague asks her to telephone him to discuss the approach to a new course. In addition, she has bent sent the provisional agenda for a meeting and asked whether she also has agenda items, and some general communications about various matters within the organisation. She works partly from home but spends three afternoons a week at the study centre. There she can see the students and maintain personal contact with her direct colleagues and members of the secretary's office. This direct and informal contact is good for relationships and helpful in dealing with matters of all kinds.

5.1 Communication

Lisa wants to do well as a teacher. That means she will regularly need to communicate with students, fellow teachers, and the staff at the secretary's office. She also feels it is important to stay in touch with her manager and the head of studies.

Communication is the transference of verbal and non-verbal communication between one or more individuals. People exchange information with each other: knowledge, feelings, opinions, preference, desires, etcetera. How does this exchange take place?
We distinguish three ways of exchanging information:
- written communication;
- oral communication;
- non-verbal communication.

5.1.1   Written communication

Written communication deals with the transference of information through messages, flyers, reports, company journals, memos on a notice board, etcetera. This information is usually disseminated electronically, for example using email, text messages, Twitter, or Facebook. The opening case shows that Lisa starts her work day by opening her email account. Assessing the project assignments handed in by her students and responding with her comments means sending those students an email. She also submits a proposal for a new agenda item and describes why it is in need of discussion. The advantage of digital communication is that it can take place independently of time and place. Whether the person addressed is physically present at work, travelling, or at home, they can receive messages (virtually) anywhere and at any time, and read and respond to them as well. Digital communication can lead to reduced direct and personal contact.

Employees who do not regularly meet face-to-face have difficulty developing team spirit or retain their commitment to an organisation. People work for more than just money – they also work because of the social aspect and the feeling of being part of a group. Digital communication may be convenient and quick, but if there are no other forms of communication, the result is social isolation. Not all employers stimulate working from home; a work method which also requires a lot of self-discipline and may complicate a supervisor's tasks with regard to addressing work or motivation related issues in time. Supervisors in those cases are lacking a direct view of what is going on.

Digital communication has caused great changes. Paper is used less and less frequently. Many organisations strive for a 'paperless office'. Fewer phone calls take place. Colleagues who would formerly knock on your door now approach you via email or text messages. Those kinds of written messages are easy to compose and easy to send to many people at once. It informalizes intercompany communication and can serve to break down barriers. Whereas scheduling an appointment with the head of a department or a manager used to be a hassle, now all it takes is a simple email. But there are also disadvantages to using digital means of

5

© Noordhoff Uitgevers bv

communication. Employees sending messages 'to all' willy nilly will result in much time lost on messages whose contents are of dubious usefulness. Many messages are deleted at a swift glance - but still take up time and attention. And those swift glances may lead to a lack of focus, causing important messages to go unheeded.

PW, JUDITH SPRUIT

Free workers

Richard de Jong, HR-manager of Dutch agricultural consulting firm DLV, supervises his 900 members of staff from a gorgeous manor in the one of the Netherlands' greenest locales. DLV has 500 long-distance workers, 400 of whom only work from home. Eighty employees are located in the manor and its three outbuildings, the others are located at one of the fifteen regional offices.
'Occasionally, I work from home, drafting invoices for example, but I am generally here at the office. Staying in touch with everyone on a day to day basis is easier for me when I am here,' says De Jong. DLV's long-distance workforce mostly consist of consultants. The idea first came up five years ago. The consultants were then still operating from 26 different regional offices, often at long distances from where they lived. DLV wanted to cut back on those costs and cut back on office expenses. These days, De Jong rarely sees his consultants face-to-face. 'But fortunately, I do know all of them. We stay in touch via email and occasionally I sit in on team meetings. Staying in touch is not as effortless as it was. Their managers inform me of the consultants' exploits and I also turn to the works council for information. They tell me a lot about what is important to the staff.'

The webcam has made direct and personal communication via digital means a possibility. This expands the list of digital tools with a microphone and a camera. Employees and supervisors can talk to and see each other using a direct connection and take part in discussions or meetings. This form of online communication is no longer written but spoken. Whether it is enough to restore and retain mutual social contact, team spirit, and commitment, remains a topic for further study.

5.1.2   Oral communication

Oral communication occurs between people who are in direct contact. Examples include phone calls, water-cooler discussions, a talk between a supervisor and an employee on the floor, a discussion between the heads of department, or weekly team work meetings. Oral communication often takes place *face-to-face*.

*"A nice job?
We don't do those around here."*

The open case shows that Lisa engages in face-to-face communication with her colleagues during meetings, with students who attend her visiting hours, and with administration helpdesk employees. She often joins those members of staff for a coffee, and the informal chit-chat keeps her appraised of goings-on in the organisation and allows her to sort out small, day-to-day matters. Other professors also often pop-in and catch-up. This direct and informal type of contact is beneficial to mutual relationship. Birthdays are celebrated with cakes from a local patisserie and many-happy-returns from the other members of staff.

5.1.3   Non-verbal communication

People convey much more in their communications with others than what they express in words. They do this with their posture, intonation, facial expressions, gestures and eye contact. We call this non-verbal communication.

© Noordhoff Uitgevers bv

EXAMPLE 5.1

What do you see?

If you look from a distance at two colleagues communicating with each other at the coffee machine, you can see from their posture, expressions and gestures whether they are, for example, arguing or chatting.

The non-verbal signals that are sent out with oral communication take place automatically. People are usually unaware of them and unable to suppress them.

EXAMPLE 5.2

Non-verbal language is powerful

A colleague has had a discussion with her manager. From the frown on her face, the way in which she slams the door and the angry way she stomps back to her desk, it is clear that it hasn't been a pleasant discussion. When a colleague asks how the discussion went, she says 'all right' and tries to put on a brave face, but she doesn't succeed.

If the non-verbal communication does not correspond with the verbal communication, doubt arouses about the accuracy of what a person says (verbal communication). In this situation, more credit is attached to the non-verbal communication. Non-verbal communication supplements what is communicated verbally, reinforcing the message or clarifying the person's intentions, for example, but it can also negate the message. It is much more difficult to maintain appearances with non-verbal signals – to act as if you are not angry when you are, for example – than with verbal signals. This is because the non-verbal signals that are sent out are unconscious. They cannot be controlled to the same extent as verbal signals. The (unconscious) observation of non-verbal signals and the impression that they do not correspond with what is being said verbally can also lead to confusion.

Non-verbal communication takes the following forms:
- **Intonation**. A person's voice can vary in volume, variaty, speed and pitch. Intonation can therefore be interrogatory, compelling, tense, relaxed, threatening, fearful, furious or friendly.
- **Posture**. A person can turn towards or away from someone else, stand close or maintain a distance, make themselves appear large or small, thereby indicating whether they are interested or not, whether wish to dominate or threaten or to remain insignificant.

- **Gestures and movements.** A person can walk and move in a relaxed or a tense manner, underline an assertion with hand or arm movements, point at something and use gestures to demand attention, ward off, greet or threaten.
- **Expressions and eye contact.** A person can appear to be happy, puzzled, furious, disapproving or distrusting. By maintaining eye contact with a someone you are conversing with, you are signalling that you are listening, interested and wish to continue the conversation.

Non-verbal communication supplements what is communicated verbally.

To a sender, non-verbal communication is an aid to clarifying the verbal message, to expressing their intentions and feelings, or to controlling the relationship with the receiver.

EXAMPLE 5.3

Signals in conversation

People do not always terminate a conversation by verbally indicating that they wish to stop. If they think this would be too impolite, they make use of non-verbal signals, such as looking away (breaking eye contact), saying nothing or averting their body. With these non-verbal signals they inform the other person that they wish to end the conversation. If the other person is sensitive to these non-verbal signals, they will respond.

Direct communication between people is rich in non-verbal signals. With telephone contact, there is far less non-verbal communication but it is not completely absent, because intonation is still used. With written communication, non-verbal communication is completely absent.

Emoticon

With electronic communication, a person can consciously send non-verbal signals along with the written message, for example by adding an emoticon, sometimes known as an emoji. This is an image – for example in the form of a smiling, angry or frowning face – which reflects the disposition of the sender. Think of using a smiley to indicate that your statement is meant to be interpreted as a joke.

5.2 The communication process

Communicating seems so natural. Nevertheless, situations occur in which communication leads to misunderstanding.

EXAMPLE 5.4

Communication

Sandra had been on holiday for three weeks. The morning she returned to work, she would have liked to talk with her colleagues about her holiday. However, the head of the department came along with a great number of new assignments. He didn't ask her anything about her holiday but simply said 'Could you deal with these assignments today?' Petulantly, she responded with the remark 'Couldn't you have given me a bit less to do?' The head of department thought: 'What did I do wrong now? It is always difficult to work with her,' and he replied, annoyed: 'Certainly not. I have a lot more work for you.'

The interaction between Sandra and her manager could have gone differently. After his request 'Could you deal with this today?', Sandra might have said 'Of course, but I will need a little time to get going again after my holiday.' Her manager could then have thought, 'Oh yes, she has been on holiday', and could have asked whether she had had a good time.

Communication
Process

To understand what can go wrong in communications between two or more people, it is necessary to look at the communication process more closely.

Figure 5.1 illustrates how communication occurs between the sender (person A) and the recipient (person B). The communication cycle is demonstrated using the following example.

FIGURE 5.1 The communication cycle between person A and person B

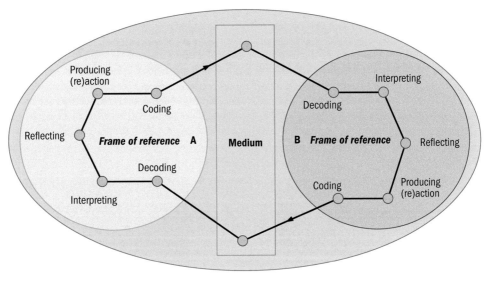

Source: © E. Wijsman en W. Molendijk

- -

EXAMPLE 5.5

Catch a movie?

Reflecting. Sender A is considering asking B to go to the movies.
Producing action. A calls B on the phone.
Encoding. A leaves a voicemail: Would you like to go to the movies?
Medium. The message proceeds to B via telephone (cable or connection).
Decoding. Recipient B hears and understands the words left by A.
Interpreting. B understands the message and the intent.

Reflecting. B considers the invitation and decides to accept.
Producing (re)action. B intends to tell A that they would enjoy going to the movies.
Encoding. Sender B leaves a message: Sure, I would love to join you.
A then decodes and interprets the message as its recipient. And thus, the cycle goes on…

- -

Reflecting and producing action
Sender A from example 5.5 is considering asking B to go to the movies with them. This consideration of undertaking an activity is known as reflection. Once A decides to contact B, they begin preparing for an action. This action may involve contacting B (phone, email, text message).

Encoding
Sender A needs to translate their desire into certain symbols, such as words or gestures. This process is known as encoding. Unclear encoding, such as mumbling, causes misunderstanding. Gestures can have different meanings

© Noordhoff Uitgevers bv

depending on the culture that uses them (context). Using the thumbs-up sign for hitchhiking can lead to an unfortunate misunderstanding in another country. Encoding results in a certain message, which is sent to the recipient. Coding can be verbal or non-verbal in nature and can be sent consciously or unconsciously. Consider gestures such as a frown or scratching your head. Messages can be one-sided or double-sided in terms of contacts. One-sided messages include advertorials, which only list a product's positive aspects. A double-sided message includes the weaker aspects of a product (or topic) in addition to the strong ones. If you are trying to convince a reasonably intelligent individual of the benefits of a certain type of car, for example, the best option is to go with the double-sided approach.

Laughter: false or genuine?

Medium
Depending on the situation and the possibilities, sender A decides which medium to use. If they encounter the recipient and ask them to join them for a movie, the medium used is the air. The words that are spoken reach the recipient in the form of vibrations transferred through the air. Examples of other media are landlines, smartphones, and computers.
It is sensible to tailor the medium to the intended target group of your communication. If you need to alert everyone in a company post-haste, you would not choose to call all of them individually. A message through a social networking website such as Twitter would work much better.

Decoding
The recipient must first decode the message before its meaning can be properly interpreted. What exactly does the sender say or write? What desire or idea are they trying to transfer?

Interpreting

In order to determine the intent or meaning the sender's message, the recipient needs to interpret the message. Is the request serious or in jest? What does the sender want me to do? What is their intention? There is a possibility of some distortion or disruption of the sender's intent, because the recipient is operating from another frame of experience. They interpret the message from their own frame of reference: their knowledge, experience, needs, feelings, conviction, and ideas. Their interpretation of the message, therefore, does not always correspond to the sender's intentions. For example, a sender may have only transferred half of a sentence before the recipient already thinks they know what is meant. One the one hand, they may be correct in their interpretation. On the other, they may be wrong – resulting in the recipient attributing an unintended message to the sender.

EXAMPLE 5.6

Selective perception

When the head of the department asked in a factual manner if she would deal with the work he had for her, Sandra decoded this as: 'He has little interest in me and doesn't even know I have been on holiday.' This decoding was responsible for her not saying 'Yes, of course. It's nice to be back, I've returned to work with fresh enthusiasm', but instead reacting petulantly.

Context also plays a role. If a recipient is a member of another (sub-)culture than the sender, they may misinterpret the message. Context can also refer to various different situations such as the differences between an assessment review and a first date. In each of those cases, how would you interpret the sentence: 'I would like to meet up again'?   Context

Reflection and producing (re)action

The recipient considers the sender's message: they reflect on it. This reflection can be a swift, nearly subconscious process, but also lead to contemplation and consideration.

EXAMPLE 5.7

Borrowing the car?

Your 18-year-old neighbour asks you to borrow your car for a day to transport 'some stuff'. You consider his request (reflection): Would it be a good idea considering he has only just started driving? Why does it have to be your car? Is he in a rush? Can you even spare your car for a day? And what is he transporting anyway? After some thought, you decide not to loan your car to your neighbour (producing reaction).

Following reflection, the recipient needs to make a decision. How will they respond? Then, the response itself takes place.

Feedback

While expression the message, the sender already receives feedback responses from the recipient. If your conversation partner were to keep furrowing their brow, you would probably adjust your use of language. If their response indicates they do not understand you story or that your intentions are unclear, you can send a new message.

During and following sending, the sender decodes the recipient's reactions and interprets the meaning of those reactions. Based on that interpretation, the sender determines what the recipient intends; reflection occurs.

Then, the sender produces another reaction to the recipient's message. All of this happens at incredible speeds.

EXAMPLE 5.8

Misunderstandings

Sandra's petulant reaction could have led to a different decoding by her manager than 'It is always difficult to work with her.' He could have thought 'She is probably a bit tired and I've ambushed her with too much work.' In that case, his reaction to her feedback would have been different.

5.3 Aspects of communication

Aspects of the message

A sender can indicate different intentions simultaneously in a message. These intentions are called the aspects of the message. We can illustrate the aspects a message may have by using Sandra's reaction to her manager's request to deal with the work he put in front of her. Her reaction 'Couldn't you have given me a bit less to do?' illustrates the following aspects of communication:

1 **Factual aspect.** The message contains factual content that can be decoded separately from the feelings. Sandra asks if it is possible to leave some on the assignments on her desk till later. Opinions or ideas can also have a factual aspect.

2 **Expressive aspect.** The message has an emotional content, with which the sender wishes to indicate how she feels. Sandra indicates by her reaction that she is irritated. The expressive aspect is often partly conveyed by non-verbal signals, such as a frowning or averted face, an angry tone, a curt response or a dismissive gesture. In electronic communication, emoticons can be used to express feelings (:) , :( ).

3 **Relational aspect.** The message expresses how the sender sees her relationship with the receiver. Sandra indicates that she thinks her manager is a rude man who has little interest in her as a person.

4 **Appealing aspect.** The message contains a desire. Sandra is trying to convey a wish to the receiver. In this case, it is not so much that wants to do less

work on her first day back from holiday, but more that she wants him to understand that he should devote a little more personal attention to her.

That not all aspects of her message are communicated effectively to the receiver is apparent from her manager's reaction. He senses that she is irritated (expressive aspect), but he does not understand why this is so (relational aspect) nor what she actually wants from him (appealing aspect).

The various aspects of a message can be identified but not isolated. All the aspects can be present in one and the same message at the same time. Many misunderstandings and arguments arise from the misinterpretation of one or more aspects of a message. These misunderstandings can be avoided by summarising how the message has been understood. The sender can then confirm or correct this.

Look at the expressive and relational aspects of this interaction.
What can you tell from their faces and posture? Who do you think is the boss? And what is the quality of their relationship?

Watzlawick et al. (1973) states that all interpersonal behaviour is communication. This means that people in social situations cannot *not* communicate. Even if someone sits silently opposite others in a train, for example, they are still communicating. Non-verbally, they clearly indicate that they does not wish to converse. This is done by looking out of the window, avoiding eye contact and averting their body from the other travellers. The message is: 'Do not disturb me.'
Organisations prefer oral communication because of the richness of non-verbal information that can be conveyed and the opportunity to give and receive instant feedback. Feedback indicates how people decode and

© Noordhoff Uitgevers bv

interpret the information received. In this way, the person who is communicating can check whether the receiver has understood everything correctly. This involves two-way communication. If the other person shows verbally and/or non-verbally, for example, that they do not understand, it is possible to address this immediately.

Two-way communication

With written communication there is one-way traffic. The sender sends a message to the receiver and usually does not receive an immediate reaction. They therefore receive little or no direct feedback. With written communication there is little or no opportunity for dialogue.

One-way traffic

Sending and receiving often occur at the same time in a dialogue.

Digital communication can also involve one-way traffic, but with a possibility to responds quickly - thus encouraging two-way traffic. Direct feedback is either impossible or restricted. Non-verbal feedback in particular is absent from digital communication. An online chat comes with greater direct interaction, and video calling turns the communication towards two-way traffic, since there is face-to-face contact. The same applies to video conferencing.

EXAMPLE 5.9

In the cloud

Lisa has recently begun using Facebook. She enjoys keeping in touch with old high school friends and send fun messages and pictures. Without noticing so, it has begun to take up more and more time. Her husband has been given a new tablet pc, and since he discovered Twitter and Instagram, he spends more and more time in the cloud.

But when was the last time they went to the cinema together?

The collection of online tools that people use to share their opinion, insights, experiences, and feelings, is called 'social media'. A characteristic of social media is that information can be shared rapidly between individuals, within groups, and between groups. In doing so, it is possible to use various media at the same time, sending texts, images, and sounds, and allowing recipients to respond (directly) and offer their feedback. The immense speed and vast range enable news (of an earthquake or a serious accident) to spread rapidly across a large group. Social media enables people to remain in intensive contact with others living on different continents and in different time zones.

5.4 Communication in organisations

In organisations, management and employees communicate constantly with each other. Through communication it is made clear what activities must be performed, how they must be performed, by whom this must be done and within what time frame. Communication is also necessary to resolve problems, to coordinate activities and to instruct, stimulate and support employees who are having difficulties in the performance of their work. Different forms of information transfer can be used, such as meetings (management meetings, progress meetings, team meetings, committee and council meetings), oral and written communications from management and instructions that colleagues give each other in order to complete a task together. All these forms of communication are intended to produce effective collaboration.

We describe two types of communication in organisations: formal and informal communication.

5.4.1 Formal communication

Formal communication includes all communication between the management and employees of an organisation that takes place via fixed channels and communication structures.

EXAMPLE 5.10

Informing and adapting

Katie Knightley is head of the Personnel and Organisation Department. Every two weeks, she has a meeting with the management team. She informs management about the state of affairs in her department and, if necessary, raises problems in her department that require a solution for which she needs management approval. The management team can put forward new activities that must be carried out by her department.

Every week, Katie also has a progress meeting with her staff. She tells them what matters have been discussed in the recent management meeting and which of these are relevant to them. She also establishes what (supplementary) activities have to be carried out that week and how these can best be tackled. If an employee has a problem she cannot resolve, she indicates that she will consult another department.

The directors of a large company do not communicate directly with employees 'on the shop floor'. They communicate with the managers directly below them. These subsequently pass the information on to their subordinates who, finally, inform the operational staff of what management has to say. This form of communication is characterised by the use of

Nodes

intermediaries. These are called nodes. The use of nodes means that communication is indirect. The larger organisations become and the more hierarchical layers they are composed of, the more indirect the

Indirect communication

communication between the top and bottom of the organisation. In small organisations, communication is usually much more direct and takes place without the intercession of nodes.

Just as there are differences between cultures in non-verbal communication, there are also differences between cultures in formal communication. In some countries (China, for example), it is not common for an employee to put a direct question to their manager. This subject is discussed further in chapter 8. An example is that it is good to know the meaning of 'maybe' differs from one country to the next; in Asian countries, it is interpreted as 'no'.

5.4.2   Informal communication

Besides formal communication networks, informal networks are also created in every organisation. For example, a certain group of employees always sits together in breaks or plays sport together after work.

EXAMPLE 5.11

Informal contacts

John regularly plays football with people from various departments and at different hierarchical levels. They form the company team and compete with other teams. Afterwards, they usually have a drink at the bar in the sports complex and talk about football, personal matters and things that are happening within the company.

Informal communication

A characteristic of informal communication is the fact that people circumvent the formal routes when disseminating information. Informal communication spreads through the organisation like a grapevine. The term 'grapevine' originated in the United States. During the Civil War, telegraph cables were loosely hung in trees, which resulted in messages getting garbled. These cables looked somewhat like grapevines. Grapevine or informal communication has since that time been associated with incomplete, garbled and inaccurate information. Nevertheless, Robbins (1989) reports the results of research into grapevines where the information passed on was 75% accurate. A characteristic of the grapevine is its speed. The passing-on of information is much faster than via formal communication channels. From various studies it appears that only a small proportion of employees (about 10%) actively function as 'liaisons' or connections. They each pass on the information to more than one other employee. There are different types of grapevine (Davis, 1953) (see Figure 5.2).

FIGURE 5.2 Different types of grapevines

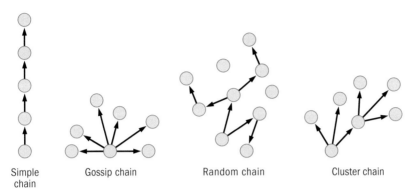

Simple chain   Gossip chain   Random chain   Cluster chain

Source: Davis, in: Stoner & Freeman, 1989

The basic type is a simple chain. All those involved pass on the information to one other person. This chain can be compared with the game of Chinese Whispers, where people whisper a message that they have just heard into their neighbour's ear. This grapevine is not very reliable. By the time it reaches the end of the chain, the information has become substantially garbled.   **Simple chain**

Another type of grapevine is gossip. Gossip is spread by one person to everyone. This type of grapevine is used if the information is of local interest and not work-related.   **Gossip**

A third type is the probability chain. The information is disseminated at random. It does not necessarily concern the person to whom it is conveyed.   **Probability chain**

The most common grapevine within organisations is the cluster chain. In this type of grapevine, the information is passed to selected people, who in turn also select certain receivers. Selection takes place primarily on the basis of trust and personal preference.   **Cluster chain**

Informal communication has both positive and negative aspects. The positive aspects are: **Positive aspects**

- **Faster resolution of problems**. In organisations there are always problems to be resolved. For example, the interests of salesmen and production workers may clash. Conflicts that threaten to arise between these two groups can be formally resolved by a management team, but they may be more quickly resolved by informal communication. People who see each other every day can discuss and resolve quite a few problems.
- **Better information**. Many people enjoy being part of an informal communication network. This often keeps them better informed of matters that play a part in the organisation than do the formal channels.
- **Greater subtlety**. Matters requiring tact or negotiation are usually better resolved via informal routes. The acquisition of appliances or a better office chair is usually a question of approaching the right people in the right way.

Employees who work a great deal from home and on the road and therefore communicate primarily electronically miss the above-mentioned benefits of informal contacts as a consequence.

EXAMPLE 5.12

Working remotely

Three hundred and fifty mobile workers in 29 European countries were interviewed by the IBM Institute for Business Value. The results of this research showed that more than 50% of mobile workers found it problematic to attend meetings and collaborate with colleagues remotely. Another significant disadvantage for mobile workers was the reduced personal contact with colleagues, in corridors or by the coffee machine. The often essential information that flows through informal networks was not available to them. One of the interviewees' greatest worries was that they were excluded from their informal networks, through which they formerly shared knowledge and discussed opportunities for the organisation.

Negative aspects

The negative aspects of informal communication are:
- **Lack of transparency.** Informal communication can be used by employees or management to test reactions to decisions. Those who are excluded may offer resistance.
- **Rumour formation.** Rumours arise when information is passed on without knowing its source. Rumours often arise in times of uncertainty. If a rumour exaggerates the negative consequences of reorganisation, for example, this can result in unnecessary fears or resentment.

EXAMPLE 5.13

Rumour mill

Things are not going well for the company, and management has met several times to discuss the situation. Rumours are circulating that management wants to downsize and that there will be a lot of redundancies, especially among lower-level personnel. The lower-level employees are furious about this. They were the victims of cost-cutting the last time, while all the people at the top and in the administrative services simply remained in place. They looked after themselves all right. Ultimately, it turned out that the rumour was partly incorrect and the anger misplaced. This time the cuts would be primarily in mid-level management and administrative services but not among lower-level personnel.

- **Gossiping.** Informal communication can be used to spread negative information about people. Gossiping can be an innocent pastime and constitute harmless social contact between employees. It is also possible to intentionally slander colleagues and damage their reputations by saying something negative about them when they are unable to defend themselves. This can lead to a deterioration in relationships at work.

BUSINESSWEEK, DIANE BRADY

Is gossip always toxic?

I have mixed views about office gossip. On the one hand, it can be a great way to gain intelligence about what's going on and who's moving where, especially if such news tends to trickle out slowly from the top. And I just read a study that said kidding around at work, especially about things associated with the job, has a positive impact on the workplace.But there's no question that straight-up gossip can cut into morale and lead to false rumors, too. Sam Chapman of Chicago's Empower Public Relations firmly believes it's toxic and, six months ago, he issued an edict to his 15 staffers to say that all gossip had to stop. (...) He just told his people that anything said about a colleague would immediately be conveyed to that person, and the source would be revealed. (...) "Chapman says the office dynamics have markedly improved since then as "people have learned how to address each other on issues."

The approach sounds a little Orwellian in execution. What if someone has ethical issues or is facing harassment from a colleague? (...) Or someone sharing good news that a colleague has e-mailed in from the road. For many people, the office is a kin to a village common. They care about the community, and they talk about its members – hopefully in a constructive or, better yet, a humorous way.

5.5   Impediments to communication

All kinds of breakdowns in communication can result in information, opinions and intentions not being transmitted properly. These breakdowns may be the fault of the person who formulates the message (the sender), the medium through which the message is transmitted (the transfer) or the person who receives and interprets (decodes) the message (the receiver). These subjects are discussed in this section. We also look at feedback in greater detail.

5.5.1   The sender

A person who wishes to inform another person or have them do something must make Their intentions known in the appropriate manner. They will by no means always be successful. The breakdown in communication is then relayed to the sender and their manner of encoding the message. The following breakdowns can occur:

- The sender uses too many difficult words or jargon, making the message too **hard to understand**.
- The sender is too **verbose**, as a result of which his actual intention gets lost and the message is **vague**.
- The sender can consciously or unconsciously hold back or distort information or pass on **incomplete** information, resulting in **partial communication**.
- The sender sends out **conflicting signals**. The sender asserts that they are not angry, for example, but looks as if they are about to explode.

Breakdown in communication

Partial communication can be the result of a lack of openness. From Sandra's reaction to her manager's request to 'deal with this today', it is not apparent to him that she is disappointed by his lack of interest. Her message therefore does

Lack of openness

© Noordhoff Uitgevers bv

not represent what she actually wishes to communicate. Lack of openness between people in organisations is primarily caused by their feelings. On the one hand, because a great deal of communication in organisations has an overwhelmingly factual character, the introduction of feelings is often perceived as disruptive or dysfunctional. On the other hand, because the expression of anger or irritation can cause upset, there is a danger of the sender's relationship with the receiver deteriorating and a conflict resulting.

5.5.2   Interference

Messages are transmitted via different media or channels. In direct interpersonal communication, three channels are used simultaneously. The voice makes use of the vocal-auditory channel. Non-verbal signals are received by eye, so the visual channel also plays a part. Sometimes people touch each other as well, in which case use is made of the tactile channel. During the transfer of the message, interference can occur. This means that the message is not received properly. De Vito (1996) described three forms of interference (or 'noise'):

1 **Physical interference.** This can occur, for example, if noise in the environment makes listening difficult, if written communication is sloppily written or if the sender is wearing sunglasses, which interfere with eye contact.

Vocal-auditory channel

Visual channel

Tactile channel

Technical aids such as microphones make communication more effective in a large group.

2 **Psychological interference.** This form of interference means that the receiver is not listening properly. This is the case if the receiver is not interested in the message or thinks that what the sender is saying is not true, for example.
3 **Semantic interference.** This form of interference is caused by the fact that sender and receiver are not using the same communication codes. This is the case if they speak different languages, for example. The use of jargon is another example of this.

Semantic interference can also occur between people from different cultures. Cultures use different codes – people often speak not only literally but also figuratively different languages – and this can lead to misunderstandings (Maznevski, 1994). Munter (1993) indicates that a distinction can be made between countries in which communication is highly context sensitive and countries in which communication is less context sensitive. In countries like China, Vietnam and Saudi Arabia, communication is highly context sensitive. People from these cultures pay close attention to non-verbal and context-sensitive signals. What is not being said can be just as important or even more important as what is actually being said. In these cultures, people are not used to a direct and explicit manner of indicating what one thinks and feels.

Highly context sensitive

EXAMPLE 5.14

Communicating differently

If you ask a Japanese person the way, they will never tell you they do not know. This would mean they would be unable to help, which is regarded as losing face. A manager will also never give a direct order to a subordinate, but rather offer a hint. Simply refusing something, showing that you are angry, or saying that another person is wrong, are examples of impoliteness, and this is also unacceptable. A great deal must therefore be expressed indirectly, which is problematic for someone unfamiliar with these rules of communication.

The Dutch have low context-sensitivity. They indicate what they think of something and what they want directly and explicitly. What is said is more important than in which context it is said. This applies to most northern European countries and the United States. A Chinese psychologist observed: 'You have to express yourself clearly and precisely in the Netherlands because you cannot expect the Dutch to understand the meaning behind the words. They take the message literally.' (Van Oudenhoven & Giebels, 2004)

Low context-sensitivity

5.5.3   The receiver

The receiver must attach meaning to the verbal and non-verbal signals of the sender by means of decoding. We have previously indicated that these signals include factual, expressive, relational and appealing aspects. What meanings the receiver gives to the signals is dependent on various factors:

Receiver

- **Knowledge of the receiver.** The factual meaning the receiver gives to the message is dependent on his or her knowledge of the subject under discussion. The use of technical jargon will be no impediment to communication if the receiver has the same technical knowledge as the sender. If this is not the case, the receiver will have difficulty in understanding the factual aspect of the message.
- **The state of mind of the receiver.** How the expressive and appealing aspects of a message are interpreted is partly determined by the state of mind of the receiver. A person who is in a good mood is more likely to perceive another person's intentions as positive than a person who is in a bad mood. When we are tired or irritated, we can interpret a neutral message as tiresome, insulting or hurtful. Tiredness or lack of interest in the subject under discussion can also lead to poor listening or listening with 'half an ear', due to which parts of the message are not properly received (psychological interference).

- **The receiver's relationship with the sender.** If the receiver's relationship with the sender is good, his assessment will more readily be positively understood by the receiver than if the relationship is poor. The receiver will also then more readily accept criticism. Nobody is fully open-minded about remarks relating to themselves. You are more likely to accept criticism that you sometimes tackle work rather haphazardly and forget things from a good colleague than from a person you do not like. In the first case, you decode the message as a well intended remark and in the second case as a tiresome and possibly even unjustified criticism.
- **The situation in which the message is sent.** It makes a difference whether something is said during a friendly conversation near the coffee machine, during an important meeting or during a performance appraisal.

Selective process

The above-mentioned factors indicate that the decoding of a message is always a selective process, where misunderstandings can easily arise about the meaning of the message and the intentions of the sender (see Table 5.1).

TABLE 5.1 Misunderstandings in communication

What the manager said	What the manager meant	What the employee heard
1 We have to make savings.	1 We must spend less money on expensive advertising.	1 There is a threat of dismissals in the department.
2 You have caught me at a bad moment.	2 I have no time now but come back in 10 minutes.	2 I do not want to speak to you for the time being.
3 Make a proper plan. I have a clear image of how it could work.	3 You are free to do this according to your own discretion. I am very curious!	3 The plan must satisfy all my requirements to be good enough.
4 I want that report as soon as possible.	4 I need that report within a week.	4 Drop everything and finish the report today.
5 Your people never have their work finished on time. Review this and resolve it.	5 Talk to them and find out what the problem is. Try to resolve it together.	5 I want to see results no matter how much conflict it causes. I have enough problems as it is.

5.5.4 Feedback

From the reactions of the receiver, the sender can deduce whether the content of his message has been understood (factual aspect) and whether his intentions and feelings have been properly transmitted (expressive, relational and appealing aspects). If it is apparent from the receiver's reactions that this is not the case, the sender can attempt to clarify his message by using different wording.

Feedback

Misunderstandings in communication can arise and persist if the feedback system does not function properly. This can be the result of absence of feedback, vague or defective feedback and defective reception of feedback:
- **Absence of feedback.** Communication restricted to the written word will often came without any feedback. There may also be various reasons why the receiver does not respond to the sender. In addition, communication may be conducted indirectly, for example through an intermediary. This will cause the sender to have to forgo direct reactions.

EXAMPLE 5.15

Unfamiliar resistance

Management has informed their employees of a major reorganisation - in writing only. This means management now has no idea about the thoughts and feelings of those employees regarding the reorganisation. These thoughts and feelings are expressed in the corridors but management does not go there. It therefore has no knowledge at all of the antipathy that has been provoked among the staff.

- **Vague or defective feedback.** Feedback loses its clarifying function in communication if it is not correctly received by the sender. This may happen if the sender fails to pay proper attention, incorrectly interprets the feedback, or rejects the receivers feedback. The sender may reject feedback if they feel threatened by it, for example.

Observing feedback signals is not easy in a large group.

EXAMPLE 5.16

Indirect response

When Sandra's manager presented her with a lot of work and nothing but the instruction to get it done, Sandra felt she was being treated poorly. However, she felt unable to clearly express why her manager's approach bothered her so. By responding with 'Couldn't you have given me a bit less to do?' she attempted to express her dissatisfaction in an indirect and unclear manner. In view of the irritated reaction of her manager, it seems that her feedback was unclear and her intended message not properly received.

5

- **Defective receipt of feedback.** Feedback loses its clarifying function in communication if it is not properly received because the sender does not notice it, interprets it incorrectly or rejects it. If the feedback is threatening to the sender, it may be rejected.

Impediments that can occur in communication are shown in Figure 5.3.

FIGURE 5.3 Impediments in the communication process

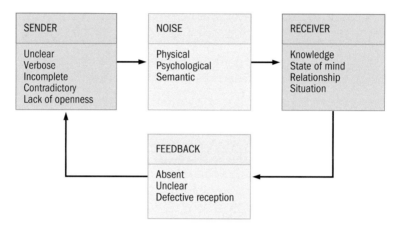

SENDER	NOISE	RECEIVER
Unclear Verbose Incomplete Contradictory Lack of openness	Physical Psychological Semantic	Knowledge State of mind Relationship Situation

FEEDBACK
Absent Unclear Defective reception

5.6 Problems in formal communication

Communication within organisations is by no means always flawless. Mistakes can be made in tasks because employees have not been properly instructed by their manager. Materials do not arrive on time because the supplier did not receive the order from the logistics department on time. A manager is indignant because an employee is absent and has failed to report sick on time.

Problems can occur in all the methods by which people in organisations communicate with each other. Some of these are caused by the previously described failings in communication between sender and receiver (interpersonal communication). Others can be caused by the way in which communication is organised and by the culture of the organisation.

Culture

If communication from the top of the organisation to that bottom and back passes through too many nodes, this can lead to the following problems:
- **Distortion.** Because the receivers of messages are always selective in their interpretation, they seldom pass the message on literally. Not only does their interpretation cause a certain amount of distortion, but their own desires and interests can also contribute to selective translation of the message.

The more nodes a message passes through, the greater the chance of distortion and of the original message arriving either wholly or partially changed.

EXAMPLE 5.17

Own rules or standards

The new management has decided that departments, services and teams can no longer have a coffee machine at their work station. Some of the machines are rather old and they are sometimes left on all night because the last person to go home forgets to switch them off. This creates an unnecessary fire hazard. This decision is announced to the divisional heads. They pass it on to the heads of department and they in turn report it to their staff. Eva, the head of the Special Products Division, who has long been annoyed by her staff's constant coffee drinking, reports to her departmental heads that coffee may no longer be drunk at the work station. Employees should go to the canteen for coffee only during coffee/tea breaks and the lunch break. Charles, the head of the Administration Department, does not like the measure. He is a keen coffee drinker and would like to be able to enjoy his favourite beverage whenever he likes. He therefore reports to his staff that their coffee machines will no longer be allowed in the department but that if anyone feels like a cup of coffee people can be designated in turn to go and get a pot of coffee from the canteen. If everyone has their own cup, they can drink coffee whenever they like.

- **Delay.** It sometimes takes a while before a message is passed on because a receiver who is a node must first do something else. Sometimes a message is also semi-consciously forgotten in the rush and people have to be reminded before it is passed on.
  The heads of the divisions pass on the new rule for making coffee at their next meeting with the heads of their departments.
- **Lack of feedback.** Indirect communication via nodes means that the original sender of the message does not know if the message has been properly received, understood and implemented by the final receivers. Management has no idea what the employees in the organisation think of the new rule and how they will react to it. In reality, the rule is implemented only by employees whose manager agrees with it and checks that it has been implemented. In other departments, there is partial or even zero compliance with management's wishes. In one department, they keep the coffee machine out of sight and continue on as before. What applies to something as trivial as drinking coffee also applies to important matters, such as a reorganisation. A lack of feedback often gives senior management the **illusion of control** over organisations. They think that passing on their wishes to the level below them will automatically lead to their implementation but they do not know exactly what is happening because they are too dependent on the (distorted) information they receive from the managers below them.

EXAMPLE 5.18

Distortion

Some Chinese emperors never ventured outside the Forbidden City (their palace complex in Beijing). They had no idea what was happening among the common people – at least, not from personal observation. They were dependent on their advisers, who often had an interest in communicating something that matched their own views and ambitions.

Culture

Good communication in organisations is impeded by a culture in which management tolerates no objections, in which they require unconditional loyalty from their subordinates and in which mutual rivalry and mistrust dominate. Lower-level management and employees will not speak out in such a culture. Employees do not say what they mean directly and are afraid to stick their necks out or make mistakes. Due to a lack of open communication, feedback is minimal. In this situation, management may be opposed if they come up with plans that are not feasible or could even have a negative effect on the organisation.

EXAMPLE 5.19

Risks for the enterprise

The head of a large company was surrounded by people who offered almost no resistance to his attempts to expand the business. For this reason, nobody pointed out the risks he was running by making a string of large acquisitions from other companies and borrowing a huge amount of money to do this. When these risks became apparent, it was too late to do anything about it.

5.7 Improving communication

We have shown that impediments to communication can arise at both the interpersonal and the organisational level. The latter is the case if communication from top to bottom and back passes through too many nodes and if there is a culture in which mistrust and a lack of openness predominate.

We shall first describe how communication at an interpersonal level can be improved and then indicate what interventions are possible at the organisational level.

5.7.1 Improving interpersonal communication

Problems in interpersonal communication are not usually the result of misunderstandings about the factual aspect of a message but of faulty interpretation of the expressive, relational and appealing aspects of the communication.

Faulty interpretations in many cases result from the fact that people who are communicating with each other think, perceive and feel much more than they convey explicitly in communication. It is as though the spoken word is the tip of the iceberg sticking out from under the water - where there are unspoken expectations, feelings, assumptions and desires.

Faulty interpretations

Sender skills

Improving interpersonal communication begins with a sender. If the sender does the following, the message that is sent becomes clearer to the receiver:

- **State the goal.** It is important that the sender indicates what the goal of the conversation, letter or email is, so that the receiver knows within what framework the message must be placed.
- **Be clear and concise.** The sender must take account of the knowledge of the receiver and adapt his message to that. It is important to avoid technical jargon the receiver does not belong to the same professional group. The sender must also distinguish between major and minor matters, so that the message is not too long or vague.
- **Be open.** The sender must indicate the feelings and desires behind what he is saying, asserting or asking.

5

EXAMPLE 5.20

Openness and self-disclosure

A manager knows that one of her employees is hoping for promotion. Unfortunately, someone else has been chosen for the higher-level position that was available and now the manager has to tell her employee that he was unsuccessful. She begins the conversation by indicating that she knows about his desire for promotion but that someone else has been chosen this time. She also indicates that she understands that he is very disappointed and that she herself finds it frustrating because in her opinion he is good enough for the position. She then explains why the choice fell on someone else and asks him what he thinks and how he feels.

In the above meeting, the manager not only informs the employee that he was not selected for the higher-level position but also shows that she sympathises with his desires and feelings. She also expresses her own feelings in the conversation and lets him know that she thinks he is competent. This encourages openness in the communication between the two and ensures that the employee's feelings do not go unexpressed. Openness about feelings by the sender in general also brings about openness about feelings by the receiver. The communication thereby becomes richer, the likelihood of misunderstanding is reduced and the chance of honest feedback is increased.

Listening skills

The receiver can reduce misunderstandings in communication by developing the following skills:

- **Good listening posture.** Good listening requires paying attention to the message. This is possible only if other matters that demand your attention are put aside. Attention must be focused on both the verbal and non-verbal signals.
- **Questioning.** If there is any doubt about the content or intention of the message, ask for clarification, for example by asking 'Do you mean that you want...?', or 'What is your intention?'.
- **Summarising.** If the message is long or complex, the receiver can summarise it and ask if the summary is correct. If this is not the case, the sender can clarify the message. Summarising is also useful for checking what a person's intentions are and be used as a means of indicating that you have been listening.
- **Expressing feelings.** By expressing their feelings, a receiver indicates how the expressive, relational and appealing aspects of the message have come across. The sender could, for example, remark 'It seems as if you are angry with me', or 'It seems as if you don't really want to give me a chance'. This requires considerable sympathy or empathy on the part of the receiver.

Summarising and expressing feelings give the sender insight (feedback) into the manner in which the content of his message and their (possibly unspoken) intentions have been received. By expressing their feelings, the receiver makes it less likely that the emotional implications of the communication remain unspoken.

5.7.2 Meta communication

Meta communication means communicating at a different, higher level. It is communicating about the way in which communication takes place. The sender may indicate how a message was intended, and the receiver can indicate why they interpreted the message in a certain way. They might say: 'Your angry remark startled me into keeping my mouth shut.' If a conversation does not proceed successfully, the participants can discuss that fact and explain to each other how their messages were intended and interpreted.

EXAMPLE 5.21

Talking things out

The manager felt rather awkward about the way his conversation with Sandra had gone. He was unhappy with his own reaction and had the feeling that something had gone wrong. So after the coffee break he asked Sandra to see him in his office. When she came in, he told her how he felt about their conversation and said that he had reacted badly. Sandra was pleased with this message and felt that her manager was paying attention to her at last. She was relieved and told him that of course she would do the work, but she had been disappointed because he had not first asked how her holiday had been and she had reacted petulantly because of this.

If the communication between one or more people has been thoroughly disrupted, it may be wiser to ask another individual, such as a coach or manager to mediate. The mediator helps the parties involved to talk openly about the way they interpret and experience each others messages. The most important factor, in this case, is clarifying the expressive relational and appealing aspects. In meta communication, people give each other explicit feedback on the way they observe and assess each other's behaviour, feelings and intentions. This feedback can, however, be rather threatening and can easily result in rejection. It can also lead to a personal attack on the giver of feedback, for example in the form of 'Yes, but you also complain all the time!' Feedback must be given in the right manner; otherwise it does not have a positive effect. Feedback can be positive when the following conditions apply:

Feedback

- The receiver is open to feedback.
- The feedback is concrete and specific and not moralising or judgemental. Not 'You always react so angrily', but rather 'When I said to you that you…, you reacted angrily and that made me feel very insecure'.
- The sender expresses his own feelings about the receiver's style of communication.

5

Good feedback follows the BFC model (behaviour, feelings, consequences). The behaviour of the other person must be described as concretely as possible, the feelings that this behaviour evokes must be stated and the consequences of this must be indicated. The feedback will lead to improvement in communication if the receiver observes the following rules:

- Try not to react immediately but ask yourself what the other person is trying to say.
- If necessary, ask questions to find out exactly what the other person means.
- Avoid immediately defending yourself or attacking the other person.
- State your own feelings about the feedback and clarify where these feelings come from.

EXAMPLE 5.22

Feedback done right

During a performance appraisal, Margret brings up the fact that she finds her employee Hank rather chaotic in his approach to his work, as a result of which a great deal of time is lost and certain tasks take too long. She illustrates her point by giving a recent concrete example of such a chaotic approach and its consequences. Hank immediately begins to defend himself by saying that he had, at the time, been swamped by urgent tasks. Margret suppresses her inclination to respond in an irritated manner. She tries to take Hank's remark seriously and asks what is causing this distress. Later, she asks his input on how it might be prevented altogether. Hank now feels that he is being listened to. He calms down and puts forward some useful suggestions that could help him to do his work better.

5.7.3   Improving formal communication

In small organisations, it is quite easy to communicate in a direct manner. This applies to both informal and formal communication. Problems with

© Noordhoff Uitgevers bv

formal communication start to increase as organisations grow in size and complexity. Vertical communication is then usually indirect and that can have negative consequences, as we have described. There are several ways of countering the disadvantages of indirect communication. These are:

- **Structural changes.** Two structural changes can make communication less indirect. These are:
  1 Make the organisational structure flatter, so that there are fewer hierarchical levels. The number of nodes through which the information must flow will then be reduced and there will be less distortion.
  2 Split the organisation into semi-autonomous units (divisions, business units). Because these units are smaller and less complex, formal communication within them likewise has to go through fewer nodes.
- **Use of other forms of communication.** Indirect communication can be avoided if the senior people in the organisation inform employees about things that are important for the organisation as a whole and/or for the employees in particular by making use of their internal electronic network, or by holding information meetings with employees. Finally, employees can be involved in important changes, such as reorganisations, by placing them in teams. These teams must then indicate how improvements can best be effected (see also chapter 11).

EXAMPLE 5.23

Involvement

A company sometimes suffers interruptions in production because there are too many changes of schedule, the supply of materials is unreliable and broken-down machines are not repaired quickly enough. Management decides that something must be done about this and puts together a team of employees from the production department, the technical department, the planning department and logistical services. This team must put forward proposals for reducing interruptions to production.

Senior managers must avoid getting their information only from the management level directly below them and placing themselves at the mercy of the interests of that management level. They will be better informed about what is happening in the organisation if they are also prepared to communicate directly with management and employees lower down the organisation (management by walking around). This not only counters the distortion of information, it also ensures that employees feel they are taken seriously and are more involved in the organisation.

Senior managers can promote openness in communication by explicitly indicating that criticism may be made of their decisions, of their style of leadership and of their plans. In this way, they show that they do not want yes-men around them and that the opinions of others matter. The example set by senior managers is decisive in the creation of openness in communication throughout the whole organisation.

Tips for managers

As a manager/supervisor, you can improve your interpersonal communication by undergoing training in the areas of sender skills, listening skills and giving feedback.

Improving sender skills
The following tips can help to improve your sender skills:
- Indicate the goals of your message, mention your motives.
- State your message clearly and concisely.
- Ask if the message has been understood or how it came across.

Improving listening skills
The following tips can help to improve your listening skills:
- Pay attention to the sender, for example by maintaining eye contact, nodding and making sounds such as 'mmm, mmm,' or 'yes, yes' to encourage the other to continue.
- Pay attention to non-verbal signals.
- If the message is not clear, ask questions.
- With a longer message, give a summary and ask if it is correct.
- Indicate what feelings the message evokes in you.

Giving and receiving feedback in the correct manner
The following tips can help to improve the way you give feedback:
- Concentrate on giving feedback about specific behaviour.
- Only give negative feedback about behaviour if the receiver is able to change it.
- Keep the behaviour and the person separate.
- Indicate your own feelings and underlying assumptions.

The following tips can help you to improve the way you receive feedback:
- Avoid immediately going on the defensive and allow the giver of feedback to finish.
- If necessary, ask questions about exactly what the other means or ask for concrete examples.
- Indicate your own feelings about the feedback.

Improving communication within the organisation
Formal communication can be improved by taking the following measures:
- Try to have information dissemination throughout the organisation via as few nodes as possible.
- Adapt the manner of communication to the nature of the message. Preferably make use of direct and oral communication and ask for feedback. Use written communication only for factual messages.
- Counter incorrect rumours by being open about such things as the course of action to be followed, the necessity for reorganisation and its consequences.
- Encourage critical contributions from employees by explicitly asking for them and responding to them seriously.

5

© Noordhoff Uitgevers bv

Summary

5

▶ The exchange of information between two or more people is called communication.

▶ Verbal communication is accompanied by non-verbal signals. These are communicated by:
- intonation
- posture
- gestures
- body movement
- facial expressions
- eye contact

▶ Communication can have four aspects:
- a factual aspect
- an expressive aspect
- a relational aspect
- an appealing aspect

▶ The exchange of information in organisations takes place:
- via fixed channels (formal communication)
- randomly (informal communication)

▶ Informal communication can spread through the organisation in different ways, such as via:
- the simple chain
- the gossip chain
- the probability chain
- the cluster chain

▶ Advantages of informal communication are:
- employees are better and more quickly informed
- employees can resolve problems more quickly

▶ Negative effects of informal communication are:
- lack of openness
- rumour formation
- gossip

▶ Impediments to interpersonal communication can be caused by:
- the sender
- interference
- the receiver
- the feedback

▶ Interference (physical, psychological or semantic) causes poor reception of the message.

▶ Defective decoding of the message by the receiver can be caused by:
- a lack of knowledge about the subject of the message
- the state of mind of the receiver
- a poor relationship between the sender and the receiver
- the situation in which the message is received

▶ Interpersonal communication can be improved if:
- the sender indicates his goal
- the sender is clear, concise and open
- the receiver has sufficient listening skills
- the receiver gives feedback on how the message has been understood

Assignments

5.1 Five people are dissatisfied with communication within their company. Read the following text and think about the background to each complaint:
- A grumbles to a colleague that she receives too little information from her boss about the decisions taken by the organisation. She is expected to pass on information in this area, but her boss rarely does this himself. This means that she learns about things too late, when she would have liked to participate at an earlier stage.
- B complains about poor communication with his boss. He has received a written instruction to do certain jobs, although other activities are not yet finished. Should he put these tasks aside?
- C thinks it is impossible to consult with management. They do not listen to anyone. Once management has formed an opinion, it is difficult to change it.
- D is annoyed with the many emails found in his in-box every day. Most of them are so unimportant that they can be deleted straight away.
- E finds that her colleagues communicate very little. They never give out useful information spontaneously. Everything proceeds strictly factually and according to fixed codes. It is impossible to find out what people really think. She noticed that there was a lot of gossip about her in the beginning.

a Indicate what went wrong in the communication process in situations A to E.
b Indicate what can be done to improve communication.

5.2 Jones is little liked by his subordinates. He is a know-it-all who cannot handle criticism. He intimidates his subordinates with this attitude and they prefer to avoid him. If he comes into the department, conversations cease and everyone pays attention to their work. No one speaks to him or asks him anything. For most of the day, he sits in his office with the door closed. When he wishes to discuss something with someone, the person must go to his office. A great deal of information is communicated via email. A regular progress meeting is held in the department but Jones leaves this to his assistant. He gives his assistant instructions about the work to be done.

a What means of communication does Jones use?
b What impediments are there to interpersonal communication between Jones and his subordinates?
c What impediments of an organisational nature are there to communication between Jones and his subordinates?

5.3 The use of social media, such as Facebook, has consequences for an organisation.

   a Do employees in an organisation change the way they interact following the use of social media and, if so, how?

   b Which possibilities and restrictions to communication within an organisation occur due to the use of social media?

   c What skills do people need to competently use (confidential) information within an organisation via social media?

6

Power and leadership

- What is power?
- What sources of power can a person have and what means of power are derived from these sources?
- In what ways is power used and what effects do they have?
- What is leadership?
- What are the different styles of leadership?
- Which forms of leadership are effective and what factors influence them?
- How can leadership be effective?

© Noordhoff Uitgevers bv

New plans

An information meeting is held for middle management. The new managing director has been in post for six months and at this meeting she wants to present her action plan and also announce a reorganisation. In her assessment, the government is going to want more and more from the organisation. The government, however, is not prepared to provide any more financial resources for this. There will consequently be no expansion of staff. This means that existing staff has to work more efficiently. She is therefore presenting a plan for achieving more result-oriented work. Middle managers will be paid according to results, their targets having been established in advance. To this end, they will have more say in how resources are spent (budgeting).

In answer to a question from a manager as to exactly how those responsible for the results can contribute to better and more efficient working, the managing director gives a lengthy and woolly explanation that leaves the questioner none the wiser. Someone else asks if his departmental budget will give any latitude to recruit more people. This is answered in the negative. It is not the intention to provide more resources; the limited resources must be used better.

Afterwards, several heads of department stay behind to talk among themselves. They honestly do not see how the reorganisation can contribute to greater efficiency. It seems more likely that they have now been landed with a problem that senior management cannot resolve itself. However, they will wait and see how it goes.

6.1 Power and influence

EXAMPLE 6.1

With renewed reluctance

After the presentation of the intended reorganisation, the middle managers stay behind, grumbling. Some of them cannot see the connection between result-oriented work and the aimed-for efficiencies. Others have the impression that the managing director's wants above all to make her mark and others think that this umpteenth organisational change will only obstruct current activities and thus cause greater inefficiency. Despite their grumbling, they accept the reorganisation because no one has the courage to object.

This example shows how people can sometimes be influenced against their will. How is it that the managing director can push through her wishes and get her subordinates to do things they cannot not see the use of? The answer to this is power. Power is the ability of person A to make person B do something that he would otherwise not have done. Power provides a person with the opportunity to exert influence over others. Only when this potential is actually used, however, is power converted into influence.

Power

Influence

Why do some people allow themselves to be influenced by others? In many cases, they do so if they think it will help them obtain something they want. Person A has power over person B if A can provide something that B finds attractive. This involves an exchange relationship. The power of A over B increases:

Exchange relationship

- the more attractive the resources possessed by person A are to person B;
- the more difficult the attractive resources possessed by A are to obtain elsewhere.

EXAMPLE 6.2

Loyalty?

Quite a few of the middle managers from the first example will nevertheless loyally go along with the proposed reorganisation when it comes down to it. Too many critical comments about the reorganisation could damage their position in the organisation. By cooperating, they hope not to spoil their chances of promotion.

6.2 Sources of power

How do people in organisations acquire the ability to influence others? They obtain this ability from the sources of power they have available. A source of power provides a person with the means of power that can be called on to influence others. In organisations, a distinction can be made between sources of power derived from the position a person occupies in an organisation and from a person's personal qualities.

Source of power

Means of power

6.2.1 Position-related means of power

In organisations, supervisors and managers occupy positions which come with certain authorities. Examples include the coordinator of a taskforce, the chairperson of a committee, or the manager of a department. These authorities present individuals with position-related means of power.

Position-related means of power

EXAMPLE 6.3

Who is leading?

The head of the Acquisitions department has been assigned to manage that department by management. They have authorised him to determine which tasks his employees should perform. He can assign tasks to those employees and review their work.

The following means of power can be assigned to a position:
- Economic means. These provide a manager with, for example, the power to give employees a higher salary and better working conditions or to make sure they achieve promotion. With economic means of power, a manager is able to reward or penalise a subordinate. If the subordinate knows that a critical attitude is penalised, he will allow himself to be influenced by his manager. This is a case of coercive power. He conforms out of fear of the negative consequences of not doing so. If the subordinate primarily does what his boss wants because of the rewards that flow from it, this is reward power.

EXAMPLE 6.4

No means of power

The head of the workshop complains about his lack of assigned resources to his wife. His management has given him too few economic means to influence his subordinates. He does not get to determine promotions or fixed contracts, since those decision are made higher up the food chain. His employees therefore do not take him seriously and, when it suits them, cut corners where they can.

- Informational means. Managers are in positions that provide them with information that subordinates do not have but which could be important to them. The higher a person's position in an organisation, the more access he has to important internal and external information. Knowledge is in many cases power. By providing or withholding information from subordinates, managers are able to emphasise the necessity for certain measures or certain activities, for example, and thereby influence the behaviour of subordinates in the desired direction. The information that a manager has can be used to convince subordinates that it is necessary to do a bit extra or work overtime. The use of informational means to exercise power can consciously or unconsciously lead to the manipulation of information. For example, to convince a subordinate of the importance of working overtime, certain facts could be exaggerated and others obscured.

EXAMPLE 6.5

Are things really going all that badly?

The managing director gathers his team. He paints them a very grim picture of the state of the organisation, and emphasises the inevitable resulting reorganisation. Some employees feel he is exaggerating; they are of the opinion that the suggested

reorganisation is much too drastic. Waiting for the economic situation to improve would also be an option. Most employees, however, are swayed by the director's bleak outlook; they place their support behind the suggested reorganisation.

- **Legitimacy.** If subordinates consider that higher-ranking individuals should automatically have the authority to decide certain matters on the basis of their position, this gives those higher-ranking individuals **legitimate power**. Once power has been legitimised, it becomes 'automatic power'. It is, for example, no longer necessary for a manager to use other means of power to get something done, such as rewarding or convincing someone.

In general, a person's legitimate power increases as they assume a higher position in an organisation. Hierarchical layering in organisations consequently creates power inequality. The automatic nature of power inequality is not a phenomenon that is encountered only in organisations. Power inequality occurs in all kinds of situations and is embedded in our culture. It is, for example, more or less taken for granted that parents have the right to decide for their children, that teachers determine what happens in the class, that a referee makessure a game proceeds according to the rules.

Power inequality

6

As a doctor, she has the power of expertise. She has positional power as well.

The degree of power inequality, and consequently the obedience shown by a subordinate to a higher-ranking individual, is not the same in every culture. Research by Hofstede (1980) into the acceptance of power inequality has shown that this differs from country to country (see Table 6.1).

TABLE 6.1 Scores of 10 countries for power difference

	Power difference
Guatemala	95
India	77
Singapore	74
Turkey	66
Belgium	65
Japan	54
United States	40
Netherlands	38
Great Britain	35
Denmark	18

A high score in Table 6.1 indicates greater differences in power between managers and employees (see paragraph 8.8).

6.2.2   Person-related means of power

Personal-related means of power are the means that people derive from their personal qualities. The following means can be used by employees and supervisors in organisation:

1 *Work-related expertise.* This consists of the knowledge and experience people can contribute to ensure the work is performed properly. This knowledge and experience enables a person to teach others, to instruct, or to help in the execution of activities.

EXAMPLE 6.6

Asking for advice

Mariam is unsure of the best way to draft a tender. She asks her superior for advice. She knows his expertise is impressive, and so is his experience with commercial companies. She is therefore more than happy to follow his lead.

---

2 *Relational expertise.* This is the ability to create and maintain a pleasant atmosphere. Employees are less likely to refuse requests by someone they like and appreciate.
3 *Collaborative expertise.* This the ability to ensure discussion and interpersonal reactions proceed well. Someone able to give proper leadership during group meetings and who offers the right task-oriented

and group-oriented contributions (see paragraph 4.9) are able to influence discussions.

4   *Appeal or charisma.* This is the ability to influence others based on one's appeal or charisma in the eyes of the other party. The greater someone's appeal, the more others are willing to do for them. Exceptionally high appeal is also known as charisma. Charismatic individuals are able to make others their followers.

Personal qualities must first be displayed and recognised before they can be used as means of power.

6.2.3   Summary overview of means of power

Figure 6.1 offers a schematic overview of means of power.

FIGURE 6.1 Means of power

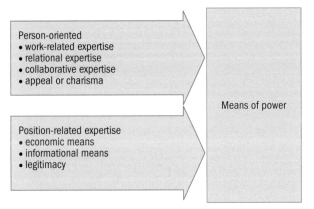

Source: Alblas (2010)

6.3 Use of power

How do people in organisations handle their means of power when they want to get others to do what is required of them? When is the attempt to influence successful and when does it elicit resistance or dissatisfaction?

EXAMPLE 6.7

Dissatisfaction

During a progress meeting, it turns out there will be overtime required next week, because otherwise a certain order will not be delivered on time. The boss says that everyone must make a contribution and that there will certainly have to be overtime on three nights. He can only be there two nights himself because he has other important appointments. Some team members grumble. They will have to miss a football training session but the boss does not regard this as significant. What must be done, must be done, and that's all there is to it. This attitude provokes a great deal of dissatisfaction.

In what ways is power used and what consequences do they have? Emans (1988) questioned management in all kinds of organisations about the ways in which they attempted to get their subordinates to do what they required of them. Four ways of using power could be identified from their answers:
- **Cooperative use of power.** People are persuaded to do something by discussing the implications with them, by indicating the benefit or the necessity of a certain measure or action and by making them enthusiastic about it. With cooperative use of power, both informational and economic means of power can be exerted. In the first case, the reason why something must be done can be explained. In the second case, it can be made clear to a subordinate that cooperation makes sense because there they will receive something in exchange (reward power).

EXAMPLE 6.8

Indicating the necessity

The managing director in the first example tried to persuade middle management to support her reorganisation proposal by indicating that the organisation would otherwise end up in difficulties. Something therefore had to be done and she proposed result-oriented work as a useful means of achieving better performance. She also indicated that middle management would be given more power to organise the work within their respective departments.

- **Confrontational use of power.** People are pressed into doing something by being threatened with negative consequences, such as a poor assessment or less chance of a bonus or promotion. With confrontational use of power, coercive power is exerted.
- **Formal use of power.** It is pointed out that a person has been given the right by the organisation to say what must be done. Reference may also be made to existing rules and norms. With formal use of power, legitimate sources of power are exerted.

EXAMPLE 6.9

Formal rules

A salesman would like to give a new client priority and he asks the head of the Production Planning department to take this into account. The latter refuses this request, informing him that the existing instructions state that orders must be handled in chronological sequence. The new client's order will therefore not be given priority.

- **Appealing to emotions.** Someone appeals to friendship, mutual relationships, loyalty or to a person's specific expertise to persuade that person to do something for them. When appealing to emotions, use is made of one's own attractiveness and relational expertise.

EXAMPLE 6.10

Flattery

The head of the Administration Department is trying to persuade an employee to take on an urgent job by indicating that this employee is the only person in the department who has the necessary skills. He also admits that he is making this request somewhat diffidently because he knows he is overloading her. But he would still appreciate it if she would do this for him. The employee feels flattered by his remarks about her expertise and, because she likes her boss a lot, she accedes to his request.

According to Emans, the four forms of use of power can be placed in two dimensions:
- businesslike versus unbusinesslike
- cooperative versus competitive (see Figure 6.2).

FIGURE 6.2 Forms of use of power in two dimensions

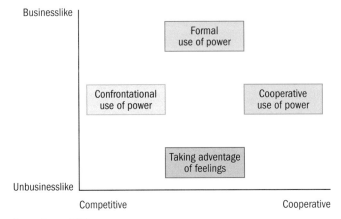

Source: Emans, 1988

Do the managers of organisations prefer to use their power in certain ways? Various researchers have shown that the cooperative use of power is by far the most popular. Yukl et al. (1996) found that the use of informational sources of power to get something done is applied in more than half of all influence situations. Confrontational use of power occurs in only a very few cases and then only if other methods have had no effect.

6.4 Effects of use of power

Why is the cooperative use of power greatly preferred and confrontational use of power almost solely applied when other forms of influence do not work? According to Emans (1988), this is because managers believe that they will achieve the best effect this way. They also suppose that they can build up or

Effect

Good
relationships

'Soft' route

maintain good relationships with their subordinates in this way. Research by Yukl et al. (1993) shows that employees' cooperation can best be obtained via a 'soft' route, by consulting them, motivating them and negotiating with them. According to Veen (1979), managers in organisations prefer a form of influence that is unnoticed or invisible whenever possible. The system of rules and regulations in organisations is directed towards getting as much as possible to happen automatically, without personal influence. Only when employees deviate from these rules or where the rules give no clear indication of the required behaviour will influence have to be exerted. Means of power must be used as frugally as possible. Yukl et al. (1996) found in their research that a manager first attempts soft methods of influence, such as discussion and persuasion or appealing to loyalty and good relationships.

Erosion

The confrontational use of power is avoided because it can strengthen the opposition of ideas and wishes and lead to a deterioration in relationships. A poor relationship with his subordinates means that a manager can make less use of other means of power, such as attractiveness, expertise and information. The manager's position of power is hence subject to erosion. The confrontational use of power puts a manager and his subordinates into a negative spiral (see Figure 6.3).

6

FIGURE 6.3 Positive and negative effects of use of power

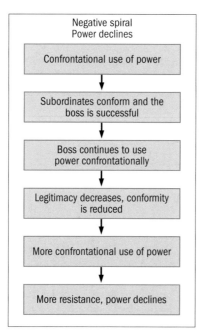
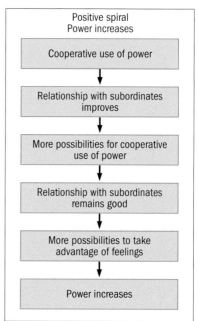

Source: Emans, 1988

Sometimes a confrontational approach is the only way to accomplish something. To make sure that their power is not eroded, a manager must make efforts to improve their relationship with a subordinate as soon as possible after the confrontation, so that the other means of power can be reused.

6.5 Use of power for political purposes

The sources of power that are attached to positions by an organisation are intended to be used in the general interest, to match the behaviour and contributions of employees to each other and to gear them to the organisational goals.

It would be wonderful if all members of an organisation and all the groups within it were of one mind and collaborated harmoniously. However, the constant need for decision-making means that differences in ideas and interests among people and groups inevitably arise. People and departments can become competitors when it comes to making decisions about a course of action to be taken, the structure of the organisation, the division of resources, the appointment of staff, the promotion mechanism and the allocation of pay for performance. In this type of situation, the decision-making process and the exercise of power and influence are no longer concerned with the general interest but with personal and group interests.

When people use their power in their own interests, they are engaging in power games. Robbins (2005) defines power games as follows:

> Power games are the use of power to influence the ratio between rewards and costs as far as possible in one's own (or the group's) favour

---

EXAMPLE 6.11

Power games

The head of the Sales Department is retiring in six months' time. One of the salesmen would like to be considered as a replacement for the job. To this end, he tries to present himself as a good salesman and a person with organisational qualities. He begins to highlight his successes and hide his failures. He also tries to butter up the departmental head by doing everything that is asked of him and to win over some of his colleagues by being extra nice to them.

There are many ways in which people can increase their political influence in organisations. Buchanan and Badham (1999b) indicate the following techniques:
- Improve image: radiate confidence, wear the right clothing, support the right actions, follow group norms, promote one's own contribution and reputation.
- Informational manipulation: do not pass on unfavourable information, retain useful information for oneself, only offer positive interpretations of one's own behaviour, overwhelm other using complex technical data.
- Turn others into scapegoats: ensure that others are to blame for any problems and that success is only due to one's own contribution.

- Connect: engage with important persons in the organisation and support their assessments and wishes. Strive for coalitions with others in order to get things done.
- Network: fraternise with people in important positions.
- Compromise: consent to the wishes of others in unimportant matters to use as leverage in important ones.
- Apply rules selectively: the reason for rejecting a request should be that it is 'against the rules', but if it comes from an important person it should be granted because of 'special circumstances'.
- Other tactics: undermine others' expertise, use force where necessary, play off certain parties against each other, use gossip to vilify others, use others to do the dirty work, keep a black book.

The effect of the use of these tactics is highly dependent on the organisational culture in which they are applied (Chapter 8). The acceptance or rejection of a certain technique relates to the value and norms that determine how people in organisations interact with each other.

Political behaviour is always found in organisations. The extent to which is occurs depends on the nature of the players and on situational circumstance. People differ in the extent to which they defend their own notions and interests at the cost of the general interest. Those with great **Ambition** ambition will be more forceful in the defence of the self than people who are more focussed on good mutual relationships. The organisational situation **Scarce resources** can also influence political behaviour. The allocation of scarce resources, such as promotions, HR and materials, and budget distribution, is a **Reorganisations** breeding ground for political games. This is also the case for reorganisations **Downsizing** and in situations in which downsizing causes jobs to be lost (Jex and Britt, 2014). Both employees and supervisors are each other's competitors in these **Performance** situations. Lastly, performance assessments can also be a cause for political **assessments** behaviour, particularly if these assessments cannot be made completely objectively.

EXAMPLE 6.12

Criticising the assessment

A number of employees in a department are grumbling to one another around the coffee machine about the way their annual performance assessment has been carried out. They think their rewards depend more on how much the boss likes them and on how docile they are than on their actual performance. They dare not express their criticism to the boss, however, for fear of an even worse assessment next time.

Senior management can also get involved in power games if they see the organisation as an opportunity to show how productive or effective they are and use it as a stepping-stone to a more senior position with another organisation. They can also be motivated by a reward structure (bonuses) to look after their own interests first.

EXAMPLE 6.13

Government measures

Senior managers can be tempted by big money and offer too little resistance to hostile takeovers. The government has therefore implemented measures to prevent senior managers from having a financial interest in the firm.

6.6 Abuse of power

For managers and employees who are adept at the political use of power, power games have no negative consequences. After all, they are the people who can most profit from them. For those who are not so adept or who are less focused on their own interests and more on the general interest, power games primarily evoke dissatisfaction and are perceived as an abuse of power.

Abuse of power

EXAMPLE 6.14

Intimidating behaviour

6

The head of a sales department keeps making advances to a female sales manager who has just been hired and is on a six-month trial. She feels intimidated by her superior's behaviour, but she knows that he is the one who will decide whether she is taken on permanently, and she really wants this job. She therefore finds it difficult to decide how to handle this situation.

An abuse of power is also perceived if employees think that matters such as promotions, assessments, the allocation of people and resources and the application of rules are no longer fair as a result of power games.

EXAMPLE 6.15

Favouritism

A team leader is retiring and their position will become vacant. Up to now, the rule has been that the most experienced team member is promoted. In this case, however, the head of the department chose to appoint their nephew, who was in another team. This caused indignation among the team's members.

The abuse of power can lead to perceived injustice. There is distributive injustice if people have the feeling that their rewards are no longer related to the effort that must be produced and to the rewards received by others.

Distributive injustice

© Noordhoff Uitgevers bv

Procedural injustice

There is procedural injustice if people have the feeling that the application of rules and procedures and the manner in which decisions are taken are unfair. This can be the case if people believe that they have been unfairly assessed, that rules apply to low-ranking staff but management pays no attention to them, or that rules are constantly adjusted for the benefit of management.

● www.beroepseer.nl

Abuse of power by managers towards employees more common than thought

The taboo around the abuse of power by managers in the business world needs to be broken. Research by lawyer and organisational expert Peter Anthonisse shows that the abuse of power is a major social issue that can be found in virtually any organisation. Both the employees and companies it affects experience its negative consequences. Antonisse gained his doctorate for his PhD thesis *Abuse of power by managers – The victim's perspective* in May of 2015 – the thesis is currently available online.

According to Anthonisse, virtually all organisations are subject to (the threat of) the abuse of power: 'Organisations should not be wondering if, but rather where, the abuse of power exists.'

In an interview with Pieter van der Meulen for the VNO-NCW West entrepreneurial network, Anthonisse mentions that, for the purposes of his research, he defined the abuse of power according to two criteria: 'Abuse is defined as a situation in which a manager's behaviour affects an employee's human dignity, for example if an employee is forced to work below their competency, or as a situation in which an employee suffers damages, for example as a result of losing their employment. It often starts as a difference of professional opinion, which subsequently continues to escalate. In none of the cases I looked into did the manager take any steps to de-escalate the situation, even though this is part of their job description.' Anthonisse suspects that the abuse of power by managers is a phenomenon that is much more common than had always been thought. 'Recent international studies among 30,000 participants shows that 55% of people feel that managers are partly responsible for creating a negative work atmosphere. This was as high as 68% in the Netherlands. And the resulting consequences affect more than just the employees concerned.'

The abuse of power can result in less work satisfaction and poorer performance by employees (Kacmar et al., 1999) and in less commitment to the organisation (Lee, 2000; Siegel et al., 2005). The abuse of power can also **Legitimate power** reduce the legitimate power of management. A manager who is authorised to select people for extra work will lose his authority if in the eyes of his subordinates he does this in a dishonest or unfair manner.

6.7 Leadership in organisations

Effective collaboration of people in organisations can only be established if the activities are distributed across those people properly, and if those activities are aligned with each other and with the goals of the organisation. In a small group, this distribution and alignment can be established relatively easily.

EXAMPLE 6.16

Friendly collaboration

While the waiters are serving meals in a restaurant, they notice that there are many more people in one area of the restaurant than in the others. The waiter in the busy area is struggling to serve all his customers properly. Other waiters, who are less busy, see that their colleague is having difficulty in coping with the work and take over some of his tasks. By doing so, they reduce his work pressure, giving him more time to serve the tables properly.

In an organisation that consists of multiple organisational units (teams, departments, agencies), employees no longer have access to everything that needs to happen to align activities to each other and to organisational goals. In this situation, people are assigned to lead others. The tasks and positions of leaders in organisations depend on their position in the organisation.

Storey (2011) differentiates between leadership of an organisation as a whole and leadership of organisational units:

1 *Leadership of entire organisations.* Top executives who manage the entire organisation are tasked with maintaining the relationship between the organisation and its environment. On the one hand, they have to be able to visualise the opportunities and threats to and from the environment; on the other, they have to be aware of the organisation's strengths and weaknesses. This involves interpreting data and estimating the significance of situations. Based on these assessments, executives have to established the goals they can and want the organisation to achieve (mission) and the methods by which those goals are to be achieved (strategy). Top executives should be able to present a clear **mission** to others and to ensure that other supervisors and employees follow and support that mission. They must also be able to design the organisation in such a way that the goals that are set can be reached through mutual effort. This involves **motivating** (see paragraph 2.4) and **designing** (see paragraph 7.1).

2 *Leadership of an organisational unit.* This involves leadership of a team, department, or agency. These leaders are responsible for day-to-day events in their organisational unit. They must establish, plan, and distribute activities. They must also encourage and support the execution of the activities. Lastly, they verify whether the execution of the activities proceeds as planned and whether the results correspond to the goals that have been set. If this is not the case, adjustments are required. This concerns the **task-oriented activities** of a manager. Leaders of organisational units are also responsible for a proper working atmosphere. This atmosphere is needed to commit people to organisations and to keep

them committed. If the atmosphere is good, there are fewer conflicts, and those conflicts that do occur escalate less quickly (see paragraphs 10.7 and 10.10). The manager uses their **relational activities** to establish this atmosphere. These activities consist of such things as showing a personal interest, being friendly, listening well, helping others, and frequently take part in deliberations.

Figure 6.4 shows a schematic overview of task-oriented and relational activities.

FIGURE 6.4 Task-oriented and relational activities of leaders of organisational units

Of particular importance is the fact that a leader should ensure there are adequate manpower, capacity, and resources for their group (department) to be able to achieve an effective execution of their required activities. Leaders who succeed in arranging these matters show their (group) department that they are able to throw their weight around upstairs. In addition, this improves the leader's influence among their subordinates.

6.8 Leadership and effectiveness

Effective leadership

A great deal of research has been done into the question 'What makes a person a successful leader?' The research has taken different approaches, focusing on the following criteria:
- **Personality traits.** According to this approach, success is ascribed to specific personality traits. Because these personality traits are inborn, it is assumed that some people are born leaders.
- **Behaviour.** Success is ascribed to a specific manner of operating. It is the style of leadership that determines success or failure.
- **Situation.** Success is determined by the requirements the situation makes on the leader. Some situations are more favourable to success than others.

6.8.1 Leadership and personality traits

Do some people have certain inborn characteristics that make them eminently suitable to be leaders? Research into the relationship between

Personality traits

personality traits and leadership ability has produced no clear picture. In different studies, more than 100 personality traits have been measured; however, it appears that not all great leaders have the same characteristics. Two successful leaders can have quite different characteristics, while of two people with the same characteristics, only one may be a good leader. Despite these conflicting findings, several characteristics have been found to be shared by many leaders – though not by all. Yukl (1998) concluded that the following personality traits were connected with effective leadership:

- A high level of energy.
- A high level of stress tolerance, self-confidence, integrity and emotional stability.
- The ability to motivate without self-promotion.
- A low need to be liked.
- High technical, interpersonal and conceptual skills.

The analysis of leadership on the basis of characteristics starts from the assumption that human characteristics are inborn and stable and that certain characteristics favour leadership. A study by Shelley et al. (1991) shows that a connection between the above-mentioned personality traits and successful leadership is sometimes, but not always, found. An explanation for these conflicting research results could be that personality traits do not precisely determine how people behave in every situation. People with the same personality traits can therefore differ in the manner in which they behave in a certain situation. It is therefore more useful to analyse what behaviour makes a person a good leader than to look at personality traits.

Research into the relationship between personal characteristics and effective leadership took a new course around the year 2000. The question became: what are the qualities required for a person to develop themselves as a leader? What are the characteristics that cause someone to rise to the surface as the leader of a group or organisation? In their study, Colbert et al. (2012) conclude that this is a matter of intelligence, a strong need to dominate, a strong ability to operate autonomously, and an ability to correctly evaluate interpersonal relationships. Leaders are also extroverted, emotionally stable, thorough, an open to experience (see paragraph 1.3). According to Van Iddekinge et al. (2009) these personal characteristics are what allows people to develop the skills and capacities needed to encourage other employees to display the type of behaviour required for quality team performance.

6.8.2   Leadership styles

People can provide leadership in very different ways. The characteristic manner in which the head of administration and the head of personnel and organisation provide leadership to their employees is called their leadership style. Research into leadership styles began in the 1970s. Stogdill (1974) identified two principal styles:

Leadership styles

- **Relationship-oriented style.** This is the tendency of leaders to orient their behaviour towards the promotion of good relationships with and among their subordinates. Good relationships are characterised by mutual trust, two-way communication and respect for the ideas and feelings of others. Leaders who score highly on this style make time to listen to their subordinates, are prepared to allow themselves to be influenced, and are friendly and easily approachable.

© Noordhoff Uitgevers bv

- **Task-oriented style.** The tendency of leaders to orient their behaviour towards the proper execution of tasks by their subordinates. Leaders that score highly on this style are highly focused on planning, instruction, description and setting norms for performance and control.

Research by Bales (1965) has shown that task-oriented and relationship-oriented leadership are not usually combined in one person. A leader who is highly task-oriented is usually not highly relationship-oriented.

Tannenbaum and Schmidt (1973) produced a different classification of styles of leadership. They identified the following two styles:
- **Directive style.** The leader give direction to activities by determining what has to be done, how it must be done and by whom. He communicates this to his subordinates.
- **Participative style.** The leader involves his subordinates in establishing the work process in his department.

The characteristics of these two styles of leadership are shown in Figure 6.5.

FIGURE 6.5 Directive and participative styles

Leader takes all decisions	Leader asks staff for information, but then takes a decision himself	Leader consults his staff and they decide jointly	Leader leaves decisions to his staff

Directive leadership ← → Participative leadership

Source: Tannenbaum & Schmidt, 1973

The two classifications described reflect different aspects of leadership. The classification task-oriented/relationship-oriented is based on what the leader focuses their attention on, in other words: *where* the leader exercises their influence. The classification directive/participative indicates *how* the leader exercises their influence; it concerns the degree of influence the leader wishes to have on the behaviour of their staff. It therefore looks as though the two classifications are incompatible, but this is not entirely true. According to Dessler (1980), there is some overlap between the classifications. In many cases, a participative style is coupled with a relationship-oriented style of leadership. Leaders who are oriented towards creating and maintaining good relationships with their subordinates will usually also consult them more and employ a participative style.

There have also been studies examining whether a directive style is better for the satisfaction and productivity of employees than a participative one. An overview of 60 studies on this topic led Locke and Schweiger (1979) to the following conclusions (see Figure 6.6):
- In 60% of studies, a participative style leads to greater satisfaction that a directive style. In 30% of cases, there is no difference; in 10%, there is less satisfaction.

- In 22% of studies, a participative style leads to greater performance than a directive style. In 56% of cases, no difference was found; in 22% of cases, performance was lower.

FIGURE 6.6 Difference in effectiveness between directive and participative leadership on the performance and satisfaction of group members

Performance	In 22% of studies greater in participative leadership	In 56% no difference between participative and directive leadership	In 22% greater in directive leadership
Satisfaction	In 60% of studies greater in participative leadership	In 30% no difference between participative and directive leadership	In 30% no difference between participative and directive leadership

Source: Alblas (2010)

It seems as though a relationship-oriented style, which is generally coupled with a participative approach, usually has a positive effect on the satisfaction of subordinates. A confusing picture arises, however, when the relationship-oriented/participative style and the task-oriented/directive style are compared in relation to their effect on performance. It appears that they are not much different.

How is it that a certain style of leadership sometimes has a positive effect on productivity and satisfaction but not always? Do circumstances play a part in this? Fernandez and Vecchio (1997) found that, with low-ranking employees, a task-oriented style of leadership was more strongly associated with satisfaction than a relationship-oriented style. For higher-ranking employees, the association was the opposite. The association between participative leadership and work satisfaction should also be qualified. Andriessen and Drenth (1992) concluded that this association is primarily found in employees who have to perform tasks that have not yet been fully established. These findings show that the nature of the situation plays a part in the effects of a certain style of leadership. Our attention therefore shifts to the question of which style of leadership is best in what type of situation.

6.8.3   Leadership and situation

In the first example, the new managing director is immediately faced with a government that is demanding more from her organisation without any increase in funding or resources. She has to act decisively in this situation because otherwise the organisation runs into trouble. Her predecessor was in a better position. He received sufficient resources from the government and was consequently able to leave the organisation undisrupted. Paying attention to the day-to-day running of the organisation was enough to keep it on the right course. His style of leadership was relational and participative.

What is a good style of leadership in one situation is not necessarily so in a different situation.

EXAMPLE 6.17

Relationship-oriented style

The head of a Production Department does not have to tell his staff how to do their work. The operational work is fully computerised and his staff are merely inspectors. They walk around, checking that the production process is running smoothly, and they intervene if breakdowns occur. How they must intervene is detailed in procedures. Task-oriented leadership is

hardly necessary and directive leadership is not appreciated. His staff know from their long experience exactly what must be done; they do not have to be told. They do, however, need a leader who interacts with them (relationship-oriented style) and creates a good atmosphere. This makes the monotony of the work more bearable.

Situational characteristics

What situational characteristics determine the style of leadership that is desirable and successful? We shall describe two approaches to this question.

Fiedler's contingency model

Contingency

Contingency model

Situational characteristics

Fiedler (1978) was the first to presume that the nature of the situation determines the style of leadership that is most successful. If the style of leadership matches the situation, there is contingency. In his contingency model, he describes three situational characteristics that, according to him, determine the style of leadership needed. These situational characteristics are:

1 The relationship between leader and subordinates. This relationship can be defined as the extent to which the leader is appreciated, trusted and accepted by his subordinates.
2 The task structure: the extent to which the task goals and requirements are clear. This concerns the manner in which the task must be executed. In a strong task structure, the task has been concretely and precisely specified, and the intended results have been clearly indicated. With a weak task structure, goals, results and methods are only roughly defined.
3 The positional power of the leader: the extent to which the position of the leader provides the necessary means of power.

To test his model, Fiedler studied different groups (basketball teams, survival groups, tank crews and the crews of bomber aircraft). He established how well these groups functioned and which style of leadership (task- or relationship-oriented) was employed.

The research produced the following conclusions:

Moderately favourable

- A relationship-oriented style of leadership produces the best group performance when the situational circumstances are moderately favourable: i.e. in which the relationship between leader and subordinates is neither good nor bad and where (a) the task is unstructured and positional power is weak or (b) the task is structured and positional power is strong.
Fiedler's supposition is that in these situations the leader must first improve relationships with the group (relationship-oriented leadership). Once relationships improve, the leader can focus on task execution.
- A task-oriented style produces the best group performances if the situational circumstances are either unfavourable or highly favourable.

The situational circumstances are unfavourable if the relationship between the leader and the group is poor, their positional power is limited and if there is a weak task structure. The supposition is that, under these circumstances, the subordinates' approach to their task must first be put right and only thereafter must attention be paid to the relationships. A task-oriented leader will ensure the best group performance in these circumstances.

Unfavourable

The situational circumstances are highly favourable if the relationship between the leader and the group is good, there is a strong task structure and the leader's positional power is strong. Under these circumstances, relationship-oriented leadership is not necessary. Even if the task is already structured, paying attention to task execution remains necessary (see Figure 6.7).

Highly favourable

FIGURE 6.7 Fiedler's contingency model

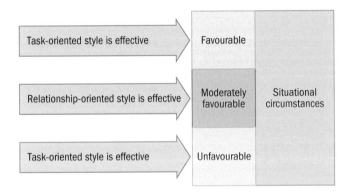

Later research into Fiedler's model confirms his results in some cases but not in others (Peters et al., 1985; Ayman et al., 1995).

The model of Hersey and Blanchard

Hersey and Blanchard (1988) likewise express the view that good leadership is situationally determined. In their model, the nature of the subordinates constitutes the most important situational characteristic. People often work together for years in a team or department. In the course of those years, they develop not only professionally but also in their attitude towards the work they are performing. If a leader is dealing with subordinates who have worked together for years and are able to plan and execute the work well without support or incentives, then hardly any leadership is necessary. Young employees who are just starting out, on the other hand, have to be trained. The manager must provide a large amount of task-oriented information, instruction, expertise or support. According to Hersey and Blanchard, the style of leadership chosen should depend on two factors:

Nature of the subordinates

1 **Ability.** The extent to which subordinates are able to independently execute their tasks properly and feel confident in doing so.
2 **Willingness.** The extent to which subordinates are motivated to perform well.

As far as the employees are concerned, the key factors are therefore 'capability' and 'willingness'.

Although these factors can be differentiated, it can nevertheless be supposed that they influence each other. Various combinations are possible, each constituting a certain level of 'task maturity'. Task maturity is the extent to which employees are able and willing to perform their activities.

Task maturity

Hersey and Blanchard identify four levels of task maturity. These are:
1 The employee is incapable and insecure and unwilling.
2 The employee is incapable and confident or motivated.
3 The employee is capable and insecure and unwilling.
4 The employee is capable and confident and motivated.

The role played by subordinates' different situations in Hersey and Blanchard's model is illustrated by the different leadership styles that go with them. The premise for this is: the more capable an employee becomes, the less their need for task-oriented leadership and the more a manager can leave to them. With unwilling or insecure employees, relationship-oriented leadership are necessary to motivate them and give them more confidence in their capabilities. With motivated and confident employees, this is less necessary. For each level of task maturity, Hersey and Blanchard indicated which style of leadership is the most effective:
1 **Telling.** Employees who are incapable, unwilling or insecure need strongly task-oriented leadership. The leader is effective if they indicate precisely what must be done and how tasks should be tackled.
2 **Selling.** Employees who are incapable but motivated and confident need a combination of task-oriented and relationship-oriented leadership. The leader should help them to increase their task abilities and convince them of their capacity to tackle the work well.
3 **Support.** Employees who are capable but unwilling or insecure need relationship-oriented leadership that is able to motivate and give them self-confidence. A manager is effective if they allows their subordinates to take part in decisions (participation) about the approach to the work and if they supports them in its performance.
4 **Delegation.** Employees who are capable, motivated and confident do not need any leadership. A manager who delegates the work to them is effective in this situation (see Figure 6.8).

FIGURE 6.8 Model of Hersey and Blanchard

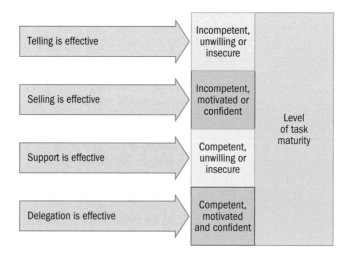

The accuracy of Hersey and Blanchard's model has partly been confirmed by research. De Jong et al. (1996) found that employees who had little ability needed more guidance. Research by De Vries et al. (2004) confirms this picture. Their results show that there is less need for leadership with employees who are capable and need independence.

In general, the research of De Vries et al. showed that the more influence a leader has with their superiors, so that they can act on behalf of their subordinates at a more senior level and provide information about what is going on at the top of the organisation, the more they will be appreciated. From the subordinates' perspective , the manner in which leadership should be exercised is primarily determined by their need for support, influence and information.

Barack Obama is a naturally inspiring leader.

6.9 Improving leadership

A leader is effective if they are able to ensure that both the productivity and the satisfaction of his subordinates is high. What actions are required to achieve this?

In this section, we discuss the following subjects: setting task goals and management by objectives, participative leadership, transformational leadership and leadership of self-managing teams.

Task goals

6.9.1   Setting task goals, and managing by objectives

As described in chapter 2, people are motivated to perform better if their tasks are challenging. According to Locke and Latham (1984), the challenge is increased if the following conditions are satisfied:
- The goal is high but remains feasible.
- The goal is precisely described.
- Regular feedback is given.
- The goal is accepted.

© Noordhoff Uitgevers bv

Management by objectives

How can a leader ensure that these conditions are met? Management by objectives (MBO) is a suitable method for this. The premise for the MBO method is that managers and their subordinates jointly establish the core objectives of their tasks and what results they are supposed achieve. The results to be achieved are subsequently defined as concretely as possible, in order to obtain a benchmark for progress checking. A schedule is then drawn up and the manner and timing of progress checks established. What ever support the subordinate expects from the leader to facilitate the unhindered performance of his tasks is also established. The MBO method involves setting sufficiently high goals, defining them precisely, getting them accepted by means of consultation with subordinates and providing sufficient feedback. A manager agrees on the following matters with their subordinates in stages (see Figure 6.9).

FIGURE 6.9 MBO, steps in the management process

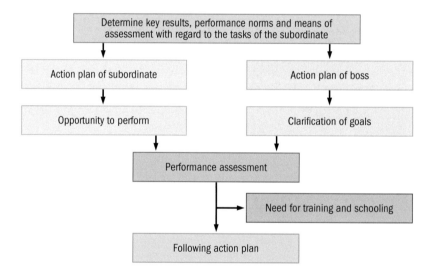

The application of the MBO method has several positive consequences for the performance of subordinates. Information is exchanged in the discussion process, thanks to which both parties obtain a better view of the task situation and the activities that must be performed within it. As a result, any excessively high expectations from the leader are adjusted and obstacles to effective task execution are identified and removed. The MBO method also offers the opportunity to assess performance accurately, because the level of performance has been precisely established. Depending on the situation and the nature of the tasks, a different amount of emphasis can be laid (Szilagyi, 1981) on for example, clarifying the goals and the schedule, or on improving control, feedback and support. By allowing subordinates to participate in the decision-making process, the leader increases the likelihood that the goals will be accepted. By also giving the subordinate the opportunity to define what support they expect from the leader in the performance of their task, the leader is better able to help the subordinate to perform well and enjoy the resulting rewards.

6.9.2   Participative leadership

The MBO method assumes participative leadership. Participative leadership is in line with a long tradition of research into the consequences of involving subordinates in the resolution of problems and decision-making. As early as the 1960s, a number of researchers emphasised that participative leadership has a positive influence on subordinates' performance and satisfaction. Miles (1965) speaks of the human resource model. Leadership should be focused on making optimal use of the knowledge and experience of subordinates. This can be done by involving them more in the planning and performance of their activities and giving them greater influence over the work they do. According to Miles, this increases the likelihood of good decision-making and support for these decisions. It also satisfies the need of the subordinates for autonomy, the chance to shape their own work situation as much as possible. By satisfying these needs, the leader increases motivation and thereby performance and, as a result, satisfaction.

Research into the effects of participative leadership has shown, however, that all the supposed positive consequences are by no means always in evidence. As described in subsection 6.9.2, participative leadership is just as often associated with deterioration as with improvement in productivity in comparison with directive leadership. Participative leadership does have an overwhelmingly positive effect on subordinates' satisfaction, however. Other factors in the situation must therefore play a part in influencing productivity. According to Veen et al. (1991), the positive consequences of participative leadership are derived from the following:

- Participative leadership improves information exchange in the organisation and this can result in better decision-making and better coordination of activities.
- Participative leadership facilitates the resolution of differences of opinion and improves relationships through the use of cooperative power.
- Participative leadership increases the involvement of employees in the decisions made and thereby their motivation to make an effort.

Participative leadership

Human resource model

Autonomy

Participative leadership

6

Unwilling employees are causing her a great deal of concern.
But is she using the appropriate style of leadership?

© Noordhoff Uitgevers bv

Research by Sue-Chan and Ong (2002) demonstrates that participative leadership leads to greater acceptance of established goals among employees and thus improves their performance.

Participation in decision-making is similarly ineffective if employees do not share the goals of their leader, if they do not wish to take responsibility for decisions, or if they distrust the leader. Furthermore, the leader must have sufficient skills to guide the group process and handle conflicts (Yukl, 1998).

6.9.3 Transformational leadership

The forms of leadership mentioned up to now and their influence on the performance of employees are in line with the idea that there is an exchange relationship between the members of an organisation. The leader should give something to his subordinates, such as support, challenging tasks and more say, in exchange for better performance. This corresponds with a transactional approach to leadership. The principle of 'something for something' applies. Conditions that are attractive to employees are offered in exchange for their performance. This approach, however, will not account for the success of certain leaders, such as Iacocca, who rescued Chrysler, and Timmer, who put Philips back on the right track. Neither of them accomplished what they did by rewarding good performance. Quite a few redundancies were necessary. The strength of their style of leadership must therefore not be sought in a transactional approach but in another form of leadership, which is called transformational (charismatic) leadership.

Transactional approach

Transformational leaders motivate their subordinates to work harder and/or do things differently and better, by:
- introducing new values and goals and indicating why they are important to the organisation;
- getting employees to put their own interests aside for the common good;
- expanding the employees' pattern of needs to other areas more favourable to the organisation.

Koopman and House (1995) call transformational leadership an approach that is based on influencing the psychological meaning of the organisational situation to the employees. The transformational leader takes into account the needs and motives of their subordinates but tries to expand this pattern of motivation and focus it more on the goals of the organisation (team, department). They do so by indicating how important these goals are for the proper functioning (or continued existence) of the organisation. In this way, they hope that the employees will reassess their activities. The leader also emphasises the importance of making a good effort for the collective interest. Through transformational leadership, the leader tries to effect a turnaround in their subordinates' involvement with the organisation. This must change from an exchange relationship (based on utility) to an ideological relationship (based on values). Employees then no longer contribute exclusively for their own benefit but for the collective good.

What made Steve Jobs such a successful leader?

Transformational leaders show a great deal of self-confidence and a high degree of commitment and ideological inspiration. They make heavy demands on themselves and their subordinates, demonstrate creative and innovative behaviour, formulate goals and tasks in ideological terms and show confidence in their employees (House et al., 1991). They are inspiring, do not stay behind their desk upstairs, but communicate directly throughout the organisation. The transformational leader practises the art of 'management by walking around'.

Transformational
leaders

6

Avolio and Bass (1999) identify the following aspects of transformational leadership:
- **Charisma/inspiration**. The leader has vision and arouses pride, confidence and respect in his employees by communicating their vision, using symbols and modelling behaviour.
- **Intellectual stimulation**. The leader provides new ideas and stimulates their employees to think critically about themselves and their work.
- **Individual attention**. The leader coaches and guides employees, gives feedback, recognises their needs and pays attention to realising their potential.

In Table 6.2, statements relating to transformational leadership are classified under the above categories (Bass & Avolio, 1990).

TABLE 6.2 Part of a questionnaire about charismatic leadership

Charisma:

- My manager makes sure that I am proud to work with him.
- My manager creates a sense of community.
- My manager speaks optimistically about the future.

TABLE 6.2 Part of a questionnaire about charismatic leadership (continued)

Intellectual stimulation:

- My manager gives me new ideas.
- My manager makes sure that I think critically about my work.
- My manager makes sure that I substantiate my opinions with good arguments.

Individual attention:

- My manager finds out what I want and tries to help me achieve it.
- My manager deals with every employee in a personal manner.
- My manager explains things to me and guides me.

A great deal of research has been done into the effects of transformational leadership (Judge & Bono, 2000). The results indicate that, compared to with transactional leadership, charismatic leadership means better motivated employees, higher levels of performance and greater satisfaction. According to House, this is primarily because the leader can communicate a belief in a better future to their subordinates and the idea that the subordinates themselves can contribute something.

A high level of work satisfaction as an effect of charismatic leadership is found in both service providers and industrial organisations (Howel and Frost, 1989; Medley and Larochelle, 1995; Sparks, 2001; Viator, 2001; Catalano, 2003).

6.9.4 The narcissist leader

Transformational leadership appears to have an especially positive effect if there is a threat to the organisation's continued existence (crisis situation). It helps if there is a top executive who can make tough calls and ensures that everyone is facing in the same direction. Transformational (charismatic) leaders can be harmful if their behaviour starts displaying narcissist tendencies. This happens if the make themselves the centre of attention, consider themselves to be the best, feel they have earned respect, and strive for admiration. Narcissist people consider themselves to be exceptional.

Narcissist
tendencies

NRC HANDELSBLAD

Beware the narcissist top executive

Every top executive is subject to a degree of self-love, or narcissism. Otherwise, they would never have made it to the top, says economist Antoinnette Rijsenbilt. A hint of narcissism ensures the right amount of vision, confidence, charisma, effectiveness, and strive for recognition. Qualities which tend to result in improved operating results. But in her PhD study at the Erasmus University of Rotterdam,

Rijsenbilts points out the other side of that coin: excess narcissim leads to a lack of counterweight from a board that should be managing and adjusting the executive. And that, says Rijsenbilt, can lead to mismanagement, or even fraud: "The narcissist executive drowns in their own reflection. An intuitive truth which I have demonstrated empirically."

Maccoby (2000) and Khurana (2002a) studied large companies which sustained substantial damage due to leaders who began displaying narcissist behaviour. They concluded that the excellent achievements by those leaders early on in their career led them to become arrogant and place themselves on a pedestal. The began feeling they had all the answers and refused to listen to other ideas. The tended to take risks and were prepared to obliterate existing strategies and work processes. They strove for power and admiration. They did not tolerate criticism and surrounded themselves with yes-men.

EXAMPLE 6.18

Narcissist behaviour

The managing director of a large retail enterprise wanted to expand the enterprise even further for his own glory. He did this by being reckless with the financial resources. The lower-ranking directors dared not offer any resistance and buffed up the figures of their own sections of the organisation. This increased the value of the shares and they were able to earn more on their share options (bonuses). After a few years it all went wrong, and as a result several parts of the company had to be sold off in order to keep its head above water.

6.9.5   Coaching leadership

A relatively new approach is coaching leadership. This form of leadership is usually connected with a result-oriented manner of working (results-accountable units). In result-oriented working, the leader and his subordinates establish the results his team or department is supposed to achieve (see also the MBO method described above). To make these results possible, the leader will have to ensure that the conditions are right. The right conditions require in the presence of sufficient knowledge and skills in the subordinates, good relationships, feedback on the results achieved and the availability of adequate personal and material resources. Coaching leadership therefore consists in the following activities:

Result- oriented working

- Bringing and maintaining the knowledge and skills present in the team or department up to standard. This can mean that the leader provides sufficient training and education for his subordinates.
- Supplying the necessary personal and material conditions for work to be able to proceed without disruption within the team or department.
- Ensuring that the results to be achieved are collectively established and accepted. The leader must also stimulate employees to achieve the desired results and give them feedback on the progress and quality of their activities.

According to Engel (2002), the essence of coaching leadership consists in the management and development of employees into a goal-oriented way of working, where barriers to effective behaviour are as far as possible removed and where employees' sense of responsibility and capacity for self-management is increased.

EXAMPLE 6.19

Coaching leadership

At the Rabobank, performance management has recently been introduced, with the aim of establishing a result-oriented way of working. A great deal of attention is paid to a development-focused training policy for both management and staff. Central to this is the desire to locate responsibilities and authority at as low a level as possible in the organisation.

The overriding vision is that such a system makes work more challenging and pleasant, increases intrinsic motivation to work and establishes the following three core values: professionalism, quality and responsibility. Senior management believes that coaching leadership can make an important contribution to realising this vision.

Research into the effects of coaching leadership (Kooning, 2007) shows that this form of leadership is positively correlated with employees' goal-orientation and intrinsic motivation to work.

Coaching leadership is highly suitable if the following conditions have been met:
1 Employees and capable and motivated (high task maturity).
2 Employees require autonomy and are able to self-manage.
3 Employees are managed by results (result standardisation).

One or more of these conditions can be present in organisations with highly educated employees (professionals), with employees who are part of semi-autonomous and virtual teams, and in organisations that introduced New World of Work (NWW). Baan et al. (2010) indicate that the role of leaders under NWW will change from an adjusting to a coaching one. In addition, leaders will need to work on solidarity and social cohesion, since there is less face-to-face contact between employees. The greater freedom offered by being able to structure one's work along one's own insight, and the reduced possibilities for leaders to monitor the execution from along the way, call for mutual trust and the employee's ability to self-manage and self-adjust. If this ability is insufficiently developed, the leader will need to help the employee develop it further.

6.10 Influence of leadership

In the discussion of leadership, the concepts of power, influence, steering, motivation and inspiration are often used. The assumption is that leadership influences the functioning of employees individually and of the organisation as a whole.

6.10.1   External influences
When it comes to the organisation as a while, the influence of top level management is exaggerated. In their studies, Wasserman et al. (2001)
Limited influence   conclude that, in this context, leaders can only exert limited influence on the performance of an organisation. Too many factors that influence the success of an organisation are barely if at all influenced by single individuals.

Relevant developments in the environment of an organisation (see paragraph 9.2.1) occur outside of the sphere of influence of top level management. Examples are developments in technology, politics, economics, competition, and the job market. If a company's environmental circumstances are good, for example in the form of a recovering economy with increased demand for products or services, then that organisation will be successful regardless of the way top level management conducts its affairs. Only if circumstances are negative does it become apparent which top executives are able to lead their organisation through these rough spots unharmed.

According to Weber et al. (2001), the exaggerated influence attributed to leadership at the top is the result of an incorrect method of attribution. Attributing is the process of establishing the cause of one's own or others success or failure (see paragraph 1.1.3). Since top level managers operate in the picture (i.e. high-profile), people tend to ascribe (attribute) to those managers any non-standard performances – both in the negative and in the positive meaning of the word. In doing so, they ignore the influence of outside factors. Top level managers will want to ascribe their organisation's good performances to their own good qualities, and the poor performances to circumstances outside their control. This distorted attribution of cause and effect is also known as the fundamental attribution fallacy.

Attribution

6

ELSEVIER, HANS CROOIJMANS

Powerless at the top

Managers overestimate their ability to influence results. External factors and 'ordinary' employees are more determinative.

Five years ago, manager Leo Berndsen was highly regarded at insurance concern Aegon. He would have succeeded Jaap Peters as chairman of the board if the current chairman, Kees Storm, had not pipped him at the post in the race for the position. What did Berndsen do? He left Aegon and became managing director of Nedlloyd. Very courageous but not so good for his reputation. Berndsen was unsuccessful there in overcoming the savage international competition and hauling the ailing transport company out of its slump by curbing its losses.
His earlier rival, Storm, meanwhile grew into a standard bearer at Aegon. Admittedly, he implemented a plan of consistent and steady growth and

acquisition. But selling remunerative life-insurance policies is these days quite a bit easier than sailing container vessels at a profit over the world's seas. Storm would probably not have done any better at Nedlloyd. There are and were no easy answers at Nedlloyd.
This is true of many companies. Managers overestimate their influence. OK, they can take a decision, that is what they were hired for, after all. Whether the estimations and expectations that formed the basis for the decision subsequently work out depends to a great extent on factors outside their control. It is wonderful to invest hundreds of millions in a super-strong fibre, but if the competition has already cornered the market, a lot of work has been done for nothing. If they have concentrated on exports to Russia, then the whole economy collapses.

(...)

In the second half of the 1990s, the economy was booming. The then top men at KPN and Ahold made use of the boom to increase the size of their organisations by means of takeovers. They were praised for their good leadership at the time and the top man at Ahold was even chosen as Manager of the Year. When the economic situation thereafter declined, it turned out that they had saddled their organisations with huge debts and they were fired and shelved as poor managers.

6.10.2   Internal factors

Internal factors

There are also internal factors that make leadership wholly or partially redundant. Certain characteristics of employees, tasks and organisations can function as a substitute for leadership or neutralise the influence of management.

This is the case in the following circumstances:
- Work processes have been largely automated and need to be performed by computer-guided machines and robots. The planning, execution, and control of the work are programmed into the operating system. These activities no longer need to be performed by a supervisor.
- Employees are highly trained, capable, and motivated, and require little to no support from upstairs.

Lastly, there is also ability of leaders and employees at lower levels of the organisation to decide to slow down or de-claw decisions made at the top, or to implement the orders differently than intended. This can have a positive effect if the decisions made at the top are unworkable or considered harmful and useless at lower levels of the organisation. These processes of interpretation and adjustment of top level decisions occur to a greater extent as the top is further removed from the lower levels of the organisation. This occurs if the number of hierarchical layers increases. The inability of top level managers to can set a company to their absolute will makes the concept of an almighty governing and controlling leader an illusion.

Tips for managers

Management at the lower and middle levels sometimes has many responsibilities but too few sources of power to exercise sufficient influence. An increase in the means of power is then necessary.

Increasing position-related and person-related means of power

A coalition with other managers at the same level can be used to obtain more position-related means of power (economic, informational, legitimate).

Increase person-related means of power by undergoing training and education in work-related and relational skills. Ensure a good atmosphere by:
- organising joint activities outside work;
- giving personal attention to and showing interest in employees;
- providing social support;
- using your influence to make the work environment for subordinates (resources, opportunities, independence, job security, work space and so on) as good as possible.

Increasing influence

Increase your influence on others by adapting your use of power to each individual and using it fairly and selflessly.

- *Adapt to the individual*: Find out what form of use of power a person is sensitive to (cooperative, confrontational, formal, appealing to emotions) and adapt your use of power to the person.
- *Be fair*: Treat your employees equally in respect of assessment, reward and the application of rules. Favour no one.
- *Be selfless*: Use your influence to promote common goals and interests and avoid focusing on your own interests.

Style of leadership

Find out which style of leadership you employ by doing the following test:

- Go to http://www.yourleadershiplegacy. com/assessment/assessment.php
- Read the descriptions of the four styles of leadership.
- Go to the Leadership Styles Questionnaire.
- Fill in the questionnaire and add up your score to work out your basic style.

6

© Noordhoff Uitgevers bv

Summary

▶ Power is the ability of person A to make person B do something that he would otherwise not have done. Power can be used to influence others.

▶ The means of power that can be used are derived from the sources of power on which a person can draw.

▶ In organisations, there are two types of power source:
- position-related
- person-related

▶ Four forms of use of power can be identified:
- cooperative (the most applied, gives the best results)
- confrontational (applied if other forms do not have the desired effect)
- formal
- appealing to emotions

▶ Use of power for one's own interests is abuse of power. It is perceived as unfair and results in diminishing commitment to the organisation.

▶ Leadership consists in:
- planning
- activation
- control
- flexibility

▶ Four styles of leadership can be identified, along two axes:
- task-oriented versus relationship-oriented
- directive versus participative

▶ The question of what makes a person a good leader was investigated from three viewpoints:
- by looking at personality traits
- by looking at behaviour (the style of leadership)
- by looking at the demands a situation puts on the leader

▶ Improving leadership in order to obtain a higher level of employee performance can be achieved by setting task goals and through management by objectives (MBO).

▶ Styles of leadership:
- participative leadership (improves relationships and decision-making)
- charismatic leadership (increases motivation among employees)
- coaching leadership (improves working conditions in a team or department)

▶ The importance of leadership for the proper functioning of organisations is sometimes overestimated. External factors can have more influence on the functioning of organisations than the manner in which leadership is given.

6

Assignments

6.1 Use of power: read the following 12 statements and indicate for each one of these to which of the four forms of use of power (see paragraph 6.3) it applies:

A boss tries to persuade a subordinate to do something by:
1   holding out the prospect of a personal favour
2   pointing out the rules
3   indicating that it has been agreed in the planning process
4   saying that it has to happen and tolerating no contradiction
5   indicating that nobody else can do it as well
6   emphasising the utility of the desired task
7   having a friendly chat
8   indicating how important good collaboration is
9   laying out the problem and asking how the person would resolve it
10   emphasising that a good assessment is important to the subordinate's future
11   indicating that a more senior boss will be informed if he does not do it
12   explaining what the problem is and indicating that there is only one solution.

6.2 Piccolo and Colquitt (2006) indicate that the positive effect of transformational leadership is best demonstrated in situations in which employees perform tasks that are characterised by variation, meaning, and autonomy.

Explain this situation-specific effect.

6.3 Education is also a field where assessments are made – specifically by teachers assessing the competency, certainty, and motivation of their students. Give your assessment of the average level of task maturity (see paragraph 6.8.3) of the students in your group.

a What do you think is the average level of task maturity of your group?

b Hersey and Blanchard indicate which style of leadership best suits which level of task maturity. Which of the styles of leadership (steering, supporting, motivating, delegating) do the teachers of your group apply? Does their style of leadership of your teacher match the task maturity of your group?

7

Organisational structure

- How is structure created in organisations?
- How can activities be distributed?
- How can activities be coordinated?
- How are responsibilities assigned and professional relationships organised?
- How is information exchanged within the organisation?
- What forms of structure exist and how are they changing?

7

© Noordhoff Uitgevers bv

Expanding the restaurant

Hillcrest restaurant is a success. Owners Anna and Bob decide to expand their business. They purchase a building on the riverfront, and have it redeveloped into a fine hospitality experience. Their restaurant now features a large dining room, a number of rooms for larger groups of guests, and a large waterside deck. In order to be able to exploit their restaurant to its optimum potential, they will need to hire more staff. The current five-person operation, being Anna, Bob, a chef, a waitress, and a dishwasher, will not be enough to accommodate the new facilities. The question is what kind of people they are after, and what tasks they would fulfill in the new restaurant. Anna and Bob are considering a separation between the activities in the kitchen, behind the bar, in the dining areas, and on the deck. They will also need to decide who to recruit for purchasing, finance and admin, marketing and reservations, sorting out (additional) staff, setting the menu, purchasing, and general management and coordination.

7

7.1 Creating structure

When – as in the previous example – a company grows, it is no longer possible for any employee to perform all the activities. There is a risk that some activities remain unfinished and others are done twice. If everyone is busy in the kitchen, table service will be neglected. If everyone is involved in drawing up the menu, they will be unable to purchase raw materials. Efficiency therefore requires a certain amount of distribution or division of activities. This subsequently brings about the necessity for coordination. By means of distribution and coordination, a certain structure is created.

Distribution

Structure

A proper execution of activities is only possible once it has been established how the tasks that need to be performed have been distributed. At Hillcrest restaurant, all activities related to ordering drinks and passing orders to the kitchen have been assigned to the bar staff. These tasks together make up the function of the bar staff. The restaurant works with a number of different functions following the expansion, such as bar staff, waiting staff, cooks, dish washers, a purchaser, and an administrator (see Figure 7.1).

FIGURE 7.1 Divison of tasks and grouping of Hillcrest restaurant

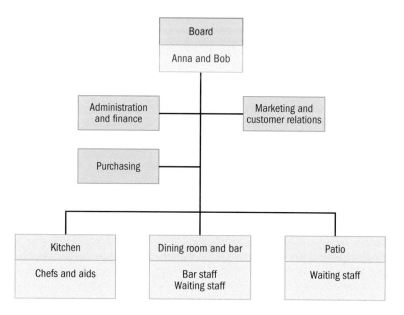

The proper execution of activities also requires that these activities are properly adjusted to one another. Distribution and adjustment applies a certain *structure* to an organisation.

As the number of jobs grows, the necessity to coordinate activities also grows. The questions here are what must be coordinated, how this must be

© Noordhoff Uitgevers bv

Grouping

done and who is to be responsible for it. Different forms of coordination are possible. By grouping jobs into departments, people who have to collaborate closely can be put together. In this way, they can keep an eye on each other and consequently determine what they should and should not be doing. Thus, the waitresses in the restaurant keep a close eye on which tables have and have not been served and therefore ensure that service runs smoothly. If departments grow and/or coordination is complicated, it can be wise to appoint someone to be responsible for coordination. In this way, the head waiter can assign the waitresses certain tables and can also indicate when it is necessary for one waitress to help another because she is very busy. If the number of departments within an organisation increases, it can be necessary to appoint someone to handle coordination between

Responsibilities job relationships

Direction leadership

departments. Creating a structure also requires establishing responsibilities and job relationships. Who should determine how the tasks are divided and coordinated? Who gives direction to the organisation and establishes the goals it will achieve and how? Who provides leadership to the employees in the organisation?

EXAMPLE 7.1

The head of the dining area is authorised to assign tables to specific waiters, and can also define how they should interact with their guests. The relationship is that of superior and subordinate. The head of the restaurant area, in turn, is the subordinate of the owners, Anna and Bob.

Lastly, calibrating and steering is not possible without communication about the nature and progress of the activities within the organisation.

EXAMPLE 7.2

Chefs working in the kitchen of Hillcrest restaurant need to be kept informed of the orders and requests from the guests visiting the dining area. The Purchasing department needs to know about the requirements of kitchen staff, and the Staff department needs to know about the numbers of people required in the kitchen and the dining area, as well as absenteeism as a result of illness or holiday time. As a result, there are weekly meetings held between different restaurant departments, for example between Anna and the chef regarding menu-setting, pricing, purchasing, and staffing the kitchen. The head of the dining area conducts short daily meetings with the waiting staff about current relevant affairs.

Not all choices made by Hillcrest regarding division, coordination, grouping, authorisation, relations, and communications, will necessarily have the desired results. Time alone will tell whether any adjustments will need to be made to, for example, the division of labour, or the way in which coordination meetings are conducted. The owners will likely make adjustments based on their experience. Once a satisfactory method of cooperation is achieved, it will stabilise and show the new organisational structure.

The requirements that need to be met in order to arrive at a new structural design are also shown in Figure 7.2.

Structure

FIGURE 7.2 Applying structure

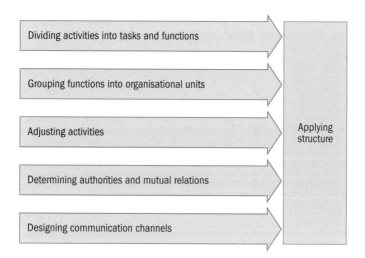

7.2 Distribution of labour

In the division of activities that is necessary in organisations to produce goods or provide services, different choices are possible.

EXAMPLE 7.3

Three departments

A department of an insurance company deals with the supply and management of company pension schemes as well as the payment of pensions. This departments' most important activities are:

- Sales: making contact with existing and new clients, drafting and issuing proposals, altering existing contracts and drafting pension scheme regulations when the contracts are signed.
- Administration: maintaining and updating the contracts of pension recipients, calculating premiums and scheduling payments.
- Payment: handling the payment of pensions.

There is a strict division of tasks in this department. The sales process is divided into five separate tasks. A salesperson makes contact with the client, a staff member from Contract Management records the client's requirements, a staff member from Tenders studies the requirements and produces a proposal, a staff member from Text-processing types this out and a staff member from Post and Archives sends the client the proposal. Thereafter, the salesperson contacts the client again and finds out whether the client wishes to accept the proposal or to make alterations. If there are alterations, the proposal goes back through Contract Management, Tenders, Text-processing and Post and Archives (see Figure 7.3).

FIGURE 7.3 Division of activities in sale of contracts

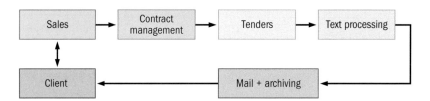

Why did the insurance company in example 7.3 opt to divide the sale of contracts into five separate tasks? Would it not have been more sensible to have all these tasks done by one person? After all, it sometimes happens that a proposal is held up or even misplaced somewhere between Contract management and Text-processing, causing a delay. If the client then asks where the proposal is, everyone hides behind everyone else.

There are various ways of dividing the activities required in an organisation into different tasks and functions. We will touch on three possible such differentiations:
- Horizontal specialisation: this determines the extent to which activities are divided into functions.
- Vertical specialisation: this determines the extent of authority a certain function carries with regard to the execution of certain activities.
- Task-broadening and task-enrichment: this determines the way in which functions can make greater use of the skills and responsibilities of employees.

7.2.1   Horizontal specialisation
Horizontal specialisation refers to the number of tasks contained in a single function. This is also known as a function's *reach*. There is *greater horizontal specialisation* if a function encompasses few tasks and, as a result, has little reach.

EXAMPLE 7.4

Greater specialisation

Initially, Hillcrest restaurant had little horizontal specialisation and a substantial reach. Following the expansion, there is now greater horizontal specialisation for employees by creating individual functions such dish washer, purchaser, and waiting staff. Thus, the reach per employee has been reduced.

There is *lesser horizontal specialisation* if an employee's function encompasses many tasks and has a large reach.

EXAMPLE 7.5

Extensive task package

A primary school teacher performs all tasks dealing with education, from designing and preparing classes to teaching, managing pupils (keeping the peace), checking and assessing pupils' work, consulting with colleagues, taking part in parent-teacher meetings, and supervising extracurricular activities.

In general, people who have completed a high level of education, such as doctors, teachers, researchers, consultants and managers, perform a function that knows only mild horizontal specialisation.

7.2.2   Vertical specialisation

Vertical specialisation refers to the extent to which employees have influence on the way in which they perform their function. This is also known as the *depth* of a function. There is *greater vertical specialisation* if the tasks that are part of a function are highly prescribed in nature. This means the employee will have little to no influence on the way they perform their function.

EXAMPLE 7.6

Assembly line work

A controller working on the assembly line at a plant nursery is tasked with removing all poor or sickly looking bulbs from the line. That describes his work in full.

There is *lesser vertical specialisation* if an employee has a lot of influence on they way in which they perform their function and verify their results. This influence, or authority, may relate to both the nature of the task approach as well as to the order of the tasks.

EXAMPLE 7.7

Self-sufficience

A plumber is informed by his manager that there is a customer who needs work done. Once on site, the plumber himself is in charge of deciding, based on the nature of the situation and the customer's demands, how to go about the job and what to start on. Once the work is completed, the plumber assesses his own work and verifies that the problem has been resolved.

In general, greater horizontal specialisation goes hand in hand with greater vertical specialisation, and lesser horizontal specialisation with lesser vertical specialisation. If there are few tasks to a function, employees tend to have little say in their execution. In this case, there is little reach or depth. This situation can offer both advantages *and* disadvantages to both the employee *and* the organisation.

The *advantages* of greater horizontal and greater vertical specialisation are that:
- The function can easily be fulfilled by a lower educated and cheaper workforce.
- The tasks that are part of the function can be prescribed and controlled precisely.
- The tast are generally simple and therefore easily to learn to do (perfectly).

The *disdvantages* of greater horizontal and greater vertical specialisation are that:
- The job becomes monotonous in nature due to the repetition of identical actions.
- Lack of influence on and control of the task performance mean the employee feels less responsible for properly performing their tasks.
- Monotony leads to increased complaints, increased absenteeism, and increased staff turnover. It also negatively impacts the relationship between employees and supervisors.
- The execution of activities becomes more susceptible to disruption.

A more severe division of tasks in function calls for additional calibration between those functions. This increases the chances of disruption in one functions causing delays in the execution of another function. This is especially true if proper performance of one function is a necessary requirement for proper performance of another function.

EXAMPLE 7.8

Dependence

If a waiter at Hillcrest restaurant makes a mistake in taking an order, then there is every chance of the bartender not preparing the correct drinks or the chef not cooking a steak to the customer's order.

The *advantages* of lesser horizontal and lesser vertical specialisation are that:
- Tasks within a function address employees' knowledge and skills to a greater degree and will therefore be perceived as meaningful and challenging.
- Employees feel greater responsibility for the quality and execution of their work.
- Employees experience greater job satisfaction.
- The execution of activities is less susceptible to disruption.

The *disadvantages* of lesser horizontal and a lesser vertical specialisation are that:
- The function requires a highly trained, expensive workforce.
- It takes more time to train and instruct employees.

7.2.3   Task-broadening and task-enrichment
The disadvantages of a greater horizontal and vertical specialisation can be negated through task-broadening and task-enrichment. Task-broadening means adding more tasks to a function and bestowing greater reach on that function. Task-enrichment means bestowing greater authority on the employee where the execution of their function is concerned, and increases its depth. Greater reach and depth lead to less horizontal and vertical specialisation.

The choice to add greater reach and depth to a function ties in with theory by Hackman and Oldham (1980) which indicates that greater reach and depth ensure that employees will be more inclined to consider their work challenging and meaningful. These employees will also feel greater responsibility to properly perform their tasks (for a more detailed description of this theory, see paragraph 2.4.2). Decreasing the severity of the horizontal and vertical specialisation also ties in with the previously discussed structural interventions intended to lead to the creation of self-guiding (semi-autonomous) teams (see paragraph 3.3.1).

7.3 Functional division

As the organisation and complexity of an organisation increases, so does the differentiation of tasks and functions. We have already shown that the expansion of Hillcrest restaurant has led to different functions in the operational field, such as cooking and table waiting, but also to different functions needed to enable the operational field, such as purchasing and staff recruitment.

When it comes to functions which enable operational activities to perform properly, there are five distinguishable functions in organisations according to Jones (2004):

1 *Support functions*: These are aimed at managing the relations with persons and parties in the environment, such as shareholders, banks, suppliers, clients, and governments.
2 *Production functions*: These are aimed at enabling the processes involved in production or service providing, and include logistics support, tech support, and quality control.
3 *Maintenance functions*: These are aimed at matters such as staffing, safety, building maintenance, sanitary facilities, and cafeteria.
4 *Adaptation functions*: These are aimed at the organisation's ability to adapt to changing circumstances, such as the development of new products or services, market research, and strategizing.
5 *Management functions*: These are aimed at applying structure and at governing, coordinating, supervising, and adjusting operations within the organisation.

As an organisation begin to increase in size and complexity, so does the differentiation between management functions. The result is the formation of *hierarchical relationships* between those functions. The effect is that new types and levels of management functions appear.

First, there is the *strategic top*. Managers at this level fulfil managerial tasks related to the determining the strategy and layout (structure) of the organisation. They must also ensure that the demands of parties in the environment, such as shareholders, capital providers, governments, and clients, are met.

Secondly, there is *middle management*. Managers at this level govern the organisational units under their supervision, such as the Production department or the HR department. They lead the departments, gather information on their performance, and relay this to the strategic top. Middle management ensures and effective and efficient execution of departmental activities and can, to some extent, be involved in the decisions taken by the strategic top.

Thirdly, there is *lower management*. Leaders at this level are responsible for the proper performance of teams responsible for goods or services. These teams are the *operational core*. Lower management reports to middle management.

In addition to these management layers and the operational core, Mintzberg (2006) distinguishes two other groups in organisations: the techno-structure and the supporting services. The *techno-structure* is comprised of specialists who design, standardise, and plan operational activities, and who perform quality control. They are also responsible for instructing and training operational employees.

The *supporting services* are employees who are not aimed at performing operational activities but at the remaining activities, such as cleaning, security, administration, IT, research and development, cafeteria management, legal affairs, etcetera.

Mintzberg (2006) has indicated the hierarchical relations within organisation, the placement of the operation core, and the supporting functions in a general, five-part structure (see Figure 7.4).

FIGURE 7.4 The five components of an organisation

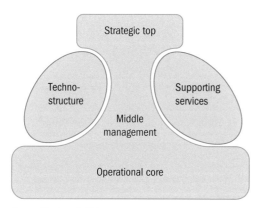

Source: Mintzberg (2006)

There can come a point in organisation's development where it becomes so large, so complex, that strategic management can no longer keep track of or be knowledgeable about everything that goes on. If this should happen, they might turn to *specialists*.

EXAMPLE 7.9

Hiring a specialist

A company decides to expand its marketing and sales to online channels. Since there is nobody in the company who knows how best to go about this kind of thing, the IT department receives reinforcements in the form of a specialist in the field. Together with the Marketing and Sales departments, this specialist is to present a plan of approach to strategic management.

Specialist aid is available in various areas. Making use of specialists when required can lead to the formation of a technostructure and supporting services, e.g. in the fields of strategy, logistics, financing, recruiting and selecting staff, and marketing. Specialists can also be hired on a temporary basis. In this case, they are not a fixed part of the organisation.

Some services (specialists), such as Human Resources, can perform a function that is both advisory and supportive. If a specialist's job is to ensure there is enough staff, their function is supportive. If their job is to inform top level management on the personel consequences of a policy change and indicate how best to go about this change, their function is advisory.

7.4 Coordination of activities

If the activities in an organisation are divided into separate tasks and jobs, the risk is run that cohesion within the activities will be lost. If division is necessary because not everyone can do the whole of an activity, then *coordination* is needed to ensure the continued cohesion between the separate tasks or jobs.

EXAMPLE 7.10

Coordination

The Sales department unexpectedly hands over a large number of orders. This forces a discussion with the Planning department to make sure if and how those orders are to be completed. The Planning department needs to confer with Production to ensure that the adjusted deadline is manageable. If the sudden influx of orders can only be completed if the Production department receives temporary reinforcements, they need to contact the HR department - who need to recruit temporary workers for the job.

Example 7.10 relates to the coordination between organisational units. However, coordination is sometimes also necessary between employees within a unit. If a person is missing from a unit due to sickness, for example, this can result in a redistribution of the activities taking place within that unit until the sick employee feels better or until a replacement has been found. Different forms of coordination are possible, such as: coordination by mutual adjustment, coordination by grouping, coordination by leadership, coordination by standardisation and coordination by formalisation.

7.4.1 Coordination through mutual adjustment

Mutual adjustment takes place via *direct communication* between one or more employees. It is aimed at ensuring they can properly fulfil their tasks and that those tasks are properly coordinated.

EXAMPLE 7.11

Lend a quick hand

The waiter taking orders from the tables along the window is busy. A large group of guests walks in, and all of them sit on the window-side. Rapid service is out of the question, so the waiter asks a colleague, who is not quite as swamped, to assist him and take the orders for tables 17 and 18 along the window.

Mutual adjustment is only possibly if employees have some degree of freedom to structure their work, and if they are able to communicate to other employees directly.

EXAMPLE 7.12

Proper communication

A crane operator on a construction site does his work on a literally different level than the rest of his team. Even though his view of the site is obstructed, he is in direct contact with another colleague who guides him through the process of lowering the boom so that the cables can be attached to steel beams. He is also notified once the beams are properly secured so he can begin lifting.

7.4.2   Coordination through direct supervision

Coordination through direct supervision occurs by assigning one person to be responsible for the proper collaboration between employees of a team, department, or agency. This person is authorised to adjust, calibrate, manage, and coordinate where necessary. Usually, this person is a *superior* (coordinator, chief, boss, head). Proper coordination through direct supervision is only possibly if the number of employees is not too large.

Fashion designer Daryl van Wouw pays attention to the smallest details.

People have a limited ability to retain an overview. The number of employees to whom a manager can give effective leadership is called their 'span of control'.

EXAMPLE 7.13

The right group size

An elderly care institution has begun working with care teams of a maximum of eleven colleagues. A team this size can still benefit from mutual adjustments and direct supervision.

Once the organisational units grow too big, structural adjustment are required. Examples are creating sub-units (teams, departments) or direct supervision of smaller numbers of organisational units. Each superior then directly supervises a limited number of people or units, preventing them from exceeding their span of control. This is known as the linking-pin structure (see Figure 7.5).

FIGURE 7.5 The linking-pin structure

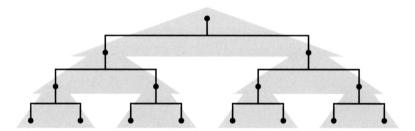

7.4.3   Coordination through standardisation and formalisation

The above-mentioned forms of coordination primarily involve coordination of the actual performance of tasks. It is also possible to achieve coordination before tasks are even allocated. They can then be coordinated by establishing rules and procedures. This is called standardisation.

Standardisation

Standardisation

There are three forms of standardisation:
- **Standardisation of work processes.** The various actions that comprise a task and their sequencing are precisely prescribed.
- **Standardisation of results.** The required results of carrying out the task are prescribed in a quantitative or qualitative sense. How those results are achieved can be determined by the employee themselves.
- **Standardisation of knowledge and skills.** Only the knowledge and skills that a person must have to perform a certain task are prescribed.

The form of standardisation that is applied in organisations is primarily dependent on the character of the tasks. If the actions can be precisely predicted, the standardisation of work processes is the obvious choice. If they are not predictable because the employee must be able to determine *in situ* how the job will be done, the standardisation of results is a more likely choice.

EXAMPLE 7.14

What healthcare is needed?

The head of the Homecare section visits a new client to assess what healthcare she needs. The client is then assigned to an employee. How this employee tackles the healthcare tasks is up to him, as long as the results are in accordance with the agreement. To establish whether this is the case, the head of Homecare regularly visits clients to find out whether they are satisfied with the agreed healthcare.

Standardisation of results of frequently applied in the New World of Work (NWW). Because employees perform their tasks at a time and place of their choosing, they can no longer be managed and monitored step by step. The solution is to manage for results.

If measurable quantities or qualities with which the end result must comply cannot be established in advance, the standardisation of results is impossible. This is the case with professionals who work in psychiatry, in the police force, in social work and youth care, for consultancies and in research departments, for example. To guarantee the quality of work, only people who have been properly trained are recruited for these jobs, so that they have the required professional skills. It is assumed that this training offers some guarantee that the work will be performed according to professional norms. This leads to standardisation of knowledge and skills.

EXAMPLE 7.15

Professional quality

An attempt is sometimes made to control the activities of professionals by prescribing or limiting results in quantitative terms. In psychotherapy, for example, there may be a maximum number of treatments per client; in universities, a minimum annual number of hours of teaching and research may be required of teaching staff. These are examples of the standardisation of results.

Through standardisation, activities can be coordinated to a certain degree. The standardisation of work processes naturally enables greater coordination, but even in this case it is by no means always possible to prescribe the activities step by step. Employees still often have sufficient latitude to coordinate their activities with those of others according to their own preferences.

Formalisation

The latitude remaining after standardisation is restricted by formalisation. Formalisation comprises the rules and regulations determining how employees must act in defined situations. Governing behaviour by rules means that coordination proceeds automatically and no consultation is necessary about who must do what in what order. In general, behaviour is

© Noordhoff Uitgevers bv

formalised in order to accomplish uniformity and make that behaviour predictable and controllable. Employees in a sales department, for example, are told what procedures must be followed if a client wishes to enter into a sales contract. These procedures include agreeing delivery times (and what to do if the client wishes to change these), negotiating prices and processing orders.

Advantages and disadvantages of standardisation and formalisation

There are both advantages and disadvantages to standardisation and formalisation. The advantages are:

Advantages

- **Predictability and control**. The more strictly standardisation and formalisation are applied in an organisation, the more precisely its activities are defined and coordinated. There is clarity about who does what in what order. The work is easier to prescribe and control. This makes the organisation function in a predictable and controllable manner. For people who like things to be clear and to know exactly what they must do and what stage they have got to, this is an ideal situation.

Manufacturing large quantities of products in a very short time according to specifications.

- **Less guidance and coordination**. Once the rules and regulations have been accepted by employees, work proceeds almost automatically along the planned route. Guidance and coordination are almost unnecessary.

The disadvantages are:

- *Lack of flexibility*. The existing rules and regulation may prevent employees from reacting flexibly to changing work requirements.

EXAMPLE 7.16

By the book

A garden furniture retail company is trying to land a new client. The client, however, is requesting shorter delivery times and greater discount than the sales agent on site is allowed to offer. As a result, the agent is forced to abandon the client, because they have too little freedom to act according to their own discretion.

- *Lack of commitment*. As employees are given less control over the way in which they perform their task, their feeling of commitment to their work decreases. A lack of commitment has a negative impact on feelings of responsibility for the proper execution of tasks and on absenteeism. It also causes increases in staff turnover rates.

Figure 7.6 presents a schematic overview of the advantages and disadvantages of standardisation and formalisation.

FIGURE 7.6   The advantages and disadvantages of standardisation and formalisation

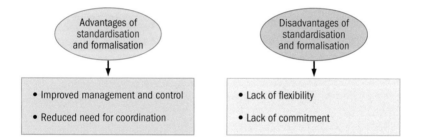

7.5 Grouping activities

Mutual adjustment through conferring directly on a worksite is only possible is people are close enough to each other to see and communicate what the others are doing. The closeness can be improved by putting them together in an organisational unit. The formation of organisational units is called *grouping*; either into departments, agencies, committees, project groups, task forces (teams) and meeting groups.

There are other reasons for grouping besides the necessity of coordination through direct conferring:
- The organisation becomes more **accessible**. The creation of additional organisational units offers a clearer view of which activities are performed where.

- Smaller organisational units enable mutual coordination through supervision, mutual alignment, and direct supervision.

In many cases, employees are grouped based on similarities in their tasks (functions), such as production, transport, storage, acquisitions, or sales. Various forms of grouping can be applied. The most suitable form depends on various factors, such as the nature and size of the organisation, the products or services supplied, the environment in which the organisation needs to function. There are several types of grouping – functional, product, market, geographical – which are discussed below, along with their consequences.

7.5.1 Functional grouping

If people who perform similar activities are put together, such as those involved in administration, purchasing, distribution and production, there is functional grouping (F-grouping).
With F-grouping, all production personnel are grouped in a Production department, all the sales agents in a Sales department and all administrative staff in an Admin department. The organisation thus takes on a functional structure (see Figure 7.7).

FIGURE 7.7 Organisation with a functional structure

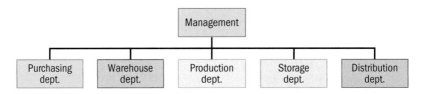

F-grouping calls for a strongly compartmentalised division into groups of activities. This compartmentalisation calls for greater attention to the coordination between the different organisational units. It needs an additional, higher layer of supervisors to properly coordinate between these units. An advantage of F-grouping is that employees with the same skills and knowledge are close together, thus drawing on, pooling, and increase each other's abilities and expertise. A disadvantage is the additional layer of management required to safeguard the coordination between organisational units.

7.5.2 Product grouping

If all the activities that are necessary to make a product or provide a service are grouped together, there is product grouping (P-grouping). The organisation is then divided into departments each of which makes its own product or cluster of similar products.

EXAMPLE 7.17

Three product groups

A company producing household appliances manufactures so many different products that its planning, execution, and control on the production process are suffering. As a result, the company has difficulty supplying its customers in time. Whereas in the past the company only produced five different products, these days that number is up to 30. The company regularly has to abandon prospective customers because its production capacity is too low. It is also becoming increasing difficult to plan production to such an extent as to be able to handle unexpected orders, order adjustments, or complaints on faulty products. To solve these problems, management has decided changing the functional structuring of the company to a product grouping. Three different, independent production groups are formed. Each product group manufactures household products which require similar production processes. Each product group has its own warehouse for the storage of materials and finished products, its own tech support, and its own planners and sales agents (see Figure 7.8). By applying product grouping, management and control become less complicated. It is now possible to better coordinate client wishes and the production of goods or services.

FIGURE 7.8 Product grouping in a company for household appliances

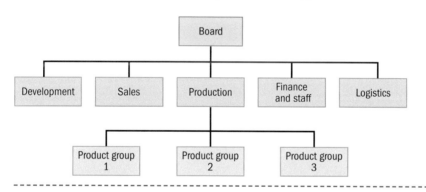

The extent to which a group is given its own techno-structure and supporting services depends on the *scope* of each product group and the extent to which *production processes* are individualised. The larger the scope and the greater the differences, the greater the chances of being allocated supporting groups or techno-structure. In many cases, part of the support will be set up at some form of centralised control, for example because it is the same for each product group. Examples include HR or Finance. An advantage of a centralised control is that specialist remain close together and thus are better able to manage their expertise. This is less easy to do if they are distributed across different product groups.

7.5.3   Market grouping

If an organisation offers products or services for markets (clients) that need to be approached in quite different ways, for example in the areas of distribution, sales and marketing, market grouping (M-grouping) may be more appropriate.

EXAMPLE 7.18

Two divisions

A company produces raw materials and semi-finished products for other companies and wholesalers, and also manufactures end products that are sold to the retail trade. Distribution, marketing, servicing and scheduling are so different for the two markets that management decides to split the company into two divisions. One division produces the raw materials and semi-finished products for companies and wholesalers and the other division produces the end products for the retail trade.

Figure 7.9 presents a schematic overview of market grouping.

FIGURE 7.9 Market grouping

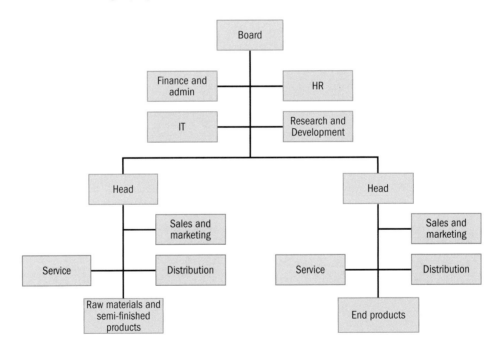

How specialist support should be structured (centralised or decentralised) in the case of M-grouping case depends on situational characteristics, as with P-grouping.

M-grouping

7.5.4   Geographical grouping

If all the activities that are focused on a geographic area are put together, there is geographical grouping (G-grouping). This grouping can take one of two forms.

G-grouping

In the first form, an organisation is divided into branches, such as Dutch, Belgian and German branches. These can be more or less independent, similar companies that sell the same thing, but operate in separate markets.

A chain of warehouses or supermarkets is another example of this. In the second form, a division into geographical areas is made within the organisation. A company marketing pharmaceutical products, for example, may be divided into departments in the Northern, Central and Southern regions of a specific country (see Figure 7.10).

FIGURE 7.10 Geographical grouping

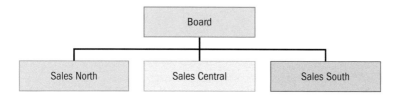

7.5.5   Consequences of grouping

The grouping of activities has a number of positive and negative consequences. The advantages of grouping are:

- **Alignment through mutual adjustment.** The natural cohesion between activities is lost as a result of the division of labour. Through grouping, this cohesion is restored, at least within each group. If the group is not too large, its members retain an overview of each other's activities. Consequently, they are able to coordinate (align) their contributions through cooperation.
- **Clarity.** The organisational structure remains clear due to the formation of departments. It is clear where every department is situated and what activities it carries out.
- **Social environment.** In large organisations, it is no longer possible for an individual employee to interact with or know everyone. Through grouping, employees are not 'lost in the crowd'. The group offers opportunities for regular social contact and can also satisfy the needs for belonging and protection, friendship and appreciation. Good group atmosphere is a fundamental condition for committing employees to the organisation.

The disadvantages of grouping are:

- **Distance.** It is less easy for employees to see beyond the boundaries of their group. The coordination of activities with employees in other groups is consequently hindered – first because there is often a physical distance from other groups (for example, they are in different buildings or on different floors) and second because there is often a psychological distance between groups. This can bring about the 'them versus us', or in-group versus out-group, phenomenon discussed earlier (see Chapter 3).
- **Differences in vision and interests.** The position that a group has and the function it fulfils within the organisation determine to a great extent how its members regard the organisation as a whole and what vision they have of its activities and their own role within the organisation and those acitivties – specifically the way in which they should work and the interests they should be furthering. Consequently, each group develops a different vision and attitudes, due to which the organisation runs the risk of fragmenting into separate pieces.

Differences in vision and interests can make an organisation into a conglomeration of 'parties'. Identification with one's own group can lead to in-/out-group differentiation and a culture of opposition. Negative images arise from resulting stereotyping, which hinders collaboration between groups. See Figure 7.11 for an overview of the advantages and disadvantages of grouping.

FIGURE 7.11 Advantages and disadvantages of grouping

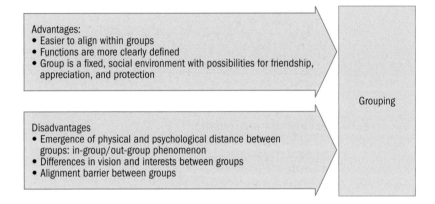

Advantages:
• Easier to align within groups
• Functions are more clearly defined
• Group is a fixed, social environment with possibilities for friendship, appreciation, and protection

Grouping

Disadvantages
• Emergence of physical and psychological distance between groups: in-group/out-group phenomenon
• Differences in vision and interests between groups
• Alignment barrier between groups

Lawrence and Lorsch (1967) studied the consequences of departmentalising. They concluded that departments will attempt to differentiate from one another, despite what their position in the organisation and their relationship to parties in the environment may be. This differentiation occurs with regard to perceived key goals, temporal perspective, and operating style. As the level of differentiation increase, mutual alignment becomes more difficult.

7.6 Responsibilities and relationships

We have previously indicated that matters of all kinds – both within an organisation and in the interaction between an organisation and its environment – need to be managed. Responsibility for managing these matters is assigned to certain people in the organisation. These people are given responsibility for specific areas of activity. As we showed earlier, senior managers, middle managers and line-managers have different areas of responsibility. As well as allocating responsibilities, the organisation must also establish the relationships between individual employees. Relationships are related to the question of who has authority over whom. In this way, the hierarchical structure of the organisation takes shape.

Responsibilities
Relationships

EXAMPLE 7.19

Relationships

The workshop managers in a production department have equal status. The production staff are subordinate to them, i.e. must answer to them and be led by them. The workshop managers, in turn, are subordinate to the head of the production department, who is subordinate to the managing director.

In theory, it is possible for everyone in an organisation to decide on everything. In practice, this is not workable – especially if the number of people in the organisation grows to the point where it becomes impracticable for everyone to be informed about or understand everything. In many cases, therefore, a certain amount of authority in day-to-day matters is delegated to certain people. This is known as vertical task specialisation. In many cases, responsibilities are associated with specific positions in the organisation and there is alignment through direct supervision. The leader (or manager) must, for the purpose of coordinating activities, be able to take decisions about such things as the sequencing of activities, the supply of materials and the pace of work.

7.6.1   Centralisation

Responsibilities and relationships can be established in different ways within organisations. The manner in which this is done determines the degree of centralisation or decentralisation of the organisation. Centralisation occurs if there is a large degree of subordination between managerial levels and if decisions on just about everything are taken at the top. These decisions are communicated from the top down until they reach the place where the tasks are to be performed. Centralisation has both advantages and disadvantages.

Centralisation

The advantages are:

Advantages

- **Overview.** Senior management has an overview of the whole and can take coordinated decisions.
- **Unity.** By taking decisions that apply to the whole organisation, senior management prevents the organisation from fragmenting into separate units that each go their own way.
- **Strategic manoeuvrability.** Because there is only a small number of decision-makers at the top and because they have a great deal of say, a decision to change course can be taken more quickly.

The disadvantages are:

Disadvantages

- **Overload.** The more the organisation grows in size and complexity, the more decisions senior management has to take. The chances of overload are then considerable. They will no longer be able to react to everything in time and delays in decision-making occur.
- **Lack of commitment.** If employees and lower-level management are not allowed to decide anything, their commitment to the organisation as a whole declines.

EXAMPLE 7.20

Losing commitment

The teachers in a large comprehensive school are being given less and less autonomy, have less and less say in what goes on and feel increasingly like mere deliverers of teaching programmes. Their commitment to the school as a whole is weakening and they are concentrating their attention and energy just on their own department.

- **Lack of awareness.** The further senior managers are removed from the organisational units about which they must make decisions, the less awareness they have of the problems that exist and the solutions that are feasible (see Figure 7.12).

FIGURE 7.12 The advantages and disadvantages of centralisation

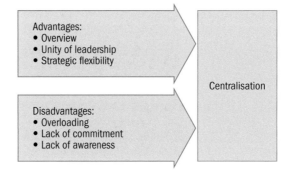

When centralisation is accompanied by a proliferation of hierarchical layers within the organisation, a particular problem can occur. The distance between senior management and the operational level becomes too great – physically, communicatively and psychologically – with the result that senior management has little knowledge of the operational processes involved in creating the products or services or of the people who carry them out.

Physical distance between management and shop floor

Physical distance

Physical distance occurs if the senior managers are in a building other than the one in which operational work takes place.

EXAMPLE 7.21

Physical distance

Senior management of a college has its offices in a building that is located at a substantial distance from the buildings in which classes are held. The managers rarely visit the locations where the actual teaching takes place and consequently know only some the teachers.

Communicative distance between management and shop floor

A large communicative distance is created if senior managers allow themselves to be informed about the state of affairs lower down the organisation via a hierarchical route. They receive information from middle managers, who in turn heard the information from leaders at the lowest level, who heard it from the employees.

Communicative distance

This large communicative distance also exists in top-down communication that arrives at the lower layers by way of middle and lower management. The major associated risk is that a message becomes distorted: in each intermediary layer, there is a potential for disruptive noise to occur due to selective perception and assessment of the received message. As a result, the final message may not come across as was originally intended (Koeleman, 2008). A second potential issue is for messages to be delayed at intermediary levels, for example if those layers become (temporarily) overloaded with information. This may result in top-down as well as bottom-up communication suffering significant delays.

Distorted

Delays

EXAMPLE 7.22

Poor communication

Some team members are increasingly having problems with their team leader, who was appointed quite recently and likes to dictate orders rather than consult with team members. This is troublesome, as increased consultation was part of the reason behind the last reorganisation. Complaints addressed to the manager by the team members achieve very little, so in the end they contact the head of the department, who promises to address the issue. The head of the department then passes on the complaint to the divisional manager at the next meeting. However, because the head of the department was the one to recommended that the team leader be appointed in the first place, he is reluctant to admit that he may have made a mistake. He therefore plays down the complaining team members as being stubborn and difficult. The divisional manager has his own ideas about the problem. His impression of the team leader is less than good, and he feels that the team leader's failure to sort out the issues within is team is down to the team leader himself.

Psychological distance between management and shop floor

Finally, there can also be a great psychological distance between top management and the shop floor. If senior managers rarely or never visit the shop floor and allow themselves to be informed at second or third hand by middle management about the state of affairs in the organisation, they become estranged from a large part of the organisation. Employees at the operational level can consequently gain the impression that 'that lot at the top have decided on something, or want to change something again, which is no help whatsoever to us down here'. In-/out-group differentiation is the result.

Psychological distance

The consequences of physical, communicative and psychological distance are illustrated in Figure 7.13.

© Noordhoff Uitgevers bv

FIGURE 7.13 The consequences of great physical, communicative and psychological distance between top managers and operational personnel

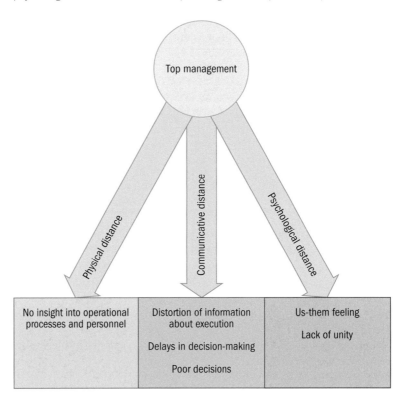

7.6.2   Decentralisation

Decentralisation

If responsibilities are shared among different parts of the organisation, decentralisation occurs. Decentralisation has two forms:
1 **Vertical decentralisation.** This is delegation to lower management levels;
2 **Horizontal decentralisation.** This is delegation to staff services or supporting services.

Decentralisation has several advantages. The delegation of responsibilities prevents overload. Senior management is given more time to concentrate on the main issues, for example on organisational strategy and on long-term planning; there is less distortion of information in communication; and people lower in the organisation, who often have a better idea of how best to tackle their work, are given more say. The quality of decision-making consequently improves. Because fewer hierarchical levels need to be involved, it also speeds up. It is consequently possible to respond earlier and better to local problems. Finally, because more people are involved in decision-making, motivation to implement the decisions increases.

Quality of decision-making

Motivation

Profit centres

One example of decentralisation is working with profit centres (PCs). These are organisational units tasked with achieving certain set objectives. Their methods, manpower, and means for achieving those objectives are left to the individual independent PCs.

● blikopnieuws.nl

Amsterdam municipality to implement PCs

So long to the current twenty-six departments, with the exception of the Administrative department. The municipality of Amsterdam will be working in four new clusters: Social & Security, Spatial & Economics, Service & Information, and Supporting Operations.
The fundamental concept behind the clusters is that they will be developed with flexibility and the specific goals and objectives of the city in mind. They will lead to a clear-cut division of labour with less overlap between the organisational units – as well as help to better assign money, time, and energy to where these are needed. The Administrative department will become a compact concern and operational staff.
Each cluster will consist of a number of profit centres (PCs). These units will team up with partnering inner-city agencies to achieve set results in specific areas – forming, for example, a Sports PC, a Youth PC, or a Real Estate PC. The operational fields of the individual PCs will be clearly delineated, which will generally help keep them small and flexible. Any changes in or discontinuations of specific tasks will be easy to implement in the relevant units.

A disadvantage of decentralisation can be that the top of the organisation loses control when decisions can be taken at all levels within the organisation. This can lead to the formation of 'empires', which are more concerned with their own interests than with the common interest. Unanimity of leadership is thereby endangered (see Figure 7.14).

Empires

FIGURE 7.14 The advantages and disadvantages of decentralisation

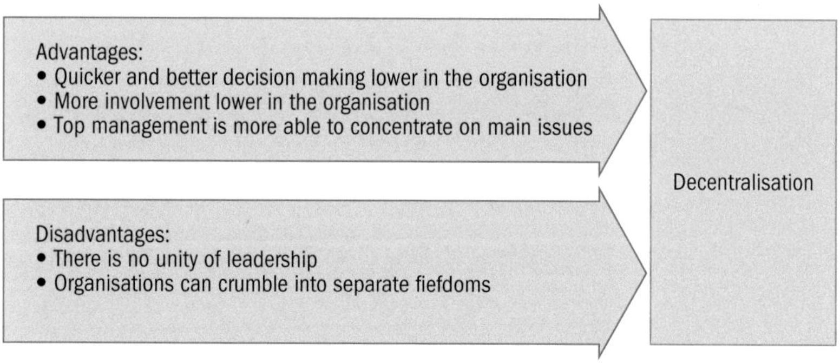

Advantages:
• Quicker and better decision making lower in the organisation
• More involvement lower in the organisation
• Top management is more able to concentrate on main issues

Decentralisation

Disadvantages:
• There is no unity of leadership
• Organisations can crumble into separate fiefdoms

The top of the organisation must therefore be very careful and selective in implementating decentralisation and constantly point out the framework within which people lower down the organisation can take decisions.

7.6.3   Choice between centralisation and decentralisation

It is impossible to give a simple and unambiguous answer to the question of what degree of concentration or division of responsibilities is necessary in an organisation. Some matters are better decided by senior management, while others can better be sorted out at a lower level. Asking for permission from the top to tackle a job in a certain sequence at the lowest level can lead to unnecessary delay and even the wrong decision, as people at the highest level may have insufficient awareness of the specific nature and circumstances of the job. In such cases, centralisation is inefficient and ineffective. The nature or scope of the decision to be taken should therefore always be taken into account in establishing who can best decide and where the responsibility for it should lie.

Matters such as deciding on prices and product range, production scheduling and techniques, hiring staff and arranging holidays can be delegated to a lower level, such as middle management. In other areas, such as finance, policy and strategy, long-term planning, research and development and mergers or reorganisations, senior management will want to take the decisions. Before deciding where responsibility should lie, the following questions should be asked:

- Who has the information that is necessary to take the decision, or who can quickly and easily access it?
- Who has the expertise necessary to take a good decision?
- How quickly must the decision be taken?
- For whom is the decision important, or for whom does it have significant operational consequences?
- How busy are the people who could be asked to take the decision?

The answers to these questions in each area of the organisation's activities will give an indication of the degree of centralisation or decentralisation that is appropriate.

In organisations that are structured around self-managing teams, this issue is tackled systematically, beginning at the lowest team level. What can be decided at this level should not go to a higher level. Only in matters requiring coordination between teams, services, or departments should the question arise of whether a team could make the appropriate decisions or whether they would be better made at a higher level. The advantage of this approach and starting point is that the first-line manager can often be eliminated, thereby removing a management layer. This shortens the chain of command in the organisation.

EXAMPLE 7.23

Self-managing teams

In an engineering works it is decided to combine certain tasks in the manufacture of products (programming, inputting, control and administration) and assign them to self-managing teams. Due to this, quality controllers and group leaders are no longer required.

7.7 Additional forms of authority and mutual relationships

In a number of circumstances, other types of organisational structure may be necessary. This is the case, for example, when tackling and resolving complex one-off problems that require a great deal of coordination of expertise, ideas and interests among different departments. If the existing structure is not suitable for this, a better structure will have to be designed.

EXAMPLE 7.24

What kind of structure is suitable?

A company has decided to launch a new product for strategic reasons. The Research Department is assigned the development of such a product, but it cannot do so alone. It needs the cooperation of the Marketing and Sales Department. It must find out what requirements the new product must satisfy if it is to be attractive to consumers and to compete with similar products offered by the competition. It also needs the cooperation of the Production Department to indicate what conditions a new product must fulfil if it is to be manufactured using current production processes. The Purchasing Department must also be consulted. They know what materials or components can be used to make the new product and what they cost. Finally, the Finance Department will have to calculate the cost price and therefore the selling price of the new product.

When the Research Department produces a design for the new product, it may be that the marketing and sales department decides that it is not attractive or competitive enough, the Production Department indicates that it will be difficult to manufacture with the existing machinery and the Finance Department comes to the conclusion that it will be much too expensive. The development process must then start again.

Under such circumstances, it is better to create a new structure in the form of a project group or matrix than to have all the departments involved working independently.

A project group is a temporary structure within the existing structure, in which representatives from different departments come together and jointly tackle a particular problem. There is usually a project leader or coordinator. In example 7.25, it was decided to put two representatives of each of the departments involved into the project group. They contribute their expertise throughout the development process and so ensure that the new product fulfils their respective requirements. The leader or coordinator keeps senior management informed about progress. Once the new product has been brought onto the market, the project group is dissolved. *Project group*

A matrix structure may be preferred if it is not a one-off problem that must be resolved but a problem with the production of goods or provision of *Matrix structure*

**Fixed
component**

services that requires an integrated approach. The matrix is then no longer a temporary structure within the main structure of an organisation; the project groups become a fixed component of the main structure.

EXAMPLE 7.25

Project groups

A company develops customised hardware and software programmes for other companies and institutions. Every assignment is different, and each client has to be consulted to ascertain their specific needs. Hardware may need to be adapted, software programmes must be designed, staff need to be trained to handle the new software and the costs of the whole programme must be established. This can only be done effectively if staff from various departments (finance, hardware, software, training) collaborate. Because collaboration is required for every assignment, working in project groups has become a standard approach and is built into the functional structure of the organisation. There are still functional groups (departments) but the employees in them are also assigned to specific projects (see figure 7.13).

Figure 7.15 shows the matrix structure of project organisation systematically.

FIGURE 7.15 Matrix structure of project organisation

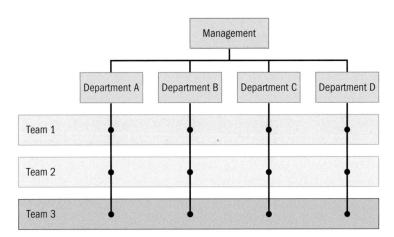

7.8 Designing communication channels

**Communication
channels**

In the structural design of organisations, it is also necessary to establish how information can be sent to and between the different parts of the organisation. Communication channels must be designed for sending and receiving all the information that is relevant for the guidance, control and coordination of activities. There are essentially three types of communication channel:

1 **Vertical communication.** Information that is relevant for the management, control and coordination of organisational activities runs via a hierarchical route. Information is passed from the top to the bottom of the organisation and back via managers, who form the nodes in the process.

   In a centralised organisation, vertical communication dominates. The top level of the organisation takes all the important decisions and resolves all the organisational problems itself. It receives and sends information in steps via management at the different levels.

2 **Horizontal communication.** Information that is relevant for the management, control and coordination of organisational activities is passed on to employees and organisational units at the same level.

   In a (partly) decentralised organisation, horizontal communication plays an important role. This is necessary if management and decision-making are to take place without reference to higher authority.

3 **Direct communication.** Employees and management at different levels and in different departments have direct contact with each other, without needing to use horizontal or vertical communication channels. This expedites the dissemination of information throughout the organisation. The use of intranet systems makes this form of communication possible. In project group and matrix structures, (see previous paragraph), there exists what is known as lateral communication.

7.9 Organic and mechanistic structures

As shown in the previous sections, when establishing an organisational structure, a choice must be made between various methods of dividing and coordinating activities, assigning responsibilities, establishing relationships and designing communication channels. The structural forms that result from these choices can roughly be placed in a dimension that runs from mechanistic to organic.

A mechanistic structure is characterised by strict horizontal and vertical differentiation of activities, by centralisation of responsibility, by extensive standardisation and formalisation and by vertical communication channels.

Mechanistic structure

In a mechanistic structure, management and control comes from above and is exercised through supervision, strict standardisation of procedures and a large number of rules (formalisation). There is a strong emphasis on adhering to rules and regulations and a strict division between operational work on the one hand and planning, management and decision-making on the other. Operational employees have little say in their own situation and they always perform the same simple tasks. This structure is a strongly interconnected system. The strict division of activities into separate tasks means that disruption or change in one task can influence all the other tasks that follow or cohere with it. The strict standardisation and formalisation of activities makes it difficult to respond quickly to changed circumstances. The different approach to the work that may be required is hindered by rules. Mechanistic organisations can easily be managed from above but the price for this is that the quality of the labour at the operational level is low and the organisation is not able to respond quickly and flexibly to changed circumstances.

Strongly interconnected system

EXAMPLE 7.26

Mechanistic structure

A company makes components for the automotive industry. In the workshop, the employees carry out the operational work according to the schedule prepared by the Production Planning Department. The checking of components is carried out by the Quality Control Department. The maintenance and repair of the machines in the workshop is done by the Maintenance Department. The workshop employees' work is rather monotonous. If something goes wrong, due to a fault in the machinery an employee is using or due to delays in the supply of components, for example, the boss has to be called in. He then contacts the head of the relevant department. Problems are discussed and resolved higher up the organisation. Communication largely follows the hierarchical route.

Organic structure

Organisations with an organic structure have slight horizontal and vertical differentiation of activities, limited standardisation and formalisation, (selective) decentralisation of responsibility and horizontal and direct communication channels.

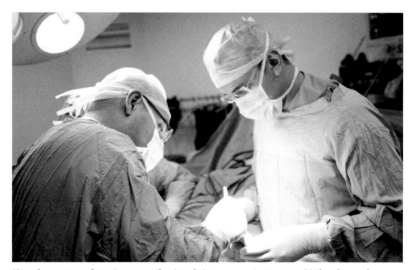

How do surgeons function as professionals in an organic structure? What form of standardisation is needed?

EXAMPLE 7.27

Organic structure

A company makes components for the automotive industry. In the workshop, the operational employees are grouped into self-managing teams. Within an overall schedule imposed from above, they do their own weekly scheduling. They also manage the supply of components, quality control and the maintenance of the machinery. Their work is consequently varied. Communication is less tied to the hierarchical route: employees in the self-managing teams can directly contact employees in other departments, without the intervention of departmental heads.

In organisations with an organic structure, coordination within and between groups takes place through horizontal and direct communication. Responsibilities are distributed and decisions are taken at lower levels. Due to their slight horizontal and vertical differentiation, limited standardisation and formalisation and the independence of the organisational units (decentralisation), these organisations are loosely connected systems. Disruptions in one part of the organisation consequently have less impact on other parts of the organisation. Because tasks are less standardised and employees have greater opportunity to vary their approach to their work, it is possible to respond more quickly and effectively to different circumstances. An organic structure therefore provides more opportunities to respond flexibly to changed requirements of an internal or external nature.

Loosely
connected
systems

The characteristics of a mechanistic and an organic structure are shown in Figure 7.16.

FIGURE 7.16 Dimensions of organic and mechanical organisational structures

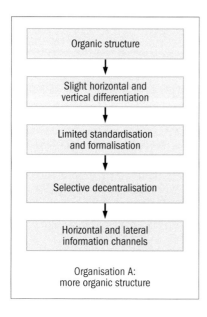
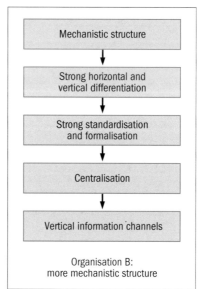

7.10 Developments in structural design

The structural form of an organisation is largely determined by the following factors:
- Size. The size of an organisation is a function of the number of its employees, the number of services and/or products it supplies and the number of markets and geographical areas it services.
- Complexity. The complexity of an organisation is a function of the complexity of its environment.
- Dynamics. Dynamics are the speed at which the environment in which the organisation is functioning changes.

© Noordhoff Uitgevers bv

To what extent each of these factors is influential and what structural design flows from them will be shown in the following sections, derived in part from the models of Greiner (1972) and Mintzberg (1983). The following paragraphs cover simple structure, functional line-staff structure, line-staff structure with P-, M-, and G-grouping, and divisional structure.

7.10.1 The simple structure

Simple
structure

A simple structure is usually characteristic of a small organisation. This structure has no staff services or supporting services and there is no strict division of labour. Standardisation and formalisation are limited. There is no middle management and communication is generally direct. Coordination takes place through discussion and supervision. The authority to take decisions is usually centralised in the hands of the owner (managing director).

EXAMPLE 7.28

The working director

A painting and decorating firm consists of an owner (managing director) and eight painters. The managing director agrees the contracts with the clients and distributes the work among his employees every week. He also regularly visits the employees to check on their progress and discusses with them any problems they may have encountered and how these can best be resolved. If necessary, he provides support. He also handles the administration and finances himself (see Figure 7.17).

FIGURE 7.17 The simple structure of a painter and decorator's business

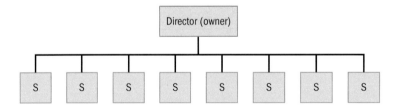

This simple, organic structure is suitable for small, non-complex organisations in a dynamic environment.

7.10.2 The functional line-staff structure

When a small organisation grows, for example because the range of products or services it supplies is expanded or the number of employees is increased, management and support problems begin to arise.

EXAMPLE 7.29

A growing company

Everything is going well with a certain painting and decorating firm. The number of painters has doubled and the owner is going to diversify into roofing. To this end, another eight employees have been recruited. The roofing work requires having more materials in stock and the warehouse where they formerly stored materials and tools is now too small, so larger premises have been found. The managing director decides to recruit a stock assistant to be responsible for the stocking and delivery of materials. He also decides to relieve himself of the day-to-day management and control of operational work by appointing a workshop foreman; and, because the administration and finances have become too complicated for him, he has hired an office assistant. The managing director can consequently focus on marketing and sales and the general running of the business.

The expansion of the painting and decorating firm by taking on more painters and opening a new roofing department confronts the owner with two problems. First, he has a management problem. The increased demands of administration and attracting clients mean that he is no longer able to provide good management, control and coordination of the operational work. Second, administration and finances are becoming increasingly complicated. He therefore has a support problem. How can these problems be resolved?

Management problem

Support problem

The solution to his management problems consist in the creation of an intermediate layer in the organisation. This intermediate layer of lower-level management will handle the day-to-day running of the operational activities (vertical differentiation). The coordination of these activities is facilitated by implementing functional grouping. The painters constitute the painting department and the roofers the roofing department. For the support problem, the solution lies in employing staff services or supporting services (specialisation). A functional line-staff structure is then created (see Figure 7.18).

Line-staff structure

FIGURE 7.18 The functional line-staff structure

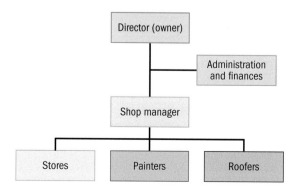

7.10.3　Line-staff structure with P-, M- or G-grouping

When organisations increase still further in size and complexity, the original functional line-staff structure faces a number of problems.

Control problem

If the work processes can no longer be properly managed from the top of the organisation (overload), there is a control problem. A number of structural approaches can then be taken to achieve better control:

- **Bureaucratisation.** Through strict standardisation and formalisation, the work processes can be better coordinated and made more controllable. Less consultation and supervision are then necessary.
Bureaucratisation has, however, the disadvantages of a mechanistic structure. If the organisation has to function in a dynamic environment and needs to respond flexibly to changing conditions, other solutions will have to be found.
- **Grouping and (selective) decentralisation.** Size and complexity can be offset by forming organisational units that are easier to manage and able to respond more flexibly to changed circumstances. This is made possible through a combination of selective decentralisation and grouping based on products, markets and geographical areas.
This combination makes the organisation into a collection of smaller, semi-autonomous units, which are easier to manage due to their restricted size and complexity (see also section 7.4.2). These semi-autonomous organisational units are also called business units, sectors or results-accountable units. Management is exercised from above through the provision of a budget for personnel and resources and by establishing the results that are expected of each unit. Selective decentralisation unburdens the top of the organisation, countering the danger of overload. Because the structure becomes more organic as a result, flexibility also increases. This structural form is more effective in a dynamic environment.

EXAMPLE 7.30

The complexity increases

The painting and roofing company is now adding paving activities to its production package. As a result, management of the operational activities has become more complicated. The workshop foreman can no longer cope with it. The organisation decides to group its activities according to products by forming three separate departments: painting, roofing and paving. Each of these departments has its own stores and specialist support (maintenance, administration and purchasing). Finances and personnel are still handled centrally (see Figure 7.19).

Figure 7.19 shows the line-staff structure with P grouping.

FIGURE 7.19 Line-staff structure with P-grouping

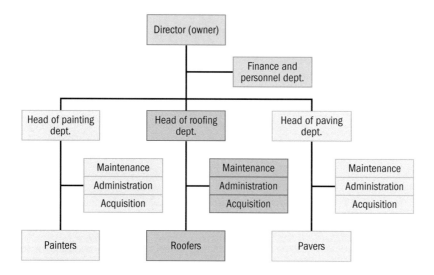

Depending on the circumstances, there are also the options of M- or G-grouping. Whether semi-autonomous units have their own specialist support or receive support from a central unit is dependent on various factors.

7.10.4   The divisional structure

When organisations grow still further in size and complexity, a divisional structure must be put in place. The semi-autonomous P-, M- or G-groups develop into separate and independently operating organisations or companies, under the umbrella of the parent company. These independent units have their own staff services and supporting services. The parent company's management provides only general guidance. It formulates a general course of action and has, for example, influence over innovation or expansion. The parent company's management is assisted by a small staff.

Divisional structure

Figure 7.20 shows the divisional structure.

FIGURE 7.20 The divisional structure

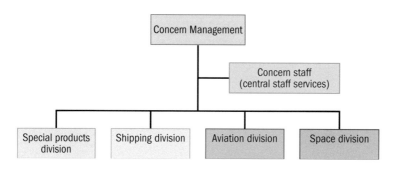

Sometimes, a division detaches itself and becomes a wholly independent company. Naturally, change is not always due to growth. When a company downsizes or splits up, it is possible to fall back on an earlier structural form. If circumstances change and organisations end up in more stable circumstances, the inclination towards bureaucratisation and centralisation will increase. If the environment becomes more dynamic, selective decentralisation will again be considered. Mergers between institutions and companies often motivate the design of a new structural form, due to the increased size and complexity of the organisation.

EXAMPLE 7.31

What is a division?

Due to its increasing size, a company that manufactures components for a wide variety of clients was grouped into departments responsible for the shipping, aviation and space travel markets. A separate research and development department was also created. Due to further growth, these groups have ultimately become separate companies (divisions), with branches in different countries (G-grouping). The staff of the parent company is in Amsterdam (see figure 7.46).

7.11 Design questions

Top level management is tasked with determining the structure of the organisation and – where necessary - to adjust is to changing circumstances. The decision to go with a structural form is not easily made, since every choice, as described in paragraph 7.9, comes with both advantages and disadvantages. Jones (2004) argues that, when designing an organisation, there should be a proper balance between the following three dimensions:
1 differentiation and integration;
2 centralisation and decentralisation;
3 standardisation and individual customisation.

7.11.1   Balance between differentiation and integration

Differentiation

Integration

Integration methods

Organisations that begin to grow in terms of size and complexity require a greater differentiation of tasks, functions, and organisational units. This differentiation may lead to coordination issues, increasing the need for greater integration. Management can employ various integration methods to arrive at a correct balance between differentiation and integration. These methods are:
- Coordinating team department activities by management;
- Coordinating between employees by way of mutual arrangement;
- Coordinating between departments by a liaison;
- Coordinating between departments by way of project organisation and matrix structure;
- Coordinating between departments by strategic apex and middle management.

– Coordinating efforts is a costly process: it requires a company to invest
time in activities that are not directly part of producing products or
services. These are additional activities that may cause a substantial
increase overheads.

Overheads

● Profielen.hr.nl

HR spending on overhead too high

HR spends too much on overhead, formation spent on their own
organisations: 42. 5%.. In other applied universities, the amount is 37%.
Overhead expenses will need to be reduced in order to free up funds for
education.
Profielen interviewed Jan Roelof, a member of the Executive Board, and
discussed the board's plans for reducing the overhead.

What is the 42% being spent on?
27.1% is assigned to generic overheads: the Executive Board (EB), line
management and secretary offices, P&O, Finances, ICT, quality care, and
legal. 15.4% is assigned to educational and research support:
educationalists, study counsellors, deans, student affairs,
internationalisation, knowledge development, the library and AV resources,
student registration and administration. These percentages are based on
the number of FTEs.

Are both percentages higher than those at other applied universities?
They are. Other applied universities spend an average of 23.8% on
generic overheads, and 13.1% on education and research support.

*The board has recently instituted a norm for overheads. Can you give us
an impression of that new norm?*
The generic overheads should be lowered to 22%, and education and
research support is to remain at 15%. This will lower our total overheads
to the same percentage as the other large applied universities: 37%.
This norm should be realised by 2016.

When structuring the organisation, management needs to determine the
extent of differentiation and associated integration required, without
causing too much of a drain on the overheads.

In paragraph 7.4.3, we discussed how the need for calibration and
responsiveness can lead to standardisation and formalisation. The positive
effects of these aspects, however, cannot be negated in terms of flexibility
and commitment. Creating separate organisational units based on P-, G-
and M-considerations can simplify the responsiveness *within* those units,
and at the same time complicate the responsiveness *between* those units. It
is therefore important to keep searching for the right balance between
differentiating and inegration.

7.11.2 Balance between centralisation and decentralisation

The balance between centralisation and decentralisation depends on the question of which decisions are to be made by top level management, and which can be delegated to lower levels. Choosing centralisation means the organisation can be managed in such a manner that the vision and strategy of the company remain in tact and that there is unity in terms of policy. The disadvantage of centralisation is that top level management can become swamped, and that supervisors and employees at lower levels of the organisation can feel stifled. Decentralisation results in an increase in flexibility in terms of adjusting to circumstances. The increase in responsibility, another result of decentralisation, leads to greater commitment to one's own work and the organisation. A disadvantage of decentralisation is that the individual organisational units can turn into little fiefdoms (balkanisation), resulting in a loss of responsiveness to other units and to the goals of the organisation. This may further regress into a loss of unity of leadership. Thus, it is important that centralisation and decentralisation are properly balanced.

EXAMPLE 7.32

Centralising

A sudden growth in turnover and in the number of types of car a certain car manufacturer produces has caused an increase in the number of division within the company – from six to nine. The necessecity of maintaining proper responsiveness (integration) within and between the divisions has lead to high costs from supporting services and managers as well as many different hierarchic levels. In order to reduce costs and reassert their grip on the organisation, the management of the concern decides to cut the number of divisions from nine to three, as well as making cutbacks in the number of managers and supporting services. The resulting consequences are a reduction in the overheads, but also a lack of creative or innovative ability, since managers at lower levels of the organisation have not retained their previous level of clout. As a result, the concern begins to drag behind its competitors after only a few years. Management therefore decides to implement selective decentralisation, allowing division managers the responsibility for the development of new models, within an established budgetairy framework.

In designing the layout of an organisation, management is tasked with finding the proper balance between centralisation and decentralisation. What that balance will be cannot be determined beforehand. The important thing is to continue making careful analyses and considerations, involving the previsouly mentioned advantages and disadvantages of either option.

7.11.3 Standardisation and mutual adjustment

Standardisation makes is possible to control employee activities and have these activities process according to plan. This is particularly true for the standardisation of work processes. An advantage of standardisation is that it requires less direct supervision and adjustments. A disadvantage is a

reduction in flexibility and commitment. Employees feel less responsible for the proper execution of their activities.
Adjustments based on mutual adjustment offer employees greater opportunity of scheduling and execution their activities based on their own insights. This increase the flexibility of the approach. A possible disadvantage is that management may lose its grip on the nature and quality of the execution. Standardisation of results or of knowledge and skills can be a solution to the aforementioned disadvantages. Both forms of standardisation can provide a certain level of guarantee for the production or service as required, while at the same time making it possible for employees to give their own take on how their work should be performed – within the established framework. It is important for management to find the proper balance between enforcing and relinquishing control when choosing between standardisation or mutual adjustment.

Standardisation helps organisations to manage employee activities, and to make sure these activities are performed according to plan. This applies in particular to the standardisation of operational processes.
The advantages of standardisation are:

Standardisation

- *Improved guidance and control.* Carefully and precisely determined and prescribed activities are easier to manage and control, and are more likely to be performed according to specifications.
- *Less coordination required.* Once work performance rules and regulations are accepted, mutual adjustments will require less coordination.

The disadvantages of standardisation are:
- *Lack of flexibility.* Rules and regulations may result in employees not being able to flexibly respond to changes to or problems with the working situation (see paragraph 7.4.3).

Coordination by mutual adjustment allows employees greater room when it comes to structuring and performing their own activities. One advantage is that it improves the flexibility of operational activities. One disadvantage is that it may cause management to lose its grip on the nature and quality of the operations. To some extent, the standardisation of results or of knowledge and skills may offer a solution to the aforementioned disadvantages. Both forms of standardisation may provide some guarantee for the production of goods or services as desired by management, while simultaneously making it possible to develop operational activities within the indicated standardised framework.

Mutual adjustment

When structuring an organisation, management is faced with the task of developing rules and regulations (standardisation) that ensure employee activities and goals are properly coordinated. Meanwhile, management should give adequate consideration to making sure that employees can address deviating situations with an appropriate response using mutual adjustments. Organisations need the correct balance to make sure employees are encouraged to approach their activities purposefully and effectively.

© Noordhoff Uitgevers bv

Figure 7.21 provides another overview of the issues management is faced with.

FIGURE 7.21 Challenges for management

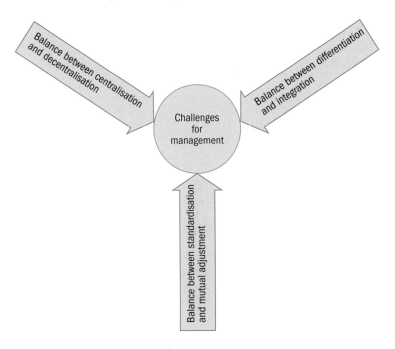

Tips for managers

Structural problems and solutions
- Excessively severe horizontal and vertical differentiation.
  Consequences: lack of motivation to work and work satisfaction, problems in the production or provision of services, absence through sickness and high personnel outflow.
  Solution: a less strict division of labour and more autonomy at lower levels of the organisation (selective decentralisation).

- Too few control mechanisms (supervision, standardisation, formalisation).
  Consequences: poor coordination within and between organisational units, scheduling and production problems (e.g. schedule is constantly revised, targets are not achieved, deliveries are late).
  Solution: hire more managers and implement more standardisation and formalisation (bureaucratisation). This solution is workable only if the size and complexity of the organisation are not too great and the organisation is operating in a stable environment.

- If structural problems are primarily the result of increased size and complexity, this can be resolved through selective decentralisation and the formation of semi-autonomous P-, G- or M-groups.

- If coordination problems are the result of one-off activities in which several departments need to be involved, implement a project or matrix structure.

- If there is a lack of flexibility in a dynamic environment, i.e. inability to respond quickly to the changing requirements of technology and/or the market, implement selective decentralisation, reduce rules and form semi-autonomous units.

Note: some of the above-mentioned problems can also be caused by defective styles of leadership (see chapter 6) and/or an unsuitable organisational culture (see chapter 8).

7

© Noordhoff Uitgevers bv

Summary

▶ Effective collaboration in organisations is possible only through:
  • division of activities into tasks and jobs
  • coordination of activities
  • allocation of responsibilities and creation of relationships
  • design of appropriate communication channels

▶ Dividing activities into tasks and jobs produces horizontal and vertical differentiation (specialisation).

▶ In allocating responsibilities and creating relationships, one can opt for centralisation or (selective) decentralisation.

▶ Standardisation can be applied to:
  • work processes
  • results
  • knowledge and skills

▶ Communication can proceed vertically, horizontally or directly. Grouping can take place on the basis of job, product, market or geographical area.

▶ Depending on the choices made, an organisation may be more organic or more mechanistic in structure, more loosely or more strongly interconnected and more flexible or rigid.

▶ The structure of an organisation is dependent on its size and complexity and the dynamics of the environment that is relevant to the organisation. A small organisation can have a simple structure:
  • one manager
  • a small number of operational employees
  • organisational units
  • (as yet) no staff services or supporting services

▶ If an organisation grows in size and complexity, a functional line-staff structure is created.

▶ Further growth in size and complexity can be managed by:
  • bureaucratisation
  • P-, M- and G-grouping
  • selective decentralisation

Assignments

7.1   Regional healthcare provider VEGA has over 600 employees who care for 1,000 mentally handicapped children and adults. The healthcare provided includes residential communities for children, residential communities and support points for adults, children's day-care centres and mobile services. There are over 40 locations. Managementis exercised through a central board of directors, a supervisory board, a family council and a works council. The healthcare services are divided into clusters: residential, day care and youth care. At the head of each cluster is a cluster manager. Under these are the location managers, who assign the group leaders to the locations. The group leaders provide leadership to their subordinates, who handle the day-to-day care of the children and adults. If necessary, they receive advice and support from experts, such as psychologists, orthopaedists, speech therapists, doctors and physiotherapists. Furthermore, there are supporting services, such as HR, economic/administrative services, technical and general support services, the communications department and consulting (see Figure 7.22).

FIGURE 7.22 The structure of VEGA

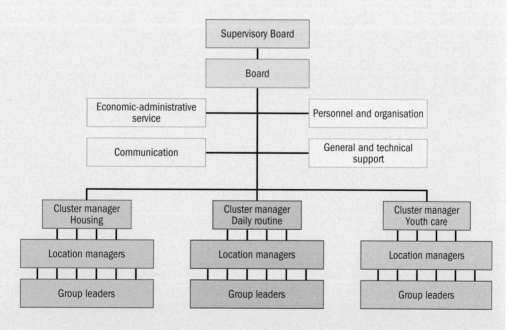

    a   How would you describe the overall structure of VEGA?
    b   Which forms of grouping does the structure of VEGA display?

© Noordhoff Uitgevers bv

c   To what extent is there strict or slight horizontal differentiation in the provision of healthcare?

d   How many hierarchical layers can be distinguished in the organisation?

e   What constitutes the staff services and supporting services?

7.2   The enormous success of his restaurant prompts the owner of *Valencia* to expand his establishment. He wants to start offering additional services, being: a tapas-bar with live flamenco and tango music, a catering department, and the upgrades to the current restaurant.

a   Which forms of grouping should the manager choose from? Which one would you choose and why?

b   What would product grouping for this business look like? Draft an organogram.

c   Which supporting services would you add? And in which form, centralised or decentralised?

7.3   The municipal government decides to proceed with the implementation of New World of Work for the Admin and Finance departments.

a   Which alignment methods does the introduction of NWW require?

b   Which leadership and management forms are suited to NWW?

c   What problems do you expect for the introduction of NWW?

8

Organisational culture

- What is culture?
- What is organisational culture?
- What types of organisational culture are there?
- What are healthy and neurotic cultures?
- How can organisational culture be established?
- How does the culture of an organisation develop?
- How can an organisation's culture be transmitted to new members?
- What is the influence of national culture on organisational culture?
- How can the culture of an organisation be changed?

8

© Noordhoff Uitgevers bv

A new working environment

Peter has just started in his job at a fashion design company. He quickly feels accepted by his colleagues. The atmosphere is cordial and people interact informally with one another and with management. On the other hand, they do work hard. Everyone makes an effort to do well for the company and no one complains if they have to work late in the evenings. All this is quite different from his previous job. He had to address management respectfully and, if there was no manager present, everyone slacked.

Melting pot?

Two consultancy firms decide to take part in a merger. All employees are attending a two-day conference to prepare them for future collaborations. The spoken language is English; one of the organisations has branches in both England and France. The Dutch employees are fine with this, but it is quite a problem for their French colleagues. The Dutch and English employees find it easy to intermingle and connect, with conversation turning positively lively at the bar. The French division, however, stands apart; they stick together during recess and other breaks, and contribute little in discussions during the workshops.

8.1 The concept of culture

Every organisation has a certain unique quality. This is noticeable after switching jobs, especially if you have been working somewhere for a long time. Peter quickly finds out that things in the new fashion company are very different from what he is used to, and he is pleasantly surprised. If two organisations with vastly differently cultures take part in a merger, the proper intergration of both organisations may be hindered. In the second example, the French employees stick together and avoid contact with the Dutch and English. This may produce problems for collaboration at a later stage. In general, mergers create fewer problems if the differences in culture are smaller.

The uniqueness of an organisation is also called the culture of that organisation. But what do we understand by culture?

Culture

When we talk about culture, we are often referring to cultural manifestations, such as exhibitions, films, theatre, music, dance and literature.

In the social sciences, the concept of culture is used differently. We see this, for example, in epithets like 'youth culture' or 'subculture'. These epithets refer to the uniqueness of certain groups of people. This uniqueness is apparent from the ways in which groups differentiate themselves, for example in their clothing, attitudes, behaviour, manners and ideas. Uniqueness becomes visible only if the group's members display a certain degree of homogeneity in their behaviour. Homogeneity within groups is the result of mutual influence and education. This is a kind of collective mental programming. According to Hofstede (1991), culture is the result of the collective mental programming that distinguishes members of one group or community from members of another group or community. The mental programming of the members of a community is focused on the creation of homogeneity in values, ideas, norms and behaviour.

Uniqueness

Homogeneity
Collective mental programming

8

● www.uchiyama.nl

Directness is not respectful

Mrs Yamanaka used to be a resident of the Netherlands for seven years; she returned to Japan in 2009. She found the most striking thing about the Netherlands to be the sense of 'order and control'. The bike paths, for example. "People have more free time, work much less, and enjoy longer holidays than compared to Japan. I began wondering why the Japanese work so much and so hard. The Dutch are direct, whereas the Japanese are indirect. I felt embarrassed on my first day of work in the Netherlands when someone casually asked me: 'Do you have a boyfriend?' The Dutch will tell you 'no' if they are unable or unwilling to do something. In Japan, saying 'no' outright can be considered poor manners, especially when you talking to a client. Instead of saying 'no', the Japanese would tell a customer: 'it would be exceedingly difficult...' or 'I shall consider it'. At first, being told no was shocking for me, because I felt as though I was being rejected as a person. But that is not the case at all: what is being rejected, is the argument."

Values   Values are principles that people within a community regard as worth striving for, such as equality, courtesy, honesty and courage. Values are profound cultural traits. They are not easy to identify and people are often
Ideas   unaware of their cultural values. Values can be derived from the ideas that people express. Parents who encourage their daughter to do her best at school imply that they think hard work and high performance are important values.

Norms   Norms are rules of behaviour that prescribe what people should or should not do. They apply to such aspects of behaviour as greeting people, giving birthday presents, holding the door open for someone and joining the end of a queue. Those who disregard norms often meet with comments or disapproving looks.

Behaviour   Behaviour that is specific to a certain culture results from the application of the culture's values and norms. Respect, for example, is expressed in various types of behaviour in China.

The uniqueness of a group or community can also be seen in the clothing they wear (an example is the clothing worn by women in strict Islamic countries) or in certain ritual greetings.

The uniqueness of a group or community can also be seen in the clothing they wear.

The transfer of culture begins at birth. Before his tenth birthday, a child has already adopted the most important values, norms and ideas of the community in which they are growing up. All the people in that community contribute to this transmission. Culture is thus collective and distinct from individual ideas.

Dominant culture   In larger communities, there are both a dominant culture and subcultures. The dominant culture comprises all the values and norms applicable within the whole community and is primarily determined by the dominant members of the community. Within the community, groups with their own subculture can also be identified. Subcultures contain the core values and norms of the dominant culture but codes of conduct (norms) can be different for each subculture.

Subculture

8.2   Organisational culture

An organisation is a small community. If people collaborate with each other for long periods, as is the case in groups (see chapter 3), a certain unity of values, norms and behaviour emerges. These then determine the organisational culture. The characteristic traits of that culture are recognisable in the specific ways in which the members of the organisation behave. Deal and Kennedy (1982) describe organisational culture as 'the way things get done around here'.

Organisational culture

Every organisation has a characteristic culture. This culture becomes apparent above all when changes take place, such as a merger. Differences in values, norms and ideas between the members of the organisations involved in the merger can cause clashes (see the following example).

NMB-PUBLICATION, J. TIBAU

Cultural differences

A Flemish and a Walloon brewery merged their businesses because it was estimated to offer them significant financial and commercial advantages. Soon, it became apparent that the cultures of both businesses were vastly different. The Walloon brewery put great stock in strong relationships of subordination, hierarchy, and a respectful attitude towards superiors. The Flemish, they felt, were undisciplined and rude. Employees of the Flemish brewery were used to participatory management. They interaction was much freer. They would occasionally hold brainstorming sessions where unconsidered remarks could be expressed without repercussion. The confrontation between the two cultures led to clashes and stereotyping. People began digging in their heels. Various grabs for power took place. At one point, the two parties tried to steal the other's market shares. This sabotage of the merger cost a lot of money and led to the sacking of 34 of the 40 members of the top executive layer on Simon [Beresford-Wylie, CEO of the new company]'s plate in this regard.

8

Cultural homogeneity within an organisation is important for effective collaboration between the members of the organisation. A sense of equality increases the employees' commitment to the organisation (Finigan, 2000; Van Vianen, 2000). Homogeneity also facilitates communication (see chapter 5), increases work satisfaction and improves relationships.

Organisations differ in the strength of their culture, which is the degree of homogeneity within them. In a **strong organisational culture**, the values, ideas and behaviour of the employees are to a great extent determined by the culture. In a **weak organisational culture**, the influence of the culture is much less.

Organisations have an interest in shared values and a strong organisational culture. Recently, companies have tended to formulate visions and mission statements in which core values have an important place. To what extent the formulated core values are shared by all the employees and are embodied in their way of working remains questionable.

EXAMPLE 8.1

Customer-friendliness?

The management of a large enterprise regularly proclaims that customer-friendliness and reliability are important values. In the company's television advertising, these values are also emphasised. This makes the workers on the shop floor laugh, because they know better.

The available resources and staff are nowhere near adequate for the ideals of management. Besides, anyone who works hard is discouraged by their colleagues with the motto 'Take your time; don't step out of line.'

Strength

As organisations increase in size, the likelihood that certain sections or departments will differentiate themselves by adopting their own subculture increases (see chapter 7). This reduces the strength of the organisational culture. The presence of subcultures can result in rivalry between departments (the in-group/out-group phenomenon), impede communication between departments and create differences of opinion about the way things should be done (see chapters 3 and 7).

8.3 Types of organisational culture

Although the culture of organisations is influenced by national culture, differences in organisational culture are still possible within one country. Various researchers have attempted to describe the characteristics of the culture of organisations. This has produced different typologies for organisational culture. This diversity is the result of different ways of looking at organisations and categorising the characteristics observed.
In this section, we discuss three typologies, each of which looks at organisations from a different viewpoint:
1 Harrison (1972) and Handy (1978) looked primarily at tasks, people, rules and power.
2 Deal and Kennedy (1982) focused primarily on the market in which an organisation operates and the type of product or service it supplies.
3 The typology of Kets de Vries and Miller (1984) was based on the personality traits of organisation's leaders.

8.3.1 The typology of Harrison and Handy
According to Harrison (1972), the organisation must take account of conflicting interests between itself and individuals. Individual interests include job satisfaction, security, influence and economic rewards. Organisational interests are focused on survival in a dynamic environment.

There are often different interests at stake, both for the organisation and for individuals, which may partly conflict with each other. The solutions that organisations find to these conflicting interests determine their culture. Harrison identifies the power-oriented organisation, the role-oriented organisation, the task-oriented organisation and the person-related organisation. Handy (1978) accepts this typology and gives the four types of culture the names of gods: Zeus, Apollo, Athena and Dionysus. Zeus symbolises the patriarch, with a charismatic personality; Apollo is the god of laws and regulations; Athena is the goddess of wisdom, who can resolve all problems; Dionysus symbolises the individualist; these four types of culture are described in more detail below:

1 Within organisations with a **power-oriented culture** (Zeus), there is a strong leader. Like a spider at the centre of a web, the leader controls the organisation. They prefer to surround themselves with loyal employees in whom they recognises themselves. Most employees try to get closer to the centre of the web. This can result in intrigues and power games.

EXAMPLE 8.2

The power of a cult leader

In a religious cult the leader is the central figure. They possess all the power and determine how the members should behave. Cult members try to improve their position, and thereby increase their power or privileges, by getting as close as possible to the leader and by making themselves liked by them.

---

2 A **role-oriented culture** (Apollo) is like a Greek temple. The foundations are formed by rules, agreements and procedures. The pillars are the different jobs and/or departments. The whole has a hierarchical structure. When the work is done according to the rules and procedures, this is perceived as correct and efficient. From the organisation's point of view, people are less important than their roles and status within the organisation. From the individual's point of view, position and status are more important than performance. This culture can be found in large, bureaucratic organisations.

3 Organisations with a **task-oriented culture** (Athena) emphasise skills and expertise. Management must be able to resolve problems. Results are more important than rules, power relationships or personal needs.

8

EXAMPLE 8.3

Result-orientation

Small start-up enterprises often have a strong task-oriented culture. The employees are building something together. There are few rules and no crystallised hierarchy. Only results count.

Is the ritual of a company party important in a person-oriented culture or a task-oriented culture?

4   In a **person-oriented culture** (Dionysus), the individual is foremost. The organisation exists for the benefit of its employees and not the other way round. The manager is the equal of the employee. Being a member of the management team does not bestow high status. Leadership is just one of many functions (the show must go on). The culture is characterised by few rules and procedures. The growth of the organisation is not an important objective. Examples of organisations with a person-oriented culture are small professional organisations with highly educated employees, such as consulting firms, law firms and partnerships.

8.3.2   The typology of Deal and Kennedy

Deal and Kennedy (1982) assume that the culture of organisations is determined by two variables: the degree of risk the organisation takes and the speed with which the organisation receives feedback about its operations.

Risk

There is a high level of risk if mistakes that are made in the production or provision of services can have serious consequences for the organisation. An airline, for example, runs a great deal of risk. If an aircraft crashes due to defective management, this can have disastrous human, financial and reputational consequences. If errors are made by a municipal administration, for example in the recording of a person's change of address, this has no great consequences for the organisation.

Feedback

There is rapid feedback if an organisation gets to hear within a short period of time whether its products or services are of sufficient quality and will sell in sufficient quantity to create a good financial position for the organisation. Some companies, for example, soon hear from their clients that a shipment of items is incorrect or has not arrived on time. They can also quickly intervene and correct the error. Government organisations often receive delayed feedback or no feedback at all if they do something wrong.

According to Deal and Kennedy, the combination of the degree of risk and the speed of feedback determines the culture of an organisation (see Figure 8.1).

FIGURE 8.1 The typology of Deal and Kennedy

	High risk	Low risk
Rapid feedback	Tough guy/macho culture	Work hard, play hard culture
Slow feedback	'Bet your company' culture	Procedure culture

We now look in detail at these four types of organisational culture:
1 The **tough guy/macho culture**: high risk and rapid feedback. This is a culture of individualists, rugged people who regularly have to take huge risks and can quickly see what the results of their actions are. Their 'macho' behaviour can be viewed as the result of uncertainty and a dangerous environment. In this culture, hard workers are generally less successful than hyperactive decision-makers; speed is more important than stamina. The 'stars' in this culture are famous for their rapid, effective action. Rituals are important. Superstition plays a role in this. Behind their success, people seek a certain 'magic'. This culture can be found in football teams and among surgeons, film-makers, property developers and people in show business.
2 The **work hard, play hard culture**: low risk and rapid feedback. Hard workers do well here. Job satisfaction is characteristic of people in this culture. Mistakes can be made; they are not dangerous, and there are plenty of new opportunities to be successful. Perseverance is important. Customer orientation is a central value. The team is more important than the individual. Results are achieved collectively. Success breeds success. This culture is seen among hotel managers, software managers and people in the automotive and consumer electronics trades.
3 The **'bet your company' culture**: high risk and slow feedback. People in this culture regularly take far-reaching decisions to which great risk is attached. It can take years before they know what the results of a certain decision are. Decisions are made by senior managers, who are in general thoughtful and respectful towards their colleagues because they need each other. In general, in this type of culture there are many meetings to discuss weighty specialist reports. Authority and technical knowledge are important. The role models have had to earn their status through many years of hard work and structured thinking. Young people have low status in this culture. This is the type of culture seen in the aviation industry, investment companies, computer manufacturers and oil companies.
4 The **process culture**: low risk and slow feedback. Work performance is often difficult to measure. People (therefore) attach importance to rules and procedures. It is more important how people behave than how they perform. The process is more important than the product. They try to avoid errors and initiative is discouraged. Punctuality is important. The

emphasis on formality in interactions is apparent, for example, in the 'initialling culture' of central government. The process culture is found in banks, legal institutions, insurance companies and accountancy firms.

8.3.3   The typology of Kets de Vries and Miller

Some organisations are not effective because their culture displays 'neurotic'

Neurotic traits

traits. These neurotic traits are, according to Kets de Vries and Miller (1984), a consequence of the personality traits of people at the top. They transmit their neurotic characteristics, such as anxiety, uncertainty, recklessness, distrust and schizophrenia, to the organisation.

Kets de Vries and Miller's typology draws on psychoanalytical terminology to establish a typology of different neurotic organisations. It consists of five

Cultures

types of cultures:

1 The **depressive culture** is based on a lack of self-confidence and a sense of failure. The atmosphere within the organisation is passive, apathetic, conservative and lacking in confidence. Everyone goes their own way. The managing director lacks the necessary leadership abilities. They may have feelings of guilt and pessimism. They shy away from important decisions. Little changes within the organisation. People have little interest in each other and quickly get discouraged.

2 The **compulsive culture** is based on the fear of losing control over what is happening in the organisation. In this culture people seem immovably focused on formalised systems for management and control. Everything is planned, each step is carefully considered; there is an obsession with information and control systems and there is an abundance of memos, schedules and budgets. The leader is often a perfectionist and is inclined to get lost in the detail and plan too much for fear of making mistakes. They can be dogmatic and stubborn; their authoritarian stance is the result of uncertainty.

3 The **dramatic culture** is based on the leader's need to be the centre of attention. Characteristic of their approach is the grand gesture. They are hyperactive, impulsive and reckless; hey have a great deal of power and are often boastful. Their behaviour can be called narcissistic. Everything revolves around them but they can never get enough admiration (see example 8.4). Employees are often poorly informed and everything is decided centrally. A proper communication network between employees is also often lacking.

EXAMPLE 8.4

'Golden boys'

Narcissist leaders can be highly productive. They are independent are self-confident enough to implement massive changes. But sometimes, their egos get in the way. Cees van der Hoeven (Ahold) was initially an effective manager, but over time became an authoritarian figure who surrounded himself with yes-men. His drive to keep expanding Ahold and buying up other companies using borrowed funds brought Ahold to the brink of disaster. Adding insult to injury was a tendency towards creative bookkeeping. Kees Storm (Aegon) was responsible for large scale fraud with respect to the sale of insurance policies, which turned out to be usurious at that.

Both managers were initially praised by their boards and acted like golden boys, earning massive premiums.

----

4 The **paranoid culture** is based on suspicion and mistrust. Employees develop a multitude of procedures for maintaining control of the business. The leader may be mistrusting by nature and confirmed in this attitude by certain traumatic events – for example, the disappearance of the market for the products the company produces or the arrival of a strong competitor on the scene. They are thin-skinned, suspicious of hidden agendas in others and aggressive in the face of a supposed attack. They are watchful of external developments, avoids risk and acts conservatively.

5 The **schizoid culture** is based on the feeling that the world does not have much to offer. In an organisation with such a culture, effective leadership is lacking. There is no strategy. People are no more connected to each other than grains of sand. Characteristic of the leader is an attitude of indifference, lack of commitment, anxiety and fickleness. People live strictly in their own little worlds. Characteristic also are aggressive outbursts within the organisation. The employees feel dependent on the leader but they show little guidance or interest. They therefore have little commitment and the organisation can become a battlefield of 'career-makers'.

The typology of Kets de Vries and Miller focuses on the harmful influence of leaders on the culture of the organisation. This suggests that the leaders at the top exercise decisive influence.

This may be the case in small organisations, but it is questionable whether one person can have so much influence in larger and more complex organisations. Kets de Vries and Miller suppose not. They assume that the defects described by them are compensated for in 'normal' organisations.

8.4 Organisational culture and effectiveness

8

Can one specific culture be found that is good for all organisations? No, because organisations differ too much in the nature of the products or services they supply, in the environments in which they operate (e.g. high or low risk) and in the phase of development they are in (young, small and dynamic or large and old). A certain culture will contribute to the success of an organisation if it fits in with the organisation's situation. We have already established this principle in connection with styles of leadership (see chapter 6). Which culture is the best depends on the following situational characteristics:

- The **phase of development** of an organisation. In a new organisation, an entrepreneurial and innovative attitude is important. A power- or task-oriented culture or a culture of work hard, play hard can be appropriate here. After a certain amount of growth, control and management will start to become more important. A role- or process-oriented culture is then more appropriate.
- The **environment** of the organisation. A dynamic and competitive environment requires a combative attitude, focused on taking risks. This fits the tough guy/macho culture. In a stable environment in which there is little or no competition, more attention can be paid to a good working atmosphere and the high quality of products or services. A person- or process-oriented culture is then preferable.
- The **nature of the tasks** that have to be performed. If these are simple, attention can be more focused on planning, standardisation and

© Noordhoff Uitgevers bv

formalisation. A role-oriented culture fits in with this. Complex tasks, for which highly-trained people are needed, are better tackled in a task- or person-oriented culture.

The organisational culture will form an impediment to the effectiveness of the organisation if the culture no longer matches the requirements dictated by the situation. If there is a transition from a stable to a dynamic or hostile environment, for example, the existing role- or person-oriented culture can be an impediment to adaptation. If the organisation grows, it can be necessary to convert a tough guy/macho culture or a power-oriented culture into a role-oriented culture.
A organisational culture can be rendered inappropriate by a change of strategy or changes in working methods. Problems can also arise if the attitude or behaviour of management contradicts new values that need to be adopted.

To find out whether an organisational culture suits the requirements of the (new) situation, it is first necessary to establish what that culture is.

8.5 Establishing the culture of organisations

How can we establish what culture an organisation has? This is not easy. The culture of an organisation can be compared to an iceberg: the tip is visible and protrudes above the water but most of the iceberg remains hidden.

The tip consists in the visible behaviour of the organisation's members. The hidden part of the iceberg encompasses their values, norms and ideas. In many cases, even the members of the organisation are unaware of these.

How can a reliable picture of an organisation's culture be obtained? Sanders and Neuijen (1987) regard organisational culture as a layered phenomenon, comparable to an onion. They call the layers: symbols, heroes, rituals, values and assumptions. The outer layer (symbols) is easy to observe (the tip of the iceberg). The deeper you go, the less visible the layers become (see Figure 8.2).

FIGURE 8.2 Aspects of culture: the layers of an onion

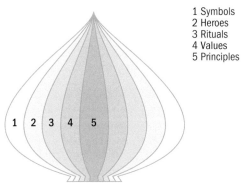

1 Symbols
2 Heroes
3 Rituals
4 Values
5 Principles

1 2 3 4 5

Source: Sanders & Neuijen, 1992

To reach the core of the onion (the organisational culture), the various layers must be peeled off. To this end, Sanders and Neuijen interviewed employees in different types of organisation and asked such questions as the following:

- Put yourself in the situation you were in when you came to work for this organisation. What were the most significant discoveries that you made in the first three months about working in this organisation?
- When is a new employee told that he fits in with the organisation? When is he told that he does not fit in?

We shall describe the characteristics of the layers of the onion in the following sections.

8.5.1 Symbols

The outer layer of the onion consists of symbols. Symbols can be words but also images, objects, attributes and other clear signs that express what is important and meaningful to the organisation. Sanders and Neuijen propose that symbols 'express what the organisation wants to be (or wants to mean)'.

Symbols

EXAMPLE 8.5

A new corporate style

Two merging hotels decide to implement all kinds of changes and introduce new symbols. A new logo is designed and a new corporate style is presented at the first joint staff meeting. All the rooms are redecorated and abstract paintings are hung on the walls. Employees are given new company clothing. These changes symbolise the desires of the new organisation.

Many symbols can be found within organisations. A few examples are:

- **Jargon**. People start to use the same abbreviations, vogue words, sayings and expressions. They differentiate themselves from other (comparable) organisations in this way. Subgroups or departments can emphasise their own identity by using different jargon.
- **Humour**. Every group of people develops a preference for a certain type of joke and way of teasing people.

EXAMPLE 8.6

Differences in humour

In the company where Peter used to work, they were partial to a somewhat bawdry sense of humour. This sometimes degenerated into crude and sexist remarks. Many of the female staff felt victimised. In the fashion house where he now works, this is not the case at all. The people here are mostly behave pleasantly towards one another and there is no discrimination between men and women.

© Noordhoff Uitgevers bv

- **Clothing and accessories.** Every organisation has a dress code. It may be customary to wear company clothing or a uniform. By wearing a suit, for example, managers distinguish themselves from uniformed employees. The suit then becomes a status symbol. Doctors distinguish themselves from nurses, for example, by wearing accessories such as a stethoscope.
- **Logo and house style.** More and more companies and institutions are implementing a house style. This often includes a logo; this is a visual representation – in the form of an animal, an object or a stylised composition – of the name of the company.

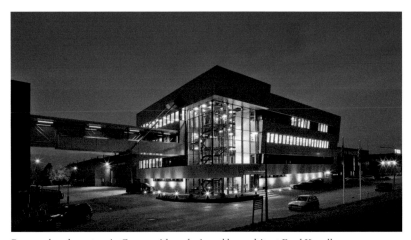

Breman headquarters in Genemuiden, designed by architect Fred Kapelle.

A house style symbolises unity externally and leads to uniformity internally. People use the same writing paper, the same design of business cards and the same type of printed material.
- **Premises.** The exterior of the company building provides some information about the organisation. Does the building makes a grand impression or is it almost impossible to find? The head office of TNT-Post is a rectangular building, an example of a 'no-nonsense' style. The head office of the Gasunie, on the other hand, features playful and unconventional architecture.

The interior of the building also radiates a certain image. There are hospitals with endless straight, empty corridors, but also hospitals with short corridors and a great deal of light, space and colour. The reception area also gives the visitor an impression of the organisational culture. A lawyer's office can exude reliability and confidence in tradition through the choice of portraits of previous incumbents and antique furniture.

8.5.2   Heroes

Heroes

The next layer of the onion is formed by heroes or role models. Examples of heroes are film stars, comic-book figures, sportspeople and political or religious leaders. Heroes may be real people or imaginary figures. Within an organisation, the heroes are the people thought to be important or who have made a contribution or displayed behaviour that is admired, such as the founders of the company or outstanding achievers. A manager who is also a hero can have a very great influence on the culture of the organisation.

Nelson Mandela will always remain a hero in the eyes of many.

In an organisation there are often also minor heroes. These are people who are noticed, stand out and embody the culture of the organisation. They get promotions and appreciation. They are regularly held up as examples to others but often also spontaneously imitated. The 'anti-heroes' are the people who do not make it within the organisation. They can provoke irritation or dislike in others. They can function as counter-examples.
To obtain insight into the heroes of an organisation, it is useful to listen to the stories or myths that are told about certain employees. Older staff who tell stories about the past can provide valuable data that is still relevant to the current culture.

8.5.3   Rituals
The third layer is formed by rituals. Rituals are habitual actions or customs **Rituals** that are thought to be important and meaningful within the organisation (see example 8.4). For example, every organisation has rituals associated with greetings and with eating and drinking during work breaks. Other examples of rituals are:
- the new year's party;
- the monthly meeting;
- the morning gymnastics session;
- awarding medals;
- decorating the chair of the person whose birthday it is.

8

EXAMPLE 8.7

Rituals

In the United States, one of the best known company rituals is the annual remuneration meeting organised by Mary Kay Cosmetics. This meeting takes place over several days on the stage of a large theatre. Saleswomen who achieve good figures are rewarded with gifts such as diamond pins, fur stoles and Cadillacs.

At an anniversary party thrown by Joop van de Ende, celebrities served dinner to the guests while the make-up artists, technicians and other backstage staff put on a show. This could develop into a regular ceremony.

(Source: Robbins, 1989)

Practices

Rituals, heroes and symbols are the three layers of the onion that are closest to the surface. Hofstede calls these layers 'practices'. They are the most visible aspects of organisational culture. The values and assumptions underlying these practices are not visible and must be inferred from observation of the visible aspects.

8.5.4 Values and assumptions

Values

Tacit assumptions

Values are things that people consider important and will strive to protect or preserve, such as honesty, politeness, loyalty and solidarity. Norms are linked to values. Underlying values and norms are what Schein (1985) calls 'tacit assumptions', assumptions of which people are no longer aware. These are ideas or presuppositions about what constitutes reality. Such assumptions can be related to our relationship with the world. Is the world safe or unsafe? Can we shape reality around us or are we victims of circumstances? Assumptions can also be related to one's relationship with other people. Are people fundamentally equal or unequal? Are they good or bad? Can they be trusted or not? These assumptions determine to a significant extent our attitude towards people.

If people in an organisation have the same assumptions, discussions of principle are no longer necessary. Furthermore, shared values and assumptions provide guidance in the resolution of problems.

● www.unilever.nl (translated)

Our vision

Unilever products impact the lives of over two billion people, day in and day out. This impact is expression in different ways. Some people feel good about themselves after washing their hair, or after tidying or cleaning their home, having a lovely cup of tea, a good meal, or a healthy snack.

The four pillars of our vision have established our company's long-term course – where we want to go, and how we are going to get there:
1 We are working towards a better future, every day.

2 We help people feel good, look good, and make the most of life through brands and services that are good for them and for others.
3 We inspire people to small, everyday acts that, when put together, can have a real impact on the world.
4 We develop new ways of doing business whose goal is to double the scope of our company, while simultaneously lowering our impact on the environment.

We have always had faith in the ability of our brands to improve the lives of people and to do what is right. As our company grows, so do our responsibilities. We realise that global challenges such as climate change are matters that concerns us all. Accountability for the wider impacts of our actions is ingrained in our values; it is a fundamental part of who we are.

8.6 The development of organisational culture

How is the culture of an organisation created? Many factors play a part in the development of a culture, such as the nature of the work and the environment in which the organisation must operate, but it is primarily created by the people who founded the organisation. Once the culture has developed, it is the (top) managers who embody, maintain or gradually change the culture.

According to the theory of Schein (1985), the culture of an organisation arises out of a learning process that is focused on finding the best way for members to interact with each other and with the environment in which they are involved. It is a process whose goal is internal integration and external adaptation.

Learning process

Ad 1 Internal integration
Internal integration is the adaptation of the activities of the members of the organisation to each other and to the goals of the organisation. In the process of integration, they learn how they must interact with each other. Once the appropriate manner of interaction has been found, this is elevated to a norm or value. Henceforth, interaction must take place in the prescribed manner.

As well as these norms or values, internal influences on the culture of an organisation include the ideas of the founders, changes in leadership, the organisation (design) of the building in which it operates and developments in working practices and communication.

Ad 2 External adaptation
External adaptation is the adaptation of the organisation to its environment. Clients, suppliers, banks and authorities may impose certain requirements, with which the organisation must comply.

EXAMPLE 8.8

Behavioural norms

If an employee falls sick, this can produce problems. Activities may be left undone, deadlines missed and other team members overloaded. The situation is made more problematic if the employee does not report sick on time and if it is not clear how long he will be absent. The rule, thererefore, is that a person must report to their manager at the beginning of the working day that they are sick and state as soon as possible how long they expect to be absent. It has also been decided that after two days' absence a temporary employee will be hired.

EXAMPLE 8.9

Discontented clients

A bank is losing clients because they are finding it more and more difficult to get anything done. The bank's opening times of the are not convenient for people with jobs, and it is difficult to contact the right people by phone. The bank considers the complaints it has received on this subject and what measures can be taken to reduce them. This results, among other things, in employees having to undergo training in customer-friendly behaviour.

External influences on the culture of an organisation include legislation by the government and the EU, other companies in the sector, market developments and mergers.

Based on the organisation's collective experiences of success and failure, common values, norms and beliefs arise about what is correct and worth striving for. The culture of an organisation is thus a product of various internal and external factors. Organisations differ from each other in this respect because they are exposed to different internal and external problems or opt for different solutions to the same problems.

Schein's theory closely matches the group development theory described in chapter 3. In a group, shared values, norms and ideas also arise. They result from the attempts of the group's members to bring about satisfactory methods of collaboration. These methods are related to both internal matters (internal integration) and the necessity to adapt to the environment (external adaptation).

Once an organisational culture has been developed, it continues to exist despite the fact that some employees leave the organisation and new employees are recruited. The culture of an organisation is relatively stable because the culture is confirmed and transmitted every day.

"Oh, look. Elly is off to give someone else a piece of her mind."

8.7 Transmitting organisational culture

The transmission and maintenance of an organisational culture occurs in several ways. It begins with the selection of new personnel.
As far as possible, employees are hired who fit in with the existing culture. In the selection process, the interview is an important way for both individuals and organisations to assess the fit. Some companies have very long selection procedures to find out whether applicants share their values, norms and beliefs. On the other hand, selection can be a means of culture change. In this case, management will want to bring in people who have accepted the new values they wish to adopt.

Selection

Staff selection is a powerful means of maintaining a culture. Management will be inclined to contract employees who fit the current established culture. An important means of gauging potential employee-compatibility with both individuals and organisations is the application interview. Some companies make use of extended application procedures to establish whether the applicant shares the company's values, norms, and notions to a sufficient degree. In a similar fashion, selection can be used as a means of changing organisational culture. In this case, management begins recruiting people who better fit and propagate the organisations new 'values'.

Socialisation

Socialisation is another powerful means of teaching and confirming desired behaviour and beliefs. Rewards and modelling by management can be important parts of this learning process (see chapter 2). Rewards are often intangible, taking the form of compliments and the granting of greater independence, for example. Punishment also plays a part, for example in the form of employees being made to do a task again, being the target of annoying remarks or receiving more supervision.

Values and norms should be accepted and internalised by an employee during the socialisation process. This is not always the case, however. Often, employees accept only 'practices or forms of expression'. They adapt but they will only conform with what they ought be doing if their behaviour is visible to others.

Education training

Education and training are also means of stimulating employees to learn desired behaviour and accept fundamental values. Some companies opt for a long probationary period for employees, with a rigorous entry programme (see example 8.10).

EXAMPLE 8.10

New leadership style

The strong growth of Fortis gave rise to problems with external adaptation (strategy and vision) and internal integration (control). Senior management decided to employ a new leadership style. The criteria that leaders would have to meet were expressed in new values and norms concerning performance, entrepreneurship, customer orientation and modelling. In this modelling, the leaders would have to show that they were positive and display courage and passion.

To achieve all this, 3,000 managers were invited to undergo an extensive training programme. The programme ended with the drafting of a personal leadership story and an action plan. Fortis was of the opinion that this training had been successful and that the commitment of senior management and its modelling had been a particularly important factor.

Modelling

Modelling is important because it is the visible manifestation of values which can be imitated by members of the organisation. It is primarily management that influences the culture of organisations through modelling. They model the beliefs and behaviour that are desirable in the organisation. How management behaves in times of crisis is crucial. Do they cope with people's issues properly? Can they help assuage others in times of crisis? Are they able to take the right decisions quickly, and communicate quickly?

Promotion and dismissal are further means of reinforcing and maintaining an organisation's culture. People who support and embody the values, norms and beliefs of the organisation are placed in central positions. Employees who behave differently are demoted or dismissed.
The organisation has other ways of maintaining its culture. Essential matters are repeatedly emphasised and the members of the organisation are given a sense of community by means of rituals. People learn that it is important always to have lunch together or to treat one another on their birthday. They can also come to value the Christmas speech by the managing director, the annual excursion or the celebration of anniversaries.

Promotion and dismissal

Rituals

8.8 Organisational culture and nationality

The culture of an organisation is not created in a vacuum. People often join an organisation after they reach maturity. They have by then been shaped by the culture of the social grouping and the society (country) in which they live. They therefore bring a number of values, norms and beliefs with them. National culture plays a part in the culture of organisations. We shall clarify this with reference to research by Hofstede (1980).

National culture

8

Clash of cultures.

Hofstede studied questionnaires issued by branches of the multinational enterprise IBM in 53 countries. Hofstede wondered whether people would make different value judgements despite working in the same organisational environment. This turned out to be accurate. The data from his research show that there are four parameters on which organisations can differ from country to country. These parameters are: degree of acceptance of power difference, individualism versus collectivism, masculinity versus femininity, and degree of avoidance of uncertainty. We shall explain these four parameters in this section, which ends with some conclusions on Hofstede's research.

8.8.1   Acceptance of power difference

To what extent do people accept power differences? Must everyone in principle be treated equally or is it accepted that higher-ranking individuals have a lot more say and a number of privileges? A high degree of acceptance of power difference is accompanied by, among other things, obedience and respect (in individuals) and a tendency towards centralisation (in the organisation). Examples of countries with large power differences are Malaysia, the Arab countries, Guatemala, Mexico, Italy and France. Low acceptance of power difference goes hand in hand with more say for employees in the organisation, which can be seen in progress meetings and less strict hierarchical relationships, among other things. Small power differences can be found in Austria, Israel, the Scandinavian countries, Great Britain, the Netherlands and the United States.

8.8.2   Individualism versus collectivism

Is individual or collective behaviour more highly valued? Within a strongly individualistic culture, values such as independence, freedom and self-development are found. Each individual is deemed to be primarily responsible for himself. In a collectivist culture, people are from birth included in strong, closely-knit groups. These groups offer lifelong protection in exchange for unconditional loyalty.

Individualistic culture

Collectivist culture

Wealthy countries, such as the United States, Australia, Great Britain and the Netherlands, score highly for individualism. Poor countries such as Ecuador, Pakistan and African countries almost all score low for individualism. Hofstede (1991) therefore states that there is a close connection between national wealth and degree of individualism.

8.8.3   Masculinity versus femininity

To what extent is there in society a division between the sexes and a differentiation of sex roles? Women in general prefer more collaboration than competition. They consider good relationships with their manager and their colleagues at least as important as good performance. They are more considerate, have more empathy and express their feelings more than men.

Feminine culture

In a feminine culture, the above-mentioned differences between men and women are less apparent. People express their feelings more and attach greater value to good collaboration and good relationships and are less competitively inclined. In a masculine culture, the differences between men and women are greater. Men are more dominant, more aggressive and more competitive and women are more emotionally and socially oriented. The differences between men and women are reinforced in cultures in which women have fewer rights and are dominated by men. Strongly masculine societies are found in Japan, Venezuela, Italy, Germany and the United

Masculine culture

States. Countries that score low for masculinity are Costa Rica, the Netherlands and the Scandinavian countries (see the following example). Cultural differences have an impact on how people work and debate in groups. The way people interact may differ from country to country.

ELSEVIER, ANNEGREET VAN BERGEN

Yankees go home!

The tendency of Dutch companies to introduce US management methods does not mesh with Dutch culture.
(...)
The question as to what energises Dutch employees – what makes them tick – can be answered using the work done by cultural investigators. They have found that the Netherlands has a feminine culture, with an emphasis on care, intimacy, personal relationships, and quality of life. The Dutch feel that living well beats winning. This is entirely different from the masculine American culture. Important aspects in those cultures are money, success, ambition, and competition: people love a winner and want to be one.
In the context of work, one difference between the citizens of the Netherlands and citizens of the US is that the former feel that appreciation from their manager is more important than a pay rise. They feel energised by an 'attaboy'. They also feel that their work needs substance more than they need a career. As a result, the Dutch mentality differs immensely from the US one. Because although neither culture feels that an uneven distribution of power is acceptable (or, in the jargon of cultural study: the power distance in both countries is minor), US culture is one of

yes-men. However, this compliant nature is not the result of respect but of self-interest. Disputing your boss' statements and showing any form of critical thinking – which comes natural in the Netherlands – is known as a CLM in the US: a career limiting move. The tendency of Dutch companies to apply US management methods and only assessing people based on targets does not mesh with Dutch culture. Particularly since there are more and more 'fast boy managers' being introduced to the scene, all of them explaining what their employees should be doing in fine detail, while giving no substantial encouragement. The only thing that seems to matter is striving for efficiency. For many Dutch people, this is disastrous. For one thing, there are no breaks in which they can recharge their batteries.
But mainly because the cold-hearted drive to be profitable does not offer them anything of substance. It does not refuel them. In fact, they become exhausted. And so, simply copy-pasting US management techniques has a counterproductive effect. If the Netherlands truly wants to retain its appeal to its working masses, then employers should start offering their employees the motivation they are looking for. That would work much better.

8.8.4   Avoidance of uncertainty

To what extent do members of a culture feel threatened by uncertain or unknown situations? This feeling of being threatened is expressed in nervous tension and a need for formal and informal rules (Hofstede, 1991), among other things. In very anxious cultures, where uncertainty is strictly avoided, 'what is different is dangerous'. There is little tolerance of deviant behaviour. People seek support in rules or absolute values. Emotions are

Uncertainty

© Noordhoff Uitgevers bv

freely expressed. In a society that allows uncertainty, rules are less strict and values more relative. People are more tolerant and cope better with conflict. Countries with strong avoidance of uncertainty are Belgium, Japan and Guatemala. Weak avoidance of uncertainty is found in Singapore and Great Britain.

8.8.5 Conclusions from Hofstede's research

The scores of the countries studied and their differences on the four parameters are shown in Table 8.1.

TABLE 8.1 Scores of 10 countries on the 4 parameters

	Power difference	Individualism	Masculinity	Uncertainty avoidance
Guatemala	95	6	37	101
India	77	48	56	40
Turkey	66	37	45	85
Singapore	74	20	48	8
Belgium	65	75	54	94
Japan	54	46	95	92
USA	40	91	62	46
Netherlands	38	80	14	53
Great Britain	35	89	66	35
Denmark	18	74	16	23

The countries with a top score in a single parameter are Guatemala (great power difference), the United States (individualism), Japan (masculinity) and Guatemala (high uncertainty avoidance). The countries that score lowest are Denmark (small power difference), Guatemala (collectivism), the Netherlands (femininity) and Singapore (low uncertainty avoidance). The big differences between the Netherlands and Belgium are striking. Belgium scores highly on power difference and uncertainty avoidance. High scores on these two parameters are a good breeding ground for bureaucracy. The Netherlands scores comparably with the United States and Great Britain on three dimensions. Only on the dimension of masculinity does the Netherlands score much lower. Hofstede (1991) describes the failure of his own application to an American company as the result of misunderstandings associated with this cultural aspect. He adopted too hesitant and modest an attitude, while the American personnel manager expected him to sell himself as strongly as possible and make it clear that he was the best man for this job.
Organisations that do business with foreign companies can benefit from studying cultural differences. When companies from different cultures collaborate, they can benefit from each other's strong points. For example:

- One company may bring precision in performance (high uncertainty avoidance) and the other supply new ideas (low uncertainty avoidance).
- A company from a feminine culture will be good at managing personnel, while a company from a masculine culture will ensure efficient manufacturing or production.

In a company with a collectivist culture, ties to the employer are strong, while in an individualistic company job mobility is greater. People are also more likely to be fired. Japanese–Dutch companies are characterised by the commitment of employees to their work, the tendency to keep people for a long time ('lifetime employment'), collective activities outside work time and strong result orientation.

The four dimensions that Hofstede describes in fact correspond to a number of basic problems which play a part in any society and have to be resolved. These are:

- How do people handle social inequality?
- How do they handle the (uncertain) future?
- What is the relationship between the individual and the collective?
- What is the relationship between the sexes?

8.9 Cultural bias

Hofstede points out that certain theories about people and organisations are strongly culture-related. Thus Maslow's theory about the value of self-development is a highly individualistic theory. In more collectivist cultures, self-development is not an important value, while solidarity with the group and the fulfilment of obligations are valued.

Culture-related

Another example is the approach to work structuring in the United States and Scandinavia. While in Scandinavian countries people work a great deal in autonomous groups, in the United States an individual approach is preferred. Americans are more highly performance oriented. This is related to their high scores for individualism and masculinity. The culture in Scandinavia, on the other hand, is highly feminine.

The bias of Western researchers studying differences in culture between countries is illustrated by Hofstede with a Chinese questionnaire. The (oriental) researchers discovered a fifth dimension to add to the four dimensions of Hofstede. This dimension is concerned with timescale and the extent to which people strive for reward in the short term or the long term. Cultures that focus on the long term attach great value to tradition, respect, hard work, patience and fulfilling social obligations. Young people owe respect and obedience to their elders and superiors. This also applies to organisations.

Timescale

Long term

Cultures that focus on the short term generate values and etiquettes that are focused on the present day. In these cultures people consider change, dynamism, rapid results, initiative and independence of thought important. There is less respect for elders, superiors and traditions. People are more impulsive and opt for consumption rather than saving.

Short term

© Noordhoff Uitgevers bv

Long-term focus: hard work in China.

Short-term focus is present in Pakistan, the Philippines, Zimbabwe, Great Britain and the United States. Long-term focus is found in China, Taiwan, Japan and South Korea. Both forms of focus have advantages and disadvantages. Short-term focus can be effective in situations requiring innovation and dynamism. A disadvantage can be that, over a longer period of time, actions are seen to be ill-advised. Long-term focus, on the other hand, can hinder change and adaptation.

When doing business in countries with a long-term focus, it is important to show respect for the values applicable in these countries. You must take your time and first develop a relationship with the people at the top of an organisation.

8.10 Changing the organisational culture

It is sometimes necessary to change the culture in an organisation. A municipal power company may, for example, need to become a private enterprise. Public companies are typically bureaucratic, with a strict hierarchy, an 'initialling culture' and internal fiefdoms; little attention is paid to efficiency and customers often have to wait a long time for attention. (In the eyes of the power companies, consumers had few rights but plenty of obligations.) The culture of this type of organisation can also be described as a role- or process-oriented culture. In order to function as a private enterprise and compete with others, a cultural shift is necessary. The organisation must, for example, think and act in a more customer-oriented manner, respond more quickly to opportunities and threats, work more efficiently and improve internal collaboration. A task-oriented culture or a culture of work hard, play hard becomes more appropriate.
In this section we discuss the extent to which cultures can be changed and how change can be effected.

8.10.1   Extent to which a culture can be changed

The culture of an organisation is characterised by stability and sustainability. If changes occur, they do so gradually and often imperceptibly. Writers on the subject have often expressed doubts as to the extent to which a culture can be changed in the relatively short term and using outside influence. They are unanimous on the point that this is not a simple matter. The culture is formed, as Schein has stressed, through an adaptive learning process. This process is natural and is determined by psychological laws. There are nonetheless opportunities to exert influence on it. It is, however, only on the outer layers of the onion that influence can be exerted. Practices (symbols, rituals and heroes) that are current in the organisation can be influenced. The deeper layers of values and assumptions cannot be changed, as they are anchored in the national culture and in the life histories of the people who comprise the organisation.

Stability
Sustainability

Practices

Values
Assumptions

The persistence of established patterns of behaviour (practices) is illustrated by the following experiment.

EXAMPLE 8.11

Socialisation of monkeys

A monkey was put in a cage. In the cage was a ladder and at the top of the ladder was a shower head that resembled a banana. When the monkey saw what it thought was a banana, it climbed the ladder and grabbed it. When grabbed, the banana (shower head) started to spray water and the monkey got wet. A second monkey was then introduced into the cage. When it tried to grab the shower head, it was chased away by the first monkey, who remembered that he had got wet doing this. A third monkey was kept away from the shower head in the same way. The first monkey, which had got wet, was now removed from the cage, so that there was no longer a monkey that had experienced getting wet. Nevertheless, new monkeys that came into the cage were chased away from the shower head by monkeys 2 and 3.

Even if the above experiment shows that behavioural patterns are persistent, a cultural change must nevertheless focus primarily on these patterns, because it is much more difficult to change the underlying values. The idea behind this is that cultural change follows from behavioural change.

8.10.2   How to effect cultural change

If cultural change is necessary, various things must be done to bring it about. We shall look at five requirements: making people aware of the necessity for change; commitment, inspiration and communication of the new vision from the top; organisational and structural support; training and reinforcement; symbols, heroes and rituals.

Making people aware of the necessity for change

Within the organisation there must be a realisation that cultural change is necessary. In a merger between two organisations, people usually experience a 'culture shock', when clashes arise between employees from the two different cultures. The necessity for change can arise as a result of internal problems or external threats.

Necessity

Vision, involvement and inspiration from the top

Vision

Senior management must formulate a clear, concrete vision that obviates what course the organisation must take. The mission (strategic path) must be clearly presented to employees. This indicates what new principles and core activities are important and what concrete measures will be taken to implement them.

Involved

It is important that senior management is personally involved in the implementation of the new cultural elements. Employees must notice that senior managers are sufficiently involved. This can be done by setting an example in a visible manner and functioning as a role model. The top man of the Mita Europa company, for example, drove a fork-lift truck himself to deliver copying machines to the stockroom during Mita Nederland's move to new premises.

Involvement alone is not sufficient. Management must also provide

Inspiration

inspiration. Good morale is important. People must be motivated and made enthusiastic about the new plans. A stimulating attitude can help in this.

Organisational and structural support

The organisation can try to enthuse the staff, or at least keep them involved, through meetings and motivational campaigns. This is necessary to obtain

Organisational support

sufficient organisational support for the changes. In any case, it is important that people are well informed and are able to contribute to the change process. The goals must be clear, meaningful and preferably attractive to them.

Structural support

Structural support is also necessary for new commercial practices. If more participation by employees and a more flexible approach to problems are required, for example, structures such as a strong hierarchy, centralised administration and regulatory rigidity must be dismantled. A more organic structure may be required (see chapter 7).

Education and reinforcement

Different skills and attitudes are not acquired overnight. It can be necessary to support the planned culture change by leading employees in the desired

Educating

direction and educating them. The belief among employees that the desired changes and their contribution to these changes will result in success is important to the organisation. To this end, some early success must be achieved and made visible. Employees need feedback on the results of their efforts. If their contribution is effective and they fit into the new culture,

Reinforcement

reinforcement is necessary to make the new behaviour take root.

EXAMPLE 8.12

Rewarding

A campaign to promote economical driving among UPS drivers started with training. The drivers were taught how to accelerate, change gear and manoeuvre more economically. Subsequently, each driver's fuel consumption was displayed every week; every month, the bonus they had been awarded as a consequence of their improvements was also indicated. After a few months, the drivers had made the new driving behaviour their own. Without prompting they would teach a new driver how to drive more economically.

Symbols, heroes and rituals

The desired culture within the organisation can be supported by new
symbols, such as a new house style and a different logo. Company clothing   Symbols
and the interior of the building can also be changed. The new logo must
represent the new values, such as dynamism and vitality, customer-
friendliness or reliability and soundness. Making the house style consistent
projects distinctiveness and unity. By making employees who have worked
hard for the change the centre of attention or bringing in top people who can
function as role models, new heroes can be created. New rituals can also be   Heroes
introduced to stimulate a new style of interaction and give the new values a   Rituals
more concrete form.

In general, cultural change takes a great deal of time and effort. Management
must deploy various resources at the same time, set an example and make
positive results visible and rewarding. A one-off campaign is usually
insufficient. Cultural change requires tenacity and endurance.

EXAMPLE 8.13

Symbols

In the merger between two management
consultancies, consultancy G, which moved
in with consultancy H, chose a pyramid as a
symbol. On the day the staff of consultancy
G moved in, a paperweight in the form of a
transparent pyramid was put on every desk.
In the canteen, a large illuminated pyramid
had been mounted on a pillar. The staff of
consultancy G told the staff of consultancy

H that the pyramid symbol, representing
wisdom, had been found in their archives
and they wanted to share it with them.
Some of consultancy H's staff responded
very positively to this. The sociability and
the non-conformism of the idea appealed to
them.

Source: Sanders, 1991

8

© Noordhoff Uitgevers bv

Tips for managers

Every organisation has a culture. Large organisations often have subcultures within each department.

Cultural typologies
Determine where your organisation or department stands according to the typology of Deal and Kennedy or Harrison and Handy. Then answer the following questions:
- Does the cultural type of your organisation fit the situation in which the organisation operates? Think about things like risks that must be taken, the feedback you receive, the requirements imposed by the environment and the nature of the activities that have to be performed within the organisation.
- What subcultures are there within your organisation? In what ways are these subcultures productive and where do they constitute an impediment to collaboration between organisational units?
- How could the culture in your department be described? Does the culture match the requirements of your department?

Changing the existing culture
Changing a culture at departmental or organisational level is approached as follows:

- Make clear what the problems are and what has to happen to resolve them (vision).
- Make clear what new values, norms and behavioural patterns are necessary in order to function better.
- Make the desired changes possible by training and educating employees, by modelling and by providing organisational and structural support for the changes.
- Make sure the new values, norms and modes of behaviour are reinforced by the creation of new heroes, symbols and rituals.

Points to bear in mind
- Take account of cultural differences in your approach to your employees.
- Be aware that such differences can result in the misinterpretation of reactions and behaviour.
- Pay a great deal of attention to these possible differences and ask for feedback (see also chapter 5) if you think something has not been properly understood.
- Be aware of cultural differences in your interactions with colleagues and partners from foreign companies.

Summary

▶ Culture comprises the shared values, norms, ideas and behavioural patterns of the members of a group or society. They are created through collective mental programming.

▶ In organisations, mental programming (of their members) also takes place. This produces an organisational culture.

▶ Different types of organisational culture can be identified, namely:
  • power-oriented, role-oriented, task-oriented and person-oriented (Harrison and Handy)
  • tough guy/macho; work hard, play hard; 'bet your company'; and process (Deal and Kennedy)

▶ Which culture is best for an organisation depends on:
  • its phase of development
  • the nature of its environment
  • the tasks that must be performed

▶ Organisations can have functional problems if they have a culture that does not match the situation they are in or if the culture starts to display neurotic traits.

▶ Neurotic organisational cultures are:
  • the depressive culture
  • the compulsive culture
  • the dramatic culture
  • the paranoid culture
  • the schizoid culture

▶ On the surface of an organisation's culture are characteristics that are visible (symbols, heroes and rituals). Underlying these are characteristics that are not visible and of which people are hardly aware.

▶ The culture of organisations arises from:
  • learning processes (successful solutions for internal integration and external adaptation)
  • influence (of important members of the organisation, such as founders and managers)

▶ Transmitting the organisational culture to new members takes place through:
  • selection
  • socialisation
  • education and training
  • modelling
  • promotion and dismissal
  • rituals

▶ A directed change of culture must begin with awareness of its necessity. Senior management must provide a clear vision, demonstrate its commitment and supply new heroes, symbols and rituals for new behavioural patterns through education and training and the provision of the appropriate organisational and structural support.

8

Assignments

8.1 Read the following article.

PW, LOUISE BOELENS

Organisational culture

US organisational psychologist and advisor Robert Quinn is well-known for his 'model of competing values'. The basis for this model is an empirical study by John Campbell and others who identified 39 factors which can be used to measure the effectiveness of an organisation. Statistical studies show that those indicators can all be grouped in one of two dimensions. The first is best summarised in short as 'flexibility versus stability', the second as 'internal focus versus external focus'. These two dimensions can be plotted as the lines of a quadrant, which can be used to classify the four main forms of organisational culture: adhocracy, family culture, hierarchy, and market culture. Quinn and his research group found that all of these elements are found in any company, but that usually one of them is the dominant element.

They developed a simple questionnaire which can be used to determine what that pattern looks like in a particular organisation, as well as what it ideally should look like. The gap between the current and the desired situations indicates the objectives of culture change actions should focus on.

a   Draw Quinn's two dimensions of two axles perpendicular to each other. Fill in the typology by Harrison and Handy on this coordinate system as best as possible. Then, fill in the typology by Deal and Kennedy.
b   Which types are hardest to place into the two dimensions, and why?

8.2 Read the following article.

PW (EDITED)

Transition to customer-centricity

A certain energy company was forced to move away from their monopoly position as the result of market liberalisation. Their new position was to be one of market-centricity. Because of its previous monopoly position, the company knew an official structure. Under the reign of this culture, the company had a highly

hierarchical setup. Superiors issued their orders and a legion of rules determined how employees should get their jobs done. To the employees, superiors and rules outranked user wishes. The new, liberalised situation required them to transition to flexibility and customer-centricity. In order to encourage that transition, all employees were offered a course on the topic, and many conferences were held to address the issues. Employees were taught 'users' had now become 'customers', and that there existed concepts like 'market-centricity', 'service', 'flexibility', and 'pricing policy'.
Then, everyone moved on to their normal, day-to-day affairs – and it turned out that little had changed.

a Which of the cultural change methods listed in paragraph 8.10 were applied in this example, and which are missing?
b Why were courses and conferences unsuccessful?

8.3 Chinese Dutchmen: from hospitality to applied university

In 2011, the Dutch Agency for Socio-Cultural Planning presented a study of Chinese citizens of the Netherlands. The 110.000-odd Chinese are faring well in the Netherlands, the study shows; in some aspects, even better than native Dutchmen and -women. One example is the fact that 85% of second-generation Chinese moves on to post-secondary education (compared to 59% of natives). Additionally, the second-generation is strongly represented in high-level functions, and knows only little unemployment (5%). Over half are best friends with a native Dutch person. And 20% no longer speak even a word of Chinese.

13% of the Chinese residents are entrepreneurs (compared to 7% for both Turkish and native Dutch residents). Two thirds of those enterprises are in the hospitality industry, 43% of whose employee records consist of employees with a Chinese background. Net labour participation is higher among the Chinese than among natives. Total unemployment is slightly higher compared to native Dutch people, but much lower compared to Turkish and Moroccan residents.

The parents of the second generation, being the first generation of Chinese in the Netherlands, struggle with the Dutch language and have relatively little contact with the natives. Chinese culture places great emphasis on education. Chinese parents feel hard work and good achievements are important. This is clearly a beneficial influence on their children's performance at school.

Less than half of Chinese residents of the Netherlands (very) strongly identifies with the Netherlands; the make relatively little use of Dutch media, do not participate much in the voluntary sector, and are not very frequently in contact with native Dutch people. The concept of family occupies a central spot in their culture. Additionally, the Chinese seem focussed more on their group of origin than on their country of origin. Homesickness and the desire to return to their native country are

© Noordhoff Uitgevers bv

uncommon. Compared to other migrant groups, Chinese residents of the Netherlands feel more accepted. They also report less instances of discrimination. Hofstede's study indicates the following cultural differences between the Netherlands, Hong Kong, Singapore, and China (see Table 8.2):

TABLE 8.2 Cultural differences

Dimension	Netherlands	Hong Kong	Singapore	China
Power distance	38	68	74	-
Individualism	80	25	20	-
Masculinity	14	57	48	-
Uncertainty avoidance	53	29	8	-
Long-term orientation	44	96	48	118

a   Describe and explain the differences between Chinese Dutch people and (native) Dutch people using Hofstede's model.

b   What is the reason for the success of the second generation?

ATTENDEE

9

Decision-making in organisations

- What are the characteristics of problems that require a decision?
- In what areas does decision-making take place?
- Why is decision-making a more or less continuous process?
- What factors influence decision-making?
- What models are there for decision-making?
- How is strategic decision-making carried out?
- How can strategic decision-making be improved?

9

© Noordhoff Uitgevers bv

Do not be shy

The management team of the Sophia healthcare institution is meeting for an hour longer than usual this week. The main topic is a possible merger with the De Fontein healthcare institution. It is a complicated, contentious and emotive issue. The managing director has indicated in memos that the organisation must work more like a private enterprise. The government wants healthcare to be subject to market forces. This means that there will have to be more negotiation with other market players, such as health insurers. Through mergers between healthcare institutions, the expertise necessary for such negotiations can be acquired. There is currently a shortage of this expertise at Sophia. Although managers realise that a merger can have great advantages, they also have objections. Will the energy that goes into such a merger be at the expense of the provision of healthcare? Will the organisation become too big and too businesslike after the merger? Is the De Fontein healthcare institution the best choice?

9

9.1 Characteristics of problems

Organisations are continually subject to meetings and discussions. Both management and care teams meet up every week. These meetings may cover a variety of mundane subjects, such as employee guidelines for reporting illnesses, as well as more difficult and complex matters, such as how to respond to changing marketing conditions. The opening case descriptions is about a merger with another institution, and how best to approach this merger: a uniquely complex issue. In order to understand how meetings in organisations take place, and how decisions are made, we first need to look at the types of problems and issues management and employees are confronted with. Therefore, we start by discussing the different characteristics of those possible problems and issues.   **Characteristics**

9.1.1   Simple versus complex

If an employee in a healthcare team is absent due to sickness, this is a simple   **Simple problem**
problem. It occurs often enough and can be resolved by distributing the activities of the sick employee among the other staff. If it is obvious that the absence will last longer than two days, a temporary worker is hired. A fixed approach is usually developed for such simple, recurring problems.

EXAMPLE 9.1

Fixed procedures

If a machine breaks down, the company employee responsible for it must inform the boss. The boss then brings in a technician from the technical department. The technician decides whether they can resolve the breakdown themselves or whether they needs to call in a technician from the company that supplied the machine.

Simple problems that occur regularly are usually tackled and resolved in accordance with a fixed procedure. These are routine matters.   **Fixed procedure**

The issue of how people within the healthcare institution should cope with the government's requirement for greater exposure to market forces is a complex one. Management has never been faced with this problem before. When they discuss it, there appear to be several sides to the argument. What exactly are the market forces in healthcare? Which market players play a role, and how? What consequences will the change have for the institution? How should it respond and how can it maintain its position in these new circumstances? These questions serve to illustrate that there is a complex   **Complex**
problem if multiple interconnected factors are all part of (the solution to) a   **problems**
problem. Because they have never had to deal with this type of problem, they cannot fall back on experience and a routine approach is impossible.

9.1.2   Certain versus uncertain

For some problems, it can be established with certainty what type of   **Certainty**
approach will lead to a solution. Hiring a temporary worker for a sick employee ensures that the work of that employee is carried out, so that the continuity of the service is assured. Continuity is guaranteed if the

temporary worker is hired from an employment agency that specialises in the healthcare sector and provides temporary workers with this type of experience.

There are also problems to which different approaches can be taken without it being possible to predict which approach will produce the best solution. After the management team has been discussing the agenda item about market forces for an hour, they still have no idea how this problem should be approached, what solutions are available and which approach will produce **Uncertainty** the desired result. This type of problem brings uncertainty. Even if they opted for a merger just because other institutions are doing the same, what consequences would this have for the institution and would they be able to maintain their position sufficiently once they were exposed to market forces? What if they were to face the challenge alone, without having to resolve all the problems associated with a merger?

9.1.3 Equal versus conflicting interests
In the case of the sick-leave problem, all the team members have the same interest, namely covering the activities of the sick team member as well as possible. If the absence is for one or two days, they can take care of things themselves, but if it lasts longer, they will need to be relieved of the extra **Equal interests** work pressure. The solution to this problem involves equal interests. They all want to achieve the same thing.

Conflicting interests Other problems can be subject to diverging interests - even conflicting ones. If a merger with another care institution goes ahead as planned, it may result in an internal reorganisation. Every choice in this respect comes with certain consequences. For example, people may be given different tasks or their position may change. They may be given more or fewer responsibilities. If one person obtains a better position, this can have negative consequences for someone else. The discussion of these issues are, as a result, a battleground for conflicting interests.

9

EXAMPLE 9.2

Conflicting visions and interests

Proponents of the merger hope that, within a larger healthcare institution, there will be more opportunities for promotion. Opponents are afraid that they will play a lesser role and stress that a smaller organisation is better for both the employees and the provision of healthcare.

9.1.4 Types of problems
So far, three perspectives have been identified from which the nature of organisational problems can be described. These perspectives (or dimensions) are:
- simple versus complex;
- certain versus uncertain;
- mutual interests versus conflicting interests

Problems that are simple, have an identifiable solution, and involve mutual interests, are easy problems. Problems that are complex, do not have an identifiable solution, and involve conflicting interests, are difficult problems. See Figure 9.1 for a schematic overview of the types of problems and their characteristics.

FIGURE 9.1 Types of problems and their characteristics

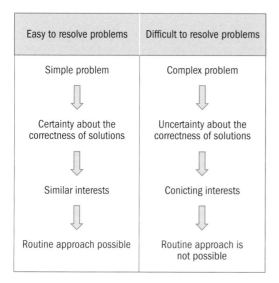

9.2 Areas of decision-making in organisations

What kinds of situation does the management of an organisationface and what sort of things does it decide about? Keuning and Eppink (1985) state that management must be active in three areas of organisation: external adaptation, structuring and internal integration (see Figure 9.2).

FIGURE 9.2 Three areas of organisation

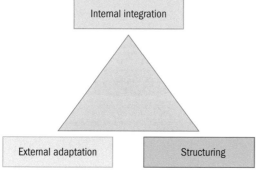

Source: Alblas & Van de Vliert, 1990

From time to time, management will have to resolve problems and take decisions in each of these areas. This involves:
- strategic decision-making;
- organisational decision-making;
- operational decision-making.

9.2.1   Strategic decision-making
Strategic decision-making is concerned with external adaptation (see example 9.3).

EXAMPLE 9.3

Surplus

Surplus slaughtering capacity arises in a pig abattoir due to a drop in demand for pork. The abattoir can respond to the situation by downsizing, by trying to acquire a larger share of the market or by just waiting to see if some of its competitors go bankrupt.

Organisations cannot operate independently of their environment. They are, for example, dependent on the labour market for the recruitment of personnel, on suppliers for the necessary materials, on banks for the provision of capital, on the government for legislation and on customers for turnover. They are also affected by the economic situation and by other organisations operating in the same market. For organisations, the environment comprises a number of players and situations (see Figure 9.3).

FIGURE 9.3 The environment of organisations

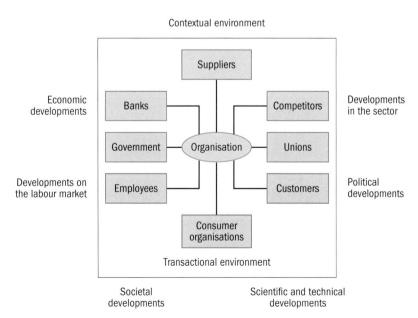

The players in society with which organisations are in contact, by whom they are influenced and on whom they themselves can exercise influence constitute the transactional environment. For most organisations, these players are its customers, the government, banks, suppliers, the labour market, competitors and interest groups (unions, consumer organisations, etc.). In the transactional environment, the various groups are not of equal importance. Their relative importance differs for each type of organisation. Non-profit organisations, such as governmental institutions, are usually little concerned with competitors. They have a monopoly position on the services they provide and they are certain of their 'consumption' by their 'customers' (i.e. all citizens). These organisations do not operate in the free market and are less dependent on their environment. Profit-making organisations must maintain their position on the free market and are consequently more dependent on their environment.

Players

Transactional environment

EXAMPLE 9.4

Competition and negotiation

Healthcare providers and educational institutions used to be non-profit organisations. They were almost exclusively dependent on the government as legislator and provider of capital. Nowadays, however, they are increasingly subject to market forces and must compete on price and quality. Educational institutions have to present themselves in competition with others on an education market. Healthcare institutions must negotiate with health insurers over the cost of their services.

Social situations that can affect organisations constitute the contextual environment. In many cases, organisations have no control over these situations. Developments can, however, affect the functioning of organisations in the long term. Concern for the environment, for example, is a response to the contextual environment.

Contextual environment

Concern for the environment increased rapidly in the 1980s. The government became involved and drafted various regulations and laws, for example in the areas of waste-processing and the use of substances and materials. Companies are consequently confronted with limitations on the use of raw materials for production and regulations for the disposal of waste products.

NRC HANDELSBLAD, MARC HIJINK

Apple's latest product is green

Apple is using its size and scope - 220 million iPhones per year - to make the electronics industry more sustainable. The company even has an ambition to be a green energy company.

Welcome to Apple's hidden factory in Breda, the Netherlands. Here, a massive, 29-armed recycling-robot disassembled incoming iPhones. This is where all of Europe's broken-down, unused model 6 iPhones are gathered and processed to reusable scrap: silver, gold, copper and tin from the motherboards, cobalt from the batteries, magnets from the speakers, and tungsten from the small internal vibrating unit.

Recycling is an appropriate process for a company that wants to come across as 'green'. During Steve Jobs' reign, Apple was limited to promoting particular products - iPods, iPhones, iPads; in a word, hardware - but has changed directions now that it is helmed by Tim Cook. The emphasis has shifted to the 'softer' side: Apple wants to 'leave the earth better than we found it.'

In the contextual environment, the following types of developments can be identified:

- **Economic developments.** Economic developments, such as changes in exchange rates and interest rates, can have consequences for purchasing power, foreign trade and innovation.
- **Scientific and technological developments.** Developments in knowledge can lead to new products and services and to different production opportunities.
- **Political developments.** Political developments can lead to different or new forms of legislation in the areas of safety, employment conditions, waste processing, taxation, and the import and export of products.
- **Social developments.** People's norms, values, ideas and needs can change. This can influence their desires in respect of the products or services they wish to consume.
- **Labour market developments.** Changes in the labour market can make it more or less difficult to recruit the people the organisation needs.
- **Business sector developments.** Developments in the business sector determine the relationships between the competitive positions of organisations in this sector.

Producing more compact cars for a better competitive position?

The contextual environment is relatively elusive for organisations. They may have little or no influence over developments that take place therein. Nevertheless, these developments can have huge consequences in the long term. An example of this already referred to is the change in attitude to the environment and the response of the political establishment, which has introduced regulations and other legal provisions designed to protect the environment. Many companies have had to change their products and their production and waste-processing methods. Organisations must not only be alert to the transactional environment, but must also follow developments in the contextual environment.

Adapting to environmental factors involves strategic decision-making. The organisation's relationship with the environment must be decided upon (external adaptation). Strategic decision-making primarily concerns the questions: What should be achieved by the organisation and how?

Strategic decision-making

EXAMPLE 9.5

Which option?

A company that manufactures pumps has is experiencing rapid growth and can no longer handle the orders it receives. There are two possibilities to accommodate such growth:
1 make the company bigger
2 build a new, similar, factory in a different part of the country.

The first option costs less and can be implemented in the relatively short term. Disadvantages of increasing the size of the current business are: less overview of the organisation, longer lines of communication, more bureaucratisation, more staff services and overheads and less flexibility. Staff

services and middle management are in favour of this option. Their position in the organisation would be strengthened. The second option is more expensive and would require more time. There are also advantages to this choice, however. If a factory is located in a different part of the country, the distance from clients in that part of the country will be reduced and distribution will be cheaper. A healthy, productive tension can be created between the two branches. The negative characteristics of a large enterprise can be avoided. The question is: Which option should be chosen?

9

Answering the question of what the organisation wishes to achieve first of all involves formulating general goals in the areas of, for example, market position, productivity, growth and continuity, and profitability. This is also called establishing the course of action. In addressing the 'how' question, management must indicate concretely with what resources and within what time frame certain goals must be achieved.

Course of action

Decisions concerning the expansion of a company or the construction of a new site are strategic. Establishing strategy is a complex matter. Many factors come into play. Because it involves long-term planning and anticipating developments, uncertainty plays a major part. Once a certain course has been taken, whether it has been successful or not can be established only after a long period. Strategy once chosen cannot therefore be adjusted or changed easily. Once a new factory has been built and so much has been invested in it, the choice cannot simply be reversed. Strategic decisions are not taken very often.

9.2.2 Organisational decision-making

Organisational decision-making

Organisational decision-making is concerned with the structuring of organisations.

EXAMPLE 9.6

Structuring an organisation

Two employees together decided to break with the cumbersome, complex, and hierarchical structure of established care homes. They designed a new type of institution, based on a smaller scale and a decentralisation of authorities. This fundamental idea was further developed in to self-guiding teams. Groups of care professionals sort out their own visits to care patients, time spent on assistance, and actual type and extent of care given. Any team that grows beyond twelve members automatically splits up into two or more new groups.

Structural problems arise if there is a need to change the division of tasks, to achieve better alignment within and between organisational units or to improve the dissemination of information throughout the organisation. Example 9.6 demonstrates that issues resulting from an excessively top-down approach to organisation can be resolved by decentralising responsibilities by forming self-guiding teams. The resulting organisational structure is flatter and has fewer hierarchical levels.

9.2.3 Operational decision-making

Internal integration

Fine tuning operational decision-making

Decisions taken at this level are in the area of internal integration. The activities are not all laid down in minute detail in the structure. It merely provides a foundation or framework within which, to a greater or lesser extent, there is room for individual interpretation of activities. In order to ensure coordination of employees' activities and their alignment with the goals of the organisation within the given structure, fine tuning is necessary. In many cases, management handles this. Fine tuning comprises, for example, scheduling work within departments, establishing performance norms, and control and guidance activities. Internal integration is achieved through operational decision-making.

This determines how day-to-day activities are to be performed.

EXAMPLE 9.7

Paid leave?

The previous holiday season came with some issues for the care team. Too many team members requested leave at the same time – which had a deleterious effect on the care provided to clients. In order to retain the level of care promised, temporary workers needed to be recruited. There was little time for any on the job training for these recruits, resulting in a slew of complaints from clients. The care team is meeting up to discuss this issue. Various solutions are offered and evaluated for achievability. The final decision is eventually made: leave is to be spread more evenly, with holiday schedules to be published earlier.

9.2.4 Characteristics of strategic, tactical, and operational decision-making

Establishing or adjusting organisational strategy is usually a complex affair. Many factors are involved and, because it involves long-term planning, it pays to look ahead. However, predicting future transactional and contextual organisational movements for the next few years is far from easy. Uncertainty plays a big part. Whether a plotted course proves to be the right one remains a matter for long-term debate. Strategic decisions and adjustments have major consequences on the interests of organisational members. Establishing or adjusting structural characteristics in the medium-run (tactical decision-making) is less complex and comes with fewer uncertainties than setting a strategy. Operational decision-making involves short-term affairs, which are usually accessible and easy to solve. The characteristics of strategic, tactical, and operational decision-making are shown schematically in Figure 9.4.

FIGURE 9.4 Characteristics of strategic, tactical, and operational issues

Strategic problems	• long-term • often one-time • highly complex • conflicting interests • highly uncertain • non-routine
Tactical problems	• medium-term • complex • relatively fewer conflicting interests • moderate certainty • non-routine
Operational problems	• short-term • frequent • simple • certain • few conflicting interests • routine

Source: Alblas et al. (2010)

9.3 Problems in decision-making

In organisations, decision-making by no means always goes well. Sometimes, decisions are taken that are disliked by a large number of staff members, decisions are taken that are not feasible or decisions are postponed for too long.

What sometimes makes decision-making in organisations problematic? It can be impeded by a number of factors, which may relate to:
• the nature of the problem;
• the nature of the decision-makers;
• the nature of the organisation.

9.3.1   Nature of the problem

In section 9.1, it was shown that problems can be placed in a dimension that runs from easy to difficult to resolve. Difficult problems are complex, evoke uncertainty and involve conflicting interests.

EXAMPLE 9.8

Uncertainty

In the case of the merger problem, some managers have an interest in the organisation remaining the same. They feel more at home in a small organisation and they can maintain their existing positions. Other managers are in favour of merging. In a larger institution, they will have more opportunities for promotion. However, it is not certain that a merger is the best solution to the problem of exposure to market forces. Perhaps there are better solutions. Or is it better to wait and see? Time will tell.

Stalemate

The more difficult a problem is to resolve, the greater the likelihood that the decision will be delayed or not taken at all. If players with opposing interests remain at loggerheads and have equal influence on the decision-making process, the result is a stalemate and the problem remains unresolved. This situation occurs more often with strategic problems than with operational problems.

9.3.2   Nature of the decision-makers

People can take in and process only a limited quantity information at one time. In a meeting to resolve a complex problem, many different issues (causes, interests, factors, solutions and consequences) are involved, and it is difficult for the decision-makers to consider them all, much less to foresee the consequences of all possible solutions. This situation evokes a number of reactions in decision-makers (March and Simon, 1958):

- **Simplification.** Some people have a tendency to reduce the problem to something simpler, for example by dividing it into sub-problems that are less complicated or by redefining the original problem.
- **Limitation of choice.** Only a small number of possible solutions may be considered. Having too many possibilities only makes the decision-making process more complicated.
- **Limitation of assessment.** The assessment of the possible solutions is superficial. The more aspects that are taken into account, the more problematic the decision-making becomes.

Reasonably satisfactory solution

By limiting the choice and assessment processes, the decision-makers tacitly agree: 'Let's not make it all too complicated because we are not yet able to see all the implications.' They are no longer concerned with finding the very best solution, but with finding a reasonably satisfactory solution.

Uncertainty reduction

According to Weick (1979), limitation of the choice and assessment processes in groups is partly caused by the need for uncertainty reduction. People prefer situations they can predict and control. But by no means all problems allow people to predict with certainty which solution is the best and will result in the desired effect. Most people find it difficult to cope with such a feeling of uncertainty. They therefore try to reduce it.

A comprehensive decision-making process, in which as many solutions as possible are contributed and assessed as conscientiously as possible, will increase the uncertainty rather than reduce it. The tendency towards uncertainty reduction will therefore result in a limited number of solutions and a supercifial assessment of their usefulness or feasibility.
This supercifial assessment may be along one of the following lines:
• Let's choose something that has been successful in the past.
• Let's choose something on which we can start work immediately.
• Let's choose something that provokes the least resistance in the group.
• Let's choose something that others (competitors) have done.

EXAMPLE 9.9

What is the competition doing?

When the government's wish that the Sophia Healthcare Institution was to be made subject to market forces was first put to the management of institution, they discussed the matter, and soon came to the conclusion that a merger might be the best solution to the problem. This was not because they had thought of this themselves but because they had looked at how other healthcare institutions had handled the same problem. Because several of these institutions were merging, it seemed as though this must be a good solution. They looked no further.

Due to the desire to keep the decision-making process manageable and the need for uncertainty reduction, only a limited choice and assessment process will be engaged in by the group. This limitation can result in reducing the effectiveness of the decision-making process. It is then to be expected that rather obvious solutions will be selected and unusual or innovative solutions have little chance.
In general, with complicated problems that evoke uncertainty, conservative choices are made.

9.3.3   Nature of the organisation

The structural characteristics of an organisation can be an impediment to a proper approach to the problem. The first impediment comes from grouping people in departments (services). If the grouping takes place for operational reasons, people with similar knowledge and skills are put together. The result of this is that each group or department within the organisation has its own specific observations and assessment of what is happening in the organisation's environment. What is observed and noticed in one department is not seen in other departments. This leads to a fragmentation of knowledge and information. Different types of information and knowledge are present in different parts of the organisation.

Fragmentation

Employees in the production department, for example, often do not notice many of the interactions the organisation has with its environment. They are more likely to observe internal events. Furthermore, their specific knowledge determines what they observe. Because they understand the machinery with which they work, they are more likely to see which machines are becoming obsolete or are likely to break down and why this would be so. Employees in the finance department, on the other hand,

© Noordhoff Uitgevers bv

mainly have an eye for the organisation's financial transactions with its environment.

Due to the boundaries between groups, observations of problems or threatening developments do not penetrate to other parts of the organisation or to the level at which these problems must be addressed. They then remain unresolved for too long.

Differences of vision and interests

The second impediment comes from the fact that grouping results not only in the fragmentation of knowledge and insight but also in differences of vision and interests. The representatives in the sales department, for example, have a different vision of the declining sales of a number of items from that of the production staff. The representatives may look for the cause in a lack of resources to promote these products properly, too high a price or the fact that the products are technically obsolete. The people in the production department consider that the representatives are not sufficiently competent and motivated to sell the products effectively. Differences of vision and interests can lead to differences in the way in which a problem (and its cause) is defined. If people want to protect their own department, to be left alone or to maintain the image of a properly functioning department, then an observed problem will be defined in such a way that other departments have caused it. If, on the other hand, the problem provides an opportunity for expansion or promotion, people will claim it as their own. If the marketing department would like to expand and spend more on advertising, a sales problem will rather be defined as a marketing problem. If an observed problem is perceived as unmanageable and it is expected that tackling it will only make it worse, or if other matters demand priority because they are more important or urgent, the problem may be defined as something that will probably resolve itself.

The American political establishment is strictly hierarchical: the president determines the course of action in broad outline; the ministers ensure this outline is implemented.

Political process

If a decision has consequences for the different groups or departments in an organisation, the interests of these groups play a large part in the decision-making process. Differences in interests between the groups increase the likelihood that the decision-making becomes a political process, which no longer involves a common interest but is determined by the prevailing group interest.

The third impediment is the hierarchical structure of an organisation, due to which there is a great distance between the decision-makers at the top and the operators on the shop floor.

Hierarchical structure

The greater the number of hierarchical layers and the more centralised the decision-making process, the greater the chance of distortion of information, overload at the top and delays in decision-making (see chapters 5 and 7). The departmental heads, who have to pass information upwards or downwards, can delay information or simply not pass it on if this suits them better. This intensifies the fragmentation of knowledge and insight. They can also play down problems that have been noticed and send them upwards in a diluted form, so that they are placed at the bottom of an often already overcrowded agenda. If there is overload, a decision must be made about which items should be dealt with immediately and which can wait. The various impediments to decision-making are shown in Table 9.1.

TABLE 9.1 Impediments to decision-making

Nature of problem	Nature of decision-makers	Nature of organisation
• Complexity • Uncertainty	• Limited intake and processing of information • Uncertainty reduction	• Fragmentation of knowledge and information • Differences in visions and interests • Hierarchical structure

What impediments to decision-making can be expected, given the nature of problems, people and organisations?

9.4 Impediments to decision-making

Impediments to decision-making are not necessarily recognised and addressed as such.

9

EXAMPLE 9.10

Not important enough

The representatives of a hardware company sometimes receive defective items back from the retail trade. They collect these items and make sure they are replaced. Because this is a normal procedure, it is not perceived as a problem about which something must be done. In the past two years, the company has increasingly experienced fluctuations in sales. Better knowledge of the market was needed. A small marketing department with a staff of two was set up. Among other things, they did intensive research into the characteristics of their existing clients and what they thought about the company's products. It emerged that the quality of the products left something to be desired and too many items had to be sent back because of manufacturing defects. When an employee from marketing discussed this with the heads of the sales and production departments, he was told that things could sometimes go wrong, but it was a rare occurrence. The head of the production department remarked: 'If you ask people what it is that they do not like, they will always point out that there has been the occasional item with manufacturing defects.

The point is that it is rare and there is no question of it happening regularly.' The marketing employee did not leave it at that and forwarded his findings to management.

They considered the situation serious enough to include it as an agenda item for the following meeting.

The various factors that can influence decision-making can give rise to a number of shortcomings that prevent the decision-making process from getting under way or make it laborious. Such shortcomings can arise in all four phases of the problem-solving process: noticing the problem; establishing the nature of the problem; designing solutions; assessing the feasibility of the solutions. In this section, we describe the shortcomings in these phases.

9.4.1 Noticing the problem

Noticing problems

Problem remains unnoticed

Problem can hang around

Before a problem can be resolved, it must first be noticed. It is possible that a problem remains unnoticed just because no attention is paid to it or because certain phenomena are regarded as 'normal' and not problematic. Even if a problem is noticed somewhere in an organisation, it is not inevitable that it will actually be dealt with. The problem can hang around in a certain department or group because nobody takes the initiative to pass it on to a higher level in the organisation. As previously mentioned, fragmentation (subsection 9.3.3) plays a part in this. A problem may also not be passed on because people do not want to reveal that they have a problem or are afraid that their positions will be in jeopardy. Differences in interests (subsection 9.3.3) are involved here. A centralised structure for decision-making and information exchange can exacerbate these tendencies.
In 2004, Shell announced that it had overestimated its oil and gas reserves. Although this problem had been noticed much earlier internally and also communicated to the top, it had not been placed on the agenda, apparently because senior management preferred to ignore it.

9.4.2 Establishing the nature of the problem

Once a problem has been noticed and placed on the agenda, a detailed assessment must be made.

EXAMPLE 9.11

What is the problem?

Why do a considerable percentage of Open University students only complete one course or a small number of courses? Is this due to poor advertising, which leads too many people to think that they can easily follow a study programme with the Open University? Is it a consequence of too little structure and too much freedom of action for the students? Was the guidance inadequate and too little focused on stimulating, supporting and retaining students? Is it

actually not a problem because these students simply did not plan to complete more than one or a few courses? At the Open University's study centres, they are inclined to look for causes involving the nature and structure of the tutoring. They would like to have more hours for tutoring. The external relationships department is of the opinion that it is an advertising problem. Perhaps the advertising campaigns could be better pitched. The board of governors is hesitant. It is in any case of the opinion that within the objectives of the Open University there must be room for students who take a

small number of courses, either out of personal interest or to improve their professional knowledge in certain areas.

What people think about certain phenomena and how they consequently define the problem are factors rgat can differ from department to department, depending on how they look at it. The more departments are involved in the definition of the problem, the more diverse the visions that are brought in. It is then to be expected that there will be different definitions of the nature and the causes of a problem. If these differences are great, it becomes difficult to produce a definition that is acceptable to everyone. Information about the nature of the problem may have to pass through several nodes and become garbled. There is then a chance that the problem will be defined wrongly.

Different definitions

Defined wrongly

9.4.3   Designing solutions

After the problem has been defined, possible solutions must be devised. The more complicated the problem and the more uncertainty it evokes, the more people are inclined to simplify it and propose a limited number of solutions. These will also often be obvious solutions, with which success has been achieved in the past. If too little use is made of the expertise of the organisation's various departments, the diversity of the solutions will be restricted.

Obvious solutions

Restricted diversity

9.4.4   Assessing the feasibility of the solutions

A choice must be made from the proposed solutions. As we saw earlier, people are inclined to reduce complexity and uncertainty. This means that only a small number of solutions will be included in the selection process and a small number of overall criteria will be applied in assessing the feasibility of those solutions. This can lead to the adoption of obvious solutions and a lack of creativity and innovation. The selection process can also be influenced by particular visions and interests, so that it is no longer a matter of the decision-makers opting for a solution that is good for the organisation as a whole, but of their focusing on their own interests.

Small number of solutions

Small number of overall criteria

Own interests

Which solution is chosen then depends largely on power relationships. If there is too much conflict, no decision may be taken at all, or a decision simply postponed.

No decision

9.4.5   Performance and evaluation

Once a decision has been taken, it must be executed and evaluated. Its implementation must be controlled to make sure that everything proceeds according to plan. After implementation it is necessary to assess whether the intended goals have been achieved (evaluation). In many cases, there is defective control and evaluation in organisations.

Defective control and evaluation

The restrictions to the various phases of problem-solving and decision-making are shown schematically in Figure 9.5.

FIGURE 9.5 Impediments to decision-making

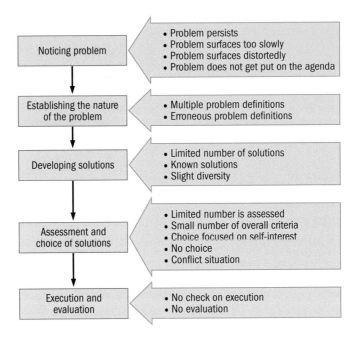

🏿9.5🏿 Decision-making models

There have been various attempts to describe the characteristics of the decision-making process in organisations. In this section, we discuss the following models developed from these characteristics
1   the rational process model
2   limitations of the rational process model
3   the garbage can model
4   the political process model
5   the covert control model.

9.5.1   Rational process model

In a company's production department, several machines suddenly show signs of failure. Production is consequently faltering and the schedule will no longer be met. In this situation one might expect discussion of the problem and the selection of a solution to involve relatively factual considerations. In this case, there is a rational decision-making process. It is only possible for a rational decision-making process to take place if the following conditions have been met:

Rational decision-making process

*   The decision-makers have the same goal.
*   There is a small number of possible solutions.
*   It can be shown objectively which solution is the best.

A rational solution is more likely to be achieved for problems that are easy to resolve than for difficult problems. If a good solution to a problem is reasonably quickly apparent, this will result in a routine approach and the establishment of procedures: in future, problem A will always be resolved in this manner.

The conditions necessary for a rational decision-making process are seldom present in organisations. There are almost always several interests at stake, and in many cases the best course of action cannot be objectively established.
If a problem cannot be resolved in a rational manner, what should the decision-making process be?

EXAMPLE 9.12

A rational solution?

In a progress meeting, the team leader says that it looks as though one of the team members will be off sick for the whole week. This disrupts the team's work schedule. Different proposals are put forward to resolve the problem, such as overtime, hiring a temporary worker to replace the sick team member as soon as possible, or adjusting the schedule to the new situation. Although it seems as though this involves factual considerations, personal interests are involved in the different solutions. The team member who does not want to work overtime proposes hiring a temporary worker. The team member who does not want to train a temporary worker for the umpteenth time suggests that the schedule be adjusted. The team leader would prefer his team to work overtime so that the schedule does not have to be adjusted and he is also not in favour of hiring a temporary worker. Because different interests are involved, the solutions cannot be objectively evaluated.

9.5.2 Decision-making as a limited-rational process
Occasionally, decision-makers are confronted with problems with the following characteristics:
- The definition of the problem-situation is probably incomplete.
- It is impossible to consider all solutions.
- It is impossible to predict the consequences of all solutions.
- The selection of solutions is influenced by personal and political factors.

Under these circumstance, there can only be a limited-rational decision-making process (March, 1988). Participants do not assess all possibilities for their usability, and subsequently choose the best one ('maximise'). Instead, they discuss the solutions one at a time, and choose the first one they feel is satisfactory ('satisfice'). Then, they stop looking.

A further limitation on the rationality of the decision-making process is caused by the uncertainty a problem evokes. As previously indicated, there is a strong inclination to reduce uncertainty. This can be done by opting for solutions that are familiar. First of all, solutions are explored that have produced success in the past. Solutions are also sought that are simple and can be implemented in the short term, or that will generate the least resistance and problems. Sometimes, this can mean simply doing nothing in order to avoid disruption and disputes.

9.5.3 Garbage can model
After observing many decision-making processes in organisations, Cohen, March and Olsen (1972) came to the conclusion that these procecsses are the opposite of rational processes. They described these processes as

© Noordhoff Uitgevers bv

organised anarchy. According to them, the decision-making process is like a garbage can into which every participant throws their own problems, preferences, arguments and solutions. According to the garbage can model, the decision-making process can be typified as:

Garbage can model

- a collection of poorly formulated and conflicting preferences (solutions);
- a process of vague selection methods based on experience, trial and error or pragmatic resourcefulness;
- involving unequal participation, where team members either invest time and energy or not, according to their interests;
- a process to which equivocal information, i.e. information that can be interpreted in different ways, is contributed.

Management is often confronted with so many problems at once that they must continually re-establish where priorities lie and how much attention and time should be devoted to each problem. Sometimes, there is actually no problem but people want to change something. A problem is then sought. Sometimes a solution is already available – for example, merging with another institution – and the nature of the problem (we are too small to maintain our position) and the arguments for the solution (others do it this way) are easy to find.

With this model, Cohen, March and Olsen give the impression that decision-making proceeds chaotically. This is not their intention. Only from the viewpoint of an outsider could the process be described as chaotic. When viewed through the eyes of the participants, their actions are based on solid factual arguments and considerations. They decide on their attention, participation, arguments and preferences according to the time they have available, their interest in the problem and the goals they wish to achieve with a solution. Because these considerations differ from participant to participant, the decision-making process seems rather arbitrary.

Time

Interest

Goals

9

9.5.4   Political process model

If different solutions are possible and it cannot be predicted which solution will be best, differences in point of view, preference and interests become involved in the decision-making process.

EXAMPLE 9.13

Opposing interests

The personnel department would like to expand by one or two staff. They could then devote more attention to career planning for employees and provide more education and training. They have put this item on the agenda of the next management meeting. Some departmental heads are in favour of the proposal but others are against. The dissenters have already asked for expansion of their own department and have been refused. The argument was that there had been cuts at operational level. Overheads must not be increased by hiring people in the support departments.

We have previously shown that an organisation can be understood as a collection of players with partly the same and partly differing or opposing interests. This is not only determined by individual factors, but is also caused by the structure of the organisation. Grouping people into departments, each of which has its own function and expertise, creates differentiation in ideas and interests.

Opposing interests

This serves to illustrate the ambivalent character of organisations (as a coalition of parties). On the one hand, the members of an organisation have the same interest (the continued existence of the organisation) but on the other, they have personal (group) interests that can conflict with those of others. When the satisfaction of the goals (needs) of the different people or groups in the organisation are concerned, people come up against a scarcity of means, in which there are more demands than can be satisfied with the available resources.

Circumstances like these cause people and groups to regard each other as competitors, potentially leading to a profit-loss scenario.

NRC HANDELSBLAD

Fighting for our existence

A glorious past is no guarantee for the future. This is the recurring message during an interview with Pieter Elbers, president-director of KLM, at their main office in Amstelveen, the Netherlands. 'As the major aviation company in a small country, our position is rather unique. But we should not feel entitled to it. We are responsible for ensuring our own continued existence. That is something we need to fight for day in, day out.'

There is plenty of fighting going on at KLM, but not in the way Elbers is talking about. Unions are butting heads with the board about working conditions and cut backs. The company is involved in a five-year operation to restore its competitive position.

Last Wednesday, KLM was subpoenaed by the VNV pilots' union. The subject: the cancellation of a pension agreement. Coming Tuesday, there are proceedings following an appeal by the FNV union regarding a temporary strike ban for the ground crews. Last week, the court forbade any strike actions from taking place until 5 September, due to terrorist threats and holiday crowds. And a third group of employees, the cabin crews, are in conflict with the board. There, the subject matter is indexing pensions, cancelling a managerial function, and more flight hours during winter.

Note that a conflict of interest is a question not only of money or resources, but also of influence, status and power. Under these circumstances, a factual approach to decision-making is hardly ever possible. The participants' task is to influence the others and guide the process in a direction that is favourable to themselves. As individuals, most of the participants have only minimal influence. Therefore, they will have to recruit fellow thinkers. The results of decision-making processes are therefore determined by the people

Forming a coalition

who succeed in forming a dominant coalition together. These coalitions can sometimes change, because the interests of a coalition can be the same in one area but not in another. The organisation then becomes a playing field on which changing coalitions are formed. Decision-making is largely a

Political process

political process in which negotiations and agreements between people (and parties) play a large part. The resolution of the problem and the decision-making process are no longer focused on the best solution for the organisation as a whole, but on achieving a solution that best serves the interests of the participants (political rationality).

● www.depolitiekedimensie.nl (edited)

Failure in decision-making at Holland University

The board of directors suggested improving the quality of education based on a specific educational concept. At its core, students needed to become self-learning, project education needed to take centre stage, and computers should be the most important tools. Despite great criticism and counter-argumentation from students and teachers, the proposal was still accepted. The top executive layer of the university was governed by a strong coalition, which sought to implement this common but nevertheless educationally disputed concept. The expertise or interests of neither students nor teachers was considered in the decision-making process.

> The decision led to many student protests against the decrease in the number of college hours, and to the departure of dozens of teachers. Other teachers attempted to subvert the plans from inside, or retreated to their own fiefdom and performed their work without any motivation.

Conflicts of interest may lead to **selfish behaviour**. Selfish (or self-serving) behaviour occurs when individual parties stop focussing on any interests except their own, causing them to lose sight of the common goal(s). This can lead to unworkable relationships and a reduced willingness and tendency to compromise. Top level management needs to make sure that selfish behaviour is kept in check and that the willingness to compromise is encouraged. This means that, being a higher authority, management will need to demonstrate they are independent and impartial, and not take part in any coalition forming.

Selfish behaviour

Following the plotting of the policy and its details in the tactical planning, management should not rest on its laurels. One the one hand, they will need to keep assessing the policy and its execution – are both living up to expectations? – and on the other, they will need to stay on their toes for events and developments with a relevant impact to the strategy.

9.5.5 Covert control model

If decision-making is controlled by chance, personal interests and ideas, and power relationships, the results become unpredictable. Nonetheless, many organisations seem to function relatively stably. This is because decision-making is embedded in the structure and the culture of the organisation. Both elements ensure a certain amount of stability because they exercise covert control, not so much over the process of decision-making but rather over the departure points of those involved. Covert control takes place in various ways:

Covert control

- By **focusing attention**. The attention paid to various matters can be directed from the top. This determines what is noticed and which problems have priority.
- Through **training and indoctrination**. The members of an organisation learn not only technical skills but also how to view and assess the organisation. They obtain an idea not only of who is considered important within the organisation, but also of what is right, good or acceptable. Decision-making is therefore influenced by the culture of the organisation (see chapter 8) and takes place within the established system of ideas, norms and values.
- Through the **structure of the organisation**. This establishes tasks, responsibilities, rules and procedures. Most decisions are taken within the existing framework of rules and agreements.

Covert control may make decision-making less random and more predictable but it does not guarantee an effective steering process beforehand or afterwards. Things can be delayed, problems are not noticed or not properly dealt with. These impediments to decision-making are the worst in strategic decision-making. After all, in this is an area in which people are confronted with the most complicated problems, the greatest uncertainty and the largest number of conflicting interests. We shall therefore indicate how strategic decision-making can be approached such that these impediments are removed.

9.6 Strategic decision-making

Strategic decision-making focuses on the organisation's course of action. What does senior management wish to achieve with the organisation and how? Determining strategy is not a strictly internal affair. Account must be taken of the organisation's environment. Because strategic policy is usually concerned with the long term, management must look ahead and anticipate changes in the transactional and contextual environments.

Having established a new policy and policy-implementation as part of the tactical plan, management should not simply rest on their laurels. On the one hand, they will need to keep reviewing whether the selected policy and its implementation meet expectations; on the other, they will need to remain focused on the future and stay alert for any events and developments relevant to the strategy.

Strategic decision-making is generally not the strongest point in organisations. Managers are usually so busy responding to day-to-day problems that they have no time to focus their thinking and decision-making on the longer term. According to Mintzberg (1973), managers' work is characterised by fragmentation. The issues they face change rapidly and often lack cohesion. Management is consequently rather more focussed on the short-term. Managers do not have time for a cohesive or profound examination of the organisation, let alone for looking ahead to the longer term. Weick (1979) also concluded that looking ahead and planning for the longer term are not part of management's usual pattern of activities.

How can we approach strategic decision-making such that these shortcomings in complex problems involving greater levels of uncertainty (see paragraphs 9.3.2 and 9.3.3) can be avoided? An approach that should improve strategic decision-making is described in the following sections.

9.7 Model for strategy formulation

Establishing or changing an organisation's course of action and carrying out the tactical planning necessary to do this is a prime example of a complex task that evokes uncertainty and in which different interests are involved. Under these conditions, it can be expected that almost all of the problems we have highlighted might occur in the decision-making process. Yet precisely because determining the course of action involves (re)defining the goals and the direction of the organisation, it is important to give it proper and thorough consideration.

Strategy formulation

Keuning and Eppink (1985) have designed an approach to the process of strategy formulation.

This model for strategy formulation focuses on breaking down the complex problem into smaller sub-problems, which can be discussed separately. This approach is in line with the systematic method (Carson and Rickards, 1979) that is used to render complex problems manageable. This method comprises the following steps:

a Divide the problem into a number of sub-problems.
b Devise different solutions for each sub-problem.
c Combine the sub-solutions into a total solution.

Systematic method

Dividing the original, complex problem into less complex sub-problems simplifies its resolution. Limitations on information absorption and processing are no longer exceeded. As a result, the inclination towards (over) simplification of the problem is offset and there is room for a more comprehensive search and assessment process. This provides more opportunities to observe the basic rule 'quality is quantity'. Quantity is achieved by formulating different solutions for each sub-problem, so that a wider range of options is available. The chance of achieving a high-quality solution is thereby increased.

FIGURE 9.6 Model for strategy formulation

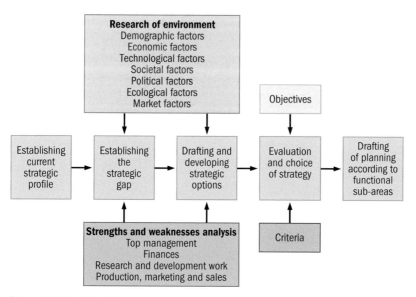

Source: Keuning & Eppink, 2011

We discuss the following components of the process of strategy formulation:
• Establishing the current strategic profile.
• Establishing the strategic gap that will be created if current strategy is maintained.
• Establishing strategic options for closing the gap.
• Choosing the new strategy from the alternatives.
• Developing the new strategy as a system of sub-plans.

9.7.1 Establishing the current strategic profile

The process of strategy formulation begins with the question of what the current strategic profile actually is. What has been the vision of the organisation in past years? In many cases, the existing strategy is not clear to the participants, or they have different impressions of it. Nevertheless, the existing strategy must first be made clear. Only then can it be determined whether the strategy is still appropriate and whether the current functioning of the organisation is still in line with it.

Clarifying the question of what management wishes to achieve with the organisation (course of action) is a condition for testing whether the current method is on the right track.

9.7.2 Establishing the strategic gap

Once the current strategy has been established, it must be ascertained whether this strategy contributes in the existing or anticipated circumstances towards good production or service provision and to the survival of the organisation. If this is not the case, there is a strategic gap and the strategy must be changed.

Strategic gap

EXAMPLE 9.14

Is the current strategy satisfactory?

At the Sophia healthcare institution, the course of action up to now has been to provide various forms of healthcare effectively in a certain region. The government specified the healthcare required and provided the money for it. Now, the government has said that market forces are to apply to healthcare. This creates a new situation in which healthcare institutions become competitors on the price and quality of their services. Their current strategy is no longer adequate in the new situation.

9.7.3 Establishing strategic options

Choosing a new strategy is not a simple matter. Many uncertain factors are involved in the choice. In example 9.15, how can the desire of the government for the application of market forces be translated into concrete aims, requirements and rules? Will a subsequent government apply the same principle? How will the organisation be financed in the future and what does this mean for its current financial position?

EXAMPLE 9.15

Confusion

There is great confusion in the Sophia healthcare institution about what strategy should be chosen. They actually have no idea what market forces are and how best to deal with them. They also do not know what will happen if their current course of action is maintained.

Strategic options can be developed properly only if sufficient information is available about the opportunities and threats resulting from the changes in the organisation's environment. To this end, research is needed in two areas. First, environmental research. What opportunities and threats are there in the areas of production technology, market development, competition, political legislation, economic developments, etc.? Can changes be predicted in these areas? Environmental research should make the opportunities and threats more easily visible.

Second, a strengths/weaknesses analysis of the opportunities available to the current organisation is necessary. Ambitious goals are easy to formulate but it is important to investigate how far they can be realised with the current organisation. What financial leeway is there for additional investment in for example, technological innovation, marketing and advertising or buying up smaller competitors? What opportunities are there for product innovation and becoming the market leader? Is the current research and development department capable of producing such innovations? Are the people in the sales department adequately equipped to use different and perhaps more aggressive selling methods? Is senior management flexible enough to develop and manage a different organisational structure and operating methods?

Environmental research

Assessment of strengths and weaknesses

Before opting for a certain strategy, different possibilities are formulated to fulfil the basic rule 'quality is quantity' in this phase.

9.7.4   Choosing the new strategy

The fourth sub-problem consists in consideration of the value of the different possibilities that have been formulated. Criteria must be developed for this. On the basis of these criteria, the feasibility of the options can be compared and a choice can subsequently be made. Criteria might include:
- financial feasibility;
- operational feasibility (potential of people and resources);
- alignment with economic expectations;
- alignment with government legislation and regulations;
- alignment with expectations concerning developments in the market and in the competition.

Criteria

In this phase, there is a risk of uncertainty reduction. It cannot be established with certainty what criteria are relevant and in what order of importance they must be placed. It may also not be possible to establish with certainty how far the possible solutions meet the criteria. Proper structuring and leadership in this phase can prevent decisions being made too rapidly and based on too few criteria (see paragraph 9.3.2). In this phase, differences in interests among the participants in the choice process can also become a problem. The model for strategy formulation offers no solution to this. However, it is possible, for example, to suppress political rationality in favour of logical rationality. First, senior management should emphasise the common interest and stand above the parties. If management participates in the conflict of interest, this will no longer be possible. Second, the participants in the choice process must be able to put their interests clearly on the table. They must be included in the criteria for assessment of the proposed solutions. As we established in chapter 4, strong support for a chosen solution is often necessary to achieve the intended effects.

9.7.5   Developing the sub-plans

The fifth sub-problem consists in detailing the chosen strategy in concrete terms. The choice that has been made has consequences for the people and departments in the organisation. Plans need to be drafted for the functional sub-areas involved in the implementation of the solution. Once a strategy has been initiated, its performance must be checked from time to time and tested against the goals. It is then possible to detect deviations promptly and make the necessary adjustments.

The model for strategy formulation is an aid to solving complex problems that evoke uncertainty. This step-by-step approach can naturally also be used for complex problems concerned not with strategic but with other types of decision-making.

9.8 Organizing strategic decision-making

Choosing

A proper approach to strategic decision-making is not just a matter of using a step-by-step method, but also a matter of choosing the right participants. What information, knowledge and awareness is required for each step? Which employees must be involved? It is important not to involve exclusively (senior) management in strategy formulation. Especially when it involves a strengths/weaknesses analysis of the functioning of the organisation, people lower down the organisation must also be consulted; otherwise management runs the risk of working with only second- or third-hand information.

Consulting colleagues and negotiating to determine strategy and mission.

If the organisation is highly centralised and information transfer follows the hierarchical route, is it necessary to set up a different – possibly temporary –

structure, in which the previously mentioned disadvantages of distortion and delay are avoided. This could be a (temporary) project group. This shortens the lines of communication and brings together the right employees from different departments. The group is tasked with discussing certain problems and formulating solutions. Employees are involved in the project on a basis of personal merit and equality. By setting up a project group, the hierarchical route is broken, which makes direct and rapid exchange of information between the different parts of the organisation possible (see paragraph 11.9).

Project organisation

9

© Noordhoff Uitgevers bv

Tips for managers

It is important to regularly check how decision-making in the organisation is proceeding. Are problems noticed in time and properly addressed?

Addressing problems
Strategic problems:
- Make sufficient time available at least once a year to redefine the current strategy, ascertain whether there is a strategic gap and assess relevant developments in the transactional and contextual environment.
- Involve the right employees in this process so that there is adequate reliable information about the internal and external functioning of the organisation.
- Create an atmosphere in which criticism can be made openly. If it emerges that the strategy must be adjusted, proceed in accordance with the model for strategy formulation.

Organisational problems:
- Find out if the problems are the result of shortcomings in the structural design of the organisation. This is the case if certain problems regularly recur – for example, problems associated with the planning and performance of services or production or with coordination between organisational units.

- Involve the right employees in the solution of the problems and maintain open communications with all those concerned.

Operational problems:
- Make sure there are regular progress meetings within organisational units and teams, in which there is open communication about day-to-day matters.

Line managers and employees must have easy access to middle and senior management. Ensure that there is an atmosphere of openness and trust within the organisation. Senior management must set an example by being open and accessible.

9

Summary

▶ Simple problems (with similar interests and an obvious solution) are easy to resolve. Complex problems (with opposing interests and with no obvious solution) are difficult to resolve.

▶ Decision-making in organisations is related to three areas, namely:
  • strategic (establishing strategy)
  • organisational (relating to structural design)
  • operational (day-to-day management, control and supervision)

▶ Problems in decision-making may concern to:
  • the nature of the problem
  • the nature of the decision-makers
  • the nature of the organisation

▶ With a complex problem involving uncertainty and opposing interests, a stalemate can arise, due to which a decision fails to materialise.

▶ With rational decision-making, the decision-makers have the same interests and factual arguments and the best solution can be established objectively.

▶ According to the garbage can model, decision-making can be characterised as organised chaos, in which participants invest time and energy according to their capabilities and desires.

▶ If there are conflicting interests involved in the decision-making, it becomes a political process. People and players can form changing coalitions to obtain more influence over the results of the process.

▶ Strategic decision-making usually concerns problems that are difficult to resolve. To minimise impediments to the solution of these problems, an approach following the model for strategy formulation must be adopted.

9

© Noordhoff Uitgevers bv

Assignments

9.1   One of the issues on the agenda of a certain management meeting is the high level of absenteeism.
The director addresses this issue by comparing absentee figures for the past two years to the average figures for the industry. The results of that comparison are grim. Absenteeism is much too high and needs to be addressed.
Several potential causes are offered:
- Some feel that work in the manufacturing warehouse is unhealthy. There is too much noise pollution, temperatures are too high in summer and too low in winter. The work is physically demanding.
- Others blame the issues on a careless selection of employees – since there are quite a few whose absentee figures are rather high.
- A third group blames lack of leadership. The metaphorical distance from the production team to the rest of the organisation is, which is detrimental to the commitment of those employees to the organisation.

All parties agree that the source of the absenteeism is the production floor.

a   Which phases of problem-solving and decision-making have been covered?
b   To what extent have these phases been covered adequately?
c   In which field of decision-making is this problem located?

9.2   Once management reaches the point of coming up with solutions to the absenteeism, suggestions abound. No sooner has one proposal been submitted than another is offered for review. The head of the Sales department interrupts the process. He agrees that it is clear the problem is mainly the result of a situation on the production floor, and not from other departments. The solution, he suggests, should be found in the same location. He feels this is a job for the team managers of the production teams. They will need to be more aware of, and respond better to, their teams calling in sick. All other suggested solutions are ignored in favour of discussing this latest idea.
Since the meeting is almost at its end, the director finishes by concluding that team leaders will need to improve their handling of absenteeism. The head of the Production department voices his doubts about this approach but is ignored.

a   Which phases of problem-solving and decision-making have been covered?
b   To what extent have these phases been covered adequately?
c   How can this solution-process be characterised, i.e. using which characteristic(s)?

9.3   On 28 January 1986, the Challenger space shuttle exploded seconds after take-off. The retrospective conclusion was that the explosion was due to a technical failure between the rocket and the shuttlecraft. In addition, those failures had been commented on by various NASA experts, who warned of launching in temperatures below 53 degrees Fahrenheit. Temperatures on launch day were considerably lower. So, what made management decide to go ahead with the launch, despite those warning signals? A reconstruction showed that the pressure on NASA to launch the shuttle was immense; that pressure meant that warnings were either not submitted to, or ignored by, top level management. They wanted to prove to their sponsors that the shuttle programme was efficient and effective, and that it was possible to perform a significant number of launches within a certain amount of time. This was of great importance to the financing of the shuttle programme. Any suggested technical improvements might have cause severe delays to the programme. Another factor was the time and energy spent on the 'Teacher in Space' programme, which meant a teacher would be joining the crew to convince the public of the shuttle's safety and successfulness.

These two factors combined meant that last-minute delays would only mean loss of face.

Indicate the factors that contributed to poor decision-making. Involve the following aspects in your answer:
a   task characteristics;
b   decision-maker characteristics;
c   organisational characteristics.
d   Which were the dominant characteristics of the decision-making process?

© Noordhoff Uitgevers bv

10

Stress and conflict

- What is stress and what causes it?
- What are the consequences of stress?
- How can stress be prevented and treated?
- What are conflicts and what causes them?
- How do people deal with conflict?
- How can conflicts be resolved?

10

The work is piling up

Sandy says: "Today my team manager sent me an email at half past four, requesting that I draft and finish a proposal for a client which had to be finished by six. Because of this, I cannot get on with other tasks, which are also urgent. The work is piling up and there's never a time when I feel I have everything under control. I will be leaving late again today and will have to give the shopping a miss. I will have to put a ready meal in the microwave because I will not have the energy to cook. I have a headache and pains in my stomach. Recently, I have been waking up in the night and lying there worrying about my work, which never seems to be finished. Next week, I have a performance appraisal – and it probably will not a good one."

Who is the around boss here?

Two hours before his regular morning shift, Charles, an anaesthetist in a regional hospital, received a phone call from the duty surgeon summoning him to an emergency childbirth requiring anaesthesia. When he arrived at the hospital, Charles noticed that this was definitely not a medical emergency. The surgeon wanted to start on time so that she could complete the delivery early. It was the third time this had happened and Charles was furious. In the presence of support staff, he loudly announced that the surgeon had better look for another anaesthetist and left.

⟨10.1⟩ Psychological load

In the first example, Sandy's work is piling up so much that it is causing her stress. This stress is a heavy psychological load and results in worry, headaches and stomach complaints.

In the second example, there is a conflict between the anaesthetist and the surgeon. Conflicts can have various negative consequences, such as irritation, frustration, lack of communication and even furious attacks. Conflicts also create a psychological load.

Ever higher demands are made on working people. The working week has become shorter but their performance must be the same or greater. Improvements are also demanded in the quality of the product or service and in people's accountability for this. Increased competition requires more customer-orientation and flexibility from employees. The environments of organisations have also become harsher. Shop personnel, receptionists, social workers, doctors and police officers are confronted with increasingly demanding and sometimes aggressive customers. Teachers have difficulty with students who are not interested in school, do not care about anything and disrupt the learning process.

In the longer term, the psychological load that an increased work load and/ or difficult working conditions impose can disrupt the balance between work load and capacity to such an extent that burn-out results.

Psychological load

10.1.1   Stress at work

Stress relates to the pressure a person experiences. Perceived pressure causes tension. The body reacts to tension by increasing physiological activity. When this does not result in lowering the tension and the physiological activity persists, exhaustion will result. Resistance to pressure declines and the risk of physical and psychological ill-health increases.

Stress

Stress at work occurs if a person cannot satisfy the demands of their work. The characteristics of the work or work situation that can cause stress are called stressors.The first example shows how Sandy is continually pressed for time and never has the feeling that she has her work under control. The stress evoked by this situation causes her headaches, stomach pains and sleeplessness.

Stressors

10

Not all pressure leads to stress in employees. One person can take more than another and some people thrive under pressure. In a department where everyone has to deliver the same high performance and therefore has the same work load, one employee will experience more stress than another. The effect is related to the extent to which a person can handle the pressure put upon him. Someone's capacity or load tolerance is determined by their ability to prevent and cope with stress. A person will experience stress at work if there is too little recovery time and if the balance between work load and capacity is seriously or protractedly upset. The perceived pressure will then result in stress reactions (see Figure 10.1).

Work load
Capacity

Recovery time
Balance
Stress reactions

© Noordhoff Uitgevers bv

FIGURE 10.1 Causes and consequences of tension at work

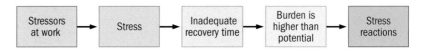

NRC HANDELSBLAD

Half of police force under constant stress

Half of the 50,000 policemen and women in the Netherlands as suffering from stress-related complaints, says an internal study commissioned by Dutch National Police. The study, which saw 13,000 participants take part over the past summer months, shows that police officers take less joy from their work than other professions in the Netherlands, and that they experience significantly more stress. The major contributing factors to work-related stress are said to be 'aggression and violent acts by civilians' (79%), 'operating below capacity' (45%0, and 'internal transgressive behaviour'. The latter category includes bullying (18%) and intimidation (15%). 'Operating below capacity' is given to mean that employees feel they are performing work below their level of training. Police officers do indicate that they take pride in their work. 86% is 'regularly' to 'always' proud to be doing the work that they do. This is the first time this type of cultural study has been conducted among police personnel. Gery Veldhuis, portfolio manager for basic teams and districts, says the results will be used to draft a workplace atmosphere improvement plan. "By continuing these measurements and monitoring the progress, we can stay on top of things. That is the only way we will be able to become an organisation of satisfied, healthy employees who continue to take the next step in making sure our nation is secure," says Veldhuis via the police intranet pages.

The following stress reactions can arise due to a prolonged psychological burden:

- **Emotional complaints.** These include dissatisfaction, irritation, anxiety, depression, nervousness and anger.
- **Physiological complaints.** These include high blood pressure and heart rate, a raised cholesterol level, muscular tension and sweating. A combination of physiological and emotional complaints can result in hyperventilation, asthma, migraine and stomach and intestinal complaints.
- **Behavioural complaints.** These include excessive smoking and drinking (alcohol consumption), overeating, impulsive behaviour and social isolation.
- **Burn-out.** This consists of emotional exhaustion, depersonalisation and diminished ability (see below).

10.1.2   Burn-out

Burn-out has become a generally acknowledged phenomenon within a relatively short time. The term was first used by the American psychoanalyst Freudenberg in 1974. He established that in young social workers caring for drug addicts depression could occur after a few years. Although these social workers were initially thought to be fit for the work, they started to display problems. According to Freudenberg, their psychological condition was probably the result of a feeling of powerlessness. He was the first to use the burn-out metaphor for this phenomenon.

Burn-out

Burn-out metaphor

In the most popular definition, burn-out is defined as a psychological syndrome consisting of emotional exhaustion, depersonalisation and diminished ability:

- **Emotional exhaustion** means a feeling of emptiness. A person feels as though they cannot go on any longer and on Monday morning already feels as though it is Friday afternoon. Their battery is flat and cannot be recharged. There is chronic physical and psychological fatigue. Emotional exhaustion is regarded as the most characteristic symptom of burn-out.
- **Depersonalisation** means that a person develops a negative, impersonal and cynical attitude towards the patients, clients or students with which they work. Whereas they were initially committed, there is now a vast distance between them and their audience because they no longer treats their audience as people but as objects.
- **Diminished ability** is the feeling a person has that they can no longer function properly at work or achieve anything of value. This is accompanied by a negative self-image.

10

Usually, people who have become victims of burn-out have a low opinion of themselves. People with burn-out normally have no energy, no longer take any pleasure in their work and derive little joy from life in general. In many cases, they cannot even enjoy their hobbies. They cannot put problems at work out of their mind, feel exhausted and dread small, day-to-day, routine actions such writing a cheque or opening the mail. They cannot concentrate properly and they find organisation difficult. With burn-out, many mental ordering principles are lost, such as setting priorities and identifying main and side issues. People with burn-out sleep badly and cannot relax. As a result of burn-out, people can suffer from neurotic complaints, such as feelings of guilt, anxiety, depression or obsession. Relational problems can also arise (Karstens, 2000).

Human professions Burn-out primarily affects people who work in the so-called human professions, i.e. in providing services/social assistance to clients, patients and students. Gradually, these people become so disappointed and exhausted that they can no longer adequately function in their profession. Burn-out has been identified in all kinds of contact-intensive professions, such as those of doctors, social workers, nurses, teachers, clergymen, police officers and security guards.

In the Netherlands, for example, 15% of all employed men and women indicates they are subject to burn-out related complaints (CBS and TNO 2015). Education is in the lead: 1 in 5 employees suffer from these issues. This is partly due to the high work load and the extant of personal involvement in the work. The lowest percentage of burn-out complaints is found in the agriculture industry.

Stress-signals: he is sombre, has stopped cracking jokes, and has been sleeping very poorly for many nights now.

Burn-out can be regarded as the result of a dynamic process between the person and the work. Cherniss (1980) identifies three phases in this process:
1 In the first phase, an imbalance arises between the demands made by the work and the person's capacity to handle them.
2 In the second phase, a reaction to this imbalance occurs that is characterised by feelings of tension, fatigue and exhaustion.
3 In the third phase, changes occur in one's attitude and behaviour towards the people with whom one works.

The change in attitude and behaviour can be regarded as a psychological flight reaction, the aim of which is to avoid being disappointed again. Teachers may develop the attitude that 'pupils are not interested in learning anyway' or 'only want to mess about'. This cynical, distant attitude is, however, not conducive to inspiring and enthusing pupils, due to which they behave even more indifferently or respond even more reluctantly. The result is that the teacher ends up in a self-reinforcing process, which only further increases their irritation, sense of inability and cynicism.

We can conclude that burn-out can be regarded as a specific stress reaction that happens over the long term and occurs in employees who collaborate professionally and intensively with other people.

Stress reaction

A great deal of research has been directed at the causes of stress and stress reactions. The results show that the causes can lie in the work and in the person.

10.2 Work-related causes of stress and burn-out

Both the nature of work and working conditions can contain stressors. A high work load, few opportunities to shape the work oneself, poor working relationships, vague work requirements, too much responsibility, insecurity about keeping one's job and limited prospects are some of these.
In this section we discuss the following work-related causes of stress and burn-out:
1   the nature of the work
2   working relationships
3   role ambiguity and conflict
4   responsibility and prospects

10.2.1   Nature of the work

In the first example, Sandy experiences a heavy work load. Due to the requirements her team manager places on her, she finds it impossible to complete all her tasks within normal working hours. She also has too little control over the quantity, inflow and scheduling of her work. She must simply wait for her team manager to bring her new tasks. She lacks any opportunity to direct her work.

There is a heavy work load if one or a combination of the following factors applies:
• The work is difficult and requires a lot of mental effort.
• There is a lot of work to do.
• The work must be done to a deadline.

A heavy work load is one of the most significant sources of stress. But not everyone who has to work hard will perceive that they have a heavy work load. According to Karasek's Job Demand Control (JDC) model (1979) (see Figure 10.2), work load produces tension and stress if it is also accompanied by lack of autonomy, i.e. the opportunity for an employee to organise his work according to his own preferences (in terms of its pace and sequence, and his approach to it). If an employee has a heavy work load and few opportunities to tackle and execute the work at his own discretion, there is little they can do to change the situation, which is an additional stressor according to the JDC model.

Work load

Autonomy

10

FIGURE 10.2 Model of Karasek (1979)

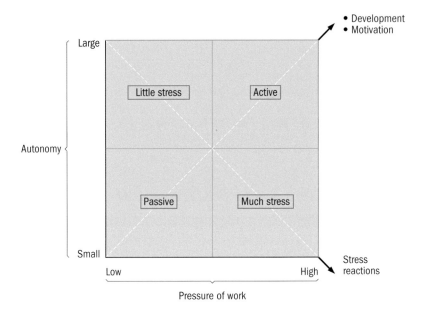

Research (CPB, 2004) shows that the combination of heavy work load and little autonomy can result in severe stress. If a heavy work load is accompanied by a great deal of autonomy, less stress is perceived only by people who have the ability to plan and execute their work themselves (Schaubroeck & Merrit, 1997).

EXAMPLE 10.1

Symptoms of work-related stress

People who suffer from work-related stress and have little autonomy score score highly against the following quotes:
- I feel like I am constantly running behind.
- I can never quite finish my work load.

- I never have a moment to relax.
- At the end of the working day I feel totally exhausted.

10.2.2   Working relationships

The people with whom one associates at work can be a major source of reassurance or stress. The relationship an employee has with their boss, their colleagues and/or their subordinates determines to a significant extent how they feel. Poor relationships arise when people do not trust each other, when there are conflicts and when people do not feel appreciated or supported. On the basis of several studies, Cartwright and Cooper (1997) come to the conclusion that poor relationships with colleagues can result in stress. Through research into the relationship employees have with their boss, Buck (1972) established that a poor relationship with one's boss produces more stress than a good relationship. A poor relationship with one's boss is characterised by a lack of appreciation, criticism without the offer of help to resolve the problem, authoritarian behaviour and the feeling that the boss favours other employees.

Nursing staff supporting each other in difficult situations.

Good relationships consist in mutual appreciation, loyalty and support in difficult situations. In particular, support from their boss and colleagues can help people to cope with stressful situations. Karasek later extended his model by adding a new variable: social support (Karasek and Theorell, 1990). This model predicts that employees with a heavy work load, little say and little social support are likely to experience stress. Social support has a so-called buffer effect, however. This means that a high level of support will mitigate or negate the effects of a heavy work load. Support is probably one of the most effective resources for countering the negative consequences of a heavy work load. Research shows that a heavy work load plus support results in less burn-out (Maslach and Leiter, 1997). The support of the boss has an influence on the stress reactions primarily of lower-level employees in the organisation. The greater the support, the fewer the instances of psychological complaints (Winnubst, Buunk and Marcelissen, 1988).

Social support
Buffer effect

Work load involves not only the quantity of work, but also the psychological demands imposed by work. Emotional load can be a part of these psychological demands. Emotional load is cited as an important cause of burn-out. Emotional load can occur in professions in which employees are exposed to accidents, death, harassment, aggression and violence. Examples are police officers, servicemen, prison officers, social workers, nurses, doctors and teachers.

Emotional load

© Noordhoff Uitgevers bv

10.2.3   Role ambiguity and conflict

Role ambiguity arises if tasks and responsibilities are not properly demarcated. If conflicting and irreconcilable demands are made on a person, there is role conflict. A personnel officer, for example, may perceive that social welfare policy is sometimes subordinate to economic goals. This produces tensions between managers and staff, making work problematic for the personnel officer. If they support social policy, this will cost money and the economic goals will not be achieved. If, however, they support the economic goals, they will be perceived by the staff as an stooge of management.

Role conflict

There are a number of situations that can result in role ambiguity and/or conflict. These are: the first job, a promotion, a change of job, a new boss or a change in the structure or culture of the organisation. Managers, especially at middle and lower levels, usually experience role problems to a greater or lesser degree. They are often trapped between the irreconcilable demands of senior management and desires of their subordinates Wong et al. 2006).

Roles should define the behaviour that must be displayed in organisations. Research (Tubre, Sifferman & Collins, 1996) shows that role ambiguity and role conflict are accompanied by tension, anxiety and the inclination to change jobs.

EXAMPLE 10.2

Role conflict

A reorganisation requires some jobs to change or disappear. The personnel manager is tasked with announcing these changes to the employees concerned. He knows that this reorganisation has produced a great deal of tension and conflict between staff and management. He argued for the creation of an attractive redundancy package for the employees who have to leave but in his opinion management considered only the economic implications of the situation. In these circumstances, he feels torn between his role as management representative and that of representing the interests of the staff.

10.2.4   Responsibility and prospects

Responsibilities

Employees and managers can be responsible for all kinds of things in organisations. Employees, for example, are responsible for the proper performance of their tasks. The leader of a number of self-managing teams is responsible for the efforts and collaboration of the team members, for the guidance of the team and for their results. Responsibility can be an important source of stress. Due to pressure from above, it is in many cases inevitable that unpleasant decisions must be communicated and implemented. It is also unpleasant if a manager has to give negative feedback to a subordinate in a performance appraisal or assessment interview, or has to use their superior rank to compel a subordinate in to making a certain effort or contribution. Such criticism can worsen relationships, which is a source of stress. Responsibility can also mean that employees or managers put themselves under additional pressure to perform as well as possible or to satisfy the sometimes exaggerated requirements of others.

Since 1990, more attention has been devoted to the question of job insecurity. Job insecurity is understood to mean on the one hand the fear of losing one's job and on the other the fear that certain aspects of one's job will change (Mauno and Kinnunen, 2002).

Job insecurity

EXAMPLE 10.3

Job uncertainty

For the team members, the formation of self-managing teams in an organisation will mean that they will have to perform more tasks and consult with each other about their approach to the work. For some managers, the implementation of self-managing teams means that their job will be abolished. They will have to re-apply for a job internally but it is questionable whether they will be hired and, even if they are, whether they will be given a comparable job. This situation creates great insecurity.

Job insecurity can have negative consequences on health, as shown by research (Burchell, 1999; Ferrie et al., 2002; Mauno and Kinnunen, 2002). According to Virtanen et al. (2002), job insecurity is associated with chronic sickness and psychological problems.

Work-related causes of stress and burn-out are illustrated in Figure 10.3.

FIGURE 10.3 Work-related causes of stress and burn-out

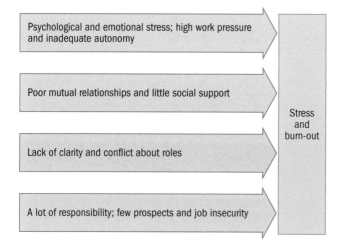

Psychological and emotional stress; high work pressure and inadequate autonomy

Poor mutual relationships and little social support

Lack of clarity and conflict about roles

A lot of responsibility; few prospects and job insecurity

Stress and burn-out

10

10.3 Person-related causes of stress and burn-out

Stress and burn-out are not exclusively caused by the nature of work or working conditions. They can be caused in part, or at least reinforced, by an employee's domestic situation or his nature.

These are person-related causes. Examples are: noise nuisance, moving house, cramped living space, financial worries, arguments, divorce, disabled partner or child, and social isolation. Such issues can weigh heavily on someone's capacity. Some people experience flexible work as a load, because it may be hard to combine work demands with household chores and care.

We will discuss the following person-related causes of stress and burn-out in this section:
- the combination of work with childcare tasks
- personality traits
- coping with stress

10.3.1 Combination of work with childcare tasks

If both partners in a family work, the division of household responsibilities and childcare tasks requires a great deal of organisation. Furthermore, women's increased participation in the labour market results in a double burden. Unlike the head of the family in former times, working women have no houseboy at home to ensure that everything runs smoothly. When they come home from work, they find a fresh task waiting for them that cannot be postponed. Even in the rare cases where women and men share childcare tasks, the burden is increased. Free time is a scarce commodity for such couples, and the distinction between private life and work begins to blur. To fulfil their childcare tasks, working parents – often designated in modern jargon as task combiners – arrange all kinds of personal matters from work. Conversely, doing overtime in the evenings or working at home at weekends becomes increasingly normal. Mobile phones ensure almost constant accessibility. Information can be sent instantly via fax, text message or email; no one has to wait until the next delivery of post. Where once matters of an urgent nature could wait a day or so, nowadays they have to be handled immediately. The pace has increased and therefore day-to-day juggling with time requires more and more dexterity. And over the past few years, the pace has been significantly quickened.

10

● www.intermediair.nl (translated)

At the end of my ropes after mom-time

Froukje (36) works as a policy officer in strategic HR-advice for the Ministry of Defence for 38 hours per week.
"Me and my partner each take care of our kids one day of the week. That may sound good, but I am at the end of my ropes after mom-time, completely spent. I like to be spontaneous and flexible. Call me up and tell me we are going on holiday tomorrow, excellent, I will set it up. But that is just not feasible with children. That is the hardest part of

motherhood for me. I need my work as a counter-balance in order to
stop me from going stir-crazy.
Lex is my remedial factor, he will tell me: 'Froukje, take it easy there.'
But we sometimes butt heads. Just yesterday, my car, which I had left in
a non-parking zone, was towed away late at night. But Lex was meeting
friends. At times like those, I can get really angry that I cannot impose
my mental picture onto reality."

Research has shown that the combination of work and household tasks can
have negative consequences on one's psychological health. It appears that
people report more burn-out symptoms when work inhibits functioning in
the home situation (Taris et al., 2001). There are also indications that people
whose domestic situation has a negative influence on their work generally
enjoy poorer health (Frone, Russel and Barnes, 1996).

10.3.2 Personality traits

Some people are more susceptible to stress due to their personal
characteristics. Think, for example, of people suffering from depression or
anxiety. Different people have different thoughts about the extent to which
they can influence their own circumstances. Some people take responsibility
for their own lives, while others seek guidance from others, or believe in fate
or in a higher power that guides their lives.
Personality traits affect the way people regard work and the way they
perceive potentially stressful situations at work. Loyal, perfectionist
employees run a higher risk of stress reactions if things are not going well at
work than employees who impose fewer demands on themselves.
Studies into the relationship between personality characteristics and
susceptibility to stress indicate that type-A individuals experience more
stress than type-B individuals (see Table 10.1).

TABLE 10.1 Characteristics of type A and type B people

Characteristics of Personality Type A	Characteristics of Personality Type B
is always busy	always has time
is often pressed for time	is not rushed or pressed for time
finds it difficult to relax	can easily relax
is highly committed to work	puts work in perspective
is inclined to perfectionism	accepts that not everything must be perfect
has a competitive nature	is not highly ambitious
is impatient and easily irritated	has patience and is not easily upset

From research it appears that type A people suffer more depression and
anxiety over role conflicts than type B people. Type A people also display
more negative reactions if things are not going well. It is therefore to be
expected that type A people are more likely to experience stress than type B
people Cooper, 2005).

Type B people

10

Exchange
relationship

Whether a person experiences a negative exchange relationship partly depends on their attitude to wards their work. A negative exchange occurs when an employee is strongly committed and expects a lot for their efforts but receives too little in return. People who work hard but feel they are rewarded too little by the organisation, for example because their salary or job has not improved or because they are insufficiently appreciated, experience stress. In some professions in the healthcare sector, there is a risk of a negative exchange relationship. Schaufeli (1990) points out that nurses are regularly confronted with difficult patients, who demand a great deal of attention and care and at the same time complain about the 'defective' care and attention they are receiving. A discrepancy between the care provided and the appreciation incurred, is a cause for burn-outs (Bakker et al., 2000).

Assistance
orientation

Exchange
orientation

If a person has an 'assistance orientation', they will be altruistically helpful and not wish to receive anything in return. A person with an 'exchange orientation' finds it important to receive sufficient reward for their efforts. People who are assistance oriented are less likely to perceive an imbalance between effort and reward than those who are exchange oriented.

10.3.3   Coping with stress

Personal characteristics are a major determining factor with regards to the way people deal with tension. Coping is a strategy used to be able to manage the tension one experiences at work. It can have varying degrees of success. Roughly speaking, there are two possible coping strategies.
The first is taking an involved approach through an active coping strategy.

This is a problem-oriented way of handling stress. According to Paffen (1996), this form of coping consists of:
- seeking solutions to problems
- seeking support
- expressing emotions
- seeking relaxation

Google employees playing pool as work-time relaxation.

The second coping strategy is one of passivity. This reaction to stressful situations consists of avoidance, withdrawal and developing a depersonalising attitude to one's colleagues and work-related individuals. A passive coping strategy consists in avoidance, withdrawal and developing a detached attitude (depersonalisation) towards the people with whom one works. Cherniss (1980) calls this a defensive way of coping with perceived problems.

People with an active coping strategy are less likely to experience burn-out than people with a passive coping strategy (Spaans, 1995).
The person-related factors that influence the development of stress and burn-out are shown in Figure 10.4.

FIGURE 10.4 Person-related causes of stress and burn-out

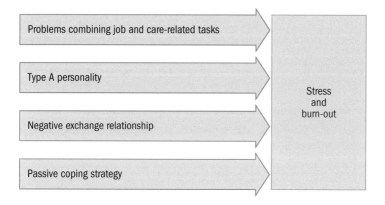

On the basis of research, Wagenvoort et al. (1998) came to the conclusion that when solutions are obvious a passive coping strategy is unfavourable for long-term well-being. Only if there are no obvious solutions can the development of a detached attitude towards colleagues and clients be the only way of preventing emotional exhaustion. This applies primarily to people facing emotional situations such as those involving death, grief, rage, disfiguration and aggression. A certain amount of professional detachment is then necessary in order to protect oneself. There must, however, be a balance between detachment and commitment.

10.4 Preventing or combating stress and burn-out

Trying to prevent stress or burn-out requires that we take certain measures. These measures can exist anywhere on the scale from work-related to person-related. They can also be sued to reduce stress, or to ensure that (the influence of) a taxing situation is removed. The following paragraph covers several of these measures:
- reducing work load and increasing control;
- providing support
- providing a clear work situation
- reducing job insecurity and making responsibility controllable
- individual measures

10.4.1   Reducing work load and increasing control

If the work load is perceived as too high, various measures can be taken to reduce the potentially resulting stress. First, one can investigate whether the quantity of work can be reduced. Sometimes, the excess work is caused by colleagues' sickness, which make it necessary to perform additional tasks. If this situation occurs too often, structural personnel solutions must be found. It can also happen that all kinds of tasks have been imperceptibly added to a job, resulting in an increase in the overal load. A fresh look must then be taken at which tasks do and do not belong to the job. The annual performance appraisal of employees can be a good opportunity to review the work load and, if necessary, reduce it to manageable proportions.

Second, one can assess whether the emotional load imposed by the work can be reduced. Emotional load can consist of aggression from clients or exposure to accidents, threats or danger. Sometimes, the emotional load can be reduced by giving an employee the opportunity to alternate tasks with a high emotional load with lighter tasks.

Annual performance appraisal

Work load
Emotional load

EXAMPLE 10.4

Reducing the load

A teacher who finds teaching too emotionally taxing due to pupils' lack of motivation and interruptions to their lessons is offered the opportunity to give fewer lessons and devote more hours to setting up and carrying out the school's extracurricular activities.
Nursing staff can be put on a roster to allow them the opportunity to alternate work at a taxing department with work at a less taxing one.

Control

Finally, one can investigate whether increasing employee control can lead to better distribution of work and so take the pressure off.

10.4.2   Providing support

With reference to the DCS model, we indicated that support has a buffer effect. Stressful circumstances at work will result in less stress if there is good support. Fenlason and Beehr (1994) identify two forms of support:

1   **Instrumental support.** This form of support consists of tangible help, such as physical assistance with work overload, information or advice about tasks that must be done, and help with resolving problems in the performance of the work. In a supermarket, there are times when there are a lot of customers at the tills. The long queues make the three cashiers who are on duty feel nervous. If the boss jumps in and opens an additional till, this reduces the pressure.
2   **Emotional support.** This form of support consists of showing sympathy for or involvement in the problems of other employees. This can help to relieve the stress created by emotional situations such those involving violence and death.
    After fatal shooting incidents, police officers are always given support so that they are not left alone with their emotional stress. According to Van Yperen and Baving (1999), in their research into burn-out in nurses, emotional support can diminish the negative feelings evoked by the work situation.

10

Support can be given by management and by colleagues. For employees lower down the organisation, support from the boss has the most effect. For teachers, the support of the school's management is very important. A study by Van Horn (2001) showed that a lack of support and appreciation from management causes teachers the most stress. A teacher can tolerate a considerable work load and stress if he knows and feels that the management is standing behind him and will help him.

It is obvious that management can play an important part in easing stressful situations and/or taking care of employees after stressful events. Which form of support (instrumental or emotional) is more appropriate depends on the nature or cause of the stress.

10.4.3   Providing a clear work situation

Role ambiguity and conflict can be resolved or prevented by the clear definition of the tasks and responsibilities that are part of a person's job. Naturally, many ambiguities or conflicts can be prevented by drawing up clear job descriptions. It is the task of management when hiring and training employees to provide them with sufficient information about the nature of the activities to be performed, the responsibilities associated with the job and how the job is linked to other jobs. A job description, however, can never guarantee good collaboration between people. On matters where interpretation can and must take place, the previously described role analysis technique (RAT) can be helpful (see subsection 4.2.2).

Job description

Role analysis technique (RAT)

10.4.4   Reducing job insecurity and making responsibility controllable

Job insecurity increases if rumours about reorganisation and job losses are circulating without senior management making it clear what is happening. Openness by senior management can reduce this uncertainty. Moreover, stress caused by job insecurity can be reduced by making available help in looking for a new job (both internally and externally) and by having a good redundancy scheme. By being clear about which jobs will change or disappear and by offering measures that show concern for the affected employees, management can greatly reduce uncertainty and stress.

Openness Help

The stress created by perceived responsibility is often the result of management lacking the means of power among to make subordinates do what is expected of them. Means of power are derived from both the position and the personal qualities of a manager. In both areas, attempts can be made to expand the means of power available. The organisation can provide a manager with more means of power, for example, by imposing more rules on the behaviour and working methods of subordinates and greater sanctions for infringements of these rules.

Means of power

10

EXAMPLE 10.5

Measures

At a comprehensive school, there are clear rules about the behaviour of pupils in class and elsewhere in school. The sanctions that are imposed for infringements of these rules are also specified. The teachers feel supported and legitimised in imposing the sanctions.

Training

It is also possible to give management more resources (e.g. a bigger budget) with which they can reward people or resolve bottlenecks in their departments. Finally, training can be offered to management by means of which they can enhance their managerial skills.

Performance appraisals are a good means of tracking down stressful situations and finding out, together with the line manager, what forms of support are required.

10.4.5   Individual measures

It is not always possible to reduce or entirely eliminate work stress by means of organisational measures. Moreover, some employees are more likely to become stressed than others. It can therefore be worth making sure that employees are better able to cope with stressful situations. There are different ways of increasing employees' resistance to stress.

Cognitive
restructuring

First, there are therapies that focus on the cognitive restructuring of work and the work situation. People are shown how to look at their work situation differently and/or make fewer demands on themselves. The following forms of cognitive restructuring can be identified:

- **Learning to think positively.** In this approach, people are taught to pay more attention to the successes they achieve. They also learn to concentrate on the processes and not just on results. Furthermore, people must not blame themselves too much for disappointing results at work. According to Maslach (1993), people in social professions are strongly inclined to ascribe failure at work to themselves instead of to external circumstances.
- **Rational emotive therapy.** The premise of this therapy is that negative feelings can be caused by irrational thoughts, desires or goals. During treatment, these thoughts, desires and goals are tracked down and, step by step, rationalised until they are more coherent with reality and the person's abilities.
- **Cognitive therapy.** This involves learning to accept things as they are. People learn that they must not saddle themselves with an unreasonable amount of commitment and responsibility. Social workers, teachers and therapists often have exaggerated expectations of what they can and/or should achieve at work. Learning to accept that reality is stubborn and does not always fit in with one's own desires is part of cognitive therapy. That expectations and goals in the social professions are sometimes unrealistically high can be attributed to the existence of a number of myths about this type of profession, according to Cherniss (1980). These are:
  - The myth of ability: people think that after obtaining a diploma they can achieve a great deal, whereas in reality their potential is disappointingly limited.
  - The myth of the ideal client: people think that clients (patients, pupils) want and are motivated to cooperate, whereas in fact they can be troublesome, aggressive or stubborn.
  - The myth of collegiality: people think they have a great deal of support from colleagues, whereas mistrust and rivalry often prevail.
  - The myth of autonomy: people think they can work independently, whereas in practice there are all kinds of rules to be abided by.

Because reality often differs from one's expectations, a shock occurs. These three therapies can puncture these myths and a person can be helped to look differently at his work situation and his own style of approach and results.

10

Nowadays, senior managers increasingly receive external coaching. They spend, for example, two hours a week with a coach, during which they discuss the situations they have encountered at work and especially those that have caused them stress. During coaching, use is often made of cognitive restructuring. Research into the effects of the above-mentioned therapies and of coaching gives a confusing picture. Both techniques reduce stress in the short term but, in the longer term, no change in overal work stress or satisfaction is experienced. It seems as though people eventually resign themselves to their situation (Cooper and Sadri, 1991; Reynolds et al., 1993).

Coaching

Finally, there are training courses that focus on physical defence. Firstly, these include sessions in which people are taught to relax (biofeedback, yoga meditation and mindfulness) health-promotion programmes, which can be focused on nutrition, exercise (fitness) or reducing one's reliance on substances such as nicotine (cigarettes) or alcohol. The latter take a step-by-step approach to influence the employee's lifestyle. Research by Keyser and Vaandrager (2000) shows a resulting drop in absence through sickness. Participants in company fitness sessions feel better and are absent less (Hottenhuis, 1998; Dam and Uyttenboogaart, 2002).

Taught to relax

Health-promotion programmes

They have less chance of contracting chronic illness. Too little exercise has the exact opposite effect: more absenteeism and a greater risk of diabetes and cardiac conditions.

10.4.6 Summary of measures to prevent or reduce stress and burn-outs

The stress and burn-our preventative measures explained in the previous paragraphs are listed schematically in Figure 10.5.

FIGURE 10.5 Measures to prevent or reduce stress or burn-out

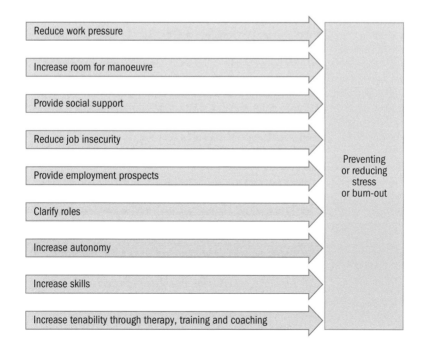

Reduce work pressure

Increase room for manoeuvre

Provide social support

Reduce job insecurity

Provide employment prospects

Clarify roles

Increase autonomy

Increase skills

Increase tenability through therapy, training and coaching

Preventing or reducing stress or burn-out

10

10.5 Physical load

Physical load

The well-being and health of employees can be threatened by various forms of physical load: on their body structure (back, legs, shoulders, wrists and neck) and on their sensations (noise, vibration and temperature).

A study by the Dutch Central Bureau of Statistics (2011) among employees in the Netherlands shows that 35% indicates they are regularly required to perform repetitive motions, 21% indicates they regularly have to apply force, and 12% indicates that they are required to assume an uncomfortable working position. The uncomfortable position combined with the application of force leads to lower back complaints. Lower back complaints are common but are characterised by a high percentage of spontaneous recovery. Problems arise if these complaints recur, as they can become chronic. The risk of this is large (estimates vary from 40 to 85%) if there is a heavy work load. Chronic back complaints lead to long-term absence from work. In the Netherlands, 16% of employees said they were afflicted with a chronic back complaint.

EXAMPLE 10.6

Physical complaints

The management of a company producing foodstuffs has had to contend with a high level of sick leave among employees in the stockroom and shipping department. From a discussion with these employees, it emerged that most of the complaints concerned the lower back. These complaints were due to heavy loads having to be lifted from an inappropriate posture and to people having to be on their feet for extended periods. Working with a forklift truck also caused vibrations and shocks.

Repetitive strain injury (RSI)

After back complaints, repetitive strain injury (RSI) is one of the commonest forms of physical load and constitutes the fastest-growing group of so-called work-related ailments. RSI is a collective term for complaints in the hand, wrist, arm or shoulder that are connected with overloading the body, usually as a result of working with a computer keyboard and mouse for long periods. Research by Blatter (2000) at the behest of Dutch research institute TNO showed that 30% to 50% of computer workers were affected by RSI to a greater or lesser extent. Hairdressers, musicians, meat processors and packers were also susceptible to RSI. RSI is caused by the combination of static posture and repetitive movement, which results in a reduction in blood flow to the muscles concerned, due to which insufficient nutrients can be transported and insufficient waste is removed. The accumulation of waste substances creates increased muscle tension and long-term excitation of the pain sensors. If this situation continues for too long, permanent damage can result.

Static posture

A study by the Dutch Central Bureau of Statistics (2011) shows that an increase in the amount of physical taxation is accompanies by an increase in absenteeism.

10.6 Reducing the physical load

Various practical measures can be taken to reduce the physical load at work; for example:
- using a **lifting and moving apparatus** if objects or people regularly have to be lifted and moved. If a person has to do frequent lifting, a course can be offered in the correct use of limbs and muscles;
- using **two or more people** if more than 25 kilograms has to be manually lifted and moved;
- setting the **correct height** for surfaces (desks, kitchen counters, cookers, monitors, etc.) on which work must be done and for the chairs used, so that it is possible to work in the correct posture;
- introducing **variation** in the tasks that constitute a job, through which working for too long in one posture or too much repetitive movement is avoided.

If substantial lifting remains a requirement, training may be a solution. People need to be show how to lift so that the muscles that are used, particularly the back muscles, receive as little adverse stress as possible. Measures that can prevent the occurrence of RSI are the following:
- The use of proper office chairs and their adjustment to the correct height for the use of the keyboard, mouse and monitor.
  - ensure that lighting is not reflected in the screen;
- The use of software programs that indicate when a break must be taken and regularly show exercises that can be done to reduce muscular tension and increase blood flow to the muscles.
- Introducing variation into the work, so that infrequently changing position and performing repetitive movements are avoided.

EXAMPLE 10.7

Variation and movement

In a laboratory, the employees can alternate their work at the computer screen with physical inspection of the production process. Because they work in a self-managing team, they are able to rotate activities and this means that they can take turns to sit, stand and walk around.

10

10.7 Conflicts at work

Just as in any relationship, people at work can sometimes disagree with each other. However, not every disagreement needs to result in conflict. Differences of opinion are normal and in most cases easily resolved. There is only a conflict if a person feels hindered, criticised and/or improperly treated by another person.

Conflict

EXAMPLE 10.8

Late again

Harry is late for a teachers' meeting again. His colleagues have just started discussing a problematic case. It concerns a pupil who, despite previous agreements, has gone back to drinking and drug-taking. Halfway through the discussion about how they should act, Harry comes in unexpectedly and immediately begins to speak loudly and persistently. He knows exactly how one should approach such pupils and one must not be too soft about it. Various colleagues feel criticised by this remark. They are annoyed by Harry's lateness, his big mouth, his know-it-all attitude and his arrogant remarks. They let Harry talk and, when he has finished, they carry on with the meeting as before.

Harry's colleagues feel hindered obstructed in their meeting about a troublesome pupil. They are annoyed that he is often late and adopts a dominant attitude. They also feel that their ideas on the way pupils should be handled are being criticised as 'wrong'. Conflict therefore begins when a person observes that his own wishes, interests or opinions are being mocked or criticised by others.

First, the possible types of conflicts are described, followed by the sources that can lead to conflict.

Differences in insight can lead to conflicts with colleagues.

10.7.1 Types of conflict

Conflicts at work can have various negative consequences. When they involve disagreement about how problems must be handled, they can result in indecision. The problems then linger and this can be harmful to the functioning of the organisation in the long term. If people feel hindered by one another and the situation is allowed to continue, it will produce tension and cause stress. This can result in a lack of collaboration, activities no longer being properly executed and people becoming ill. In these cases, the conflict is destructive.

Destructive conflict

Conflicts are not always negative. If people can have an open discussion about a conflict that has arisen, this can result in the resolution of unworkable situations or poor methods. This is primarily the case where process- or task-oriented conflicts about the content of, approach to and goals of work are involved. If the resolution of these conflicts is successful, they are constructive. If process- or task-oriented conflicts are to be constructively resolved, the differences of opinion must not be too great or continue for too long.

Constructive conflict

If a conflict takes place between, for example, a boss and an employee or two or more employees, this is called an interpersonal conflict. This is the nature of the conflict between Harry and his colleagues. A conflict between teams, departments or services is an intergroup conflict.
Parties in this case refers to two or more individuals or groups.

Interpersonal conflict

Intergroup conflict

EXAMPLE 10.9

Troublemakers?

Competitive prices, good service and quick delivery can be important conditions for attracting new clients. Employees in the marketing and sales departments rely on them when they make promises to potential clients. However, the finance and planning departments are sometimes obstructive. To them, what marketing and sales promise is not always possible. Internal agreements have been made about the pricing of products and it is not possible to deviate from them just like that. The production schedule is usually drawn up a month in advance and suddenly producing something for the benefit of a new client is not possible. The staff in marketing and sales feel that they are being unduly hindered in their efforts to attract clients by the rigid and inflexible attitude of the people in finance and planning. The latter, however, think that the 'fast' boys and girls in marketing and sales take no account of anyone else and believe theirs is the most important department in the company.

10

The types of conflict are shown in Figure 10.6.

FIGURE 10.6 Types of conflict

© Noordhoff Uitgevers bv

10.7.2   Sources of conflict

All kinds of circumstances can produce conflicts in organisations. External and internal circumstances can be identified. External circumstances are related to the environment of the organisation. Environmental factors can, for example, exert pressure on the organisation to change its course of action. Within the organisation, the question of how they should respond to this pressure arises.

External circumstances

EXAMPLE 10.10

Government intervention

Teachers complain that the government is always wanting to make changes in education. This often results in heated discussions in educational circles about how they should deal with the government's latest demands. Conflicts can easily arise between teachers and managers on various topics. Should they loyally follow the wishes of the government? How will they find the time to implement the changes? Who is responsible for what?

Various internal circumstances can cause conflicts. People and groups are in most cases dependent on other people or groups for the performance of their work. This mutual dependence can be a source of conflict. This is the case, for example, if one person or group is unable to deliver a contribution that makes the proper functioning of another person or group possible.

Internal circumstances

EXAMPLE 10.11

Rigid attitude of colleagues

Harry's lateness and his dominant presence frustrates the progress of the team meeting. The inflexible attitude of the planning department frustrates the wish of marketing and sales staff to offer new clients an attractive package.

10

Other internal circumstances, such as defective forms of communication and leadership, abuse of power and vague rules, can likewise be sources of conflict. Bad communication can result in activities not being carried out in the right manner or at the right time. This can cause friction, which can easily result in blame. Management may exploit its position of power and treat subordinates inequitably or ungraciously. Employees may feel hindered by unnecessary or inefficient rules. Reward systems may be perceived by employees as unjust if they find that they are disproportionately remunerated.

Sources of conflict

Circumstances that can create conflicts can be classified into the following types:

- **Instrumental conflicts.** These are circumstances related to the methods that must be used in the organisation.
  The instrumental question 'How should we respond to the government's desire for renewal in education?' can result in conflict between teachers and managers, as can the question 'How should we deal with a pupil who has committed an offence?'
- **Conflicts of interest.** This source of conflict is related to the distribution of rewards in the organisation.
  In many organisations, employees must vie with each other for limited resources such as pay increases, promotions, budgets and space. Gains of one often come at the expense of another.

EXAMPLE 10.12

Mobilisation of fellow thinkers

An older teacher applied for a vacant management position within the school administration. To his amazement, the decision was made to hire a younger teacher with less experience. The older teacher was not going to take this lying down and sought the support of a number of his colleagues. Jointly, they requested a meeting with the managers who had hired the young teacher. This meeting resulted in vehement debate and accusations of favouritism.

- **Power conflicts.** Power struggles concern the question of who in the organisation should decide about certain things.
  People may dispute with each other about who should be responsible. An employee may think that his boss should not interfere in the way he works, as long as everything is completed on time and he produces good work.

EXAMPLE 10.13

Who is the boss?

Charles, the anaesthetist, believes that the surgeon is not entitled to decide in a spur of the moment when he should turn up. There should be a some negotiation with him well in advance.

- **Relational conflicts.** Relationships can lead to conflict when one person is irritated by the behaviour of others.
  A dominant but sloppy person like Harry can quickly irritate his colleagues through his attitude, even if this is not at all his intention. Conflict can also be created by harassment and other forms of

mistreatment. Finally, a person can become irritated by a lack of effort from colleagues (freeloading). This is especially the case if the person has to compensate for this lack of effort. Relationship conflicts can also be the result of personality clashes. Some people just do not like each other.

EXAMPLE 10.14

Harassment

In stereotypically male-dominated professions, such as the army and the police force, female members are frequently exposed to annoying, discriminatory remarks and harassment from their male colleagues. Outward appearance, sexual identity, or religion can also be exploited as a source of harassment; personal belongings are destroyed, compromising pictures are passed around, or social media is used for slanderous purposes (cyber bullying). Employees who do not conform to group norms may also find themselves the subject to harassment.

The sources of conflict are shown in Figure 10.7.

FIGURE 10.7 Sources of conict

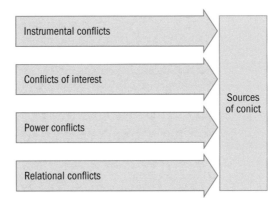

10.8 Conflict management

In the first example, there is a conflict between an anaesthetist and a surgeon. The anaesthetist feels badly treated by the surgeon. Despite the fact that the anaesthetist is a highly trained professional, the surgeon treats him like a subordinate, who must turn up when the surgeon wants him to. The anaesthetist has been irritated by this for some time. Now that he has had to turn up early yet again and finds the surgeon has invented an excuse, he has had enough. He departs in a fury and leaves the surgeon without support.

The conflict perceived by the anaesthetist can be approached in different ways. Perhaps the surgeon was completely unaware of her authoritarian behaviour and the irritation this evokes in others. In that case, a conversation about his feelings could help to resolve the conflict. This approach would be less successful if the surgeon thinks she has the right to dictate to others when they must come in. It could then turn into a quarrel and an upset relationship. The anaesthetist could also accept the situation and hope that things will improve. In fact, however, he avoids conflict with the surgeon by leaving.

There are several possible forms of conflict management, being: fight, collaboration, compromise, avoidance, and concession. There are several relevant dimensions to consider for each of these strategies. The first is the extent to which a party's interest in conflict management is their own or that of others. The second is the question of (lack of) assertiveness in handling the conflict. The third is the question of whether a party is prepared to take a positive or a negative stance (see Figure 10.8).
The different forms on conflict management are explained below.

Conflict
management

FIGURE 10.8 Forms of conict handling

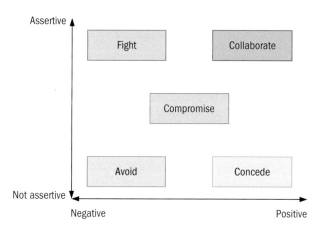

10.8.1   Fight

In the case of fight, the parties involved in the conflict are said to have an assertive and negative attitude. They also champion exclusively their own interests.

10

EXAMPLE 10.15

Championing one's own interests

If the anaesthetist confronts the surgeon about her authoritarian behaviour, he is behaving assertively. If the surgeon thinks that she has the right to determine when her colleagues must be ready to work, she is championing her own interests. The anaesthetist is championing his interests if he does not accept this and demands that the surgeon plan the timetable in consultation with him.

Win-lose situation

Opposition creates a win-lose situation. If one party wins, it automatically means the other party loses.

10.8.2 Collaboration

Win-win situation

In collaboration, the parties defend their own interests and those of others at the same time. They deal with conflict assertively and positively. The parties are concerned with each other's interests and try to attain a solution that is positive for both parties. This is a win-win situation. Collaboration can be a good approach if both parties are striving for the same goal and need each other to achieve it. There is then a common interest. Collaboration is possible if people have regard for each other's wishes and interests and they are positively minded.

EXAMPLE 10.16

Joint interests

If the anaesthetist has any regard for the wishes of the surgeon in the area of scheduling activities and the surgeon can empathise with the feelings of the anaesthetist, the foundation for a solution has been laid. They can then agree that they will, as far as possible, produce a weekly schedule together. If there is an urgent case, the surgeon will not immediately summon the anaesthetist but will first indicate what kind of case it is so that they can decide how best to handle it.

10.8.3 Compromise

Negotiation

Acceptable compromise

If the conflict is about the division of scarce resources, not every party is able to achieve maximum results. A win for one is a loss for another. In this situation, one can try to make the winning and losing acceptable to the different parties. One then strives for a compromise, where each party concedes something to the other. This approach can also be described as negotiation. In negotiations, neither party strives for the maximum for himself but for a reasonable share. We also call this process working towards an acceptable compromise.

10.8.4 Avoidance

Lose-lose situation

If the parties in a conflict do not attempt to resolve it, there is avoidance. They do not act assertively and no attention is paid to their own interests. This is a lose-lose situation. People who avoid things are usually afraid of confronting others and quarrelling. They may also feel powerless and see no possibility of improving the situation. Sometimes, however, this form of conflict management is chosen because it is the most sensible choice in the given situation. For example, criticising one's manager will have bad consequences in the next reorganisation or performance appraisal. A person can justify avoidance by pretending that the conflict is not really very serious. Psychological adaptation then takes place.

EXAMPLE 10.17

Keeping things positive

The group members do not say anything to Harry about his lateness or his obstructive behaviour. They are afraid of his reaction and they want to keep a positive atmosphere in the group. It is better to act as if everything is going well than to discuss it.

10.8.5   Concession

With concession, one's own interests are put aside for the benefit of the interests of the other party. One is positive but not assertive. People who concede are perhaps afraid of depriving others or of standing up for themselves. They are compliant and tend to want to make others happy instead of fighting for their own interests.

Some people use concession as a strategy in which they meet others on secondary issues in exchange for support on more important ones. It is also possible to come to an explicit arrangement where one party gets their say in one issue, but only if they are willing to concede on the next.

10.9 Conditions that influence conflict management

If subordinates have a problem with the behaviour of a superior, they are more likely to choose avoidance, concession or collaboration than opposition. For superiors, it is the other way round. If they have a conflict with subordinates, they are more likely to fight (Euwema, 1992). Here, it is the power difference between the parties that influences their choice of conflict management. The superior acts to protect their position and is focused on control and winning. Collaboration, avoidance and concession are viewed as losing and would undermine the position of power. By opposing the superior, the subordinate runs too great a risk of upsetting the relationship and incurring sanctions from the superior. The subordinate is therefore more likely to opt for other forms of conflict management.

Power difference

Personality traits can also play a part in the manner in which a person deals with conflict. People who are competitive and assertive are more likely to opt for opposition. Those who are not assertive are more likely to opt for avoidance or concession. Those who are cooperatively inclined will be more likely to collaborate.

Personality traits

Finally, one's assessment of the situation affects one's choice of the form of conflict management. How important is the conflict, how much leeway can one offer, how will the other party react and what positive or negative consequences will a certain form of conflict management entail?

Assessment of the situation

10

In some cases people cautiously try to talk about a conflict. If there is no response from the others, however, they withdraw. They quickly conclude that nothing can be done and that to persist in opposition, for example, will have too many negative consequences. They prefer to avoid confrontation. In groups in which the members need to collaborate intensively, avoidance can ensure that the collaboration continues reasonably well. The source of **Latently present** the conflict then remains below the surface and latently present. This entails the risk that an accumulation of small irritations can cause it to erupt. Irritation suppressed for too long comes to the surface in an explosive manner, and this makes the calmer forms of conflict management impossible.

Which strategy a person will ultimately choose to resolve a problem therefore depends on his position, his personality traits and his assessment of the situation.

10.10 Escalation of conflicts

Conflict escalation When feelings of irritation are suppressed for too long or the parties in the conflict are inclined to defend their own interests strongly and/or confront the other about their behaviour, a conflict can escalate. Even if the parties at first intend to resolve it calmly and cooperatively, it is possible for things to get out of hand. The following processes are involved in escalation:

1 **Polarisation of viewpoints.** If one party puts forward a viewpoint with great certainty, the other party will be more inclined to adopt an opposing viewpoint with great certainty, even if they are not in fact so certain about either viewpoint. The parties distance themselves from each other and polarisation occurs.
2 **Hardening of positions.** The parties criticise and reproach each other. Their interaction degenerates. If they are attacked, they seek arguments to bolster their own viewpoints, due to which they become even more convinced that they are right. Adopting a viewpoint a little closer to the other party is then no longer possible.
3 **Widening the conflict.** The parties are inclined to involve other issues in the conflict. Whereas it was originally a conflict about whether they were in favour of educational reform, for example, the more the conflict escalates, the more other issues are involved, such as poor management and an excessive work load.
4 **Increase in parties to the conflict.** The parties have the inclination to involve other parties in the conflict. In a conflict between an employee and his boss, the employee tries to mobilise a number of his colleagues to support him in his attempt to oppose the boss.
5 **Destruction.** The parties are increasingly inclined to no longer defend their own interests or the interest of others, but to cause damage to the other party, even if that also damages their own interests (see figure 10.9).

Figure 10.9 shows the phases in the escalation of conflicts

FIGURE 10.9 Phases in the escalation of conicts

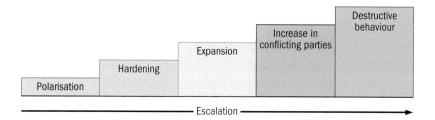

If the parties are still talking fairly reasonably about a conflict issue, a satisfactory resolution is possible. If one of the parties becomes more recalcitrant or principled or if emotions are aroused, escalation threatens. The principle of reciprocity, the inclination to treat others as you are treated by them, intensifies conflict. It then becomes increasingly problematic to resolve the conflict to the satisfaction of all those involved. After a time, the other party can do nothing right. Even if rapprochement is attempted, this is interpreted as a cunning new trick. The parties are therefore irreconcilably opposed and are no longer inclined to concede anything.

Principle of reciprocity

10.11 Organisational intervention in conflict resolution

Conflicts between people and groups are usually unavoidable. In many cases, people resolve the conflicts that arise between them or choose to ignore the problem (avoidance). Sometimes, a conflict has so many repercussions that measures are taken by the organisation to resolve the conflict or to make sure that such conflicts are prevented in the future. For these cases, there are three possible approaches: indirect and direct intervention, and negotiation.

10.11.1 Indirect intervention

With indirect intervention, the conflicting parties are kept out of range of each other and measures are taken to prevent similar conflicts in the future. These are measures in the organisational context.

Indirect intervention

10

EXAMPLE 10.18

Prevention through regulation

The departure of the anaesthetist caused an upheaval in the organisation. The manager of the department concerned tried to discover the cause of the conflict. He concluded that there was an cooperation and power problem and drafted rules about how surgeons should in future plan their work with their colleagues.

Structural interventions

Vagueness

Indirect measures are necessary if a certain type of conflict occurs frequently and if its cause is vagueness in the definition of tasks, responsibilities, rules, regulations or norms. Structural interventions are then necessary to remove such vagueness, such as:

- clearer demarcation of tasks and responsibilities for all jobs and departments;
- clearer rules and regulations governing collaboration and behaviour between employees and towards clients;
- clearer lines of control and authority.

Regulating mechanisms

Norms Rules and procedures

If conflicts continue to arise despite these structural interventions, regulating mechanisms can be applied. These regulating mechanisms also consist of norms that relate to, for example, privacy, correct behaviour and how men and women should treat each other. Regulation mechanisms consist of rules and procedures that must be followed if conflicts arise. Rules determine, for example, the manner in which clients must be handled. Procedures relate to appealing against sanctions and complaint handling.

EXAMPLE 10.19

Handling complaints

If a student at the Open University thinks that their work or exam has been unfairly assessed, there is a clear incident reporting procedure. There is also a clear procedure for handling the complaint.

Finally, people or committees with a mediating role can assist in the resolution of conflicts. Examples are a complaints committee, an ombudsman, a confidential advisor or the works council.

10.11.2 Direct intervention

Direct intervention

In direct intervention, people or committees take action to make sure that a conflict is resolved. Different forms of direct intervention can be identified, such as power intervention, arbitration and mediation.

Power intervention

Power intervention

In power intervention, the solution to the conflict is left to a party that stands above the conflicting parties. This can be a manager but also a committee or the management board of an organisation.

EXAMPLE 10.20

Transfer

Ultimately, Harry's colleagues became so irritated by his behaviour that there was an explosion. Discussions got so out of hand that an unworkable situation was created. The conflict had escalated and the parties remained entrenched. The organisation's board of management made the decision to transfer Harry to a different department, so that he no longer had to work with the team.

Various measures can be used in power intervention, such as transferring or firing people, appointing new team leaders and changing the composition of groups. A condition for power intervention is authority.

Arbitration

In arbitration, a person or committee is appointed to give a decision on a point at issue between the parties. It can be agreed that this decision is binding. Arbitration functions somewhat like a legal decision. Opting for arbitration often originates from a number of failed attempts to find a solution between the parties is possible. The arbitrator will first endeavour to see if a compromise between the parties is possible, so that the negative consequences of the proposed solution are minimised and neither of the parties feels too much like a loser.

Arbitration

Mediation

Mediation can be regarded as a form of arbitration under the leadership of a person (or party) that stands outside the conflict. The mediator attempts to make the conflict discussable and resolvable. The mediator should be an independent person from outside the organisation, with sufficient skills to get the stalled process running again. The mediator is not concerned with the content of the conflict but focuses on changing the communication between the parties, so that they are able to find a solution themselves.

Mediator

Independent person skills

EXAMPLE 10.21

Mediation

When the situation in Harry's team worsened, the manager decided to employ a mediator. He proposed this to his team and, hesitantly, without much hope of success, the team members agreed. The mediator first interviewed the conflicting parties separately and thereafter convened a joint meeting.

A mediator must have sufficient skill to make conflicts discussable and resolvable. They must be able:

- to maintain an independent and impartial attitude;
- to bring latent conflicts into the open, by first interviewing the conflicting parties separately and subsequently encouraging the participants to air their grievances, opinions and irritations;
- to cope with vehement feelings and pilot the parties into quieter waters after a confrontation;
- to clarify the intentions and wishes of the parties and enable mutual understanding of them;
- to emphasise common goals and interests and change a competitive attitude into a cooperative one;
- to separate issues.

10

Will it remain neutral?

Mediation makes heavy demands of a person. They must be able to motivate the parties to clarify the conflict and air emotions and desires, they must not apply any pressure, they must ensure that the conflicting parties have an equal hearing, and they must remain neutral towards the parties, so that they are not perceived as helping one more than the other.

10.11.3 Negotiation
Negotiation often applies to conflicts over the division of scarce resources, where the parties are seeking priority. These include conflicts over pay, overtime rates, performance bonuses, severance pay and promotion, for example.
It is possible for two people or parties to negotiate directly with one another, but it is also possible for an intermediary to be used, who assumes leadership of the negotiation process.

Two types of negotiation can be used in such situations: distributive and integrative negotiation.

Distributive negotiation

Win-lose
situation

Distributive negotiation concerns a win-lose situation. If one party receives more, the other party receives less.

- -

EXAMPLE 10.22

Winning or losing?

An employee negotiates over her salary and other employment terms with the owner of the enterprise. Her additional requirements will come at the expense of the income the owner can derive from his enterprise.

- -

In general, there can be negotiation only if both parties have a target and a   **Target**
margin for negotiation. The target is the maximum that the employee wishes   **Margin**
to obtain from the negotiation and the margin is the gap between the target
and the minimum the employee is prepared to accept. Note, however, that
during the process of negotiation both targets and margins can change. The
employer also has a target and a margin at the beginning of the negotiation
process (see Figure 10.10).

When there is no overlap between the margins of the two parties, achieving
agreement is problematic. The negotiations will then fail unless both parties
widen their margins.

FIGURE 10.10 Onderhandelingsruimte

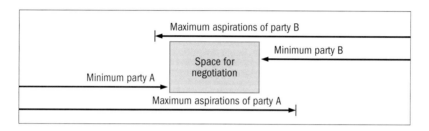

During the negotiation, certain temptations or threats can be used to change   **Temptations**
margins. Threats include on the one hand a strike, walk-out, work-to-rule or   **Threats**
resignation, and on the other transfer, dismissal, closure or relocation of
parts of the company. Temptations include offering higher performance or a
reduction in pay or perks to counter the threat of company relocation.

Integrative negotiation
With integrative negotiation the possibility of a win-win situation exists.   **Win-win situation**
Usually, there is some sort of exchange.

- -

EXAMPLE 10.23

What is on offer?

A manager may negotiate with an employee   wishes only if the manager has something
over additional overtime or an unwelcome   to offer, such as extra holiday, more
shift during Christmas or New Year. The   privileges, a bonus or prospects of
employee will accede to the manager's   promotion.

- -

If a conflict can be resolved by integrative negotiation, this is preferable to
distributive negotiation because the relationship between the conflicting

parties then improves. The parties must adhere to the following principles during the negotiations:

- **Leave room to manoeuvre.** Do not adopt an immovable attitude because then you will have no room for negotiation.
- **Separate the people from the problem.** Do not make it a personal conflict but remain focused on goals and results.
- **Put yourself in the other's place.** If you indicate that you accept the intentions of the other, the other party is also more likely to accept yours.
- **Seek solutions that take both interests into account.** This increases the chance of a win-win situation.
- **Employ objective criteria.** In the assessment of possible results in terms of time, effort and rewards, use as many objective criteria as possible.

Tips for managers

More and more demands are being made of employees. The psychological burden of a heavy work load and/or difficult working conditions can result in stress and burn-out in the long term.

Risk factors for stress and burn-out
Be alert for signs of stress. People may start to behave differently or be absent more often. You can use the performance appraisals with employees to pick up on signals and problems but you must also keep your eyes and ears open in the day-to-day work situation. Use the following checklist to detect risk factors and signs of stress:

Work-related stressors
- vague duties and responsibilities (role ambiguity)
- heavy emotional load
- heavy work load
- heavy physical load
- little influence or autonomy
- little support and appreciation
- a lot of responsibility
- job insecurity
- poor prospects

Person-related stressors
- problems combining work and childcare
- heavy demands on one's efforts and performance (perfectionism)
- high expectations of the positive consequences of one's efforts
- problems handling stress (coping)

Stress and burn-out signals
- health problems
- irritationwith work and colleagues
- increased smoking and drinking
- increased absence
- less commitment to work

Approach to risk factors

Work-related approach
- Make more detailed definitions of tasks and responsibilities (role clarification).
- Provide more support.
- Reduce work load by better scheduling and/or expanding personnel.
- Hold more progress meetings and increase employees' influence and autonomy.
- Spread responsibilities.
- Provide clear information about the nature and consequences of reorganisations.
- Pay more attention to the consequences of reorganisation for employees.
- Give employees more positive feedback and appreciation.
- Adapt work stations to reduce the physical effort required and improve working posture.
- Provide training in lifting and operating machinery (including computers).
- Explain career prospects and offer education and training, including stress-reduction training.

Person-related approach
- Discuss with employees how work and childcare can be better integrated.
- Curb employees' expectations of high performance and rewards.
- Advise employees about ways of reducing stress, e.g. exercise and relaxation.

Detecting conflicts
Conflicts can be a source of stress and have a paralysing effect on employees and on the organisation. Do not allow conflicts to escalate or persist. Use performance appraisals to detect conflicts. Be aware: employees are not likely to tell you

10

everything and are not inclined to bring conflicts into the open. You must be alert for the following types of conflict:
- about goals and methods of work (of employees, teams, departments and the organisation as a whole);
- about salary, promotion, budgets, space and other rewards;
- between individuals, teams and departments about respective contributions;
- about responsibilities and leadership;
- between colleagues and team members about behaviour and attitudes.

Resolving conflicts
Conflicts can lead to paralysis if they escalate, but different approaches must be used to discuss and resolve them.

In the case of conflicts between individual employees or within teams, you must find out the following:
- What is the conflict about and who is involved?
- How do the conflicting parties regard each other in terms of their intentions and wishes?
- How are the parties coping with/managing conflict?

On the basis of this conflict analysis, you can determine which type of conflict resolution is most suitable.
You can act as an arbitrator and bring the parties together to discuss and resolve the conflict. This can be done only if you are not party to the conflict and are regarded by the conflicting parties as neutral. If the conflict has escalated or arbitration has not had the desired effect, a mediator can be employed. In both cases, the following interventions are necessary to resolve the conflict:
- Encourage the parties to discuss and resolve the conflict.
- Emphasise mutual dependence and common interests.
- Clarify the good intentions of the parties.
- Resolve breakdowns in communication and mutual misconceptions.
- Propose solutions if appropriate.

Direct forms of conflict resolution are:
- Power intervention: if a rapid solution is necessary and/or the parties are no longer inclined to resolve the conflict.
- Mediation: If both parties are still able to engage in civil discussion
- Negotiation: if the conflicting parties cannot work it out themselves but are still prepared to resolve the problem.
- Indirect intervention: if conflicts are the result of vagueness about such things as tasks, responsibilities, rules and regulations.

10

Summary

- Stress at work can occur if someone can no longer satisfy the demands imposed upon him by his duties.

- Burn-out is a specific form of stress and is characterised by:
  - emotional exhaustion
  - diminished ability
  - depersonalisation

- Stress, if it is the result of long-term exposure to stressors, can result in the following complaints:
  - physiological complaints
  - emotional complaints
  - behavioural complaints
  - exhaustion

- Measures to reduce the risk of stress or burn-out include:
  - reducing work load
  - increasing control of the work situation
  - providing support
  - reducing job insecurity
  - increasing prospects
  - providing clear role descriptions
  - providing more sources of power
  - increasing resistance to stress by therapy, training and coaching

- Physical load can be reduced by:
  - the use of lifting and transportation devices and/or the provision of lifting training
  - interventions that ensure a proper working posture
  - introducing variation into work
  - reducing noise and improving temperature control in the workplace

- Conflicts can be constructive or destructive to the functioning of people and organisations. They can take place between people but also between groups.

- Sources of conflict include:
  - instrumental circumstances
  - competition
  - power struggles
  - relationships.
    In many cases, different sources of conflict are intertwined.

- Forms of conflict management are:
  - opposition
  - collaboration
  - compromise
  - avoidance
  - concession

- Conflicts escalate if:
  - the parties adopt a hostile attitude towards one another
  - their positions become entrenched
  - the conflict expands
  - more parties become involved
  - the inclination to damage the other party dominates

- Conflicts can be resolved through:
  - indirect intervention: this consists of structural changes and the introduction of regulation mechanisms
  - direct intervention: this consists of power intervention, arbitration, mediation and negotiation.

10

© Noordhoff Uitgevers bv

Assignments

10.1 Jean Pierre works as an air-traffic controller at a large international airport. Every day, thousands of people's lives depend on the quality of his work. Almost every day there is a near-accident. To prevent a disaster you have to think quickly and remain calm. Now that he is over 30, he is one of the oldest people in the control tower. There are few air-traffic controllers over 40, so he knows he has only a few years of service left. He has tensions in his private life, too. He is going through a protracted divorce. A medical check-up has discovered a stomach ulcer. Furthermore, he has high blood pressure. He has recently been fantasising about the possibility of starting a business with a friend. But he no longer wishes to work with other people.

   a What stress factors of a personal and organisational nature do you recognise in this situation?
   b Is there a buffer effect here?
   c What strategies can Jean Pierre use to handle stress?
   d What opportunities does he have to become less stressed in his work situation?

10.2 Read the following recommendations by Van Bergen (2000) to counteract or cure burn-out:
   (1) 'Not every task is worth doing perfectly. You also do not always have to do everything that is asked of you, no matter how flattering it is to be asked to do difficult jobs. Sometimes it is wiser to disappoint people and say "no".'
   (2) 'Do not cut all the down time out of the production process but also provide "idle time". This gives employees the opportunity to rest.'
   (3) 'Make sure there is proper guidance for newcomers. Teach them to have realistic expectations of their work and let them also see that work does not always go smoothly for others.'

   a What work-related interventions do you recognise in the above recommendations?
   b What person-related interventions do you recognise in the above recommendations?

10.3 HR has noticed that many of the secretaries at a certain company are dealing with feelings of isolation and loneliness. Changes brought about by New World of Work have resulted in a significant reduction in social contacts. It is hard to talk to supervisors face-to-face, and people taking part in fewer team building-activities. The managers now set their own calendars, making it that much harder for their secretaries to schedule meetings with customers and other relations. This is a cause of frequent issues. Many secretaries are unwilling or unable to address these issues publicly. They want to preserve what little positive atmosphere remains. And because of the lack of good mutual contact, each of them feels as though they are the only one dealing with these problems.

a Which types of stress are the secretaries dealing with?
b Which style of conflict management are the secretaries using?
c Which individual differences in stress management can be expected to exist between secretaries?
d Which approach would you recommend to reduce individual stress?
e Which organisational approach would be suitable to reduce stress? Would you make use of a mediator?

10

11

Organisational change

- What developments occur within organisations and in their environment, and what consequences do they have?
- What is planned organisational change?
- What can organisational change focus on?
- What resistance can there be to change and how can willingness to change be increased?
- What strategies for change can be employed?
- How can the change process be given a structured form?
- How can management organise and manage change?

11

© Noordhoff Uitgevers bv

New times, different approach

Dutch mail service PostNL records a 30% drop in deliveries over the past ten years. One the one hand, this is due to the digitisation of mail traffic; on the other, it is due to the emergence of competitors on the postal delivery market. In order to stay afloat in the Dutch deregulated postal market, PostNL will need to offer competitive pricing combined with good quality and service. Initially, PostNL used an extensive cost management programme to stay on top of the reduction in income due to shrinkage of the market. But from 2005 to 2006, the organisation was forced to consider wage reductions and a reorganisation of the postal delivery system. In 2012, this led to the implementation of a reorganisation scheme consisting of the following changes:

- The closing of 171 regional preparation centres and 330 delivery offices, to be replaced by nine larger Central Preparation Locations, where mail bags for postal delivery personnel are packed.
- The old-school postman or woman who, in addition to delivery also took care of sorting their route, will be dispensed with. Instead, part-time postal delivery personnel now pick up their mailbags from smaller pickup points.
- Business post, such as that sent by banks, telecom companies, and similar, are only delivered on Tuesdays, Thursdays, and Saturdays.

11

11.1 Necessity for change

Organisations do not operate in a vacuum. They need clients to sell their products or services to and to earn money from. That money is necessary to continue production. After all, raw materials must be purchased, power paid for, wages paid and loans repaid. Every hiccup in the flow of money is a threat to the survival of the organisation.

This view of organisations fits in with the 'open system' investigative approach which focuses on the transactions between organisations and their environment. Katz and Kahn (1978) point out that organisations are open systems, which derive their energy from the environment and owe their continued existence to the functions they can fulfil in their environment. The emphasis of their investigation is on the manner in which this energy is obtained, flows through the organisation and ultimately produces products and services. This flow can be described in terms of input, throughput and output (see Figure 11.1).

Open system approach

FIGURE 11.1 The organisation as an open system

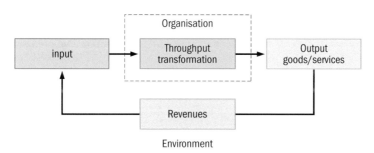

Through its activities, an organisation obtains energy (money). This energy is necessary for the acquisition of resources. With these resources, the organisation is able to maintain the cycle of input, throughput and output. There is therefore an exchange relationship between the organisation and its environment.

Exchange relationship

The fact that an organisation is functioning properly – that is to say, is putting a good product or service on the market and has sufficient turnover to maintain this cycle – is, however, no guarantee of its continued existence in the long term. A product can become obsolete. The competition can produce a better product. The public's tastes can change. The economy can decline, as a result of which people have less to spend. All these environmental factors can reduce turnover and compel the organisation to take a different approach.

An organisation therefore interacts with its environment, and the nature of that interaction determines whether the organisation can continue with its activities. The environment is also subject to change, and these changes – as demonstrated in the first example – have consequences for the organisation.

Interaction

11

The following example makes it clear how much changes in this interaction can influence the functioning of an organisation.

EXAMPLE 11.1

Book sales in decline

Swering is a large bookseller in a Dutch university town. The company has departments serving diverse groups of clients. In addition to literature and leisure, there is a department for science books and textbooks at Bachelor and vocational training levels. In recent years, the managing director has seen a number of changes that have made him consider the future of the company. These changes include:

- Book sales are declining nationally.
- Sales of leisure books (travel, hobbies, etc.) have grown strongly in comparison with those of literature. They now comprise more than half of the general-interest books.
- Book sales via the Internet have grown strongly.
- People increasingly borrow books from public libraries.
- More and more books are sold via channels other than booksellers, such as book clubs and supermarkets.

In the media, there is increasing interest in literature (book week, literary prizes, bestsellers); nevertheless, about half of Dutch people over 18 never buy books. It looks as though the trend towards borrowing books or acquiring them via other channels will increase. The question is how the booksellers will respond to this trend.

⑪.② **Causes of change**

Example 11.1 shows that a number of factors can lead to the necessity for change. For the bookseller these include public taste, a reduction in spending power, and technological developments that make other forms of selling possible. These are all external causes. Organisations are, however, not puppets of their environment. They are also collaborations of people, each with their own ideas about the structure of the organisation, its reward scheme, styles of leadership and the nature of work. These internal factors can also lead to the necessity for change.
In this section, we discuss both external and internal causes.

External causes

Internal causes

11.2.1   **External causes**

What is an important environmental factor for one organisation may not be so for another. Customers are very important to a company that makes kitchens, but for a municipal service organisation the mayor and aldermen are more important 'environmental factors'.
Various developments in the environment can force organisations to adjust their policies or operating procedures. First, there are the clients, whose tastes, preferences, or purchasing power determine which products or services they will procure.

Customers

Through legislation, regulation and subsidy, the government and government institutions affect the environment of many organisations. Legislation in the area of environmental requirements and the organisation's provision for the safety, health and welfare of employees have had a big influence on, for example, production processes, the arrangement of work stations, the allocation of tasks, and the way sick employees are dealt with.

Government

EXAMPLE 11.2

The customer decides

Supermarkets precisely record which items are sold in what quantities. Customers determine which items do well and which do not by their purchasing behaviour. Sales patterns enable the supermarket to shift its range in the direction of the more successful items and so adapt to customer preferences.

Technological developments can affect countless processes. One example is the use of microchip technology to automate production processes, store information and disseminate it within organisations and improve and accelerate interactions between employees and between the organisation and its environment.

Technological developments

11

© Noordhoff Uitgevers bv

NRC HANDELSBLAD

Postal sector decline continuing rapidly

The downfall of the Dutch postal sector is continuing unabatedly. During the presentation of the year figures, CEO Herna Verhagen of market leading company PostNL was forced to acknowledge that the number of postal items delivered over the past year had gone down even more rapidly than had initially been anticipated: an 11.9 percent decline, leaving only 3 billion items. These results mean that Verhagen's expectations for the near future are even bleaker than before. The formerly state-owned company is looking at a postal market decrease of 9 to 12 percent per year. At that rate, in ten years the number of postal items will have dropped below one billion items – in thirty years, it will have fallen below 100 million items.

This is still some ways to go, and PostNL is trying desperately to come up with ideas to compensate for their loss of income – last year, revenue on Dutch postal items went down by nearly 5%, and came to 2.16 billion Euros. Over the next few years, the concern is looking to cut back on fixed costs by 75 million, as well as increase the prices of postal items. In principle, the cutbacks will not mean additional layoffs. Nevertheless, PostNL has found a possible growth market in the digital age: the delivery of smaller parcels, related to online shopping. The revenue of the parcels department came to 803 million Euros last year, which is 10 percent more than in 2012. Parcel volumes went up by 6.7 percent.

Competitors

Competitors must also be taken into account. If they bring newer or better products or services onto the market or supply similar products or services more cheaply, an organisation will have to react accordingly (see example 11.3).

Economy

Finally, the economy has an important effect. In times of prosperity, organisations can expand and invest in new products or services. In times of economic decline, this is more problematic.

EXAMPLE 11.3

11

Cheap competition

When Ahold noticed that its market share was declining because its competitors were much cheaper, it decided to go on the offensive and reduce the prices of a large number of its products. This was accompanied by an extensive advertising campaign. Because of the smaller profit margins that resulted, however, there had to be staff cuts.

NRC HANDELSBLAD

Fugro adjusts ambitions and implements reorganisation

268 million loss over first 6 months

Fugro (soil surveys, cartography, underwater works) is adjusting its ambitions for growth and implementing a drastic reorganisational process. This should help improve the concern's results substantially.

This was said by CEO Paul van Riel this morning during an elaboration on the unsatisfactory semi-annual figures. Following last month's profit warning, the announcement did not come as a surprise, but the extent of the disappointment became clear this morning: at 1,187 million Euros, the turnover was nearly 20 million Euros higher than that over the first 6 months of last year, but results went from 110 million Euros in profit over the first 6 months of 2013 to a loss of 268 million over the past 6 months.

The main reasons for this were the one-time write-offs on below-expected activities, especially in the geoscience division (seismic surveys).

Fugro places the blame for the setback on the poor oil and gas market conditions, which account for approximately three quarters of the company's turnover. Major energy concerns are starting to postpone or cancel investments, leading to fewer jobs for subcontractors.

11.2.2 Internal causes

The necessity for change can also arise from new insights into the manner in which the activities of employees can best be organised to integrate with each other and with organisational goals. New insights may, for example, be related to the style of leadership, the division of tasks or the motivation of employees. It can also be a case of resolving problems, such as inefficiency in production or the provision of services, staff shortages, too high an outflow of qualified personnel or discontent among employees about the way the organisation is being run.

© Noordhoff Uitgevers bv

In some countries, secondary school teachers have, for some time, been objecting to the constant increase in the size of schools. They perceive this as detracting from their influence on the school's organisation and consequently as a reduction in their autonomy.

EXAMPLE 11.4

Increase in scale

After just under 20 years of growth in the size of secondary schools, some schools now have thousands of pupils and hundreds of teachers. These developments in secondary education have resulted in changes to the structure of schools. From flat, informal organisations, they have evolved into hierarchically layered organisations. Many matters in which teachers used to be involved are now decided at a higher level. Teachers have increasingly become simply implementers of education policy and their involvement in the school's organisation has consequently declined. The result of these changes is that they are becoming alienated from the organisation, are less loyal and are more often absent. Because of this a shortage of staff has arisen and teachers' work load is increasing. Lessons are frequently cancelled and this undermines pupils' motivation.

A heavy work load and the feeling that they have less say in their own work situation arouse the desire to reduce the negative effects of increased size. There are also more and more calls for a reduction in school size, greater autonomy for teachers and less regulation by government.

In a call centre, people are often paid by the number of contacts or the number of sales. This can lead to a heavy work load and stress in employees.

The internal and external motivations for organisational change are shown in Figure 11.2.

FIGURE 11.2 Factors of influence on the decision to change

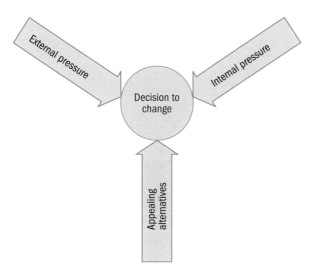

11.3 Deciding to change

Organisational issues do not always lead to organisational changes. Minor problems, such as an employe calling in sick or a machine tool failing, are resolved by, for example, deploying temporary workers or contacting tech support. In some cases, the workload of a sickly colleague may even be shelved in the hopes that they will soon get back to full health. This is known as an *ad-hoc approach*. It is also possible for larger or prolonged issues to remain unaddressed, simply because an organisation is unsure of how to fix them or because there is a hope that the problem will simply go away, for example through an economic boom or an important competitor filing for bankruptcy.

Many companies only feel that it is necessary to address a problem once it has become so urgent that it can no longer be avoided. The term organisational change in this chapter is used to describe changes to certain work methods which apply to multiple people and/or organisational units, and whose implementation becomes permanent in nature.

What are the deciding factors in proceeding with organisational change? Three factors can be distinguished, namely:
a **Internal pressure**. As the number of employees dissatisfied with the organisation grows, the internal pressure to change increases.
b **External pressure**. As the threats coming from the outside environment of the organisation grow, the external pressure to change increases.
c **Availability of alternative options**. As the ways of solving a certain problem become clearer, the desire and tendency to address this problem increases (see Figure 11.3).

11

FIGURE 11.3 Factors of influence on the decision to change

- External pressure
- Internal pressure
- Appealing alternatives

→ Decision to change

EXAMPLE 11.5

Concerns for the future

A company that manufactures pumps has a few managers worried, fussing about the future of the company. They have found that the number of competitors is growing, that the market share of certain types of pumps is shrinking, and that economic growth is stagnation. As of yet, the order portfolio has still remained sufficient to continue operations and to keep turning a profit. But any further decrease in market share

combined with a continue economic downturn might have some very negative consequences. This sense of dread is more subconscious than conscious and, so far, there have not been any members of management willing to be the first to submit it for discussion in a board meeting. Everyone is fully absorbed by day-to-day affairs, leaving this problem undiscussed.

11.4 Planned organisational change

Comprehensive changes, such as introducing new technology into production or the provision of services, expanding the number of departments or services and reorganising a company, do not usually happen

all by themselves. Once a decision has been taken to implement a certain large change, planned organisational change must take place. This process has the following characteristics:
- It is goal-oriented: the company has a situation in mind that it wishes to realise.
- It is comprehensive: several members of the organisation and/or several departments or services are involved.
- It is planned: the necessary activities are established, assigned to people, sequenced and planned over time.

In many cases, planned organisational change is a process that is tackled in phases.
In this section, we discuss the following phases:
1 orientation
2 diagnosis
3 planning
4 execution
5 evaluation

11.4.1   Orientation
In the orientation phase, one explores whether there is sufficient motivation to change the functioning of the organisation. We have already indicated that the motivation can be a desire to give shape to new insights or solve problems with which the organisation is confronted. In such cases, it is necessary to investigate whether the desires are so strong or the problems so serious that there will be sufficient support to do something about them. Initially, this means support from the top of the organisation.

New insights

Problems

Support

If it turns out in the orientation phase that there is insufficient support for change, this can result in abandoning the intended organisational change. If the senior management of an organisation imposes its wishes against the will of important members of the organisation, it runs the risk that at a later stage organisational change will encounter resistance, be insufficiently radical and fail to produce the desired results.

EXAMPLE 11.6

Can we keep this up?

PostNL attempted to address the shrinkage of the postal market by cutting costs in the context of their existing working methods.

Once that became untenable, management decided a drastic organisation and structural change were in order.

11

11.4.2   Diagnosis
When it has been established that an organisational change is necessary, the question arises what changes must take place and what results they must produce. If the desire for change originated from a problem, its cause must first be established.

When the causes of the perceived problems are clear, a focused search can be made for an appropriate solution. Determining organisational change involves establishing the desired situation on the one hand – what one wishes to achieve with the change – and identifying the changes that are necessary to achieve this end on the other.

Desired situation

Change

EXAMPLE 11.7

A new mission

At a banking institution, senior management wishes to draft a new mission. This new mission will incorporate three core values: professionalism, quality and responsibility. They think that the new mission can be given shape by middle management switching to an integral and results-oriented form of leadership. This, they hope, will lead to better market penetration, more customers and better performance by employees.

11.4.3   Planning

Once it has been established what situation is desired and what changes must be implemented, it s then necessary to work out what concrete interventions are necessary to accomplish the change. This involves making a plan of action.

EXAMPLE 11.8

Planning

In order to implement an integral and results-oriented form of leadership, senior management decided to begin by holding an information meeting with middle management. At the meeting they explained to middle management what their desires (new vision) were, how these desires must be realised and what result-oriented working means. After the meeting, training was organised for middle management. During the training, the new style of leadership was explained in more detail. Middle management was also schooled in the skills necessary to provide result-oriented leadership. During the next six months, they regularly met under the leadership of a trainer to discuss how they were coping with the new style of leadership. They could also indicate what problems they had encountered and discuss how best to approach them.

Plan

If the desired situation is very different from the current situation, a plan of action is essential. In a plan of action, the following must be established:
- The concrete changes that are necessary to achieve the desired situation.
- The order in which the changes must be made.
- The timing of the changes. It must be clear when a change must be started and when it must be completed.
- Who is responsible for the proper performance of the changes.

The plan of action must ensure that the desire for change does not get bogged down in a quagmire of good intentions.

11.4.4   Implementation

The change plan is carried out in the implementation phase. Plans may look wonderful on paper but they have to be realised. There are countless examples of wonderful plans that have not produced what was expected because of defective execution.

The text about police reorganisation shows that a plan is necessary but not a guarantee for success. The people responsible for its execution must perform their managerial tasks efficiently. Sometimes, however, they have to do this work alongside their usual management tasks and they therefore have too little time to devote to it. Sometimes they lack skills. In these cases, there is a great risk that the management of the change will be inadequate and the change itself consequently defective.

How to develop a helicopter view?

NRC HANDELSBLAD

Police reorganisation stagnating

Dutch minister Opstelten seems poised to over-stretch himself with the intended merger of the 26 Dutch police corps into a single national police entity.
Yesterday, Opstelten (member of the VVD party) sent a promising letter to the Dutch Lower Houses of Parliament, filled with grand terms such as 'enrichment', 'actualisations', 'strike and realisation plans', 'change processes', and 'key issues'. The actual current state of affairs was described in various committee and inspection reports, which the minister sent along by way of appendix. The way in

11

which the 26 corps are to be structured into one single national corps is a 'difficult, if not impossible, assignment'. Despite the best efforts of the police force, 'we are being confronted by the boundaries of what is possible'. The police are lacking in the manpower and expertise needed to lead such an enormous organisation. The reorganisation schedule is unclear. Its objectives are overly ambitious. This means that plans are constantly in flux, leading to even more uncertainty. 'There is a risk that the final objectives of the national police force will not be met.' Although the political branch (being Opstelten) is assigning more tasks and

priorities to the police force, it is not assigning more manpower.

Gerard Bouman, the chief of the national corps, is less delicate than his political superior. 'Trying to change the engine and wheels of a car while it's in motion' is how he describes the change from 26 regional corps and one national corps into a 50,000 officer and 15,000 employee strong single National Police Corps. No wonder that there are inevitable problems with 'the most complicated ever national service reorganisation'. There are continued problems in the ICT department, and absenteeism is at high levels.

11.4.5 Evaluation

Changes are implemented to achieve improvements in the functioning of an organisation and achieve the goals it has set for itself. After a time, it is therefore desirable to evaluate whether the changes went according to plan and have resulted in the intended improvements. Two forms of evaluation are necessary:

Evaluation

- Process evaluation. This evaluation establishes whether the change plan is being properly executed. Shortcomings in execution can be tracked down and rectified if necessary.
- Product evaluation. This evaluation explores whether the intended goals have been achieved. Can employees now cope better with the administration of the organisation or with the computerised information system? If not, what additional changes are necessary to achieve this? Has the intended increase in turnover been achieved and has this resulted in a better financial position for the organisation?

Process evaluation must take place regularly, so that adjustment takes place in time and the organisation does not continue to plod down the wrong road. Product evaluation is done at a later stage, when the changes have been carried out. This evaluation can supply meaningful data only if the goals to be achieved have been stated in measurable terms. The objective 'making the company healthy again' is too vague. It is necessary to quantify the objective such that progress can be properly measured. Examples of this are: 'an increase in turnover of 10%', 'reducing production errors in articles to 2%' or 'driving down absence through sickness to below the average for the sector'.

The phases of planned change are shown in Figure 11.4.

FIGURE 11.4 Phases in planned change

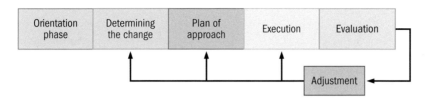

FIGURE 11.4 Phases in planned change

11.5 Types of change

Depending on the reasons for change, changes can be made in the structure of the organisation, in relationships between departments or groups or in relationships with groups in the external environment (external orientation) (see Figure 11.5).

FIGURE 11.5 Three approaches for changing

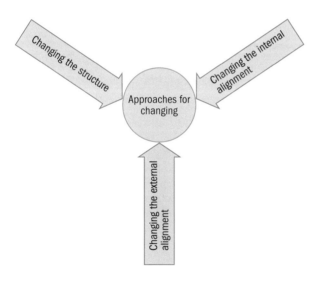

11.5.1   Changes in structure

One of the ways of accomplishing changes in the functioning of an organisation is to make a change in its structure. The structure of an organisation is an important factor in the functioning of its constituent parts. Their behaviour and style of collaboration and decision-making are to a great extent determined by the organisational structure. Employees can come and go but their jobs continue to exist. If the structure changes, the activities or forms of collaboration of the members of the organisation change too. If structure is the trigger, change is primarily a structural design problem.

Structure

Design problem

11

EXAMPLE 11.9

A change of structure

In secondary education management strives for a minimum size of 600 pupils per school. Such a size lets them offer a full range of study programmes. The increase in scale is not without consequences for the internal organisation of the schools. There will be three more hierarchical layers because of the increase in the need for coordination between departments. These management layers require more support in the areas of administration, finance and personnel. Scheduling will have to be organised more from above. What was formerly a fairly flat organisation, with much informal and interpersonal communication, is now a hierarchical organisation in which many more things are handled formally and distantly.

A change in structure is, however, no guarantee of the successful resolution of an organisation's problems. A new structure must also result in improved decision-making or a more effective style of leadership, for example.

EXAMPLE 11.10

A different style of leadership

Electro Ltd was faced with two problems: frequent sick leave and frequent defects in its production of technical appliances. Management assumed that an insufficient sense of responsibility among employees was the cause of these problems. They decided to create self-managing groups in the production department. These were small groups of operational employees who were collectively responsible for the production of a limited number of household appliances. The intention was that every week, on Monday morning, the groups would meet to discuss the scheduling of the work for that week and matters such as filling in for employees who were off sick or on holiday. They would also be responsible for the quality of production. To this end, they had to perform quality checks on the appliances themselves. The boss of the production department was assigned a different form of leadership in this structure. His role shifted from prescribing exactly what the production staff must do to making sure that the conditions under which the self-managing groups operated were as favourable as possible. This was a shift from a directive form of leadership to a guiding and coaching role.

11

It will be obvious that this new work structure at Electro BV did not occur spontaneously. It required the ability of the employees to collaborate and avoid conflict. The boss of the production department also had to learn to provide a different kind of leadership. Only then would the new structure produce the intended effects.

11.5.2   Changes in internal relationships

Example 11.14 shows that structuring work differently is a condition for the improved performance of employees, but that it is not sufficient to bring about the intended changes. It is also necessary to teach employees how they should collaborate and make decisions and how they must take responsibility for the quality of the production. In addition, the departmental heads in production must learn how they can be more supportive and less directive. These are changes in internal relationships.

Internal relationships

For team members as well as managers, a change in attitudes and ideas is necessary. Such a change can also be described as culture change.

Culture change

EXAMPLE 11.11

Relationship problems

After a few months, Electro Ltd came to the conclusion that the task groups did not function well (product evaluation). The members of the task groups blamed their boss. He was still directing too much instead of supporting and coaching. The boss blamed the group members. They were unable to collaborate properly. There was too much quarrelling about details and meetings took too long and produced too few concrete decisions.

11.5.3   Changes in external orientation

Problems with groups external to the organisation, such as suppliers, customers, competitors, subsidy providers and banks, can be approached and resolved by means of changes in external orientation. This can mean, for example, that other suppliers are brought in or that different agreements are made with current suppliers about prices, quality and delivery times. It can also mean penetrating the market more intensively (e.g. through advertising) or organising sales differently. This is related to the question of how the organisation can best control input and output for the benefit of effective and efficient functioning. In many cases, in order to make changes in external orientation, changes in structure and internal relationships are also necessary.

External orientation

EXAMPLE 11.12

A different relationship with customers

Electro Ltd wants a better relationship with its customers (retail trade). This requires better service and faster delivery. To achieve each of these goals, a change in structure is required. Faster delivery requires changes in production methods and better service requires a different way of handling products that are returned with defects. Internal relationships must also change, and a more customer-oriented attitude must be developed.

11

In many cases, adjustments to external factors, as shown in example 11.15, also require adjustments to the structure or internal orientation. Therefore, Electro Ltd's approach can be described as a mixed approach to the change

Mixed approach

process. Various factors played a part. External changes required a change in structure but this also required a change in internal relationships and a different attitude towards clients.

11.6 Two approaches to planned change

Higgs and Rowland (2005) studied the ways in which organisational change is addressed. They concluded that there are two distinct perspectives:

1 **Top-down versus bottom-up.** A top-down approach means that top level management decides on, initiates, and dictates the change. A bottom-up approach means the need for change is established by lower organisational levels, with those levels also being involved in setting the change approach.
2 **Scheduled versus developing.** A scheduled approach starts by determining exactly what change is required. Then, relevant change is implemented according to a plan. A developing approach does not set all details beforehand. As the change process proceeds, changes in targets or operating procedures may evolve as notions change or situation demands.

These perspectives can be seen in two different approaches to the change process: the design process and the development process. Both approaches are discussed in this paragraph, which also address the difference between and the effects of both approaches.

11.6.1 The design approach

Design approach
In the design approach, (senior) management, possibly assisted by an external advisor, determines what the desired new situation is and which new organisational structure is most suitable. A team of senior managers analyses the business processes and establishes the desired processes or performance. With the aid of advisors, a new blueprint is made for the structure of the organisation. When this blueprint has been drawn up, the change is implemented. The design approach is a one-off, linear process. The change process ends when the new structure is implemented. There is a clear separation between designing a new organisation and implementing one (Boonstra, 1991). Changes are set by the top level of the organisation.

11

EXAMPLE 11.13

Result-oriented management

In a government institution, senior management, assisted by an organisational advisor, decided to resolve the problem caused by reducing personnel due to cutbacks but needing to provide more service. Senior management attempted to solve this problem by implementing result-oriented management. The managers of the various divisions and sectors within the institution would be given responsibility for determining, within an established budget, how to deploy the available people and resources to achieve certain results within their division or sector. They would henceforth be paid according to those results and it would be up to them to steer their staff in the appropriate direction.

Research into the effectiveness of the implementation of this organisational change shows that the heads of the divisions and sectors who had to provide result-oriented leadership were hardly ever consulted about the nature of the change, even though they were responsible for its proper execution. In addition, they had little idea of exactly what result-oriented leadership meant or how they should provide it.

In a design approach, the execution of the planned change is seen as the responsibility of management lower down the organisation. However, lower-level management has little or no involvement in determining the nature of the change. The design approach is primarily a top-down approach.

Top-down approach

Top-down implementation of a new organisational structure. All ideas come from the top, and are then presented to the rest of the organisation as faits accompli.

11.6.2 The development approach

In the development approach, one does not work towards a new situation predetermined from above. There is no detailed blueprint of the new organisational structure. Establishing goals, developing an appropriate organisational design, and planning and implementing the necessary changes are achieved through discussion and negotiation, in which the different levels in the organisation participate. Collectively seeking solutions is an important part of the change process. There is no strict division between design and execution. The desired new situation is roughly sketched out and the new organisational form is not worked out in detail in advance. There is always room to adjust the goals and design during the process. Establishing goals and designing and implementing changes are intertwined and can be regarded as a self-repeating (iterative) process. There is a gradual change, in which the lower levels of the organisation are involved. The change process is only planned in outline and is flexible enough to make interim adjustments possible. The development approach is a mixed top-down and bottom-up approach. Information goes both from top to the bottom and vice versa.

Development approach

11

Mixed top-down and bottom-up approach

11.6.3 Differences and effects

The differences between the design approach and the developmental approach are shown in Table 11.1.

TABLE 11.1 Design and development

Design approach	Development approach
• New organisational design as a blueprint	• Improve from within the existing organisation
• Top-down	• Use of knowledge and insight of personnel
• Solution-oriented	• Problem-oriented
• Stable final situation	• Increasing the capacity for change
• One-time linear process	• Continuous iterative process
• Strict norms and planning	• Pay attention to capacity for change
• Abstract models (concrete methods)	• Concrete methods (abstract models)
• Emphasis on expert knowledge	• Use of knowledge of materials
• Separation of design and implementation	• Smooth transition between phases

The design approach usually involves a limited objective, namely the resolution of problems by means of restructuring the organisation. In its development process, attention is more focused on changing patterns of action and processes. By arriving at a diagnosis and devising a solution by consulting all interested parties, the development approach has a supplementary objective: teaching employees to resolve problems in the organisation themselves. Problem-solving skills are improved and thereby the ability to tackle future problems.

Various researchers (Homans, 2005; Ten Have, 2004; Duren et al., 2005) state that a development approach produces better results than a design approach in many cases because the development approach increases the participation of stakeholders and implementers of the change.

Together with colleagues, you develop ideas that might improve the organisation.

This ensures that:
- they have a clearer view of the necessity and nature of the changes, due to which their resistance to change is lessened;
- their motivation to implement the changes increases;
- plans are realistic and can be executed with the available manpower and resources;
- it is clear what conditions must be fulfilled to give the change a chance of success.

11.7 Impediments to the change process

A great deal of research has been done into why some change processes go well and others go badly. This research has identified various factors that can impede or advance the change process. From the perspective of change management, we shall indicate two areas that impede change: organisational shortcomings and individual resistance. These are covered in the following subsections. We also explore reactions to change.

11.7.1   Organisational shortcomings

The proper execution of a change plan requires good management and guidance of the change process. Managing the change process is not a simple matter because it concerns something new that happens only once and that, as a result, has to be carried out in addition to normal management tasks. Because day-to-day events usually already demand enough attention, nobody likes having supplementary tasks. Impediments to good management and guidance of the change process include the following:

Management and guidance

- The goals of the change are too vague to give proper direction to the activities that are necessary.
- The planning of changes is not detailed enough.
- It is insufficiently clear who is responsible for effecting the required changes, or those responsible have too little time and/or too few management skills.

Change can also be hindered by a lack of resources. The creation of a new situation is often accompanied by considerable costs or requires resources and expertise that are not available within the organisation. These then form an impediment to the proper execution of the change. Finally, it is possible that several changes are taking place at the same time employees and managers can be so busy that they lack the time and energy to devote sufficient attention to everything.

Lack of resources

Several changes at the same time

11

NRC HANDELSBLAD

Too many changes at once

In November of 2004, the Dutch VHMF union insisted that undersecretary Wijn reflect carefully on the issues of organisation and automation.

'So much work needs to be done that the question is whether the systems and the people using the systems will be able to keep up. It is one of the biggest concerns in

© Noordhoff Uitgevers bv

the workplace,' said former VHMF-chairman Jo Engelen following his annual address in 2005.

In 2005, Jenny Thunnissen sent all employees a letter, in which she admitted that management had become 'slightly adrift' from the staff. And that they were in the process of two reorganisations and three major automation projects. 'But we ought to have realised that you would be the ones having to process all of those changes and cutbacks. And that, especially during these circumstances, we should have provided greater support.'

Whittington and Mayer 2002 studied 50 enterprises which implemented a reorganisation between 1992 and 2000. The study found that, in some companies, reorganisations took place every three to five years. This led to the following phenomena:

1 The positive results from the previous reorganisation evaporate once the organisation starts new initiatives.
2 The improvements established during the previous reorganisations are unable to take root if a new reorganisation is implemented.
3 Employees become tired from continually having to be confronted with new and different losses, and thus loose their willingness to recommit to a reorganisation.

11.7.2 Individual resistance

Resistance to change

Acceptance of the need for change by the people who have to implement it cannot be taken for granted. In many cases all kinds of resistance to change are encountered in organisations. No matter how tiresome this resistance is, it cannot be ignored. Changes can have all kinds of negative implications for employees, such as:

- **Economic disadvantages.** In the new situation they may be required to produce more for the same salary and they will therefore feel that they are moving backwards. Their jobs or positions can also be threatened.
- **Fear of the unknown.** For many employees the existing situation is a safe situation. They know what is expected of them and they have accumulated sufficient skills to fulfil these expectations. It is possible that the new situation will put different demands on them, and it is questionable whether they will be able to fulfil them with as much success as now.

11

● www.penoactueel.nl

Reorganisation leads to breach of psychological contract

The expectations of employers and employees with regards to mutual obligations often come under siege during reorganisations. A breach of the so-called psychological contract can have devastating consequences to an organisation (Freese, 2007). This is the conclusion of a PhD study by Charissa Freese at Tilburg University, the Netherlands. The psychological contract encompasses all unvoiced, but in no sense unimportant, obligations of organisations to their employees and vice versa.

Involving employees in reorganisations
Freese recommends that organisations involve their employees in scheduled changes at an early stage, thus offering them a clear view of what will be expected of them during and after the reorganisation process.

- **Threat to existing relationships.** Changes can result in employees getting different colleagues or a different boss. If they have built up good relationships in their current situation, they will have to break them off and it is questionable whether they will enjoy equally good relationships in their place. Change can also mean that department heads lose some of their authority.
If, for example, the change in an organisation involves the creation of self-managing groups, as with Electro Ltd then management must transfer part of its authority to the group. Less leadership will be necessary and it is obvious that some managers will perceive this as digging their own grave. They will consequently have reservations about the change.
- **Changing habits.** People cling to their established ways of working and interacting with each other. Breaking with these habits is usually perceived as disruptive. The more strongly habits are ingrained in employees, the more problematic the change will be for them.
The introduction of New World of Work (NWW) has brought about many changes to a certain HR department and its employees. Suddenly, there are no more fixed workplaces and desks; only flexible workstations are now available. Nor are there any fixed working hours, fixed meeting times, or fixed storage areas for individual dossiers. It takes getting used to, with some employees still decorate the flexible stations in such a way that they resemble their own, personal space – even though that is not the idea.
Adding insult to injury are employees at other departments and supervisors, who still have their own spots they are regarded with no small amount of jealousy.
- **Lack of support.** Changes are often devised and put on paper 'upstairs'. Why this is necessary is by no means always clear to those lower down. What are the problems the desired change is supposed to resolve? Lack of knowledge of the 'why' and 'how' will not increase acceptance. It may be that people see that change is necessary but do not see how the proposed measures can achieve it.

The organisational and individual impediments to change are listed in table 11.2.

11

© Noordhoff Uitgevers bv

TABLE 11.2 Organisational impediments and individual resistance to change

Organisational impediments	Individual resistance
• vague, poorly developed goals	• economic disadvantages
• inadequate planning	• fear of the unknown
• poor performance management	• threat to existing relationships
• defective interim evaluation	• changing habits
• lack of resources	• lack of support
• too many simultaneous changes	

11.7.3   Reactions to change

The reaction of an organisation's members to an intended (imposed) change can range from stiff resistance to eagerness to cooperate. Their reaction is explained by the theory of planned behaviour (Ajzen, 1991, 2001). According to this theory, a person's reaction towards an intended change is determined by their attitude to the change, the ideas of others (social norms) and the extent to which the person thinks they themselves is capable of implementing the change (see Figure 11.6).

Theory of planned behaviour

FIGURE 11.6 Theory of planned behaviour

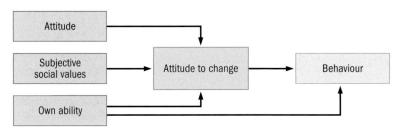

Source: derived from Ajzen, 2001

Attitude

An attitude is a view that a person has about an object, person, institution or event. This attitude is formed by cognitive and affective reactions. Cognitive reactions in the case of organisational change relate to the knowledge the person has of such matters as goals, methods and the consequences of the change. The more an employee agrees with the goals and methods and the more positive the expected consequences are, the more positive his attitude is likely to be. Affective reactions are the emotions evoked by the proposed change.

Social norms

Social norms comprise the (expected) ideas of the people in one's immediate environment. In organisations these are usually colleagues and managers. These ideas influence an individual's own ideas in accordance with the extent to which the individual is prepared to be influenced by and conform to the attitudes of others.

Perceived own ability

The extent to which a person thinks they are capable of adopting (new) behaviour required by the change depends on its estimated difficulty as well as the person's self-esteem.

These three factors, according to Ajzen, equally determine the degree of resistance to change or the degree of willingness to work towards change.

Research into the explanatory power of this theory has not always confirmed this, however (Armitage and Conner, 2001; Ajzen, 2002). According to a study by Oude Veldhuis (2004) of an intended reorganisation of an institution in the healthcare sector, it appeared to be emotional reactions (attitude) that were most determinant of resistance to or acceptance of change. Perceived capability had less influence, and social norms had none at all. This was in contradiction to other research, in which it was established that the attitudes of colleagues do influence a person's willingness to accept change (Metselaar, 1997).

Individual resistance factors can easily be placed in the theory of planned change. These resistance factors and the model provide indications for the manner in which an organisational change can be introduced and implemented such that resistance factors are minimised and willingness to change increased. This is the subject of the next section.

Willingness to change

11.8 The role of management in change processes

Organisations can be assisted in change processes by an external advisor but can also initiate and implement the process themselves. When a change is tackled by an organisation, it must first establish who is responsible for the process and will manage, guide and control its execution.

The execution of a change process is called change management. In its approach to change management, the organisation must ensure that reasons for resistance are minimised and motivators for willingness to perform the desired changes are maximised.

Change management

Therefore, it is important awareness of a problem and the need to address this problem among members of the organisation, to create support for the nature and direction of a change, and to remove any impediments to the change process. The importance of these conditions was established by the study by Whittington and Mayer (2002). They concluded that the results of many major organisational changes are disappointing because too much attention is paid to the introduction of new, costly information systems and complex new structures, the 'hardware' of the reorganisation; while too little attention is paid to the employees tasked with giving form to the reorganisation. The 'software' is neglected. Only one in five reorganisations paid sufficient attention to employee participation when established the nature of a change and its implementation.

Adequate attention to the 'software' of the change process will more likely be present in a development-approach than in a design-approach. A development-approach involves greater numbers of people in the design and implementation of the change, which improves the chances of obtaining their support. We will discuss the tasks of change management and indicate issues of particularly notable importance when it comes to increasing support and decreasing resistances, during all of the following phases of the change process:
- determining the desired situation;
- establishing the required changes;
- planning, driving, and adjusting the change process.

11

NRC HANDELSBLAD (EDITED)

PostNL postpones reorganisation

Dutch mail service PostNL has postponed the earlier announced reorganisation. This is the outcome of an evaluation of the problems caused by the reorganisation implemented by the board over the past three months. Initially, the organisation was scheduled to close 172 delivery offices over the course of this year. Instead of a fine network of delivery office, mail would be sorted from six larger sorting centres and nine central preparation sites. Central preparation locations are vast warehouses where tens of thousands of mailbags are filled largely automatically. PostNL's major reorganisation will be replaced by a number of small-scale pilots. This autumn, pilot results will be evaluated, and the course of any other potential reorganisation will be discussed.

11.8.1 Defining the desired situation

When defining the desired situation, the organisations aims must be described as precisely as possible. In this phase, particular attention must be paid to generating support for the change. First of all, middle management must be informed. Middle management is therefore crucial in obtaining sufficient support. Do they stand behind the principles on which the desire for change is based? Are they sufficiently aware of the necessity to tackle the perceived problems? Are they of the opinion that the desired situation can be achieved with the proposed change?

How important their judgement is becomes apparent from the previously described situation with the tax authorities. If several members of middle management do not favour the proposed change, the chance of a successful change is not very great.

11.8.2   Establishing the necessary changes

Once the desired situation has been defined, how this situation is to be achieved must be worked out. What changes in tasks, responsibilities, circumstances and procedures are necessary? How should they be implemented? If substantial changes must be implemented in several departments or services, a trial run in one department or team might be considered.

Through a small-scale trial run, less burden is placed on the organisation than when a substantial change is implemented. The trial run also produces knowledge about the manner in which the change can best be approached. Management learns from mistakes and from the obstacles it encounters. Finally, a trial makes it possible to assess whether the change will result in the desired new situation – for example, better production, a more flexible response to demands from the market or greater motivation and satisfaction among employees.

Trial run

Changes in an organisation always bring unexpected side effects, which can be positive or negative. Sometimes, the negative side effects are so great that they nullify the intended positive effects of organisational change.

Side effects

EXAMPLE 11.14

Side effects of change

The senior management of a company handling the sale and service of three major makes of car decided to set up a separate sales organisation for each make, with separate showrooms, and also to create separate workshops for repair and maintenance. The mechanics would have to be divided among the three makes and must henceforth specialise in one. The idea was that clients would then be better informed and assisted. The unintended side effect was that overheads were greatly increased by the requirements for additional receptionists, salesmen and managers and more buildings. These costs had to be passed on to their clients. The maintenance and repair services shrank. Where the organisation was formerly able to deploy the mechanics flexibly if there was more work for one make of car than for another, this was no longer the case in the new situation. Now, some clients had to wait too long for service and maintenance.

11

It is good to consider the possible side effects caused by organisational change in advance. If negative effects can be expected, it is necessary to find out whether they can be avoided and what measures are necessary to achieve this.

Above all, an important part of this phase is not only to make clear what changes are necessary and what their results should result be, but also to obtain sufficient support and reduce possible resistance. The chance of this is greater if the initiators of the change (management, employees) are sufficiently informed and involved in determining the nature of the change and the manner in which it must be implemented (Piderit, 2005). After all, they know best what is possible in the operational area, what potential obstacles there are and how they can best be cleared away. It is important in this phase to remove uncertainty among employees about whether they can perform the new tasks. Providing training and education and the creating opportunities to practise and experiment are necessary for this. Above all, it will help to remove uncertainty and doubt if you indicate that everything does not have to be executed perfectly straight away, but that this is rather a learning situation and provides an opportunity for employees to make improvements to the plans.

11.8.3 Planning, coordination, evaluation and adjustment of the change process

The execution of a change plan requires planning and coordination.

Planning
Coordination
Planning makes it clear what activities must be performed, by whom, in what order and within what time frame. Coordination of the performance of the planned activities is then necessary. One must also investigate whether the performance is running according to plan and the goals are being achieved. If interruptions occur, one must find out what the causes are and

Adjustments
what adjustments are necessary. To enable the implementation to proceed according to plan, the following questions must be answered affirmatively:
- Is it sufficiently clear to those involved what activities must be performed and in what order?
- Is it sufficiently clear within what time frame the various changes must take place?
- Is it clear who is responsible for the coordination, evaluation and adjustment of the change process?
- Are people alert enough to notice obstacles to the change process in time and devise effective solutions for them?

To obtain an affirmative answer to these questions, it is important that a great deal of attention is paid to planning, supervision, evaluation and adjustment of the change process in this phase of change management. The managers responsible will need to invest a substantial proportion of their time in this.

Strong resistance against change can be a signal to reconsider that change. This is especially the case for top-down implementation in which management, prior to the change, has done little to nothing to involve employees and management lower down in the organisation (Piderit, 2005).

11

NRC HANDELSBLAD, ANNE-MARTIJN VAN DER KAADEN

Change is not an exact science

Companies often do not realise that organisational change is should be a tailored process, says professor of organisational change Wouter ten Have.

'What works for Tesco will not necessarily work for Asda.' And customers almost always notice at least a little of what is going on.

11.9   Creating a structure for handling change

Planned change has the character of a temporary and extraordinary activity that is not part of the standard repertoire of an organisation. It usually involves matters that go beyond the scope of departments. Various groups or layers in the organisation can be involved in the change. It is therefore advisable to regard the planned change as a project and set up a separate structure to handle it. A suitable structure is a steering committee-working group model. We shall discuss this structure in this section. Finally, we shall discuss the execution of the changes.

Structure for handling change

Steering committee-working group model

11.9.1   The steering committee-working group model

A steering committee consists of a limited number of senior managers, who are responsible for the change process: for diagnosing the problems and defining the desired changes. The working groups consist of line-managers and employees who must implement the changes. These groups must furthermore develop the desired situation at local level (department, shift) and to this end must make concrete proposals for changes in tasks, methods, procedures, result evaluation and so on. The steering committee is authorised to approve the proposals put forward by the working groups, possibly after proposing changes itself and consulting with the teams. The steering committee should monitor the cohesiveness of the proposals and ensure they are attuned to each other and to the desired situation (see Figure 11.7).

Steering committee

Working groups

FIGURE 11.7   The steering committee-working group model

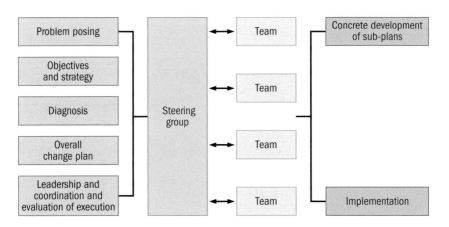

In this structure, there are both a top-down and a bottom-up approach. The change is overseen by the top of the organisation but its execution and performance are managed from below. In this way an effective interaction is created between the hierarchical levels of the organisation. The wishes of senior management are assessed at the operational level for their feasibility and possible consequences. The advantages of this method are twofold. People at the operational level are best able to establish whether proposed changes are feasible, what bottlenecks there are likely to be and how they can be resolved. By becoming participants in the change process, people commit to the solution of the problems, and this reduces resistance and increases acceptance of and support for the change. Kuipers (1975) speaks in this connection of a 'shuttle strategy'. The premises and conditions are formulated by senior management (steering committee), after which other parties have the opportunity within that framework (working groups) to influence the sub-goals and their realisation. This method corresponds with the previously described development approach.

11.9.2   Management of changes

When the change plan has been made, its execution can begin. This is delegated to the working groups. The steering committee, however, remains responsible for execution and can agree with the teams when progress will be evaluated, so that bottlenecks can be identified and adjustments made to the plan and its execution. Setting up effective progress monitoring is of crucial importance. After all, everything may look simple on paper but things are usually more complicated in practice. Every change, no matter how well thought out, is an experiment with an uncertain outcome. There can be all kinds of obstacles on the road that cause delays or necessitate adjusting the plan. Precisely for these reasons, it is good to be clear about what one wishes to achieve but not plan it in too much detail. This leaves room to learn from experience and adapt if necessary.

Conditions for effective change management are:
- The desired end situation and the sub-steps to be taken to achieve it must be concretely formulated so that they are measurable and can serve as norms. Only then can one properly establish whether the norm has been achieved or departed from.
- The progress must be checked with sufficient regularity that people do not go too far down the wrong path but can adapt in time.
- Progress control must be seen as a means to improve the process and not as a means to assess people. Only then will there be open communication and will employees be able to air their problems and doubts.

11.10 Reducing resistance and increasing support

An important factor for the success of a change process lies in the willingness of management and employees to implement change. We have already indicated that resistance to change can result in problems with implementation: for example, employees may delay the process or do things differently than was intended. It is therefore vitally important to reduce or avoid resistance and thereby increase support for the change. The following activities in change management can contribute to this:
- **Increasing problem awareness.** The employees in the organisation must be informed about the risks of the existing situation continuing. The more effective this information process is, the more the existing situation will be perceived as problematic and the greater will be the willingness to change.
- **Increasing participation.** The more employees in the organisation have been able to influence the change plans, the greater their commitment to the selected change. However, a choice will always have to be made about who are to be involved in the thinking and decision-making. In most

11

Support

cases, it is neither possible nor desirable to involve everyone in everything. Where too low a degree of participation can result in poor decisions and evoke resistance, too high a degree of participation can result in chaos and ineffectiveness.

- **Reducing uncertainty**. The new situation can mean that jobs, positions, tasks, responsibilities and relationships will change. This can evoke uncertainty among employees. They may question whether they can accomplish their new job properly, for example. It is necessary to anticipate this by providing clarity as early as possible in the process and by providing the necessary support or training and guidance. It can also be beneficial to provide some space for experimentation and learning. It must be explained that employees do not have to perform all the new tasks perfectly straight away but will be given time to learn them.

- **Increasing information and communication**. The above-mentioned points require that employees are always informed as fully as possible and that they can express their ideas, doubts, desires and uncertainties. There is a greater likelihoodthat something can be done to address these expressions. The change will not be perceived as something that has been concocted 'upstairs' and has now been imposed upon the forces on the shop floor. Information provision and communication are important during a change process. Clear explanation to the employees involved of the necessity, nature and consequences of the changes can increase support and reduce uncertainty about what will happen. Clarity about the expected situation also provides the opportunity to anticipate and possibly take steps to cope with the new situation. Buurma et al. (1999) conclude from research into the role of communication in organisational change that organisations that have undergone a successful change believe their success to be 50% to 70% attributable to the quality of the internal communication.

11

- High levels of communication over the course of the change process can help reduce resistance among employees, as long as the following conditions are met (Giangreco and Peccei, 2005):
  - Employees should be made to feel properly treated.
  - Communication should offer a rational basis for an assessment of personal costs and gains, which should come to a net positive result.
- **Increasing rewards.** The new situation must be attractive to employees economically, socially or in respect of the quality of their work. Participation in the change should be rewarded. Redundancies must be avoided as far as possible, unless an attractive redundancy package can be offered.

EXAMPLE 11.15

Claim: Support from a direct superior is crucial for the success of a change.

Imagine: your manager returns from a meeting with the board, saying: 'Well gang, you will not believe what those guys upstairs have come up with now.' Dollars to donuts that his team will not be chomping at the bit to comply. Research shows that support from a direct superior is a very important factor in the involvement, satisfaction, and productivity of the staff.

It is possible for a manager to disagree, of course. But in that case, they would serve the company better by saying: 'Here is what needs to happen, how do you think we can get there?' Since employees often feel insecure in times of chance, managers should be attentive, for example by positioning themselves as approachable and compassionate, and by using employee input where possible.

The use of a steering committee–working group model increases the participation of middle management and people on the shop floor. They then have the opportunity to exert influence on the nature and direction of the change. This increases support. They can also contribute their expertise to the execution of the change and to the creation of the conditions that are necessary for its success. This is all the more true if the participants see the necessity for and support the direction of the change. If there are too many different ideas, the use of a steering committee-working group model can result in a fight for power, lost time and vague decisions.

11

Tips for managers

If there is a desire to implement organisational change, the following questions need to be addressed (orientation and implementation phases) and action taken (planning phase).

Orientation phase
- What problem or desire is the change intended to solve or satisfy?
- Are there sufficient indications that the intended change will lead to the desired result? If not, should it be pursued?
- Are other changes being implemented, due to which too much disruption will occur in the organisation with this new change?
- What side effects could the change have? Can negative effects be expected and what must be done to avoid or counteract them?
- Can the same desired situation be achieved by implementing smaller changes, which require less time and energy and take effect sooner?
- Is adequate opportunity given for critical remarks about the intended change and its possible effects and are they taken seriously?

Planning phase
- Set up a structure to manage the change by means of a steering committee and working groups. Put the right people (in terms of expertise and skills) in these groups.
- Determine what functions the groups will have in the change process in respect of devising a solution to the problem and breaking down the solution down into concrete activities.
- Make a diagram which sets out when which groups must produce what solutions (information), so that progress control is possible.
- Establish who is responsible for the control, coordination and progress monitoring of the activities of the working groups. Do those who are responsible have adequate managerial skills and time for this?

11

© Noordhoff Uitgevers bv

Implementation phase

- Has the selected solution (organisational change) been broken down into concrete steps to be taken? Is it clear what new situation is desired in terms of structures, tasks, jobs, communication and leadership, etc.?
- Has the nature of the change been sufficiently communicated to those involved so that they know what consequences it has for their tasks, responsibilities, job and position within the organisation?
- Is there sufficient support for the change by the people involved? Are any steps needed to increase support and reduce resistance, for example, through education, training and support?
- Is the change process adequately managed, supported, coordinated, checked and if necessary adjusted? Is there sufficient progress control?
- Is it possible first to implement the selected change on a small scale? One can then establish what potential obstacles there are and, if necessary, come up with a different method of execution, and one can also establish whether the change has succeeded in solving the original problem.

Execution on a small scale is usually easier to manage and less expensive in terms of time and manpower. Obstacles can more easily be detected and removed. If the anticipated effects do not occur, it will be known that the original plan is not workable. Adjustment is then still possible. Avoid change for change's sake.

Summary

▶ The necessity for change can be brought about by external and/or internal factors. External factors are:
- Customers or clients are no longer satisfied.
- The government produces new legislation.
- Technological developments necessitate changes in the products or services supplied.
- Competitors are changing strategy, due to which they constitute a threat.
- The economy is growing or shrinking, due to which new opportunities or threats arise.

Internal factors are:
- discord between management and employees
- changed ideas about, for example, the organisation of work and the style of leadership

▶ In a planned organisational change, the following phases can be identified:
1 orientation
2 diagnosis
3 planning
4 execution
5 evaluation

▶ Organisational change can take place through:
- a design approach: senior management establishes the changes that are necessary and subsequently implements them in a top-down process
- a development approach: use is made of the knowledge and insights of management and employees lower down the organisation

▶ Organisational impediments include:
- too vague or too few concretely developed goals
- too vague or too rushed planning of changes
- too little management and adjustment of the change process

▶ Individual resistance arises through:
- fear of economic disadvantage
- fear of the unknown
- feeling that existing relationships are threatened
- feeling that habits are to be broken
- lack of support

▶ Management must play a guiding role in the change process and must also:
- establish what the desired new situation should be
- establish the changes that are necessary for this
- implement the changes by planning, managing, coordinating, controlling and adjusting

▶ Individual resistance can be prevented or reduced by:
- increasing awareness of the problem and its consequences
- increasing participation in the change process
- reducing uncertainty
- increasing information and communication
- increasing rewards

11

Assignments

11.1   Read the following article.

NRC HANDELSBLAD (EDITED)

Education saved, Amarantis disbanded

Amarantis is no more. The Dutch educational giant has been split up into five new schools. Once the new schoolyear starts, the doors will be reopened. And that has been a real point of uncertainty these past months, as the conglomerate was struggling with a 90-million Euro debt. "During the first months, it was unclear whether we would be able to keep offering education in any form. We had to regain the trusts of all the parties who no longer had faith in Amarantis: the banks, the Ministry of Education, local officials. Once they showed they were willing to look for a solution together, we set to work in April. I soon felt that there would be only one way to safeguard any offer of education: a reorganisation followed by a restructuring of Amarantis into logical units. Over the coming months, we will be reviewing the ways in which we can align our education to complement the trainings offered in the regions in which the individual units operate. We need to take into account the human dimension. The vast conglomerates that have emerged over the past decades have often led to alienated staff, teachers in particular. Honestly, education is not improved by a 3% efficiency gain requiring a merger. Education benefits from good, committed teachers – they are the ones who make the difference."

a   What was the direct cause for Amarantis to reorganise?
b   What other indirect cause for restructuring an organisation into smaller components is also mentioned?
c   Which starting point did Amarantis use as the basis of their organisation?
d   Is this an example of a design approach or a development approach?

11.2   The approach to a structural change in an organisation is as follows:
Phase 1 The necessity for change, as well as the vision and objectives of the new organisation, are expressed by the management team. The new structure is described in broad outline. The departmental head responsible for the implementation of the change incorporates these into a report, which is submitted to the various communication nodes in the organisation. These nodes can respond to it and, if necessary, adjustments can be made on the basis of their reactions. After adjustment, the report is submitted to the board of management for approval.

Phase 2 Personnel from middle and lower levels of management are involved. Two section heads are made responsible for this process and they will be assisted by a personnel consultant.

Phase 3 The operational work and the staff and supporting services are further organised. Small working groups are assigned responsibility for small parts of this. A (yet to be appointed) project leader will manage and coordinate the groups in collaboration with the newly appointed management.

Phase 4 A year after the implementation of the change, an evaluation takes place. On the basis of this evaluation, adjustments can be made.

a   Which form of approach – design or development – was chosen here?
b   Which type of change structure has been used here?

11.3   Electro Ltd manufactures electronic components. In recent years, the company has shrunk from 800 to 450 employees. This shrinkage had various causes. In the first place, there was a decline in the economy and therefore in demand for electronic products. In the second place, there was increased competition. In the third place, in the company's productivity was too low, which made the price of the manufactured components too high be competitive.

In 2008, a new managing director was appointed. He decided to take steps for the survival of the company in the short term and growth in the longer term. He hired an organisational consultant. The consultant's brief was to produce a plan for the creation of a modern, flexible, customer-oriented and productive organisation.

The consultant started with a strategic orientation round. The company director and heads of departments participated. Objectives were specified and translated into concrete goals in the short and longer term. The consultant then formed a steering committee. This group had to initiate, manage and evaluate the process of change. The group also had the task of handling internal and external information concerning the change process.

The third phase consisted of analysing the problems. The goal of this phase was to determine what problems could be resolved in the short term and what changes were necessary for this. Five groups of ten employees were formed to this end. These groups had first to produce a bottleneck analysis and subsequently make proposals for improvement. The steering committee inventoried the proposals from the five groups and drafted a plan for the change process.

The fourth phase comprised the execution of the plan. The steering committee opted for three main types of action. First came 'quality now' action, focused on improving the quality of the products. In each group, the employees had the task of reducing product defects through better observation, faster intervention and greater care. Second was 'improvement action' – as proposed by the working groups – that could be implemented relatively simply and quickly. This was focused on better coordination within and between groups and departments, so that decisions could be taken and breakdowns resolved more quickly and machinery used more

11

© Noordhoff Uitgevers bv

efficiently. Third came 'renewal campaigns' focused on redesigning the production process. For the execution of these three types of action, a project team was appointed in each department. Because by no means all the activities proceeded according to plan and people generally wanted to do too much at once, a project coordinator was soon appointed and the working groups were assisted by the consultant. The consultant helped with the management of the projects and taught the groups to draft concrete plans, indicate priorities and manage and control performance. Employees who were not in the working groups were kept informed about the plans through wall posters, meetings and written information focused on the change activities.

a   Changing an organisation can be regarded as a solution to a structural problem, a problem of internal relationships and/or a problem of external orientation. Which was it at Electro LTD?

b   What external causes determined the decision to implement change? (see section 11.2)

c   What was done to discourage resistance to change and increase willingness to change?

d   Which phases can be identified in the planned approach?

e   To what extent was there a design or a development approach in this case? What reveals this?

f   What was the nature of the structure created to manage the change process? Show this by means of an organisation chart.

Integral case

The following case offers many examples of subjects covered in this book. The case is intended to test your knowledge and insights. Read the case, and then answer the questions.

New World of Work: Bricks, Bites and Behaviour in Ede

The Dutch municipality of Ede began a New World of Work (NWW) pilot in 2011. Inspired by other examples, cutbacks, lack of space, and the overall zeitgeist of flexibility, autonomy, and enterprise, the municipal government has announced their NWW pilot as a way of 'working flexibly according to time and place, in a culture of trust, with supervisors relinquishing control and managing for results'.

Employees need greater freedom and flexibility (where and when do I want to work), and the municipal government wants to be an attractive employer. In addition, the municipality wants to contribute to a customer-centric approach (for each job, consider: who am I doing this for, and whom/what do I need?).

Part of the town hall has been renovated to accommodate the process. There are no more individual workplaces. There are tasteful, appealing rooms with empty desks, some with desktop computers. Depending on their activities, employees select a 'concentration', 'administration', or 'collaboration' workstation. Each employee has a locker and a single cupboard shelf. Paper dossiers have been digitised is possible. People leaving their workstation for more than 45 minutes must relinquish it to the next interested person. Each department has its own zone, with a lounge and kitchen, for lunches or office parties. Supervisors have been trained in making results-based agreements.

It took nine months to complete the preparatory process, with employees intensively involved in the design and impact of NWW. Sixty employees operated in four taskforces: Culture, Management, Housing, and IT. The municipality organised a personal development route for employees and supervisors. The municipal government was convinced that behaviour and attitude would be the critical factors in determining the success of this undertaking.

In their implementation of NWW, other municipalities sometimes hit a wall because they were so preoccupied with (bricks) and IT (bites) that they forgot the importance of employee behaviour. The desired behaviour for employees in Ede is self-sufficient, self-corrective, and assertive. Employees also feel it is important to address unwanted behaviours in others. The municipal government wants its employees working together instead of marking individual territories. One potential issue is 'limited' availability as a result of flexible working hours.

Questions

Refer to the indicated chapters of the book to answer the questions.

1 The municipal government of Ede has the following profile of desirable employee behaviour: autonomy, responsibility, flexibility, and entrepreneurship. What type of personality fits that profile? Which personality characteristics could cause issues? (Chapters 1 and 2, consider the Big Five.)

2 How would you motivate the staff members subject to the changes? How do you generate enthusiasm from them? (Chapters 1 and 2)

11

3 What would be the changes for management? Which type of behaviour, skillset, and style of leadership would be best suited to relinquishing control and managing for results? (Chapter 6)

4 Would you expect communications within the organisation to become *more* informal, or *less* informal? Would communications between staff and customers (citizens) become *more* informal, or *less* informal? And what is the role of social media in this process? Who should be the party controlling social media (Chapter 5)

5 Would you expect *more* hindrance or *less* hindrance to organisational information provision and decision-making? (Chapter 5 and 9)

6 What hindrance could NWW cause with regards to physical, mental, and semantic noise? (Chapter 5)

7 To your mind, what is the dominant culture among most municipal or other small, regional government agencies? What would be the desired culture for the renewed organisation? Use Deal and Kennedy's theory in your answer and involve Handy and Harrison if you can. Which issues do you expect to come up? Which approach would you choose? (Chapter 8)

8 NWW can also be a source of stress and conflict. A secretary work-meeting shows that secretaries feel lonely. They miss their (fixed) workstations and the contact with their managers. They are annoyed with the growing number of failed and duplicate appointments, since managers have taken greater control over setting their own calendars. Which stressors apply to this situation? What would be your recommended stress-reducing approach? (Chapter 10)

9 Assume that the municipality is planning to implement NWW across the entire organisation, applying it to all staff. What issues would you expect (e.g. us-them groups)? (Chapters 3 and 4)

Offer the municipal government of Ede your advice on how to approach this organisational change (Chapters 8 and 11)

11

Bibliography

Ajzen, I. (1991). The Theory of Planned Behavior. *Organizational Behavior and Human Decision Processes,* 50 (2), 79-211.

Ajzen, I. (2001). Nature and operations of attitudes. *Annual Reviews Psychology, 52,* 27-58.

Ajzen, I. (2002). Perceived behavior control, self-efficacy, locus of control, and the Theory of Planned Change. *Journal of Applied Psychology, 32,* 1-20.

Alblas, G. (1998). *Veranderingsmanagement.* Issue Paper, 15 November. Deventer: Kluwer Bedrijfsinformatie.

Alblas, G. & Vliert, E. van de (1990). *Doelmatig organiseren.* Groningen: Wolters-Noordhoff.

Alderfer, C.P. (1969). An empirical test of a new theory of human needs. *Organizational behavior and human performance,* (4), 142-175.

Alderfer, C.P. (1972). *Existence, relatedness and growth: Human needs in organizational settings.* New York: The Free Press.

Allport, G. (1954). *The nature of prejudice.* Reading, MA: Addison-Wesley.

Altink, W.M.M., Greuter, M.A.M. & Roe, R.A. (1990). Hoe werven en selecteren Nederlandse bedrijven? *Gids voor personeelsmanagement,* 6.

Andrews, J.D.W. (1967). The achievement motive in two types of organizations. *Journal of personality and social psychology,* 6, 163-168.

Argyris, C. (1969). The incompleteness of social psychological theory: Examples from small group, cognitive consistency, and attribution research. *American Psychology,* 24, 8 93-908.

Armitage, C.J. & Conner, M. (2001). Efficacy of the Theory of Planned Behavior; A meta-analytic review. *British Journal of Social Psychology,* 40, 471-499.

Asch, S.E. (1956). Studies of independence and conformity: A minority of one against a unanimous majority. *Psychological Monographs,* 70, (9), whole no. 416.

Avolio, B.J. & Bass, B.M. (1999). Re-examining the components of charismatic and transactional leadership using the Multifactor Leadership Questionnaire. *Journal of Occupational and Organizational Psychology,* 72, 441-462.

Ayman, R., Chemers, M.M. & Fiedler, F. (1995). The contingency model of leadership effectiveness: Its level of analysis. *Leadership Quarterly,* summer, 147-167.

Bales, R.F. (1953). The equilibrium in small groups. In: T. Parsons, R.F. Bales & Shills, P.M. *Working papers in theory and action.* Glencoe: Free Press.

Bales, R.F. (1965). Task roles and social roles in problem solving. In: I.D. Stenier & M. Fishbein (eds), *Current studies in social psychology.* New York: Holt, Rinchart & Winston.

Bandura, S. (1977). Self-efficacy: Toward a unifying theory of behavioral change. *Psychological review,* 84, 191-215.

Bass, B.H. (1954). The leaderless group discussion. *Psychological Bulletin,* 51, 465-492. Bass, B.M. & Avolio, B.J. (1990). *Manual: The multifactor leadership questionnaire.* Palo Alto, CA: Consulting Psychologists Press.

Bergen, A. van (2000). *De lessen van Burnout. Hoe word je er beter van? Een persoonlijk verhaal.* Utrecht: Het Spectrum.

Berger, G.P.A., Marcelissen, F.G.H. & Wolff, Ch.J. de (1986). *VOS-D, Vragenlijst organisatiestress.* Nijmegen: Stressgroep publikatie, 36.

Berger, J., Conner, Th.L. & Fisek, M.H. (1974). *Expectation states theory: A theoretical research program.* Massachusetts: Winthrop.

Blake, R.R. & Mouton, J.S. (1964). *The managerial grid.* Houston: Gulf.

Blake, R.R. & Mouton, J.S. (1968). *Leiderschapspatronen.* Utrecht: Het Spectrum.

Blatter, B.M. (2000). *RSI klachten in de werkende populatie: de mate van voorkomen en de relatie met beeldschermwerk, muisgebruik en andere IT-gerelateerde factoren.* Hoofddorp: TNO Arbeid.

Blauw, E. (1989). *Het corporate image.* Amsterdam: De Viergang.

Bloemers, W. (2008). *Het psychologische onderzoek.* Amsterdam: Ambo.

Boonstra, J.J. & Allegro, J.T. (1991). Integraal ontwerp van een klantgerichte verzekeringsmaatschappij. In: P.M. Storm et al., *Organisatieontwerp.* Heerlen: Open Universiteit.

Borman, W.C. & Motowidlo, S.J. (1993). Expanding the criterion domain to include elements of contextual performance. In: N. Schmitt & W.C. Borman (eds), *Personnel selection in organizations.* San Francisco: Jossey Bass.

Borrendam, A. van (1990). Werken met cultuur and kwaliteit bij een dienstverlenend bedrijf. In: Swanink, J.J. (ed.), *Werken met de organisatiecultuur, de harde gevolgen van de zachte sector.* Schiedam: Scriptum Management.

Bouchard, T.J., Barsaloux jr., J. & Drauden, G. (1974). Brainstorming procedure, group size, and sex as determinants of problem-solving effectiveness of groups and individuals. *Journal of Applied Psychology*, 59, 135-138.

Brouwers, A. & Evers, W.J.G. (1999). *Burnout bij cliëntgerichte beroepen. H.R.M. in de praktijk.* Issue paper, 19. Deventer: Samson.

Buurma, H. & Jacobs, C.W.J.M. (1999). *Integraal management.* Utrecht: Lemma BV.

Byrne, D. (1971). *The attraction paradigm.* New York: Academic Press.

Campbell, J.P. & Pritchard, R.D. (1976). *Motivation theory in industrial and organizational psychology.* Chicago: Rand McNally.

Carson, J.W. & Rickards, T. (1979). *Industrial new product development.* Farnborough: Gower Press.

Catalano, P. (2003). The relationship between charismatic and transactional leadership and job satisfaction in an aerospace environment. *Dissertation Abstracts International, Section A: Humanities and Social Sciences,* 63, 2612.

Cherniss, C. (1980). *Staff Burnout: Job stress in the human service.* Beverly Hills: Sage.

Chin, R. & Benne, K.D. (1970). General strategies for effecting change in human systems. In: W.G. Bennis, K.D. Benne & R. Chin, *The planning of change.* London: Holt, Rinehart & Winston.

Cohen, M.D., March, J.G. & Olsen, J.P. (1972). A garbage can model of organizational choice. *Administrative Science Quarterly,* 17.

Cooper, C.L. & Sadri, G. (1991). The impact of stress counseling at work. In: P.L. Perrewe (ed.), *Handbook of Job Stress (Special Issue), Journal of Social Behavior and Personality,* 6 (7), 411-423.

Dam, E. & Uyttenboogaart, H. (2002). Investeren in bedrijfsfitness en extra arbozorg levert Gasunie 300 procent rendement op. *Rendemens, 5,* 22-25.

Dansereau, F. (1995). A dyadic approach to leadership: Creating and nurturing this approach under fire. *Leadership Quarterly, 6,* 479-490.

Davis, K. (1953). Management communication and the grapevine. *Harvard Business Review,* 43-49.

Dayal, I. & Thomas, J.M. (1968). Operation KPE: Development of a new organization. *Journal of Applied Behavioral Science,* 4, 473-506.

De Zaak, jaargang 16, nr. 6, blz. 29. Interview www.studentenwerk.nl (2007).

Deal, T. & Kennedy, A. (1982). *Corporate cultures, the rites and rituals of corporate life.* Reading Mass: Addison-Wesley.

Deci, E.L. (1975). *Intrinsic motivation.* New York: Plenum Press.

Deci, E.L. & Ryan, R.M. (1985). *Intrinsic motivation and self-determination in human behavior.* New York: Plenum Press.

Delbecq, A., Ven, A. van de & Gustafson, D. (1975). *Group techniques for program planning.* Glenview Ill.: Scott, Foresman.

Dessler, G. (1980). *Organisation theory: Integrating structure and behavior.* Englewood Cliffs: Prentice Hall.

DeVito, J.A. (1996). *Messages, building interpersonal competences.* New York: HarperCollins Publishers.

Dubin, R., Champoux, E. & Porter, L.W. (1975). Central life interests and organizational commitment of blue collar and clerical workers. *Administrative Science Quarterly,* 20, 411-421.

Dubin, R., Hedley, R.A. & Taveggia, C. (1976). Attachment to work. In: R. Dubin, *Handbook of work, organization and society.* Chicago: Rand McNally.

Duuren, H. van & Manen, H. van (2005). *Integraal veranderingsmananagement.* Assen: Koninklijke Van Gorcum BV.

Elizur, D. (1984). Facets of work values: A structural analysis of work outcomes. *Journal of Applied Psychology,* 69, 379-389.

Ellemers, N. (2000). Betrokkenheid bij het werk: een kwestie van verstand of gevoel? *Nederlands tijdschrift voor de psychologie,* 55, 296-309.

Ellemers, N., Gilder, D. de & Heuvel, H. van den (1998). Career-oriented versus team-oriented commitment and behavior at work. *Journal of Applied Psychology,* 83, 717-730.

Emans, B. (1988). *Machtgebruik.* Rijksuniversiteit Groningen.

Erez, M. & Early, P.C. (1987). Comparative analysis of goal-setting strategies across cultures. *Journal of Applied Psychology,* 72, 658-665.

Erez, M., Early, P.C. & Hulin, C.L. (1985). The impact of participation on goal acceptance and performance: A two-step model. *Academy of Management Journal,* 28, 50-66.

Euwema, M.C. (1992). *Conflicthantering in organisaties.* Amsterdam: VU Uitgeverij.

Fayol, H.F. (1950). *Administration industrielle et générale.* Paris: Dunod.

Feldman, D.C. (1984). The development and enforcement of group norms. *Academy of Management Review,* 9, 47-53.

Fenlason, K.J. & Beehr, T.A. (1994). Social Support and Occupational Stress: Effects of Talking to Others. *Journal of Organizational Behavior,* 15 (2), 157-175.

Fernandez, C.F. & Vecchio, R.P. (1997). Situational leadership theory revisited: a test of an across-jobs perspective. *The Leadership Quarterly,* 8, 67-83.

Fiedler, F.E. (1978). The contingency model and the dynamics of leadership process. In: L. Berkowitz (ed.), *Advances in experimental social psychology.* Vol. 11. New York: Academic Press.

Finegan, J.E. (2000). The impact of person and organizational values on organizational commitment. *Journal of Occupational and Organizational Psychology,* 73, 149-169.

Forsyth, D.R. (1983). *An introduction to group dynamics.* Monterey: Brooks/Cole.

Forsyth, D.R. (1990). *Group dynamics.* Brooks/Cole Publishing Company.

Freudenberger, H.J. (1974). Staff burnout. *Journal of Social Issues,* 30, 159-165.

Frone, M.R., Russel, M. & Barnes, G.M. (1996). Work–family conflict, gender, and health-related outcome: A study of employed parents in two community samples. *Journal of Occupational Health Psychology,* 1, 57-69.

© Noordhoff Uitgevers bv

Glasl, F. (2001). *Help! Conflicts.* Zeist: Christofoor.

Goldthorpe, J.H., Lofwood, F., Bechhofer, F. & Platt, J. (1968). *The affluent worker: Industrial attitudes and behavior.* Cambridge: Cambridge University Press.

Gordon, M.E., Pryor, N.M. & Harris, B.V. (1974). An examination of scaling bias in Herzberg's theory of job satisfaction. *Organizational Behavior and Human Performance*, 11, 106-121.

Gramsbergen-Hoogland, Y.H. & Molen, H.T. van der (1992). *Gesprekken in organisaties.* Groningen: Wolters-Noordhoff.

Gramsbergen-Hoogland, Y.H., Blom, H. & Molen, H.T. van der (2005). *Conflicten in organisaties.* Groningen: Wolters-Noordhoff

Greenberg, J. and Baron, R.A. (2003). *Behavior in Organizations.* New Jersey: Pearson Schooling.

Greiner, L. (1972). Evolution and revolution as organizations grow. *Harvard Business Review,* 50, 37-46.

Grumbkow, J. van (ed.) (1988). *Arbeid in verandering.* Heerlen: Open Universiteit.

Guzzo, R.A., Jette, R.D. & Katzell, R.A. (1985). The effect of psychological-based intervention programs on worker productivity: A meta-analysis. *Personnel Psychology*, 38, 275-291.

Hackman, J.R. & Lawler, E.E. (1971). Employee reactions to job characteristics. *Journal of Applied Psychology Monograph*, 55, 259-296.

Hackman, J.R. & Oldham, G.R. (1975). Development of the job diagnostic survey. *Journal of Applied Psychology*, 60, 159-170.

Handy, C. (1978). *Gods of management, the changing world of organizations.* London: Souvenir Press.

Harrison, R. (1972). Understanding our organization's character. *Harvard Business Review*, 119-128.

Herman, J.R. & Hulin, Ch.L. (1973). Managerial satisfaction and organizational roles: An exploration of Porter's need deficiency scales. *Journal of Applied Psychology*, 57, 118-124.

Hersey, P. & Blanchard, K.H. (1988). *Management of organizational behavior.* Englewood-Cliffs: Prentice-Hall.

Herzberg, F., Mausner, B. & Snyderman, B. (1959). *The motivation to work.* New York: Wiley and Sons.

Hickson, D.J., Hinings, C.R., Lee, C.A., Schneck, R.E. & Pennings, J.M. (1971). A strategic contingencies theory of intra-organizational power. *Administrative Science Quarterly*, 16, 216-229.

Hinings, C.R., Hickson, D.J., Pennings, J.M. & Schneck, R.E. (1974). Structural conditions of organizational power. *Administrative Science Quarterly*, 19, 22-44.

Hofstede, G. (1980). *Culture's consequences; International differences in work-related values.* Beverly Hills: Sage Publications.

Hofstede, G. (1991). *Allemaal andersdenkenden: omgaan met cultuurverschillen.* Amsterdam: Uitgeverij Contact.

Holmes, T.H. & Rahe, R.H. (1967). The social readjustment scale. *Journal of Psychosomatic Medicine*, 11, 213-218.

Holzhauer, F.F.O. & Minden, J.J.R. van (1985). *Psychologie, theorie en praktijk.* Leiden: Stenfert Kroese.

Homan, T. (2005). *Organisatiedynamica. Theorie en praktijk van organisatieverandering.* Den Haag: SDU.

Horn, J.E. van (2001). *Teacher burnout, a flickering flame: an empirical study among teachers from a social exchange perspective.* Delft: Eburon.

Hottenhuis, A. (1998). Bedrijfsfitness gaat stress te lijf en verhoogt collegialiteit en band. *UT-nieuws*, 5, 1-4.

House, R.J. (1971). A path–goal theory of leader effectiveness. *Administrative Science Quarterly*, 16, 321-338.

House, R.J. & Mitchell, T.R. (1974). Path–goal theory of leadership. *Journal of Contemporary Business*, 3(4), 81-97.

House, R.J., Howell, M.J., Shamir, M.J., Smith, B. & Spangler, W.D. (1991). *Charismatic leadership: a 1990 theory and seven empirical tests*. Philadelphia: University of Pennsylvania.

Howell, J.M. & Frost, P.J. (1989). A laboratory study of charismatic leadership. *Organizational Behavior and Human Decision Processes*, 43, 243-269.

Interfutures, facing the future. Mastering the probable and managing the unpredictable. (1979). Paris: OECD.

Janis, I.L. (1972). *Victims of groupthink: A psychological study of foreign policy decisions*. Boston: Houghton Mifflin.

Jonge, J. de & Kompier, M.A.J. (1997). A critical examination of the demand-control-support model from a work psychological perspective. *Interactional Journal of Stress Management, 4,* 235-258.

Jonge, J. de, Kompier, M., Furda, J. & Feuvers, M. (1997). Psychosociale werkkenmerken en gezondheid. *Nederlands Tijdschrift voor de Psychologie*, 52, 27-41.

Joppen, R., Brand, W. & Schreurs, P. (1992). *Omgaan met stress*. Baarn: Trion.

Judge, T.A. & Ferris, G.R. (1992). The elusive criterion of fit in human resources staffing decisions. *Human Psychology*, 77, 261-271.

Kacmar, K.M., Bozemann, D.P., Carlson, D.S. & Anthony, W.P. (1999). An examination of the perceptions of organizational politics model: replication and extension. *Human Relations*, March, 383-416.

Karasek, R.A. (1979). Job demands, job decision latitude, and mental strain: implications for job design. *Administrative Science Quarterly*, 24, 285-308.

Karasek, R.A. & Theorell, T. (1990). *Healthy work: stress, productivity and the reconstruction of working life*. New York: Basic Books.

Karstens, C. (2000). *Omgaan met burnout*. Rijswijk: Elmar.

Katz, D. & Kahn, R.L. (1978). *The social psychology of organizations*. New York: Wiley.

Keijsers, J.F.E.M. & Vaandrager, L. (2000). *Gezond leven: stand van zaken en voorstel voor programmering*. NIGZ.

Kelley, H.H. (1972). *Causal schemata and attribution process*. Morristow: General Learning Press.

Kerr, S. & Jermier, J.M. (1978). Substitutes for Leadership: Their Meaning and Measurement. *Organizational Behavior and Human Performance*, December, 375-403.

Kessels, J.W.M. & Poell, R.F. (eds) (2001). *Human Resource Development*. Alphen aan de Rijn: Samsom.

Kets de Vries, M.F.R. & Miller, D. (1984). *De neurotische organisatie*. Amsterdam: M. Muntinga.

Kets de Vries, M.F.R. & Miller, D. (1985). De neurotische stijl van de leider. *Psychologie*, (4).

Keuning, D. & Eppink, D.J. (1985). *Management en organisatie*. Leiden: Stenfert Kroese.

Kluytmans, F. (2003). *Leerboek Personeelsmanagement*. Groningen: Wolters-Noordhoff.

Kolb, D.A., Rubin, I.A. & McIntyre, J.M. (1984). *Organizational psychology: an experimental approach to organizational behavior*. Englewood Cliffs: Prentice-Hall Inc.

Koning, E. (2007). *De invloed van werkkenmerken, een persoonskenmerk en coaching leiderschap bij de Rabobank Flevoland*. Heerlen: Open Universiteit.

Koomen, W. (1988). Relaties tussen groepen. In: R.W Moretens & J. von Grumbkow (eds), *Sociaal psychologie*. Groningen: Wolters-Noordhoff.

Koopman, P.L. (1992). Charismatic leadership, motivation and performance. In: H.K. Thierry, P.L. Koopman & H. van der Flier, *Wat houdt mensen bezig*? Utrecht: Lemma.

© Noordhoff Uitgevers bv

Koopman, P.L. & House, R.J. (1995). *Charismatisch leiderschap in organisaties.* Utrecht: Lemma.

Kornhauser, A. (1965). *Mental health of the industrial worker.* New York: Wiley.

Kotter, J. (1982). *The general manager* . New York: The Free Press.

Kuip, R. (1992). Verwende twintigers. *Intermediar,* 36, 4 Sept.

Kuipers, J.H. (1975). *Bedrijfsvoering door werkoverleg.* Alphen a/d Rijn: Samsom.

Lammers, C.J. (1983). *Organisaties vergelijkenderwijs.* Utrecht: Het Spectrum.

Latané, B., Williams, K. & Harkins, B. (1979). Many hands make light the work: The causes and consequences of social loafing. *Journal of Personality and Social Psychology, 37,* 822-832.

Lawrence, P.R. & Lorsch, J.W. (1967). *Organization and environment: Managing differentiation and integration.* Boston: Division of Research, Graduate School of Business Administration Harvard University.

Lee, H.R. (2000). An empirical study of organizational justice as the mediator of the relationships among leader-member exchange and job satisfaction, organizational commitment and turnover intentions in the lodging industry. *Retrieved,* January 20.

Leigh, J.H., Lucas, G.H. & Woodman, R.W. (1988). Effect of perceived organizational factors on role stress-job attitude relationships. *Journal of Management,* 14, 41-58.

Lewin, K. (1951). *Field theory in social science.* New York: Harper & Row.

Locke, E.A. & Henne, D. (1986). Work motivation theories. In: C.L. Cooper & I. Robertson (eds), *International review of industrial and organizational psychology.* Chichester: Wiley,1-35.

Locke, E.A. & Latham, G.P. (1984). *Goal setting: A motivational technique that works.* Englewood-Cliffs: Prentice-Hall.

Locke, E.A. & Schweiger, D.M. (1979). Participating in decision-making: one more tool. In: B.M. Staw (ed.), *Research in organizational behavior.* Greenwich: JAI Press.

Locke, E.A., Cartledge, N. & Knerr, C.S. (1970). Studies of the relationship between satisfaction, goal setting and performance. *Organizational Behavior and Human Performance,* 5, 135-158.

Lord, R.G., DeVader, C.L. & Alliger, G.M. (1986). Meta-analysis of the relationship between personality traits and leadership perceptions: An application of validity generalization procedures. *Journal of Applied Psychology,* 71, 402-410.

Maesen de Sombreff, P. van der (1990). *Testwijzer, het gebruik van de psychologische testen bij personeelsselectie.* Assen: Van Gorkum.

Man, H. de (1992). *Organisatiecultuur.* Heerlen: Open Universiteit.

Manz, C.C. (1992). Self-leading workteams: moving beyond self-management myths. *Human Relationships,* 45 (11), 1119-1140.

Marcelissen, F., Madsen, A. & Schlatman, M. (1988). *Werkstress, voorkomen en bestrijden.* Den Haag: Ministerie van Sociale Zaken en Werkgelegenheid.

March, J.G. & Simon, H.A. (1958). *Organizations.* New York: Wiley.

Maslach, C. (1993). Burnout: a multidimensional perspective. In: W.B. Schaufeli, C. Maslach & T. Mareks (eds), *Professional burnout: recent developments in theory and research.* Washington DC: Taylor & Francis.

Maslach, C. & Leiter, M.P. (1997). *The truth about burnout: How organizations cause personal stress and what to do about it.* San Francisco: Jossey-Bass.

Maslow, A. (1943). A theory of human motivation. *Psychological Review,* 50, 370-396.

Maslow, A. (1954). *Motivation and personality.* New York: Harper and Row.

Mayo, E. (1945). *The social problem of an industrial civilisation.* Cambridge, Mass.: Harvard University Press.

Maznevski, M.L. (1994). Understanding our differences: Performance in decision-making groups with diverse members. *Human Relationships, 47,* 531-552.

McGregor, D. (1960). *The human side of enterprise.* New York: Mc Graw Hill.

McLelland, D.C. (1971). *Assessing human motivation*. Morristown: General Learning Press.
McLelland, D.C. (1976). *The achieving society*. Princeton: Nostran-Reinhold.
Medley, F. & Larochelle, D.R. (1995). Charismatic leadership and job satisfaction. *Nursing Management*, 26(9), 64JJ-64LL, 64NN.
Meertens, R.W. & Grumbkow, J. von (eds). (1988). *Sociale psychologie*. Groningen: Wolters-Noordhoff, Heerlen: Open Universiteit.
Metselaar, E.E. (1997). *Assessing the willingness to change; Construction and validation of the DINAMO*. Proefschrift, Amsterdam: Vrije Universiteit.
Meyer, J.P. & Allen, N.J. (1997). *Commitment in the workplace: Theory, research, and application*. London: Sage.
Miles, R.E. (1965). Human relationships or human resources. *Harvard Business Review*, 43, (4), 148-155.
Mintzberg, H. (1983). *Designing effective organizations*. Englewood Cliffs: Prentice-Hall.
Mitchell, T.R., Rothman, M. & Liden, R.C. (1985). Effects of normative information on task performance. *Journal of Applied Psychology*, 70, 48-55.
Mochel, H. (1990). *Stress*. Kampen: Kok.
Moreno, J.L. (1943). Sociometry and the cultural order. *Sociometry*, 6, 299-344.
Munter, M. (1993). Cross-cultural communication for managers. *Business Horizons*, May-June, 69-78.

Nadler, D.A. (1987). The effective management of organizational change. In: J.W. Lorsch (ed.), *Handbook of organizational behavior*. Englewood Cliffs: Prentice-Hall.
Nuttin, J. (1981). *De menselijke motivatie: van behoefte tot gedragsproject*. Deventer: Van Loghum Slaterus.

Osborn, A.F. (1953) *Applied imagination*. New York: Scribners.
Oude veldhuis, A.M. (2004). *Veranderingsbereidheid: een positieve kijk op weerstand tegen organisatieverandering*. Heerlen: Open Universiteit.
Oudenhoven, J.P. van & Giebels, E. (2004). *Groepen aan het werk*. Groningen: Wolters-Noordhoff.

Paffen, M.J.A. (1996). *Stresspreventie*. Deventer: Kluwer.
Perrow, C. (1970b). Departmental power and perspective in industrial firms. In: Zald, M. (ed), *Power in organizations*. Nashville (Tenn.): Vanderbilt University Press.
Peters, L.H., Hartke, D.D. & Pohlman, J.T. (1985). Fiedler's contingency theory of leadership: An application of the meta-analysis procedures of Schmidt and Hunter. *Psychological Bulletin*, 97, 274-285.
Peters, T.J. & Waterman, R.H. (1985). *Excellente ondernemingen*. Utrecht/Antwerp: Veen.
Pfeffer, J. & Salancik, G.R. (1975). Determinants of supervisory behavior: A role set analysis. *Human relationships*, 28, 139-154.
Pinto, D. (1990). *Interculturele communicatie*. Houten: Bohn, Stafleu, Van Loghum.
Podsakoff, P.M., MacKenzie, S.B. & Bommer, W.H (1996). Meta-Analysis of the Relationship between Kerr and Jermier's Substitutes for Leadership and Employee Attitudes, Role Perceptions and Performance. *Journal of Applied Psychology*, August, 380-399.
Prein, H. (2002). *Trainingsboek conflicthantering en mediation*. Houten: Bohn Stafleu van Loghum.

Raad, B. de and Doddema-Winsemius M. (2006). *De Big 5 persoonlijkheidsfactoren, een methode voor het beschrijven van persoonlijkheidseigenschappen*. Amsterdam: Nieuwezijds.
Reiche, H.M.J.K.I. (1982). *Stress aan het werk*. Lisse: Swets and Zeitlinger.
Reynolds, S., Taylor, E. & Shapiro, D.A. (1993). Session impact in stress management training. *Journal of Occupational and Organizational Psychology*, 66, 99-113.

Robbins, B.P. (1989). *Organizational behavior*. Englewood Cliffs: Prentice Hall.
Robbins, S.P. (2005). *Gedrag in organisaties*. Amsterdam: Pearson Schooling Benelux.
Robertson, I.T. & Smith, M. (2001). Personnel selection. *Journal of Occupational and Organizational Psychology, 74,* 441-472.

Sanders, G.J.E.M. (1991a). Werken met organisatieculturen bij fusies en overnames. In: J.J. Swanink (ed.), *Scoren met cultuurverandering*. Schiedam: Scriptum Management.
Sanders, G.J.E.M. (1991b). De kunst van het cultuuronderhoud. In: J.J. Swanink (ed.), *Scoren met cultuurverandering*. Schiedam: Scriptum Management.
Sanders, G.J.E.M. & Neuijen, B. (1987). *Bedrijfscultuur: diagnose en beïnvloeding*. Assen: van gorkum.
Schabracq, M.J., Winnubst, J.A.M., Perreijn, A.C. & Gerrichhauzen, J, (1995). *Mentale belasting in het werk*. Utrecht: Lemma BV.
Schachter, S. (1951). Deviation, rejection, and communication. *Journal of Abnormal and Social Psychology, 46,* 190-207.
Schaubroeck, J. & Merrit, D.E. (1997). Divergent effect of job control on coping with work stressors: The key role of self-efficacy. *Academy of Management Journal, 40,* 738-754.
Schaufeli, W.B. (1990). *Opgebrand: over de achtergronden van werkstress bij contactuele beroepen – het burnout-syndroom*. Rotterdam: Ad. Donker.
Schein, E.H. (1985). How culture forms, develops and changes. In: R.H. Kilman (ed.), *Gaining control of the corporate culture*. San Francisco: Jossey-Bass.
Schein, E.H. (1988). *Process consultation, Volume I: Its role in organization development*. Reading, Mass.: Addison-Wesley.
Schiemann, W.A. (1984). Major trends in employee attitudes toward compensation. In: W.A. Schiemann (ed.), *Managing human resources and beyond*. Princeton: Opinion Research Corporation.
Schmidt, F.L. & Hunter, J.E. (1998). The validity and utility of selection methods in personnel psychology: practical and theoretical implications of 85 years of research findings. *Psychological Bulletin, 124,* 262-274.
Schoenmakers, I.A.M. and Koopmans, F.A.J.(2004). *Operationeel personeelsmanagement*. groningen: Wolters-Noordhoff.
Schwab, D.P. & Dyer, L.D. (1973). The motivational impact of a compensation system on employee performance. *Organizational Behavior and Human Performance, 9,* 215-255.
Schwenk, Ch.R. (1984). Cognitive simplification processes in strategic decision-making. *Strategic Management Journal, 5,* 111-128.
Seegers, H.J.J.L. (1986). *De assessment center-methode: een bruikbare vernieuwing in het personeelsbeleid*. Malden: GITP/Focus BV.
Sell, M. van, Brief, A.P. & Schuler, R.S. (1981). Role conflict and role ambiguity: Integration of the literature and directions for future research. *Human Relationships, 34,* 43-71.
Sessa, V.I. & Jackson, S.E. (1995). Diversity in decision-making teams: All differences are not created equal. In: M.M. Chemers, S. Oskamp & M.A. Costanzo (eds). *Diversity in organizations: New perspectives for a changing workplace*. Thousand Oakes, CA: Sage.
Shaw, M.E. (1979). *Group dynamics*. New York: McGraw-Hill.
Shelley, A.K. & Locke, E.A. (1991). *Leadership: Do traits matter? Academy of Management Journal*, May 1991, 48-60.
Sherif, M., Harvey, L.J., White, B.J., Hood, W.R. & Sherif, C.W. (1961). *The Robers Cave experiment: Intergroup conflict and cooperation*. Middletown CT: Wesleyan University Press.
Sitskoorn, M. (2007). *Het maakbare brein*. Amsterdam: Bert Bakker.
Sleebos, E. & Ellemers, N. (2000). Effecten van cultuur, taakrespect en sociaal respect op betrokkenheid en inspanning in taakgroepen (ongepubliceerde onderzoeksgegevens).
Spaans, M. (1991). *Als werk een zorg is: een theoretisch onderzoek naar stress en burnout bij psychiatrisch verpleegkundigen*. Groningen: Andragogisch Instituut, Rijksuniversiteit.

Sparks, J.R. (2001). Explaining the effects of charismatic leadership: an exploration of the effects of higher order motives in multilevel marketing organizations. *Journal of Organizational Behavior,* 22, 849-869.

Steensma, H., Knippenberg, D. van, Borsboom, T. & Son, M. van (1993). *Groepspsychologie.* Rijksuniversiteit Leiden: DSWO Press.

Stemerding, A.H.S. (1975), *Begeleiden van groepen.* Alphen a/d Rijn: Samsom.

Stogdill, R.M. (1974). *Handbook of leadership.* New York: Free Press.

Susman, G.I. & Chase, R.B. (1986). A socio-technical analysis of the integrated factory. *The Journal of Applied Behavioral Science,* 22, 257-270.

Szilagyi, A.D. (1981). *Management and performance.* Santa Monica: Goodyear.

Tajfel, H. & Turner, T.C. (1986). The social identity theory of intergroup behavior. In: S. Worchel & W.G. Austin (eds), *Psychology of intergroup relationships.* Chicago: Nelson-Hall.

Tannenbaum, R. & Schmidt, W.H. (1973). How to choose a leadership pattern. *Harvard Business Review,* May-June.

Taris, T.W., Houtman, I.L.D. & Schaufeli, W.B. (2001). Risicogroepen en risicofactoren van burn-out. *Tijdschrift voor Bedrijfs- and Verzekeringsgeneeskunde,* 9(6), 163-170.

Ten Have, S & Ten Have, W. (2004). *Het boek verandering.* Amsterdam: Academic Service.

Thibaut, J.W. & Kelley, H.H. (1959). *The social psychology of groups.* New York: Wiley.

Tibau, J. (1992). Zijn culturen te fuseren? In: *Fusie, integratie en cultuur,* NMB-Publicatie, February.

Torn, J.D. van der (1986). Management in het krachtenveld van de organisatie. *M & O, Tijdschrift voor Organisatiekunde en Sociaal Beleid,* 40, 48-501.

Tubre, T.C., Sifferman, J.J. & Collins, J.M. (1996). *Jackson and Schuler revisited: A meta-analytic review of the relationship between role stress and job performance.* San Diego, C.A.

Vechio, R.P. (1987) Situational leadership theory: An examination of a prescriptive theory. *Journal of Applied Psychology,* 72, 444-451.

Veen, P. (1979). Bedrijfsdemocratisering en invloedsprocessen: Macht slijt. *M & O, Tijdschrift voor Organisatiekunde en Sociaal Beleid,* 33, 452-467.

Veen, P., Alblas, G. & Geersing, J. (1991). *Mensen in organisaties.* Houten: Bohn Stafleu Van Loghum.

Vestergaard, R. (1992). Hogerop in de hamburgerhiërarchie. *PW Personeelsmanagement Magazine,* 34-35.

Vianen, A.E.M. (2000). Person-organization fit: The match between newcomers' and recruiters' preferences for organizational cultures. *Personnel Psychology,* 53, 113-148.

Viator, R.E. (2001). The relevance of charismatic leadership to non-traditional accounting services: information systems assurance and business consulting. *Journal of Information Systems,* 15, 99.

Vis, J. & Ploeg, H.M. van der (1985). *Stress in bedrijfsleven en onderwijs.* Lisse: Swets and Zeitlinger.

Vliert, E. van de, Euwema, M.C., Dispa, J.J. & Vrij, A. (1988). Een framing verklaring van conflictgedrag van boven- en ondergeschikten. *Gedrag en organisatie,* 1.

Vonk, R. (2007). *Sociale psychologie.* Groningen/Houten: Wolters-Noordhoff.

Vossen, H.P. (1988). *De operationele groep.* 's-Hertogenbosch: Interne publicatie Adviesgroep Koers.

Vries, E. de, Roe, R.A., Taillieu, T.C.B. & Nelissen, N.J.M. (2004). Behoefte aan leiderschap in organisaties: wie heeft het en waarom? *Gedrag & Organisatie,* 17 (3), 204-226.

Vroom, V.H. (1964). *Work and motivation.* New York: Wiley.

Wahba, M.A. & Bridwell, L.G. (1976). Maslow reconsidered: A review of research on the need hierarchy theory. *Organizational Behavior and Human Performance,* 15, 212-240.

Wall, T.D., Jackson, P.R., Mullarky, S. & Parker, S.K. (1996). The Demands-Control model of job strain: A more specific test. *Journal of Occupational and Organizational Psychology,* 69, 153-166.

Waters, L.K. & Waters, C.W. (1972). An empirical test of five versions of the two-factor theory of job satisfaction. *Organizational Behavior and Human Performance,* 7, 18-24.

Weick, K. (1979). *The social psychology of organizing. Reading* (Mass.): Addison-Wesley.

Weiner, B. (1979). A theory of motivation for some classroom experiences. *Journal of Educational Psychology,* 71, 3-25.

Wheelan, S.A. (2004). *Group processes: A developmental perspective.* Boston: Allyn and Bacon.

Wijsman, E. (2005). *Psychologie en sociologie.* Groningen: Wolters-Noordhoff.

Willis, R.E. (1979). A simulation of multiple selection using nominal group procedures. *Management Science,* 25, 171-181.

Winnubst, J.A.M., Buunk, B.P. & Marcelissen, F.H.G. (1988). Social support and stress: Perspectives and processes. In: S. Fisher & J. Reason (eds), *Handbook of life stress, cognition and health.* New York: Wiley.

WRR. (1977). *De verdeling en waardering van de arbeid.* 's-Gravenhage: Staatsuitgeverij.

Yang, K.S. (2003). Beyond Maslow's culture-bound linear theory: a preliminary statement of the double-Y model of basic human needs. *Nebraska Symposium on Movivation,* 49, 175-255.

Yankelovich, Skelly & White (1984). Employee attitudes in the workplace. *Business Week,* Feb. 20.

Yperen, N.W. van & Baving, H.H. (1999). Burnoutsymptomen bij verpleegkundigen: de relatie met werklast, regelruimte en sociale steun. *Gedrag en gezondheid,* 27, 4, 174-187.

Yukl, G. (1998). *Leadership in organizations.* London: Prentice-Hall.

Yukl, G., Falbe, C.M. & Youn, J.Y. (1993). Patterns of influence behavior for managers. *Group and Organizational Management,* 18, 5-28.

Yukl, G., Falbe, C.M. & Youn, J.Y. (1996). Patterns of influence behavior for managers. In: R.M. Steers, L.W. Porter & G. Bigley (eds) *Motivation and leadership at work .* New York: McGraw-Hill Comp.

About the authors

- -

Gert Alblas is an social and organisational psychologist and used to be a university lecturer at the University of Groningen and the open University of the Netherlands. He currently works as a writer. He has written several books on psychology, management, and organisation for Noordhoff Uitgevers.

Ella Wijsman is a psychologist specialising in organisational psychology and management theory and taught at various (vocational) universities. In addition, she also designed and coordinated management trainings and provided training and coaching in both the profit and non-profit sectors. She is the author of *Psychology & Sociology*, a standard reference work in this branch of study in the Netherlands.

- -

© Noordhoff Uitgevers bv

Index

© Noordhoff Uitgevers bv

© Noordhoff Uitgevers bv

© Noordhoff Uitgevers bv

Illustration acknowledgement

Image Research: Daliz, Den Haag, The Netherlands

Photo's:
Shutterstock, New York: p. 10, 12, 19, 24, 25, 38, 48, 65, 85, 86, 126, 128, 129, 144, 166, 168, 173, 176(l), 186, 227, 229, 240, 290, 294, 301, 342, 366, 378, 400, 417, 429
iStockphoto / Getty Images, Londen: p.16, 31, 36, 44, 46, 50, 55, 59, 60, 96, 97, 115, 119, 132, 149, 151, 176(r) , 179, 180, 189, 202,204, 207, 225, 238, 245, 254, 270, 286, 288, 307, 322, 324, 347, 350, 356, 358, 362, 390, 398, 402, 408, 418
Jaco Klamer / Hollandse Hoogte, Den Haag: p. 33
Copenhagen Zoo / Y&R / Copenhagen: p. 49
Dreamstime, San Francisco: p. 62
Jull Baars / Nationale beeldbank, Amsterdam: p. 68
Experiment van Asch: p. 100
Peter van Straaten / Kbizz, Baarn: p. 171, 305
Carl de Keyzer / Hollandse Hoogte, Den Haag: p. 251
Breman Machinery bv / Van der Berg Architecten, Genemuiden: p. 300
Corbis Historical / Getty Images, Londen: p. 312
Rick Nederstigt / ANP Photo, Rijswijk: p. 336
Kafxkafx / Nationale Beeldbank, Amsterdam: p. 360
Blend Images / Getty Images, Londen: p. 365
Google: p. 370
Fugro N.V., Leidschendam: p. 405
Chris Pennarts / Hollandse Hoogte, Den Haag: p. 406
Michel Porro / Hollandse Hoogte, Den Haag: p. 411
Post NL: p. 424

Technical drawings:
Integra, Pondicherry, India